Fantastic

Laurence Leamer is the prominent
author of many bestsellers, including
The Kennedy Women, *The Kennedy Men*
and *Sons of Camelot*.

    He lives in Washington, DC, and
Palm Beach, Florida.

Also by Laurence Leamer

Fantastic

The Life of Arnold Schwarzenegger

Laurence Leamer

Pan Books

To Helen Leamer, my mother, and Ivanka Ostojic, my mother-in-law

and

In memory of Bruce Murphy, 1959–2004

First published in the United States 2005 by St Martin's Press, New York

First published in Great Britain 2005 by Sidgwick & Jackson

This updated edition first published in paperback 2006 by Pan Books
an imprint of Pan Macmillan Ltd
Pan Macmillan, 20 New Wharf Road, London N1 9RR
Basingstoke and Oxford
Associated companies throughout the world
www.panmacmillan.com

ISBN-13: 978-0-330-43962-6
ISBN-10: 0-330-43962-6

Copyright © Laurence Leamer 2005, 2006

The right of Laurence Leamer to be identified as the
author of this work has been asserted by him in accordance
with the Copyright, Designs and Patents Act 1988.

All rights reserved. No part of this publication may be
reproduced, stored in or introduced into a retrieval system, or
transmitted, in any form, or by any means (electronic, mechanical,
photocopying, recording or otherwise) without the prior written
permission of the publisher. Any person who does any unauthorized
act in relation to this publication may be liable to criminal
prosecution and civil claims for damages.

1 3 5 7 9 8 6 4 2

A CIP catalogue record for this book is available from
the British Library.

Printed and bound in in Great Britain by
Mackays of Chatham plc, Chatham, Kent

This book is sold subject to the condition that it shall not,
by way of trade or otherwise, be lent, re-sold, hired out,
or otherwise circulated without the publisher's prior consent
in any form of binding or cover other than that in which
it is published and without a similar condition including this
condition being imposed on the subsequent purchaser.

Contents

Acknowledgments

I would like first like to thank Governor Arnold Schwarzenegger. When I finished my research, Schwarzenegger allowed me several interviews. He answered every question that I asked him. He neither sought nor received any special consideration. He is in no way responsible for my interpretations, and this is in no way an authorized book. Maria Shriver also gave me an interview, and I would like to thank her, too.

A biographer is dependent on the perceptions of many people. If this book is any good, it is because a great number of people have been honest with me. I have been writing books for several decades, and I have a pretty good sense of when people are dissembling or holding back. I had the feeling that most people I interviewed were talking from the depths of their human experience.

I was fortunate in interviewing almost all of Schwarzenegger's close friends and associates. I talked to them and others in Graz, Thal, Schladming, Munich, Los Angeles, Sacramento, San Diego, New York, Columbus, and Boca Raton. Each one of the friends I should rightly acknowledge in at least a paragraph, but let me just list their names, including them among acquaintances, professional associates, and others who talked to me or helped in other ways: Alfred Gerstl, Heidi Gerstl, Dr. Karl Gerstl, Franco Columbu, Albert Busek, Reg Park, Jon Jon Park, Dianne Bennett, Joe Weider, Betty Weider, Barbara Outland Baker, Charlotte Parker, Joel Parker, Charles Gaines, George Butler, Lou Pitt, Sven-Ole Thorsen, Frank Zane, James Lorimer, Jean Lorimer, Neal Nordlinger, Paul Wachter, Jake Bloom, James Cameron, Representative David Dreier, Mike Murphy, Landon Parvin, Herta Kling-Schmidbauer, Franz Hörmann, Sepp Heinzle, Karl and Elif Kling, Mark Arax, Douglas Kent Hall,

Frank Zane, Kurt Marnul, Joan Goodman, Franz Baumgartner vulgo Großhofbauer, Peter Urdl, Johann Strebel, Dr. Jur. Heinz Anderwald, David Anderwald, Anthony Shriver, Bobby Shriver, Tim Shriver, Eunice Kennedy Shriver, Dan Samson, Gary Ginsberg, John Connolly, Mickey Kaus, Burton Hersh, Rick Wayne, Bill Pearl, Kurt Shusterich, Dan Moldea, Gene Mozee, Dick Tyler, Bill Dobbins, Mike Uretz, Wendy Leigh, Lou Ferrigno. Bobby Zarem, Lawrence Kubik, Theo Hayes, the late Dr. Herbert Kramer, Patricia Seaton Lawford Stewart, Franz Wisner, Jill Stewart, Eric Morris, Craig Rumar, Dino De Laurentiis, David Pecker, John Milius, Jerry Lopez, Bill Grant, Sandahl Bergman, Raffaella De Laurentiis, Rabbi Marvin Hier, Sandy Gleysteen, Barry Golson, Larry Grobel, Ronald Shusett, Paul Verhoeven, Danny Hernandez, Rob Stuzman, Margita Thompson, Sheryl Main, Charles Fleming, Mike DiGiovanni, Anita Busch, Sid Ganis, Duncan Clark, Danny Simon, Dr. Hans-Moritz Pott, Ann Louise Bardach, George Gorton, Kiki Gorton, Governor Gray Davis, Arthur Laffer, Yvonne Abraham, John Carroll, Senator Tom McClintock, Arthur Grace, Bill Bradley, Gary Cohn, Joe Sappell, David D. Kirkpatrick, Charlie LeDuff, Senator John Burton, Robert Leamer, Mary Francis Leamer, Daniela Leamer, Antonio Mantilla, Assemblyman Keith Richman, Assemblywoman Sarah Reyes, Donna Lucas, Pat Clarey, John Jackson, Leticia King, Armand Tammy, Joe Mathews, the late Bruce Murphy, Dan Lurie, Win Paris, Mary Ann Dolan, Charly Kahr, Larry Thomas, Ben Weider, Bruce Kluger, Melvin Sokolsky, Wayne DeMilia, Representative Dan Lundgrum, Dennis McDougal, Lucy Penny, Suzanne Irwin, Donna Reeder, Elizabeth Mehren, George Linder, Kristina Rebelo Anderson, Hil Anderson, Mike Feldman, Jack Romero, Carla Hall, Bob Delmonteque, Daniel Weintraub, Terry Todd, Jan Todd, Mayor Hermann Kröll, Peter Nicholas, Margaret Talev, Rabbi Abraham Cooper, Gigi Goyette, and Debra Breslow Grace.

There were a number of sources who asked to remain anonymous. I am of the school that believes that if you are unwilling to affix your name to your opinions, then you had best be quiet. There are exceptions, and I think a few anonymous quotes in a book of this length is acceptable. I assure you that if these people had given their names, there may have been consequences to their personal or professional lives.

I would like to express my gratitude to Kim Beckwith, a graduate student at the University of Texas, who under the direction of Terry and Jan Todd researched the unique collection of bodybuilding magazines and other research materials at the Todd-McLean Physical Culture Collection at the university. I also must thank Don Spencer, who transcribes my tapes with great sensitivity. And once again I could not have done the research on this book without Zoot Software. I would like to give a tip of the hat to its inventor, Tom Davis. I have dealt with many executive assistants in my life, but I have never dealt with anyone better than Kris Lanner Liang in Governor Schwarzenegger's office.

I am deeply blessed in the friends I have. Several of them read all or part of this manuscript. The biographer Nigel Hamilton read the pages with the detailed concern of an editor and was immensely helpful. The author Burton Hersh made his astute suggestions. Barbara Gasser, an Austrian journalist from Graz, not only had many insightful comments but traveled with me to Austria and served as my interpreter and guide. If the pages that take place in Austria are vivid, she has much to do with that. California syndicated columnist Jill Stewart read the political chapters and offered her strong insights. My brother, Professor Edward Leamer, read the campaign and political chapters and had his valuable criticisms to offer.

I made several friends out of this project. One of them was Schwarzenegger's longtime publicist, Charlotte Parker. She was a wonderful guide to the intricacies of public relations, and I learned a great deal, and not only about Schwarzenegger. I traveled to Columbus, Ohio, to interview James Lorimer, and not only did I discover a great American city, but a great American.

I owe special gratitude to my friends at *Congressional Quarterly*—Robert Merry, Mike Mills, and Jeff Stein—who provided me with credentials for the 2004 Republican National Convention so I could be on the floor the evening that Governor Schwarzenegger gave his talk. That week in the evenings Rita Cosby, Tomaczek Bednarek, and Janet Donovan were marvelous companions to all the Republican festivities.

When my mother, Helen Leamer, was a student at the University of Chicago in the 1930s, she helped earn her way by copy-editing manuscripts for the University of Chicago Press. At the age of eighty-seven, she was the first person to copy-edit this manuscript.

In the computer age, good copy-editing is a dying craft, but I was blessed with one of the best in Steve Lamont. I have never met him, and for all I know he may be eighty-seven years old or a precocious eighteen-year-old, but whatever his age, he watched over my words with immense concern. I am also fortunate in that George Butler has allowed me to use so many of his marvelous photos, available at Contact Press.

When I began this project, I felt unwanted by New York publishers. No one thought that Schwarzenegger was worthy of a full-scale biography, no one but Diane Reverand, the executive editor of St. Martin's Press. She understood that this man was a phenomenon, and her contributions to this project are immense. Her assistant, Regina Scarpa, handled the details with consummate skill and cheery resolve. St. Martin's president and publisher Sally Richardson backed this project to the hilt. John Murphy, the publicity chief, grasped its potential the moment he was handed the manuscript, and he and his associate Gregg Sullivan developed a sterling publicity campaign. The marketing campaign directed by Matthew Baldacci and his associate Carrie Hamilton-Jones may well be the reason you heard of this book. I also must note my appreciation to Joy Harris, my agent.

I also would like to thank Lufthansa Airlines. The German carrier is the only airline with a direct flight from the United States to Graz, and it was a pleasurable journey. In Graz, I stayed in the Grand Hotel Wiesler, where manager Hubert Aumeier not only showed me gracious hospitality but one evening provided accommodations in the grand suite where Schwarzenegger stays. As a biographer I have traveled extensively researching my subjects, but this is the first time that I slept in one of their beds, and a good night's sleep it was indeed.

I often say that I should dedicate every one of my books to Vesna Obradovic Leamer, my wife, but never has she contributed more than she did to *Fantastic*. I could never have done this book if Vesna had not taken care of everything else in our lives. She was endlessly supportive, and if these pages have any merit, she deserves much of the credit.

PART ONE

The Vision

The Vision

CHAPTER ONE

The American Dream

As California Governor Arnold Schwarzenegger stood at the podium of the Republican National Convention in August 2004, scanning the vast assemblage, everything was fantastic. Arnold's favorite word was *fantastic*. Of course, his wife, Maria Shriver, was "fantastic," but so was working with his predecessor and archrival, former Governor Gray Davis, during the transition. Now that Arnold was in office, every Californian would have a "fantastic job." When a judge ruled that he had violated campaign laws and would have to repay $4.5 million out of his own pocket, that was "fantastic," too.

Arnold was washed in waves of applause that began directly in front of him in the Ohio delegation. They knew him as the greatest bodybuilding champion in history, who had come to Columbus each spring since his retirement to put on a bodybuilding and sports competition. Behind the Midwesterners stood his own California delegation, many wearing T-shirts reading I'M WITH ARNOLD. Beyond them were other delegations that considered him the most exciting new political figure in their party. And back up in the upper reaches of Madison Square Garden were many to whom he was primarily a movie star celebrated almost everywhere.

Arnold looked out beatifically on the huge hall. This was his first public test as a national political figure and the most important speech of his life. He had been given a key slot, Tuesday evening at ten o'clock, the first speaker on prime-time network television. He had been governor of California for nine and a half months, elected in a controversial recall election. As far as he was concerned, he had done a fantastic job. He was wildly popular and had made Californians feel good about their state once again. It was all about competition, and standing there was like moving up from the California title to the national championship or the Olympics. He was shining. Everyone was looking at him. Everyone was wondering, could he hack it? Could he make it on this great stage?

Arnold's enormous head on the great television screens in the Garden looked like a giant icon. His head was so large that it was a visual signature that could be seen from afar. His hair, already turning gray a quarter-century ago, was dyed the most peculiar shade of brown. The six-foot, two-inch-tall politician had orange-brown skin, a color that was also a shade unknown to nature. He had a tucked face that was the work of either a master plastic surgeon or a generous God who had decided to bestow eternal youth on one mortal. However bizarre these elements might have seemed individually, they came together in an immensely powerful image.

Fifty-seven-year-old Arnold Schwarzenegger was a man of the most extraordinary public discipline. The look of youthful exuberance and energy was, in part, an act of pure will. He had a slow, purposeful walk. He almost never hurried. He held his stomach in tight to promote the lean look of youth. His discipline set him apart—surely from most men his own age, many of whom were already counting the days to retirement.

Arnold's first starring role in Hollywood had been in 1982 as Conan the Barbarian. In his action/adventure films, Arnold had slain his enemies by the hundreds. To his audiences who had seen him as the world's greatest action star, he seemed immortal, impervious to pain, attack, flame, bullet, or natural disaster. His most famous character, the Terminator, was a robot, but Arnold projected himself onto the world like a Terminator with a heart, a suprahuman, constantly reinventing himself, regrowing his aging parts so he seemed eternally young.

Arnold waved to Maria and their four children, all impeccably dressed for their father's great moment. They were seated next to former President George Herbert Walker Bush, a man Arnold admired as much as any living figure in American politics, and the governor waved to him, too.

Maria was here this evening to honor her husband, but she was a Kennedy/Shriver, member of a family with two great faiths, the Catholic Church and the Democratic Party, and she would not give up either. The Republicans were no more comfortable with her then she with them, and not once this evening was her image shown on the in-house television screens. Maria had shoved a microphone in Senator John McCain's face after his defeat in the Super Tuesday primaries four years earlier and asked him, "How do you feel?" Many among the delegates remembered that the Arizona politician had snarled at her to get out of the way, and she was escorted out, actions that were applauded by some of the Republican faithful.

Arnold knew there were those out there among the 2,509 delegates, the thousands of others in attendance, and the 30 million watching on television who expected him to falter, to expose himself as a celebrity playing in a league where he did not belong and in a game he barely understood. Arnold took that as just another challenge. He became the greatest bodybuilder of the modern era by the most meticulous preparation, including working out more each day than any of his opponents. He became the biggest movie star in the world by the same kind of concern over every last detail of his films, from the script to the marketing to the publicity. He entered politics the same way, scoping it out over a number of years, planning his attack, and when opportunity opened up, going for it.

To prepare for this evening, Arnold probably devoted more hours than any of the other politicians who spoke at the convention. For weeks he had spent hours with his speechwriter and staff, tinkering with phrases, debating concepts. Longtime Reagan speechwriter Landon Parvin had been brought in to write the speech, but Maria was dissatisfied with the original draft, and the speech went through many revisions. Parvin wanted to begin the address with a joke about Maria's uncle, Senator Edward Kennedy. "People ask me if I still lift weights," Arnold was to say. "Absolutely. Just the other day, I lifted two hundred and eighty-five pounds. I lifted Ted Kennedy out of his chair." The joke would have brought the house down, but Maria would not allow her uncle to be mocked.

The week before the convention, in Sacramento and Los Angeles, Arnold practiced the speech again and again, working over the nuances of his delivery. Monday night he arrived at the convention in downtown Manhattan at midnight with his entourage and walked into the eerily empty Garden. In the belly of the arena, where a stray journalist could not possibly find him, he worked with the technician handling the teleprompter and ran through the address once again. Then he walked into the arena itself and up to the podium and stood there. He saw in his mind's eye what it would be like as the crowd exploded with cheers.

As he stood there, warmed by the ovation, it was just as he imagined it would be. He was bathed in adulation. There were even hundreds of blue signs emblazoned with the name ARNOLD. Wherever he looked out upon the immense gathering, he saw his name. As his eyes fell for an instant on the glass teleprompter, he was startled. The blue background from the hundreds of signs showed through the screen, and he could not see the words. He knew his speech, but he had not memorized it. He did not panic or turn in a frantic gesture to an aide. He was in the moment. He would find a way.

"Thank you, thank you," he said. He had a consummate awareness of his image, and he turned slowly so that everyone would see his profile, capturing him in their minds. "Thank you . . . What a greeting!"

"This is like winning an Oscar!" Arnold said as the applause died down. "As if I would know!" Arnold believed that "modest" was the appellation that the mediocre gave themselves to hide their mediocrity. This moment of self-deprecation was totally calculated. As he saw it, if he could get a laugh from making fun of himself, he would achieve instant commonality with the audience, winning a kind of capital he could use later on in his speech.

"My fellow Americans, this is an amazing moment for me," he said, turning serious. "To think that a once scrawny boy from Austria could grow up to become governor of California and stand in Madison Square Garden to speak on behalf of the President of the United States—that is an immigrant's dream. It is the American dream."

There in three sentences was the essence of his life, the essentials of his message, and the foundation of his political faith. He conveyed these sentiments with an elevated sense of joy and optimism that affected almost everyone around him, and he had those emotions at a time in modern politics when almost no one else did. That, too, he was conveying to this audience.

Three days before, up to half a million Americans had marched in opposition to the war in Iraq outside this arena, many of them believing that the best and only way to be heard was to shout in the streets. The President, who had authorized this war, was accused by his foes of being a slacker who had used his father's influence to avoid risking his life in Vietnam. His Democratic opponent was charged by political enemies with exaggerating his heroic record in that tragic conflict. It was a dispiriting time in which Democrats and Republicans tore mercilessly at each other, and many Americans seemed ready to believe the worst of the motives of those who sought to lead them.

"I was born in Europe, and I've traveled all over the world," Arnold said. "I can tell you that there is no place, no country, more compassionate, more generous, more accepting, and more welcoming than the United States of America." Since the terrorist attacks of 9/11, these public professions of patriotism had become a standard ritual of politics, but few of these assertions had the authenticity of Arnold's.

Arnold was a true witness to the greatness of America and what freedom could mean, and he held this convention the way no one else had yet. The delegates put down their blue Arnold placards, and Arnold could see the teleprompter, and he was fully in the moment. He had played many roles, but the character he played best was his own creation: the giant, mythic Arnold Schwarzenegger who stood onstage that evening. He focused relentlessly on whatever he was doing. He was giving the speech of his life, imbuing it with every ounce of his controlled emotional power.

He told the audience what it had been like growing up in Austria, when he had seen Soviet tanks in the streets and experienced firsthand the repression of liberty in a socialist country. Arnold was a loving son of Austria and had kept dual citizenship. This exaggerated picture pleased his audience in America as much as it displeased those in his birthplace.

When Arnold was working on the speech, some of Bush's people recommended that he not say that when he came to United States in 1968, he had heard Richard Nixon campaigning for President and found him "a breath of fresh air." Since his disgraced resignation in 1974, President Nixon's name was one that Republicans rarely invoked. Arnold did not care. He said to himself, "The hell with that. I'm not embarrassed by anything that has had an effect on me, and therefore I will not stay away from that." That was the truth of his life, and he was going to speak it, and so he did. There were many in the audience who still revered Nixon. They left the hall that evening remembering the one man who spoke the former President's name when no one else would. One of those was Nixon's daughter Julie Nixon Eisenhower, who said that she was "moved to tears by Arnold's immigrant story and by the fact that thirty years later my father's legacy—and the impact he had on our party—still resonates."

In twenty-three minutes, Arnold had to do many things—among them, prove his fidelity to President George W. Bush. Time and again he invoked the President's name and proved to any who doubted it that he was a stalwart supporter. Arnold also sought to bring the disparate elements of the party together. He was a Republican governor in a state largely controlled by Democrats, and he was here "trying to find the middle ground." He had to do that "without rubbing it in their faces, putting it in their eyes, and at the same time helping the President." In California, he had won the support of right-wing members of his party who would have deplored almost any other Republican candidate who held liberal views on social issues—pro-choice, pro–environmental movement, pro–gay rights. "We can respectfully disagree and still be patriotic and still be American and still be good Republicans," he told the delegates. He sought to reach beyond his own party to independents and Democrats and to move them with the passion of his ideas.

Arnold has an impish quality that no amount of power, no seriousness of position or theme, can change. In July, when he was fighting to pass a budget through California's Democrat-controlled legislature, he called members of the opposition party "girlie men." Some accused Arnold of resorting to "blatant homophobia," but he meant the phrase as a gibe at what he considered weak-willed politicians who would not come to meaningful compromise.

He wanted to use the phrase again at the convention, but when Bush's handlers vetted the speech, they sought to veto its inclusion. They were incapable of appreciating the irony that they were embodying the very definition of "girlie men." Arnold held tough and let it be known that even if the phrase was not in the formal speech, he might just decide to say it extemporaneously.

"To those critics who are so pessimistic about our economy, I say: 'Don't be economic girlie men!'" he said, receiving the biggest ovation of the entire speech. He knew it would be a great applause line, but he also wanted to signal that he "was not apologetic about it at all."

Arnold insisted that there be humor even in the most serious of moments, not because he was a frivolous man but because he saw that humor was one of the engines of the human spirit. Nothing—not a toast, not a speech, not even a funeral or a memorial service—should be untouched by it. But the purpose of this speech was a serious one: to invoke his own life as a witness to the greatness of his adopted country, to reach for the deepest truths of his own life to inspire his nation and to advance himself as a major national political figure.

"My fellow Americans," Arnold said at the end of his speech, "I want you to know that I believe with all my heart that America remains 'the great idea' that inspires the world. It's a privilege to be born here. It's an honor to become a citizen here. It's a gift to raise your family here, to vote here, and to live here."

The cheers and applause rose to an ovation, but Arnold did not linger. He walked offstage as purposefully and as deliberately as he had entered onto it. He knew that he had done precisely what he wanted to do. He could never say so publicly, but he believed that there was a vacuum of leadership in his adopted country. There had been a vacuum in California, and he believed that he had more than filled it. As he looked on the horizon, he saw no one with the strength, confidence, energy, and belief to lead America in the twenty-first century. All that held him back from actively aspiring to the highest office in the land was the constitutional prohibition of foreign-born citizens becoming President.

He believed he had been chosen for a special role in the world. He wanted more than anything to leave that stage with people thinking that maybe he was the one. Though he was an immigrant and was not born here, maybe he was the visionary. Maybe the American people would change the Constitution so that he could lead them.

PART TWO

The Bodybuilder

CHAPTER TWO

A Man from Thal

On summer weekends, families from Graz often journeyed over the wooded hill from the Austrian city to a diminutive lake in the village of Thal. There they swam in the Thalersee, rented wooden rowboats, or ate ample meals of pork loin and fried potatoes in the restaurant by the side of the lake. In the summer of 1963, as the visitors took their half-hour constitutional around the lake or sat in the outdoor café with their coffee and strudel, near the boathouse a group of young men in swim trunks lifted weights and exercised, performing a theater of physicality. They hung from the tree branches and did vigorous series of chin-ups. They held one another's feet for repetitions of sit-ups. The young men were "bodybuilders," practicing an obscure sport for which there was not even a word in German.

Eyes inevitably focused on one of the youths. He was an inch or two over six feet tall. He had short-cropped brown hair; thick, lengthy eyebrows; deep, expressive eyes; a separation between his front teeth; and sensuous lips that often seemed poised between a laugh and a sneer. If the sixteen-year-old looked much like any other teenager from the village, he had other qualities that made him an imposing presence beyond his age and station. He was developing the most muscular body of them all and had an awesome exuberance. His enthusiasm was a benediction that he spread on all within hearing—his fellow bodybuilders, the weekend strollers, everyone from the giggling young women to the serious walkers with their carved walking sticks and lederhosen.

The young man's name was Arnold Schwarzenegger. His father, Gustav, was the police chief in Thal, a modest position overseeing two deputies.

Arnold's mother, Aurelia, was a housewife. He lived with his mother and father and his elder brother, Meinhard, in the upstairs of a home owned by a local nobleman. The centuries-old house was in disrepair and had no indoor plumbing, a lack it shared with most residences in Thal.

"Where I started was a little farm community outside the Austrian town of Graz," Arnold reflected. "Now, that may make you think of sunny hillsides with buttercups dancing in the breeze, and happy children with rosy cheeks, eating strudel. But that's not what I think of. First of all, strudel was a luxury. It was right after World War II, and the country was absolutely devastated and destroyed. We had no flushing toilet in the house. No refrigerator. No television. What we did have was food rations—and British tanks around to give us kids an occasional lift to the elementary school."

In the four-room Hans Gross Volksschule, the children wore patches on their hand-me-down clothes and passed their books down from class to class. "Arnold learned how to get along with the little money he had," recalled Peter Urdl, one of his classmates, now mayor of Thal. "But nobody at the time had all that much money. In the beginning, his mother had her hands full just to keep him fed."

Arnold was thrice a provincial. He was a citizen of an Austria that before defeat in World War I had been the center of the Austro-Hungarian Empire, overseeing the destinies of 67 million Europeans. In the late 1930s, many Austrians had hoped to restore their nation's greatness in an alliance with Nazi Germany, but the Austrian-born Adolf Hitler led them into a disaster unprecedented in their history. The Austria that Arnold was born into on July 30, 1947, was a despairing, defeated country occupied by the Americans, British, and Russians. The crews on the tanks that rolled through the countryside spoke English, for the region was part of the British zone of occupation.

Arnold was also a provincial in that he was born in Styria. The southeastern region of Austria had been the watchtower against the invasion of the Turks of the Ottoman Empire. When the Muslims retreated, Styria lost its historic importance. As early as the end of the eighteenth century, Graz was already becoming a backwater, a place where, one writer noted, "most of the people . . . [lost] the desire to pick up their walking staff and continue wandering." Even so, Graz remains the second-largest city in Austria, with a population of 250,000.

The Alps helped wall off the region in geographic and cultural isolation. Other Austrians caricatured the Styrians as "the wild people beyond the Semmering." Other German speakers sometimes find the Styrian dialect unintelligible and vulgar, like a hillbilly accent. The critical listener does not hear the words themselves, but the accent marks its speaker as uneducated and backward.

Arnold was also from a village hidden beyond a large hill that isolated Thal from Graz itself. Even now the community remains largely unchanged from the years when Arnold lived there, revealing a soothing commonness of form and purpose. For the most part, the homes are set well apart from one another across the slope of the hill, the orange-tinged tile roofs making the houses look like a series of stepping-stones across a landscape of pasture, farm, and forest. There is nothing of the bold reds of a Vermont barn. It is all subtle shades, pastels blending in with the verdant greens of the grass and forestland.

Thal was a bucolic, pastoral setting for a boy's life, everything within reach and comprehensible, the lake half a mile from Arnold's home, the school in the same building that housed his father's police station, his friends' homes visible from most places in Thal. From Arnold's upstairs bedroom window, he looked out on what could have been a stage setting for a Wagnerian opera, a few cows grazing in the pasture, wooded landscape mysterious in the morning haze, and to one side of the tableau the spire of a ruined castle where Arnold played hide-and-seek as a boy.

If the small Catholic church in the upper reaches of the village is Thal's symbol of faith, then the Café-Restaurant Thalersee is its symbol of sociability. When the outsiders had gone back to Graz, the restaurant became a gathering place for the locals. Even on an August Sunday afternoon with the tables full of weekenders, Austrian custom reserved one table in the establishment, the *Stammtisch*, for the owner's chosen guests. It might be a regular group of men, local officials, or relatives, but one sat at that table only by special invitation.

Almost no one came into the Café-Restaurant Thalersee for a hurried meal. At some of the tables, the words were witty, the conversation animated, but even if it was not, the pleasure was simply in being there. Arnold's mother worked in the kitchen sometimes, but there were not the social distinctions of an urban, more stratified society. Almost everyone in the village was welcome at the restaurant, from the one family of nobility who had an estate to the village drunk. It had been that way long before Arnold was born, and it would be that way decades after he no longer lived there.

There is a strong centrifugal pull to Thal. People do not want to leave to venture forth in the unknown world beyond. Generation after generation, they stay there. When a home is for sale, it is much preferred to sell to a relative or close friend of someone in the village itself. It is a homogeneous place;

the villagers look as if they are from one large family. They are hospitable to those they think might be one of them, but uncomfortable and nervous with those they deem outsiders. They are deeply conservative, finding comfort in a present that is full of the past.

Gustav was a large man who dominated his family in a way that he could not dominate the world beyond. Arnold's obsession with physical size and strength surely comes in part from his father, whose sheer mass suggested that heft and muscle translated into power and potency in the world and control over those on whom he passed his gaze. Arnold fondly remembers how, as a little boy, he dressed up in Gustav's police uniform. "I was a little kid standing on a chair, and the jacket was hanging down, like a raincoat, all the way to my toes," Arnold recalled. "I had this hat on which covered me all the way to my nose. I always played dress-up with his uniform."

When Gustav walked upstairs into the Schwarzenegger home, wearing his police outfit, he insisted on discipline and order in the most minute details of family life. He sought perfection in his sons, and perfection was a goal that was forever receding. He pushed his sons to develop an interest in classical music and took them to museums on Sundays. This was all an endless chore to Arnold. He preferred to go to movies, especially the features his father told him not to see. Arnold snuck in to see films that children were not permitted to attend by walking in backward when theatergoers were leaving.

It was bad enough having to go with his parents to a concert or a museum, but even worse was that afterward his father made him write a ten-page report on what he had just seen. "He would correct it all over the place," recalled Arnold. "'This sentence makes no sense.' 'Write this word fifty times.' 'You made a mistake.'"

If his sons did not polish his shoes and burnish his brass belt until they gleamed, Gustav ordered them to do the job over again and punished them for their inadequacy. Arnold had to be home at a certain time, his pace homeward quickened by the prospect of a cuff to the ear if he was even a minute late. Gustav took immense satisfaction in meting out what he considered just punishment. Other parents were strict, too, but most Thal youths did not have the curfew that Gustav imposed on his sons, nor the myriad duties and obligations.

It was not just at home that Arnold feared the sting of reprimand. He recalled vividly the Parents Day when one father walked into the schoolroom, slapped his son without even a word, and walked out again. In school, some of the teachers taught with sticks in their hands, ever ready to use them on an unruly pupil. The students' worst fear was of a female math teacher who delighted in coming up from behind and whacking them on the head. Arnold was a feisty, irrepressible boy, and he received more than his share of raps on his large head.

"My hair was pulled," Arnold recalled of his home life. "I was hit with belts. So was the kid next door. It was just the way it was. Many of the children I've seen were broken by their parents, which was the German-Austrian mentality. Break the will. They didn't want to create an individual."

"I have seen one kid almost get his ear ripped off right in front of me because he was fighting with someone else," Arnold said. "I think it was a very much more brutal time." Although Arnold is surely correct that the corporal punishment he received "would now be called abuse," his solace is that everyone was getting walloped, too, and that his was just a typical German-Austrian childhood.

There is no way to calibrate whether Gustav's beatings were worse than those handed out by other fathers, but what is probably true is that young Arnold suffered more than many of his peers. He might have seemed at times an oafish lad, but he was preternaturally sensitive to everything around him. The best evidence of that is not in his contemporaries, who saw nothing of it, but in the man he became, a man with extraordinary insight into the motivation and character of other people. That is one of the qualities that has helped him advance in the world, and it is a quality that began in his difficult childhood years.

"I rebelled against my father," Arnold said. "When he said white, I said black. When he wanted my hair short, I wanted it long." It was not just his father that the youth was rebelling against, but the subjugation of the spirit and physical brutality that masks private pain.

It was the boy who felt the pain and it is the man who found the understanding many years later. "I think being a disciplinarian, being a military guy, made my father more intense in some ways, more into the discipline thing," said Arnold. "But with the punishments, the next day he would shower you with gifts. He was a very generous guy. He was always handing out money, a schilling here and a schilling there, or going into town and buying something or doing wonderful things for our mother on Mother's Day or for Christmas. But he still had that side of being a soldier in the Second World War, with all the wounds, with the shrapnel still in his legs and body. He was in tremendous pain a lot of times. He drank because of that. There was all of that, which, of course, as a kid, I wasn't much aware of, only later on. And so I know that the key thing always is that you know that your father was a good human being."

There was one matter that was not discussed in the Schwarzenegger house, and that was Gustav's membership in the Nazi Party. Millions of Austrians in the thirties believed that Hitler would bring order and discipline to the world, but only a minority of them joined the Nazi Party, as Gustav did in 1938, four months after the annexation of Austria. As a police officer, he surely found it advantageous to carry a party card. Moreover, he was precisely the kind of conservative, insular, proud Austrian to whom Hitler appealed.

One indication that Gustav's beliefs in Nazism went deeper is that in May 1939 he volunteered for the Sturmabteilungen (storm troopers), and served as a master sergeant in a military police unit on both the eastern and western fronts. The Feldgendarmerie were nicknamed the "Chained Dogs," a vivid rendering of their reputation in subduing occupied peoples. Gustav left the military in 1943 after being wounded. After the war, there were tens of thousands of former soldiers like Gustav who may have witnessed war crimes or participated in atrocities. The Allies had neither the time nor the political will to investigate each one of these hollow-eyed veterans. Almost all of them returned to civilian society, where they almost never talked about what they had seen and done. In 1947 Gustav was cleared sufficiently to return to police work.

In civilian clothes, Gustav was a nondescript middle-aged man with a receding hairline and an unprepossessing manner, but in uniform he was transformed. His other uniform of choice was that of the Graz Gendarmerie Musik, the police brass band in which he played the trumpet, sometimes leading the uniformed group though the streets of the provincial capital.

In Thal a celebratory dinner at the Café-Restaurant Thalersee, a wedding feast or holiday dinner, was a lengthy, convivial affair in which Welschriesling and schnapps flowed as freely as the conversation. It was hardly a matter for social ostracism to imbibe until flush-faced, but Gustav's drinking was of a different sort. He was an angry drunk, and there were rumors in the village that when he wended his way home in the evening hours, he beat his wife. Despite these tales, Arnold has no memories of his father hitting his mother.

One of Arnold's schoolmates recalled the time he discovered Gustav passed out. The boy removed the police chief's pistol and fired it into the air, which did not wake Gustav. The villagers of Thal might gossip mercilessly among themselves but not to outsiders, and they protected a man who was a danger to himself, to his family, and to the community as a whole since he was police chief. He was eventually transferred from the village, though he never had the epaulets of authority cut off, his name disgraced.

Arnold's elder brother, Meinhard, was enthroned in his father's mind as his favorite son. Meinhard was a year older than Arnold and not only larger through their childhood but robustly healthy, whereas Arnold was often sick. He was handsome in a way that Arnold was not, with a winsome charm that he could turn on and off on cue. Gustav's championing of his elder son was the worst of gifts to Meinhard, endowing him with an arrogant lassitude and the belief that he could pluck whatever he wanted from life without even a down payment in effort. He was the school bully, tormenting those weaker and smaller. His merciless teasing began at home, where Arnold had to learn to stand up to not only his father's pedagogical cuffing but his brother's cruel words. Outside the house, Meinhard faced a world that would not tolerate his abuse as his younger brother did, and he graduated from surly intimidation of his peers to full-fledged delinquency and tenure in a reformatory.

The emotional neglect Arnold received from his father, the brutal hazing from his brother, and the secret shame of Gustav's drunken binges could have emotionally crippled many youths. Instead, Arnold developed an ability to turn his head from what was negative and hurtful and always to look beyond. To compensate for what he lacked as a child, Arnold also developed an insatiable hunger for the love, applause, and affirmation he could never receive from his father.

His childhood friends do not remember Arnold as anything but a normal boy, full of humor and pranks. "He was a rascal, surely, but that's very normal," recalled classmate Franz Hörmann. "He played a few great pranks. He was part of every prank." Like his friends, Arnold was a mediocre student who gauged his success more by avoiding his teachers' censure than by academic achievement.

For all Thal's exquisite beauty, there was nothing that led away from the village, no legendary figure of accomplishment who had once lived there, no teacher who filled the spirit with a vision of a grander life, no inspiring neighbor who had reached beyond the narrow confines. On the far side of the village stood a castle owned by a family of German nobility who visited occasionally, but they were a species far beyond the aspirations of the people of Thal.

Arnold's emotional salvation lay largely in his relationship with his mother. "Arnold was a mama's boy," said Sepp Heinzle, another classmate. Aurelia had been a childless widow with a serious, gentle demeanor, slightly protruding teeth, and a stolid frame when she met Gustav after the war. Twenty-three-year-old Aurelia married her forty-two-year-old suitor in October 1945.

The bachelor Gustav already had four decades to become a narrow martinet, and Aurelia assumed the most traditional of wifely roles, obedient to her older husband's wishes, deferential to his suggestions.

If ever once Aurelia complained about her lot or sat befuddled at her condition, there is no one who recalls it. Almost everyone who knew Arnold's mother says that she was "simple." They do not mean that she was simple-minded but rather a woman of a few compelling concerns—her husband and her children—who built her life around them. She was not an educated woman, but she had a natural dignity. When she worked in the kitchen at the Café-Restaurant Thalersee to earn some extra schillings, she was "Frau Schwarzenegger," as she always would be.

Arnold could have gone the route of his father and brother, an oppressive bullying presence, but it was his mother who taught him empathy and tenderness. When one family of outsiders moved to the village, their daughter, Herta Kling-Schmidbauer, felt ostracized by many of her new classmates. Arnold befriended her, staying close to the woman for decades to come. Arnold tried to be a dutiful son but wanted only to get away from his mother and father and what he considered the claustrophobic world of Thal. It was not until his father's death in 1972 that he truly began to value his mother. He talks about her now with an emotional intensity that he brings to only a few things in his life.

"With my father's death, it dawned on me that my mother had struggled her whole life," Arnold said. "She was a child through the Second World War. When she married my father and had my brother and me, there was no food around. She had to run for twenty miles around just to get a little piece of butter or some food that she could feed us, because otherwise we would die. And then to sell off their little belongings just to get enough food. I mean, it was horrible, it was unbelievable the hardship that my parents went through. And when I was sick, she carried me over the mountain to Graz to the doctor at midnight in a rucksack on her back. So what was life really for her? It was a continuous struggle."

Aurelia was not a child during the war, but in her son's recollections she was. There is no mountain between Thal and Graz, only a wooded hill, but in Arnold's mind, it is a mountain. His mother may not have gone twenty miles foraging for food, but to her son it seemed an epic journey. And if she had not found provisions, her family would not have starved but only gone hungry. But that is how Arnold remembers a childhood full of unspoken fears, and at base this is not sentimental recollection but emotional truth. His mother's lot had been a hard one. She had loved her husband and her sons, and she had lived for them and not for herself.

Arnold's real school in Thal was not the banal classroom, but the village and the people in it, and he learned long and well. He has the same instinctive conservatism as most of the villagers—not a political statement, but an emotional commitment to the stability of life and a belief that in times of need one looks first and last to one's family and neighbors. He has the endlessly convivial habits of the villagers, spending hours with his friends and acquaintances, kibitzing in a manner tedious to most Americans. What sets him apart from others who leave their birthplaces in search of larger lives is that wherever he journeys, he remains a man from Thal.

CHAPTER THREE

The Hedgehog

By the time Arnold headed off to Knaben Hauptschule Fröbel in Graz after the eighth grade, his life had already been set out for him, the parameters marked on one side by his father, who wanted his second son to become a police officer, and on the other by his mother, who thought he had best become a carpenter. The high school he attended had the advantage of being geographically nearest to home, but it was one of the worst high schools in Graz. Some of the other parents in Thal sent their sons and daughters to better public schools in the city, but Arnold's interest in academics was so minimal that it was hardly a matter of consequence whether he went to Fröbel or not. He also worked in an apprentice program as a carpenter, taking a crucial step in following his mother's aspirations.

Graz is a walker's city with a labyrinth of streets, and the famous Schloßdsberg, the ruins of a great fortress, looks down upon the ancient roads from a hill above the old city. Arnold did not have the time, the money, or the inclination to stroll the byways. He was usually on one purposeful journey or another. On one occasion, fourteen-year-old Arnold saw a bodybuilding magazine in a store window that featured Reg Park starring in a Hercules movie on its cover. The producers had made the film to exploit the success of another bodybuilder, the American Steve Reeves, who had become a worldwide star in a series of similar toga-and-sandals sagas.

"I scraped up the *pfennigs* that I had left and bought that magazine," Arnold recalled. "It turned out that Hercules was an English guy who'd won the Mr. Universe title in bodybuilding and parlayed that into a movie career—then took the money and built a gym empire. Bingo! I had my role model! If he could do it, I could do it! I'd win Mr. Universe. I'd become a movie star. I'd get rich. One, two, three—bing, bang, boom! I found my passion. I got my goal."

Arnold had already been working out in a gym and at the lake in Thal. Surely, if he had not glanced into the store window, he would have come across something else that would have sparked his obsession. He was not a man to learn from books or abstract ideas but from identifying with what he considered admirable individuals. It simplified his life journey and focused his energy and mind. "Reg became my idol," Arnold said in 1976. "In time, I would base my whole bodybuilding future on Reg. Everything that I dreamed of was embodied in Reg Park. I couldn't have had a better hero to inspire me."

Modern bodybuilding began with the Prussian Eugene Sandow, who had developed himself into the idealized proportions of classical Greek sculpture. The celebrated showman Florenz Ziegfeld featured the muscular German in "the Sandow Trocadero Vaudevilles" in which he flexed his muscles and performed feats of strength in the nude except for a leaf-like appendage over his genitals. At the Chicago World's Fair in 1893, he stood daubed with white powder in front of black velvet, a living statue. Sandow was a unique phenomenon, winning not only fame but social and cultural acceptance in Europe and America.

There had been others who carried on the same tradition, including an impresario of bodybuilding, Bernarr Macfadden, who held a famous show at Madison Square Garden in 1903 and started *Physical Culture*, the first American magazine devoted to muscular development. Although bodybuilding in the early 1960s had hundreds of thousands of adherents, it was still perceived by many as a theatrical adjunct to serious sport. One of its champions, Frank Zane, has gone so far as to call it "performance art." Some consider bodybuilding not a sport at all to be included in the Olympic Games. The athletes are judged not by how many pounds they lift, how far they heave a javelin, or how fast they run, but by a committee of judges evaluating how they look, how well defined their muscles are, how flawless their forms are. It is natural that the highest reward for a bodybuilder is to end up like Reeves or Park, starring in films in which their bodies do most of the performing.

Most bodybuilders begin, as Arnold did, as teenagers, and usually from much the same mind-set. Growing up in Austria, Arnold never saw the famous comic book ads for Charles Atlas, "the world's most perfectly developed man," and his technique of "Dynamic-Tension." The ads, based supposedly on Atlas's own life, featured a cartoon in which "a 97-pound weakling," lying with his girlfriend on the beach, has sand kicked in his face by larger, tougher youths. Thanks to "Dynamic-Tension," the weakling builds up his body, successfully confronts his tormenters, and gets the pretty girl. Few boys who have seen that ad ever forget it, for it plays brilliantly to the self-doubt in the struggle for manhood.

There is another theme common among many of the greatest body-builders: a deeply troubled relationship with their fathers. On some level, their fathers do not accept their sons' manhood, and the sons seek in body-building to assert their masculinity in such a profound, pictorial way that their fathers can no longer deny them. This, like the layer of muscle on a self-perceived weakling's form, is a struggle that is rarely fully successful. "Maybe I was competitive with my brother or trying to prove something to my father," Arnold said. "But it doesn't really matter. Something was there that made me hungry."

Arnold is a connoisseur of his own story, yet as much as he enjoys lovingly reciting the details of his rise, he is far from introspective. Even as a teenager he chose never to look back at what was unpleasant, whether specific episodes in his past or the psychological realities of his own life. From his early years, he had a merry, exuberant temperament that drew people to him. That spirit seemed a gift from a distant place where Arnold had never been. The logical Freudian conclusion would be that Arnold has repressed the darkness of his childhood and overlaid it with a giddily positive spirit, but he bridles at those who would make facile psychological judgments about his character. "I wouldn't overthink it," he said. That is his mantra about every-thing that is unpleasant and unchangeable. He is not a child of the American culture of blame. He accepts his childhood and moves on.

"Some people are by nature depressed or optimists and some are funny by nature and some aren't," he said, as close to analyzing himself as he ever gets. "I think my body produced the right combination of chemicals. I found joy in my life. My chemistry was right. There are people I know who are on med-ications to try to get some of this. I just by nature happen to have this gift from God."

Arnold's observation about body chemistry is supported by contemporary psychology. Intense physical exercise is considered a major antidote to depres-sion, as effective as or more effective than drugs. And yet to credit body chem-istry is just as inadequate an answer as the psychological. There is equally a spiritual dimension. In her book *Exuberance: The Passion for Life*, Kay Redfield Jamison writes about those rare individuals who have such a passionate love of life that they transform it for all of us. It is this sheer joyous assault on life that many great men have had, from Theodore Roosevelt to Winston Churchill. This exuberance makes "the exploration of the universe more likely: it fuels anticipation; overlooks or minimizes risks and hardships; intensifies the joy once the exploration is done; and sharply increases the desire to recapture the joy, which in turn encourages further forays into the unknown."

Arnold delighted in himself, and out of that delight came many gifts.

Bodybuilding was the vehicle that carried Arnold away from Thal. He was a natural athlete who could have made his mark in any number of sports. He has said that he liked bodybuilding because it was not like soccer, which required him to share his acclaim with others. With bodybuilding, the glories were his alone. There was another reason that was probably even more important. Arnold was a profoundly controlling person, who needed sovereignty over all aspects of his life. He had no teammates in bodybuilding. He alone determined how he worked on his triceps or built up his deltoids, or whatever muscle he sought to expand or define.

Arnold maneuvered to meet Kurt Marnul, the reigning Mr. Austria and the closest thing in Graz to the bodybuilding elite. Marnul was a flamboyant, charismatic figure who tooled around Graz in a sports car with a voluptuous blonde by his side. Marnul was proof positive that with a great body came great sexual opportunities. Marnul invited his young acolyte to train at the Graz Athletic Union in the bowels of Graz's Liebenauer Stadium. The rudimentary structure had concrete floors, no heating, and equipment copied from pictures in the American muscle magazines. Although Arnold celebrated the solitary, competitive nature of a bodybuilder, he did not like to be alone and was a natural participant in the boisterous camaraderie of the sport. Bodybuilders usually have a workout partner, and Arnold enjoyed the banter and manly fraternity.

When Arnold looked back on those days, he realized that joining the Athletic Union was the first decision he had ever made on his own. Arnold admitted later that he was "literally addicted." The union was closed on weekends, so Arnold rode his bicycle into Graz, broke a window in the building, and worked out by himself in the darkened gym.

Marnul says that he introduced Arnold to synthetic male sex hormones known as anabolic steroids, which are used to grow skeletal muscle. Steroids were developed in the 1930s and served an important medical function to treat hypogonadism, when the testes do not produce enough testosterone for normal growth. Russian and other Eastern European weight lifters began using steroids in the early 1950s, achieving records impossible without the drugs.

For bodybuilders, steroids were a miracle drug, enabling them to bulk up in ways that no amount of physical effort could duplicate. In the early 1960s, anabolic steroids were not illegal, but they were not something that reputable doctors prescribed for healthy adults. Steroids were already the drug of choice for serious bodybuilders, giving them the competitive edge that could be achieved no other way. Although there are anecdotes about Arnold's mindlessly gobbling down steroids like potato chips, that was hardly his standard approach to anything involving his chosen sport. As unseemly as it may appear for the thirty-two-year-old Marnul to have introduced fifteen-year-old Arnold to steroids, it was nonetheless a rite of passage, a sacrament in his newfound religion.

Arnold's mother was upset at his obsession, thinking that she was losing her son and that he might be hurting himself. "When I discovered what he was doing, I was concerned that it might be harmful to him," she reflected. "As a baby, Arnold was always sick with one of the child illnesses."

Arnold's father tried to throttle his obsession by limiting his trips to the gym, but Arnold built a mini-gym in the unheated basement of his house. Waiting for the bus to Graz in the morning, he struck poses and trained while his peers watched. In the hours he served his apprenticeship as a carpenter, he happily picked up heavy loads of lumber. During lunch hour, he turned the timber into his makeshift heavy weights. "We used to joke around, 'We don't need a forklift, we have Arnold,'" said his friend Franz Baumgartner vulgo Großhofbauer. If Arnold's friends asked him to join them in an after-school soccer game, he usually refused, lecturing them that fast running would hurt his muscle development. At night, he rode his bicycle back into Graz to work out until the late hours.

"You'll see! I'll be like this," he vowed to his friends, pointing to a picture of Reg Park. "I'll become Mr. Universe and go to America."

"Yeah, sure you will," his friends laughed, letting Arnold indulge in his reverie.

Arnold did not have that much time for his old friends any longer. He had a new circle of bodybuilder friends, several of whom became crucial figures in his life. In the popular nineteenth-century Horatio Alger stories, the hero inevitably rises out of poverty after being befriended by a wealthy older man. The tales have been mocked for their refusal to deal with harsh socioeconomic realties of life in the Gilded Age, but they may have been more realistic about how people advance than the critics suggest. Arnold's rise is in some ways a series of linked Horatio Alger stories, in which he uses what he has learned from one mentor to move to the doorstep of another mentor, and then move on again. He takes on part of their being as his own, and moves on when he has learned everything there is to learn.

Arnold's closest friend among the bodybuilders was Karl Gerstl, a twenty-year-old medical student in Graz. It was an unlikely friendship: a shy, studious doctor-to-be and a young high-school student on a career track to become a carpenter. Dr. Gerstl insists that there was difficulty with neither the gap in age nor the level of education. "Arnold has always been a personality," Dr. Gerstl reflected. "Among the friends, Arnold was the leader. I was five years older, but he was the leader. The difference in age made no difference."

Karl was so impressed by his younger friend that he invited him home. Arnold met Karl's parents and hit it off immediately with Alfred Gerstl, a complex, sophisticated man of a type Arnold had never met before. Arnold stayed overnight so often that he became subject to the same strict house rules as Karl. In Austrian society, this was an unusual occurrence, doubly so since the Gerstls were Jewish. Arnold's feelings for his mentor were such that in 2004 he signed a photo to him, "From your second son." Yet in Arnold's 1977 autobiography, he does not even mention Gerstl's name. As Arnold admits, it has taken many years for him to mature enough and to gain enough wisdom to appreciate what Gerstl gave him.

Alfred was a cosmopolitan mixture of cultures and faiths. In the late nineteenth century, Alfred's grandfather Dr. Ignaz Gerstl had sailed to New York City to study medicine. He had a remarkable voice that led to careers as a bass-baritone at the Metropolitan Opera and a celebrated cantor. He traveled the world, giving performances, and died in Graz during World War I. Alfred's father fell in love with a Catholic woman, who converted to Judaism before they married in the Graz synagogue. As a Jew, he could not obtain a position with the Austrian Federal Railway. To advance himself, Alfred Senior converted to Catholicism, and his wife reverted to her former faith.

At the beginning of World War II, Alfred was enough of a Catholic to avoid being sent to a concentration camp and worked as a toolmaker in a chain factory. When he was drafted into the army, he went underground, serving as a courier for anti-Nazi partisans.

There had been two thousand Jews in Graz when Alfred left. When he returned there were fewer than a hundred. Alfred says he rejected joining the leftist Social Democratic Party because he was told he had fought Hitler for religious, not political, reasons. It was his first indication that the endemic anti-Semitism of his homeland had not died but had merely been muted. He joined the Conservative Party. He was in several respects an outsider. "To the Catholics I was a Jew," he said. "To the Jews I was a Catholic."

Gerstl is a profoundly conciliatory human being, the fact that he returned to Graz being only the most obvious indication. Gerstl believes in developing all aspects of a person, his mind beyond all else, and his body, too. He worked with his son and his friends who pursued bodybuilding and karate. Although

Gerstl was a small businessman with a tobacco shop, his deepest interest was politics. He saw it not as a way to social and economic advancement, but as a vehicle to transform his nation. In his living room convened an eclectic group of former partisans, politicians, activists, and intellectuals to discuss the questions of the day, represented by everything from an anarchist to conservatives such as himself.

Neither Karl nor Arnold said a word during these discussions. If they would have preferred to be working out instead of listening, they hardly dared say so. "When Arnold talked with Alfred, he was quiet because he saw an elevated personality, but he was like a sponge quiet," said Dr. Gerstl. "Arnold was not shy. Arnold never was shy. He never knew any fear, but I was the one who was more introverted. He was always outgoing."

Arnold saw in that living room a family model so unlike the authoritarian rule of the Schwarzenegger home. There was openness, nowhere more startling than when Gerstl broke into song in a voice inherited from his cantor grandfather. Gerstl insisted that after his son and his best friend worked out, they listen to serious music recordings, including two of the great voices of the time, the half-Jewish Austrian tenor Richard Tauber and the Romanian Jewish tenor Josef Schmidt. If that did not make Arnold an immediate lover of classical music, it gave him an understanding of a cultural world far beyond his own.

In his many hours in the Gerstl home, Arnold dreamed only of his next workout, but he had been exposed to an exalted vision of politics and of life. "We paid very little attention, but as time goes on it has an impact," Arnold said. "The mind is like a tape recorder. He [Gerstl] would be talking about classical composers, Beethoven and Mozart. And he would talk about tolerance and about the Second World War. He was educating us in a way. He could reach me much better than my father."

Arnold would go on to meet many of the most celebrated people in the world, but he rarely sat with a more extraordinary group of people than those to whom he listened those long evenings in the Gerstls' apartment. They were men who did not see themselves as the passive recipients of history, but individuals who believed that they had the possibility of putting their strong marks on the world. Although Gerstl had a distinguished political career, becoming a senator and twice president of the Bundesrat, the Austrian Senate, no period of his life does he remember with more excitement and insight.

One of the other regulars at the Gerstls' was Helmet Knaur, a big, boisterous, redheaded anarchist whom the Nazis had imprisoned in the notorious Strafkolonie 999 labor camp in North Africa. Knaur, who came from a wealthy Austrian family, was rescued by the British and brought back to Austria, where he fought against the Nazis. He was a bodybuilder fluent in English who translated some of the American bodybuilding magazines for Arnold.

Knaur never fully recovered from the trauma of war, yet to Arnold and the other young men, the former prisoner was a formidable human being. Knaur raged against those crypto-Nazis who remained at the levers of power in the new Austria. He combined body and mind with action, and he had a major effect on Arnold. "Arnold was influenced by the fact that I was in the resistance and my brother was in a concentration camp," said Gerstl, "but he was mainly influenced by Helmut Knaur, who was a great anti–National Socialist and inspired these young people."

It is a measure of how much Arnold was affected by the man that his whole idea of faith changed. One day Knaur handed him *Pfaffenspiegel*, an anticlerical book filled with the myriad misdeeds of priests. Arnold was not much of a reader, but the treatise affected him. Knaur had his own deep insights into the human psyche. When they were discussing the book, he asked his young protégé if he prayed to God for a good body.

Of course, Arnold said. Knaur made the telling point that if he wanted a champion's body, he would have to build it himself. It was as if Arnold had been cheating, asking someone else to lift a part of his weights. Arnold returned home to tell his parents he was no longer going to Mass on Sunday. His mother was distraught at losing her son to bodybuilding, and now he was apparently replacing the Catholic religion with a newfound faith.

"Knaur had a big impact on me," said Arnold. "He was a large, fat guy. I thought he was cool, because he was so big. All of the bodybuilders admired him, because he was the most sophisticated. He was a free spirit and very liberal. He would bring *Playboy* magazines to the lake. He would find ways to educate you and to talk about knowing various languages. He introduced us to women, to girls at the lake. He wanted to make sure we got together with girls."

The guests in the Gerstl living room shared a common belief in a new democratic Austria that would bury the swastika so deeply that it could never be resurrected. The evils of Nazism reach further than anti-Semitism, but that was one of the fascist core beliefs, and it had found fertile soil in Styria for hundreds of years. At the behest of the leaders of Graz, in 1496, Emperor Maximilian I expelled the Jews, declaring that "the Jews had too often shown serious disrespect of the sacraments, and had tortured, martyred, and killed Christian children and taken their blood and used it for their obstinate, malignant nature." The Jews had been allowed to return, but always as sojourners.

Though the Holocaust had left only a few witnesses to the horrors of the gas chambers who returned to the streets of Graz, undercurrents of anti-Semitism still existed. The Jews were no longer accused of taking the blood of Christian babies, but there were many who believed that Jews controlled the banks and the newspapers, the secret presence that manipulated the lives of the good people of Styria.

To Gerstl and his friends, there could not be a truly democratic Austria if society was infused with this conspiratorial delusion. At the Teachers Academy in Graz, Director Franz Göbhard was educating the next generation of teachers about Nazism. Since the subject was not discussed in most of the students' homes, Dr. Göbhard's words were a revelation. The lectures had such an impact that they offended the neo-Nazis and ultrarightists, who considered these truthful accounts as treasonous slander and marched on the town center, attacking the professor. The group of men whom Arnold befriended quickly organized a counterdemonstration and marched to the Herrengasse themselves and chased the neofascists away.

One of those running alongside Arnold was Kurt Marnul, who remembers his young companion as both "outraged—so filled with rage against the Nazi regime"—and also "a very reserved boy" whose "only interest was in shaping his body in hopes of one day becoming Mr. Universe."

To Arnold, bodybuilding was the world. In Sir Isaiah Berlin's famous essay "The Hedgehog and the Fox," the historian of ideas argues "there exists a great chasm between those, on one side, who relate everything to a single central vision, one system less or more coherent or articulate, and, on the other side, those who pursue many ends, often unrelated and even contradictory." Arnold was a hedgehog who pulled most of his meaning, purpose, faith, ambition, and ideas out of bodybuilding. For almost anyone else, it would have been like divining water from the desert sand, but Arnold filled his glass up. When he said years later that everything he knew from life he had learned from bodybuilding, he was not far from wrong.

Arnold listened to Marnul's lectures on nutrition with intense interest and heeded his precepts, treating his body like a machine that had to be fueled properly. He treated sex the same way, as a bodily function that he needed and wanted regularly. There was a rudely hedonistic quality to the bodybuilders. As young as he was, Arnold was invited to their parties and provided with suitable companions for the evening. On the Thalersee, he picked up young women, had sex with them, and dropped them back at the lake, never to see them again. "I saw the other bodybuilders using them in this way, and I thought it was all right," Arnold said. "We talked about the pitfalls of romantic situations, serious ones, how it could take away from your training."

By the time Arnold appeared at his first bodybuilding competition at the leading Graz hotel, Steirer Hof, the teenager was transformed. He did not win first place that evening but was the most promising younger bodybuilder in Graz. He took home a trophy, and his mother, who had been worried about her son's bizarre obsession, finally saw value in his efforts.

Aurelia was worried not about Arnold's body but about his soul. It was a small village, and his mother knew more than she wanted to about her son's sexual pattern. That was a mother's legitimate concern, but his father's attitude was bizarre and unsettling. "Jesus Christ, you should see some of the women my son's coming up with," Gustav told his friends, as if bragging about his own virility.

Since he was a little boy, Arnold had been a natural leader, and that was even truer now. Everyone wanted to be around him, in part because wherever he went he had an impish, cheerful manner that made things come alive. He was fearless and daring. One evening he and his classmate Peter Urdl drove their mopeds into Graz to see a movie. Returning through a driving snow, Urdl swerved to avoid hitting a car, and both youths were thrown off the little scooters. Arnold jumped back on his moped, but Urdl decided he would walk back to Thal.

As genial as he was, Arnold had a humor that he wielded like a knife that cut only others. If you were inside the sacred circle of friends, you were probably protected from the worst of it, but if you were not, he could be merciless in his jibes and pranks.

On one occasion he went into the Kastner & Öhler store in Graz to buy a new jacket for his *Trachtenanzug*, his traditional Austrian wool suit. He purposely asked the salesman for a size too small. The clerk was complimenting Arnold on how fine he looked when the seam split in the back. "No, that one doesn't fit me," he said, and the story entered into the growing myth of Arnold.

CHAPTER FOUR

Helping Hands

As soon as eighteen-year-old Arnold arrived to begin his year of obligatory military service on October 1, 1965, he set himself apart from the other inductees. While he and his fellow trainees were trying on their army uniforms, Arnold decided to pull the same trick on the Austrian army that he had pulled on the clerk in Graz a few months before. He purposefully crunched his shoulders so that the jacket would tear, in so doing calling attention to his distinctive body. It did just that, creating a murmur and laughter among the other fledgling soldiers about this giant who had landed unassumingly in their midst. That evening in the barracks, one of the other recruits, Johann Strebel, had the misfortune of sleeping in the bunk bed beneath Arnold. His two-hundred-pound body pressed the springs so far down that the mattress was practically in Strebel's nose.

Arnold had all the attributes for success in the military. He was in superb condition, able to go effortlessly through calisthenics and other physical training that had others panting and doubled up in pain. The discipline was a costume he enjoyed wearing. And yet back in the barracks when the day was over, Arnold was a rollicking, joking raconteur, highly popular among the men. He held no higher rank than the other inductees, but they looked up to him. One evening when there was a fight brewing, he marched at the head of his company to the anointed field. His mere presence calmed down the opponents and ended the prospects of a brawl that could have had serious disciplinary consequences.

In the continuing pattern of Arnold's life, an older man came forward to help ease Arnold's way along his chosen path. In this instance, it was an officer fascinated by bodybuilding and awed by Arnold's extraordinary physique. He set up a small gym where he could work out with Arnold.

Arnold fit his massive frame into the ordered, disciplined life of the military. He seemed the least likely soldier to go AWOL in the midst of basic training, but in late October Arnold pulled himself over the fence and set off to compete in the junior division of the Mr. Europe championship in Stuttgart, Germany. He had so little money that he had to settle for a third-class train that rolled slowly through Germany for a day, stopping at local stations. Arnold had never left Austria before, and the trip was an adventure in itself. He was perfectly aware of the consequences of deserting his company, if only for a few days, but nothing would prevent him from testing himself against the best young European bodybuilders of his generation.

At Stuttgart, the fans at the Wulle Rooms considered the event as authentic as any other sporting event, but to most others it remained a bizarre spectacle—these muscular young men standing in swim briefs, shorn of body hair and covered with a thin coat of oil, flexing their overwrought muscles. It was where Arnold belonged, loving the brilliant flash of attention, appreciating the adulation that he felt was rightly his.

Not only did Arnold win the championship as Junior Mr. Europe that day, but he met two of the crucial people in his life. The first, Albert Busek, was only three years Arnold's senior, but he was far older in the ways of the world. Busek had come from Munich along with his boss, Rolf Putziger, a businessman who owned a leading health club and a bodybuilding magazine. Busek was a wiry, literate man. Although not a bodybuilder himself, he had a deep appreciation and understanding of the sport. He realized immediately that in Arnold he had seen someone astonishing. "I was interested in Arnold as a great athlete to bring him to Munich," Busek recalled. "I talked to Arnold about it." Busek also talked to Putziger, who agreed that Arnold would be a valuable addition to his gym.

When Arnold walked onstage to receive his trophy, he was joined there by Franco Columbu, who that same day had won the European power-lifting championship. Columbu was a five-foot, four-inch-tall, 170-pound Sardinian. Although Franco had arrived in Germany only three years before, he was less an outsider to this world than was Arnold. Franco lived in Munich, where he was working as a bricklayer. He knew all the bodybuilders and power lifters, and it was unthinkable that this kid had shown up and won.

"Who are you?" Franco asked, standing there, holding his trophy. "Where you come from?"

"Oh, I'm not from here," Arnold said. "I'm from Austria."

"Oh, I'm from this tiny village in Sardinia," Franco said.

"Yeah, well, I'm from a tinier village outside Graz," Arnold snorted. "Only two hundred people!" For the first of many times he had one-upped

Franco—by cutting Thal to a tenth of its size. Columbu had an ebullient sparkle to his dark Italian eyes, an aggressiveness tempered by his incongruously sweet demeanor, and a bouncing, optimistic stride.

If there is love at first sight, there is surely friendship at first sight, and that is what it was between these two men that evening. They had the same rough-hewn, masculine bodies that perfectly mirrored their spirits. Although twenty-four-year-old Franco was six years older than Arnold, they were peers in every other way. Franco had the same resolute spirit as Arnold, a man of the most compelling optimism who had already achieved far more than most men of his background. His father was a shepherd, who sold his three hundred sheep when he went off to war and put the proceeds in the bank. When he took out his savings at the end of World War II, inflation had rendered him only enough liras to buy three sheep. Instead, he purchased an old horse and made his living as an itinerant peddler, selling beans and potatoes from town to town in baskets made by his wife. Franco was an only son who became a champion boxer as a teenager. Like Arnold, he did not like a sport in which he was dependent on others—in this case, managers and trainers. He left for Germany, because there he could find a job.

That evening Arnold went out to a big beer hall with a small group including Albert and Franco. "It clicked like the chemistry," said Columbu, who was training in the unfinished Munich gym that Albert was managing. "Arnold kept telling me what he's going to do, the kid is going to get out. I identified with that. If I stayed in Sardinia, I might have a million sheep and be a millionaire with sheep, but I didn't want that. Arnold [was] the same. He said, 'I want to come to Munich and train with you.' "

Arnold did not even have enough money for a return ticket, and he had to borrow funds from his newfound friends to get back to Austria. As Arnold took the long, tedious train ride, he carried back with him a trophy and a future in Munich. Until that point, everyone in his life had considered his goal of becoming a great bodybuilder an aberrant and dangerous fantasy. Even his mentor Gerstl had a limited vision of Arnold's prospects. "Freddy would say, 'Arnold, just remember I always have a job ready for you. You can be the swim master at the biggest swimming pool in Graz,' " recalled Arnold " 'You will have the security of the pension and the health care.' "

Clutching the trophy in his hands, Arnold had the physical manifestation of his future. In his conversations with Busek, he knew that when his military service was over, he would pursue his destiny in the capital of Bavaria. In the next months, he kept in touch with Albert by letter.

Arnold climbed back over the fence at the army base as if he imagined he could walk into the barracks with his absence unnoticed. He was observed as he dropped over the wall and escorted to the brig, where he spent a week in a cold cell with only a blanket for company.

As tedious as those days were, Arnold's life was proving to be a ladder in which the rungs led only upward. By the time he left confinement, he was the most celebrated soldier on the base. Instead of condemning him for his dereliction of duty, his superior officers praised him as an exalted figure who had exhibited the kind of daring conduct that could be used on the field of combat as well. "I had become a hero, even though I had defied their rules to get what I wanted," Arnold reflected later. "That one time, they made an exception."

This was another remarkable aspect of Arnold's life. He could do things and say things that would have merited the most onerous consequences for anyone else. He could turn the malignant into the benign, and the malicious into the kindest sentiment. Arnold trained as a tank driver and enjoyed being part of a five-soldier team on the Korean War–era vehicles. He was so strong that he was the only man who could single-handedly put chains on a tank. He got the best of his assignment as a tank driver, too. In the afternoons when his comrades were cleaning the tanks and performing other tedious duties, Arnold was deputized to work out. He kept at it four or five hours a day, using some equipment that he had brought from home.

For the first time in his life, Arnold had all the food he wanted. Shoveling gigantic portions of meat into his mouth, he put on twenty-five pounds of muscle. And every day, every repetition, every spoonful of food, every ingestion of steroids moved him away from the Austria of his birth.

"From my earliest recollection, I've always had a tremendous hunger and desire," Arnold reflected. "It was just there. I feel it was a combination of my upbringing, my heredity, competition with my brother, and the frustration of growing up in a little country. I despised growing up in a little country. That's the reason I left Austria. I did not want anything about my life to be little."

By the time Arnold headed off to Germany after his year in the service, he was a monstrous 225 pounds. In the Europe of the mid-sixties, few men had such mammoth muscular bodies, and people often viewed him as either a formidable figure or a freak of nature.

Arriving in Munich on August 1, 1966, Arnold was confronted by a great city beyond anything he had ever known. He was a small-town boy almost overwhelmed by the polyglot realities of the Bavarian metropolis, the anonymous crowds, and the ceaseless bustle.

Arnold's new employer, the genial Putziger, squired his newest employee around the city in his Mercedes and invited him to stay in his fine house. Putziger was a homely man with a nose that dominated his small face, and tiny eyes squinting behind large glasses. It took Arnold several days to realize that Putziger was attempting to seduce him, a mark of Arnold's naïveté and the gym owner's subtlety. "Putziger had agreed immediately to bring Arnold to Munich, but his thinking was young guy, good-looking, easy win for him," said Busek. Putziger was always on the prowl for young men at his club, using guile, money, and other blandishments.

When Putziger asked him to sleep in his bedroom, Arnold could no longer pretend that he did not understand what was happening. It was a common scene in that world, a poor bodybuilder—which was the common lot—propositioned by a rich gay gentleman. In this instance, Putziger sweetened his suggestion with enticing prospects. Other bodybuilders had shared that bed before Arnold, and with the businessman's assistance, they now were no longer merely the marginal denizens of Munich but had their own gyms. Putziger painted an even more grandiose picture for Arnold, saying that through that bedroom door lay the portal to greatness as a bodybuilder and perhaps even a movie career. It was an alluring package, all in exchange for sexual compliance.

Arnold's immediate problem was not a movie career but a job, and he desperately needed to maintain some semblance of a relationship with Putziger. It would have been understandable if he gave the matter consideration for a moment at least. After all, he was a man of limitless ambition willing to run great risks to achieve his goals. By everything he said then and later, he was outraged by Putziger's offer. He left the house prepared to pay the price for his refusal, even if he lost his job at the newly opened gym. He went to Albert and asked his help. "Arnold was mad as hell," said Busek. "I fixed the problem. Putziger wanted to throw him out."

Arnold moved into a windowless cubbyhole in the gym that previously had been used to store vitamins. There was hardly enough room for his small cot. "Why you got such a little bed?" Columbu asked, looking at Arnold's legs hanging a foot over the end of the cot. "It must come from Sardinia," Arnold explained. For the two new friends, it was one raucous put-down after another, so many jokes that when they were working out it was a vaudeville show in the gym.

The two men had an almost magical rapport and a congeniality and impish exuberance that spilled over to almost anyone who came near them. They were both poor men and foreigners in a country not always known to be welcoming to impecunious outsiders, but they didn't care.

After several weeks Arnold had enough money to rent a tiny bedroom in a modest apartment. It was about as low a circumstance as one could have without living on the street, but the gym was the theater of Arnold's life. Arnold had an energizing impact on those around him, and he created an excitement in the gym that had not been there before. "We called him the 'muscle locomotion,'" said Busek, "because within two weeks everybody had a much higher level of energy working out. He was immediately the center. He had this outstanding talent, and everybody who had eyes knew that this was one outstanding body. Then there was his drive and personality. First you see the body, and you are impressed, and then you see him working out and acting, and you are totally impressed. It was his attitude, his will to arrive at his goals, that impressed you."

Bodybuilders are frequently criticized as being no more true athletes than professional wrestlers, poseurs who display the illusion of strength rather than its steely reality. In Arnold's instance, this was simply not true. In 1966 he won the heavyweight division of the International Powerlifting Championships, just one example of his authentic strength and athleticism.

Arnold, like most great athletes, did not have the patience to train amateurs, to squander his efforts on the Munich businessmen and wannabes who envisioned themselves developing muscles like their hero. His real life consisted of the hours before his work at the gym, when he trained seriously with other true bodybuilders.

Among the goodies that Putziger had dangled before Arnold's eyes when he first arrived in Munich was a trip to the Mr. Universe bodybuilding contest in late September 1966 in London, where he expected Arnold to sit in an orchestra seat and observe the stage on which one day he might compete. Arnold told his would-be patron that he intended to go not as a spectator but as a competitor. When he walked out of Putziger's house that day, he had walked out of his one sure way to get to England. "If it hadn't been for Albert, I wouldn't have been able to compete in the Mr. Universe contest," Arnold recalled. "I was working in the gym with Putziger, who did everything to stop me. Putziger wanted to throw the application away. Albert caught it some way, and I filled it out, and he sent it to London."

Years later Arnold's proudest boast was that he "did not have to kiss ass," though early in his life he had often stooped to ingratiate himself. He had only a few weeks before the Mr. Universe competition in London, and he knew almost no one in Munich. He stood one evening in the street outside the home of Reinhard Smolana waiting for the champion bodybuilder to return home. The previous year Smolana had won Mr. Universe in his weight division, and Arnold wanted to tell the man of his exalted dream to go compete himself.

Invited inside, Arnold was a compelling witness for his own story. That evening after Arnold left, Smolana made up his mind. Not for the first or the last time, a generous colleague took up the cause of this outsider blessed with energy, playfulness, a refreshing guilelessness about his ambitions, and willful determination. Calling his friends, Smolana began to collect the necessary money to send the youth from Graz to England—and show the Brits and the Americans a thing or two.

CHAPTER FIVE

Paying the Price

As Arnold's cab pulled up at London's Royal Hotel, where the 1966 Mr. Universe contestants were staying, he recalls there being "at least fifty huge guys standing outside the glass doors," apparently waiting for him. Many of the leading bodybuilders in the world "crowded close, grabbing and feeling my arms and talking in at least ten different languages." Perhaps a crowd should have been there welcoming him with wild enthusiasm, but no one else has anything like that recollection. "No one knew him, and no one knew he was coming," said Dianne Bennett (she and her husband, Wag, were the leading couple of British bodybuilding).

What anyone outside bodybuilding would consider a whopping untruth was in part the natural rhetoric. The whole idiom of discourse in bodybuilding was and is exaggeration, expanding everything—from the size of one's biceps to the magnitude of the applause. It was a genial conspiracy that afflicted almost everyone in what was at that time a tiny, marginalized world. It was an effective way of moving people. Arnold inflated his truths to such a size that anyone could see them. His hyperbole began with bodybuilding, but it expanded to cover this whole life and the world beyond.

Even as he began his bodybuilding career, Arnold was already carrying this further than it had gone before. The contest itself became a landmark in Arnold's budding career because it challenged the young bodybuilder to pull out precocious psychological as well as muscular tactics—before he even went onstage.

Arnold met his main opponents for the first time at the prejudging, the first and most important part of a bodybuilding competition. It is there that the judges grade the contestants on various parts of their bodies. It is a long, tedious process. Except for the opponents, their entourages, officials, and the press, there generally are few spectators; but for the competitors, this is the crucial part of the process.

Backstage was a place of tense anticipation for the competitors. Their bodies were being oiled so that their physical form took on an otherworldly, defined quality it did not have in the gym. Then they began pumping up, working to expand their muscles to create the maximum presentation to the judges. "It is a visible process and a riveting one," writes Charles Gaines. "Watching a muscle after working it, he [the bodybuilder] can *see* the freshly oxygenated blood flooding the tissue, spreading and flushing the skin, creating the condition known as a pump—the sacramental engorgement of muscle that is an outward and visible sign of growth."

As Arnold pumped himself up, he watched the other contestants. For all his hyperbole, when it came to the realities of bodybuilding, Arnold was as fair and accurate in evaluating himself and the others as any of the judges. The competition from across the Atlantic was formidable. Arnold had a vision of America as a land of skyscrapers, giant people, and endless vistas. When he saw the greatest of the American bodybuilders that day, it was a physical manifestation of that image. Arnold felt they looked like "special creations of science," a peculiarly American science that created these superhuman creatures.

Arnold carefully observed the most formidable of his challengers, Chet Yorton. The American's body not only was oiled but had a brown sheen, a preternaturally dark color that could not have been obtained merely by tanning. Each muscle group seemed to stand apart, with veins standing out like marble in beefsteak. As for Arnold, he had what was an almost plump veneer in comparison. Arnold's hair reminded Rick Wayne, a professional contestant, of "Prussian militarism when the cut of the day was Beatle, and his skin was white enough to light up the dark." If the trophy were awarded to the most courteous of the competitors, Arnold would have won hands down. His lack of English made him seem deferential and self-effacing, characteristics that Arnold did not consider virtues and that he was rarely accused of possessing in later years.

The judges found it an extremely difficult call to choose between Arnold and Yorton. One of the judges, the legendary American bodybuilder John C. Grimek, decided not to vote in the obviously close competition. Grimek knew Yorton and believed that he might have been considered biased. In the modern bodybuilding world of which Arnold became the prime creator, such a gesture would be considered a betrayal of friendship.

"Considerable time was spent calling out both of these men for body comparisons and checking various body parts," Grimek wrote later. "A few of the judges got up and stood behind the area where I sat in order to get a better look. I heard two judges discussing the merits of each man, and more than anything else, husky Yorton came through to victory on the merits of his fine calves!"

The judges did not announce the winners of the prejudging. The finals took place at the Victoria Palace Theatre before nearly three thousand spectators the next evening. As the bodybuilders prepped themselves for the minutes of posing, young, untried Arnold should have been the most nervous. As much as he anticipated going onstage, the nineteen-year-old saw this as a moment to learn from other bodybuilders. Although few of them spoke German, he had a friend from Munich there to translate for him.

Arnold had impeccable instincts to seek out whoever could help him. He approached Rick Wayne, who though only five feet eight inches tall, packed two hundred muscular pounds on his frame. Wayne was from the Caribbean island of St. Lucia. Before going to London, Arnold had never seen a black with an Afro hairdo, and he had rarely met anyone so articulate about his chosen sport. Wayne was a talented journalist as well as a bodybuilder, with a philosophical view of the sport deeper than many of his peers'. Arnold asked Wayne questions about the nature of bodybuilding in a humble, supplicating manner, a novice seeking wisdom from one of the elite.

Arnold wanted to know about the leading American bodybuilders. Although the interpreter relayed the Austrian's curiosity about such celebrated bodybuilders as Dave Draper, Larry Scott, and Bill Pearl, it was clear that Arnold was preparing for the inevitable challenge. When the conversation turned to a comparison between Steve Reeves and Reg Park playing Hercules, Arnold's championing of his South African mentor came across as a championing of himself. Arnold considered Reeves too pretty, too refined, too handsome, and too perfect to play the elemental Hercules. Reg, by contrast, had rawness to him, an edge, and a fundamental force—essential components of what Arnold considered a true Hercules.

To Wayne's surprise, Arnold predicted that he, Arnold, would win the Mr. Universe competition. Even in translation it did not sound to Wayne to be hollow posturing, but rather a confident assertion. Before going onstage, Arnold asked a final question: "Do you think a man can get whatever he wants?"

The question stunned Wayne, who had seen enough of the world to have a quick and certain answer. "A man's got to know his limitations," he replied.

As soon as the answer was translated, Arnold shot back, "You're wrong."

"What do you mean, I'm wrong?" Wayne said, growing mildly irritated at this arrogance.

"A man can get anything he wants," Arnold declared definitively, "provided he's willing to pay the price for it." Then he turned on his heels and went to prepare to take his place onstage, leaving a speechless Rick Wayne behind.

As Arnold waited to go onstage, he saw for the first time the extent that body-building was an amalgam of sport and show business. Dianne Bennett had put together a group of young women from her gym called the Glamour Girls, who lifted weights to Roy Orbison's "Pretty Woman." An acrobat performed and several comedians regaled the crowd while Miss Britain herself took a bow. Interspersed in the variety show came the bodybuilding championship.

When Arnold walked out onto that stage, he was a bigger presence than he had been only a few weeks before. He was not only bigger physically but larger in the manner in which he exhibited himself. He had never posed be-fore such an audience, and he was carried out onto the stage on a great wave of applause. The adulation sent a warm rush through his body. He had only three minutes in the spotlight, but it was enough time to make a lifelong im-pression, to realize that "it made the entire four years of training worthwhile." Before the cheering spectators, he was not what he seemed back in the hotel, a German hayseed wearing silly, ill-fitting corduroys, looking like a boy play-ing in a world far beyond his comprehension.

Arnold's posing techniques were rudimentary, culled largely from Ameri-can bodybuilding magazines. He was more than comfortable wearing nothing but black briefs on the great stage. As he breathed in and flexed his pecs, he also seemed to breathe in the applause and the acclaim, puffing himself up with it as no other bodybuilder did.

Arnold made such a formidable impression and the applause was so ex-tended that he was called back for an encore. He did not win that evening but came in second to Yorton, by any measure an astounding achievement.

Arnold returned to Munich a newfound celebrity. He embraced the goal of going back to London the following year, determined to win the amateur Mr. Universe title. Already in January 1966 he had been on the cover of the Ger-man muscle magazine that Busek edited; now he was on the move—upward. When he walked down the broad avenues of Munich, it was with a confident stride worthy of a young millionaire. When he worked out, he was the man whom people watched over their shoulders.

As good as he had a right to feel about his young life, Arnold still found him-self criticized by his father. "Why do you write so big?" his father asked, refer-ring to one of Arnold's letters to his parents. "You don't want to write more?"

"No, it was just my handwriting like that," Arnold replied.

"Yes, but now you're grown up," Gustav said, as if doubting that fact. "You're not anymore in grammar school."

Arnold was a revered figure in the Munich sports world, but in his father's eyes he was a son who could not even write a decent letter.

One major reward of bodybuilding was that Arnold could see dramatic results in his physique. He could see his lower-body muscle groups growing each day. Until then he had been building his upper body, the most visible signature of his physique, but now it was his legs that he had to develop as the worthy foundations on which stood his massive frame. Never for one moment, however, did he lose sight of his real goal—competitive victory.

Arnold sought in almost every aspect and every moment of his life to challenge someone and to best him. He trained with a partner with whom he could have a mini-Olympics every day. His expectations were not only high but relentless—even ruthless. If his prospective partner showed up late to the gym even once, he was gone.

No one Arnold ever partnered with in Munich (or anywhere else) was as perfect a psychological and physical match as Columbu. They were an inevitable duo—Lone Ranger and Tonto, Batman and Robin—in which Columbu's diminutive size advertised that he was always the second lead.

Arnold had convinced Columbu that he should begin serious bodybuilding training. What held the Sardinian back in his competition with Arnold was the aesthetics of height; it was almost impossible to beat a man nine or ten inches taller. As they developed their bodies, Columbu was probably Arnold's superior, pound for pound. As it was, Columbu did not have Arnold's brilliant psychological acumen, the bag of tricks that he was willing to play on all his competitors, even his closest friend.

In the gym, there was constant gamesmanship between the two men, endless banter that masked the seriousness of their endeavor. "Look in the mirror," Arnold scolded as a tired Columbu stopped doing squats lifting 400 or 500 pounds. "See those guys watching? They're from Italy, and they see you quitting in the middle of a set. What will they think?"

The men may not have been from Italy and they may not have been watching, but that was enough to push Columbu to do ten reps. "You're a lazy bum!!" Arnold yelled when he finished, pushing his partner to do at least half a dozen more.

On other occasions when Arnold left for a few minutes, Columbu added ten-pound plates to the bar that Arnold was lifting. Arnold would return, struggle to do his reps, not realizing that he was lifting twenty pounds more than he had before—but doing it nevertheless.

That minor deception exemplified what Arnold considered a basic reality of life itself: a person could do far more than he thought he could. Pain was the proof that what he was doing was right and that he was pushing beyond the parameters of the possible. He walked through a crucible of pain, and no one who would not walk through with him was his equal.

"When Arnold did squats, sometimes he would faint," Busek said. "He didn't know his limit. He knew his limit when he fainted. But without fainting, he didn't know the limits."

What saved Arnold's compulsively excessive workouts from being exercises in masochism is that even in the most agonizing of moments, he exuded joy. He projected that quality in whatever he was doing, and that more than anything drew people to him.

Even in his first months in Munich, his full psychological makeup was in place, his philosophical mind-set and his life's agenda. He was like a young general with a war plan so tailored to his strengths that he would deviate from it not one iota, no matter the momentary vicissitudes of battle. Few, if any, had a full sense of the magnitude of Arnold's vision. As gregarious as he was, as willfully extroverted, he was alone with his ambition. He had consciously distanced himself from his parents. Women were interchangeable. As important as Busek and Columbu had become, there was a subtle distance, places in the heart and soul to which they did not gain admission.

Unlike many bodybuilders, Arnold not only fit comfortably into his enlarged physical self but had a manner that made him seem even bigger. What to some sounded like boasting was to him merely an honest recitation of the truth, as he saw it: magnified, dramatic, dynamic. And yet for a man of such ego, he could be extraordinarily perceptive and empathetic toward others, in pursuit of what he could take in value from them. "He learns from other people," said Busek. "He has the ability to pick up the good things like an elephant who with his trunk pokes into anything that's important and sucks it in."

Arnold's focus on whatever lay before him was extraordinary, from an exercise in the gym to a casual conversation with a stranger. His focal point was locked in, because even the most trivial of moments led to a higher focus, and that higher focus led to something far beyond it. Thus, when a companion ran a few yards to catch a tram, Arnold walked ahead at his same steady pace, prepared to wait for the next streetcar. He was trying to gain weight, and it wasn't good to jolt his body—his passport to the future.

CHAPTER SIX

The Trickster

Aman sauntered into the Munich gym one day with a belly the size of a beer keg resting precariously on pencil-size legs and told Arnold, "I want to be a champion." Arnold looked the man up and down and told him he definitely had the makings of one of the immortals and that he would train him to enter the Mr. Germany competition taking place in only a few weeks.

Arnold told the man that to impress the judges, he should yell. The louder he yelled, the more impressed the judges would be. When he leaned forward in a pose, he should shout, "Ahhhhhhhh!" in deep guttural tones, and when he stood up tall to do a double bicep pose, he should emit a high-pitched "Ehhhhhhhhh!" And with each pose he should step closer and closer to the front of the stage until he stood within a few feet of the judges, screaming at the top of his lungs. "During the training Arnold would hit him on the leg and say, 'Louder, louder,'" recalled Columbu. "We told him to stick the stomach out."

The man was an apt pupil, and on the evening of the Mr. Germany contest, he proudly walked onstage with the other contestants and posed in a manner that had never before been seen in a bodybuilding context—and has never been seen since.

Arnold's reputation as a prankster grew alongside his fame and physique. He greased barbells so it was impossible to lift them. He told a bodybuilder that to look like a champion, he must eat ever increasing mixtures of ground-up nutshells and salt; the young man did so with devastating consequences. In his unremitting pranks, Arnold resembled the classic archetype of the trickster, a mythological character found in Greek legends, African tribal

tales, American Indian myths, and American folklore. He is Hermes stealing
Apollo's cattle. He is Brer Rabbit with his Tar-Baby.

The tricked did not see things the same way the trickster did. What to
Arnold was the often-pathetic gullibility of his victims was to them the trust
that their esteemed trainer would give them worthy advice. Arnold had no intention of allowing others to presume on his friendship and affection. Just as
his aggressiveness with women was more about power than sex, so was this
endless gamesmanship another way of asserting his sovereignty over his
world. He was making fools of those who had the audacity to think that they
could follow too closely on the trail that he had laboriously blazed. Yet for all
that, Arnold possessed the knack of behaving in ways that in anyone else
would seem mean-spirited, petty, and even dangerous, and he used his magnetic charm to transform his actions into amiable anecdotes that embellished,
rather than spoiled, his legend.

Arnold enjoyed the spectacle of uncertainty over what he would do next.
In a bodybuilding exhibition in Germany, Arnold flashed what appeared to be
a Nazi salute in the midst of his posing. It was hardly a public admission of his
devotion to the Führer, but the act was greeted with little applause and much
unease. Afterward, backstage, Arnold told Rick Wayne: "These people are
nothing without an Austrian to lead them." Wayne found Arnold's contemp-
tuous comment funny, and the whole matter was forgotten. It was, however,
typical of the almost reckless bravado that exemplified Arnold. He pushed
and probed beyond what was permissible, and then dismissed his actions
with defiance and moved on.

Soon after Arnold returned from London, Putziger told him that he had
decided to get out of the gym business and concentrate on his magazine and
supplements. He asked if Arnold wanted to buy him out. Arnold had no
money and was in no position to walk into a Munich bank for a loan, so instead he found people willing to help and was able to take over partial ownership of the gym. It was an impressive accomplishment, especially since he
had done it while refusing to become Putziger's lover.

In Europe many people thought of bodybuilders the way many Americans
considered motorcycle groups: self-conscious outlaws spoiling for a fight.
Arnold considered it an amiable diversion to have a few liters of beer and then
face off with belligerent punks, who thought they would test their mettle
against Arnold and his buddies. When he and his friends made their way
through the beer-sodden during the famous Munich revel Oktoberfest, he
was a walking provocation.

Arnold was sauntering through one of the giant Oktoberfest tents when a
drunken American ran into him. There was as much give as tackling a house.

Arnold kept on walking, an action that the American took as a provocation. Lunging at Arnold from behind, he grabbed him by the neck. Arnold pushed him off, turned, and faced the little man who stood before him, fists at the ready. Arnold smiled almost imperceptibly, slowly took off his shirt, and then flexed his muscles. The American put his fists down and invited Arnold and the others to dinner.

Arnold had the Germanic love of the woods and went off with his body-building friends to work out on weekends. To him, it was communing with the primitive, wild soul of man that had long been domesticated. They brought girls with them to cook the massive meals and to have sex with.

Even in the streets of Munich, when he wanted attractive women, Arnold did not squander his time on civilized patter. He simply said, "Do you want to have sex?" When a woman asked to see him with his shirt off, Arnold said that he would be delighted if she would do the same, a request that was at times granted. Arnold had to assert his superiority, to women as well as men. He made most of his boastful requests for sex in the presence of his male friends, simultaneously demonstrating his power over the women while duly impressing his friends.

Although Arnold was able to build up the gym business, he had already set his sights far beyond success just in Munich. He ingratiated himself with the most powerful individuals within his vision. He was daringly assertive with people who would have intimidated most teenagers from his modest background. After he finished second in the Mr. Universe contest in England, he met Wag and Dianne Bennett, prominent gym owners devoted to bodybuilding. The Bennetts became figures like Gerstl and Busek, studiously devoted to Arnold's advance, sharing vicariously in his success. Wag had been one of two judges who had voted Arnold first and had been the first man in Britain to bench-press 500 pounds, both qualities that immediately impressed the young bodybuilder.

The Bennetts were a genial couple totally lacking in British reserve. They invited Arnold to stay with them and their six children in their home above their gym, a converted church in East London serving as a temple of new-found faith. Since there wasn't an extra bedroom upstairs in the living quarters, he slept on the bed settee in the front room. "His corduroy trousers were a poor fit, because he was growing so fast that he resembled Li'l Abner," Dianne Bennett recalled. "He couldn't get shirts to fit him, so I had to make them in fluorescent lime and yellow Crimplene."

"He came from a stern background, and he loved the informality that you could lie on the floor and eat your food and the kids would climb all over you," said Dianne Bennett. Wag Bennett taught Arnold that he must add a new element to bodybuilding, posing to music with lights dramatically sil-houetting him. At first Arnold wondered what this had to do with sport, but once he realized that this show-business aspect would help him win, he added a whole new component to his performance, posing to the theme music from the film *Exodus*.

To the Bennetts Arnold poured out his hopes, including his aspirations of one day meeting his hero, the South African bodybuilder Reg Park, who in 1958 and 1965 had won the professional Mr. Universe title to which Arnold aspired.

As soon as Arnold returned to Germany, he began writing letters to Park, something he had held off from doing for years. "Before that, when I was just a young bodybuilder, a nobody, I hadn't been sure he would bother to answer," Arnold explained his reasoning in his autobiography. He had had no intention of writing Park as a mere fan and risking rejection. Instead, he had waited for the time when he could at last write as a colleague. That moment, he reckoned, had now come.

Soon afterward, Park received a call from Bennett. "There's a kid from Austria, who is a sensation, and you're his hero and he idolizes you," Bennett said. "If I put on a show in London, will you come over and guest-star the show with him?" Bennett had already lined up a series of shows in Scandinavia for the Yorkshire-born Reg, and it was an easy matter to send an acceptance.

Arnold had influenced Park and Bennett to create a show in which one of the greatest, most celebrated bodybuilders in the world would share the stage with a teenage novice. Arnold had employed a shrewd ploy to advance himself, but he had done so largely in order to learn from a master. Arnold was no book reader. People were his reading matter. Getting to know Reg was like checking a book out of the library that he had long wanted to have.

"I consider myself a sponge," Arnold said. "I'm extremely good at absorbing information. I was always hungry to hang out with people who were smart and to learn from them. With my background, I had to do a lot of learning. It was like the world was one big classroom. That's not just a metaphor, but it's a real thing."

It was a measure of Arnold's good fortune that it was Reg's portrait he happened to see in that shop window in Graz, for in the whole history of bodybuilding, other than the immortal Sandow, he could not have found a better model than the South African. The two men had the same kind of body, and as they saw it, a moral force emanated from their bodies. They were raw, rough-hewn, tough men in both body and spirit.

"Steve Reeves was the typical hero, but I picked Reg," said Arnold. "I admired what I read about him. He was not only an incredible bodybuilder, he was the strongest bodybuilder in the world. He bench-pressed over five hundred pounds. And he had a family. None of the other bodybuilders had families that I ever read about. They were on the beach and running around with surfboards. It was written that Reg had a great wife and he was lecturing at the university in South Africa."

When Reg arrived at the gym in London, Arnold said that he had "this foolish self-conscious smile on my face. I just kept looking at him and smiling—almost like when a girl has a crush on a boy and she doesn't know what to say; she just has this smile on her face. I was absolutely speechless. I was afraid to talk. I ran around like an excited little kid, looking at his muscles, trying to talk to him."

Arnold was not a man who exposed his emotional vulnerabilities, and there perhaps has been no other time in his life when he has so openly admitted his weakness. He had found in Park a father figure who was like a little boy's model of his father when Dad was the most powerful and perfect of men. As great a bodybuilder as Arnold became, and as proudly committed as he was to his chosen sport, it was equally a means to achieve a powerful sense of traditional manhood.

While Arnold was dumbstruck with awe at meeting Reg, his hero was a man of reserve that strangers often thought was shyness or aloofness. The best that Reg managed was a wave in Arnold's direction before he returned to his workout.

Arnold and Reg had hours to overcome their mutual apprehension during their tour together. A magical transference took place whenever Arnold stood next to those more powerful, more celebrated, than himself. After a week touring England with his idol, Arnold had achieved a prominence he had not had before, not simply as the world saw him but as he saw the world. Afterward a reporter asked Park what he thought of young Arnold. "Well, this kid could be the greatest of all times. He's young. He's got potential, he's got charisma, and the crowd liked him."

Arnold sought to push himself ever closer to the man who stood at the peak to which he was ascending. "I understand you bring out the current Mr. Universe to South Africa," Arnold said.

"Yeah, we do a barnstorm where we do every city hall, Johannesburg, Cape Town, Port Elizabeth, East London, Durban. It's good for my business."

"If I win, would you bring me out?" Arnold asked.

"Sure," Park said. "With pleasure."

CHAPTER SEVEN

Mr. Universe

A rnold was obsessed with power, with the pure physical manifestation of
power in his body and with the powerful men who dominated the world.
He had begun calling himself "Arnold," in the third person, but this was not
so much a royal manner as one of the many ways he motivated himself. By ob-
jectifying himself, he could train "Arnold" even harder. He developed new
exercises and motivational techniques, utilized special equipment, chose different venues for training and various training partners—whatever it took to
keep "Arnold" on a relentlessly focused course. He trained five or six hours a
day, a full-time job in itself, and then had all his other obligations at the gym,
as well as the good times in the evening, almost as much an imperative as
training and work. He was a philosopher of competition who saw that these
hours of training were the great competition, and training began when most
people thought it was over.

It is possible that there have been other bodybuilders who worked as hard
as Arnold, but no one worked harder. He wasted no time, and he considered
driving within the speed limit a waste. One of Arnold's friends was a maniacal
driver who thought nothing of steering his car up on the sidewalk and then
back down again before careening down the street. Arnold followed his lead,
picking up enough speeding tickets that his license was in jeopardy.

Arnold returned to London in the fall of 1967, where he believed only Dennis Tinerino, the new American heir apparent, stood between him and the
crown. Arnold was going to seek whatever edge he could in this competition.

For the first time, he began a level of gamesmanship, of sheer trickery, of sub-terfuge, that had never before been seen in bodybuilding. He did not try to hide his actions but proudly admitted them afterward.

One of the judges in the competition was Arnold's mentor Wag Bennett. "He was helping me, giving me instructions, psyching me up," Arnold said. Bennett not only stayed a judge but actively conspired with Arnold about how he could win.

Busek had press credentials for his bodybuilding magazine. "I sent him out as a spy to locate Tinerino and see how he looked," Arnold proudly disclosed later. Bennett's and Busek's actions were not only patently unfair, but they were unnecessary. That was true of most of Arnold's endless trickery in the years to come, a seeming waste of his energy and will that diminished the gen-uine quality of his victories. In terms of psychological self-pumping, the scheming was vital. Arnold needed to feel and portray himself as standing on a plane far above his opponents, a master manipulator able to pull the strings of fate and to needle his opponents into fatal errors.

When it was time for the crucial prejudging, Arnold was asleep in his hotel room. Bennett called Arnold and woke him up. Clutching his swim briefs, Arnold ran down to the lobby and joined his competitors a minute before the deadline.

The reason the prejudging at a bodybuilding competition takes place in a largely empty auditorium is that it is bereft of drama and excitement. Arnold, with his gift for self-dramatization, pumped himself up emotionally by turn-ing the event into an epic psychological drama. While the two top contestants waited backstage, Arnold said that Tinerino asked Arnold how he felt. "Fan-tastic!" Arnold recalled saying. "It's the kind of day when you know you're going to win." Tinerino remembered it a little differently. "I was going through my routine, and I looked in the mirror and here was this larger-than-life body-builder saying, 'I vant you to get out of the vay. There's not enough room for the two of us. I vant to pose here. The best man shall win, and you're looking at him.'"

Arnold liked to believe that his little verbal ripostes were like pinpricks in a balloon, but it is more likely that these gestures pumped Arnold up far more than they deflated Tinerino. As Arnold walked onstage, instead of standing in the lineup, he walked forward and began shaking hands with the judges.

After being admonished to join the other contestants, Arnold made a point of standing next to Tinerino onstage, observing his every move. After Tiner-ino posed, Arnold did a kind of counterprogramming, highlighting every as-pect of his body that bested the American's, a lean, confident winner's presentation. When it came time for the final pose, Arnold continued surreptitiously observing Tinerino, topping him with his own poses, checkmating his opponent's every turn.

The next evening in the same theater in which Arnold had finished second the year before, he was awarded the amateur Mr. Universe title. "I was twenty years old, and I was already the greatest and the best," Arnold claimed in his autobiography, but that was not strictly true. There had been a higher competition, and sharing the podium that evening was the American Bill Pearl, winner of the *professional* Mr. Universe title.

Arnold was focused so completely on what he was doing that his was the only reality, but as he stood next to Pearl, he could not rightfully consider himself "the greatest and the best." To deserve that title, he would have to defeat such men as Bill Pearl.

"I would think Arnold was in awe of me," said Pearl, recalling his prowess. "At that particular time, there was only one hot dog at the top. I happened to be the hot dog at that time." Yet even the professional Mr. Universe, looking at the twenty-year-old amateur, knew his own days were numbered. "Well," he confessed candidly, "I knew that Arnold was probably going to take my place in the industry."

Arnold was not yet the champion of champions, but he was already leader of the bodybuilders. After the finals he suggested that the thirty or so competitors jump in their cars and taxis and head down to Trafalgar Square to show the skeptical British just what bodybuilders were all about. In the center of London some of the bodybuilders ripped off their shirts and began posing. Franco decided to perform his favorite trick. He picked up one end of a Fiat, and one of the other bodybuilders picked up the other, a feat impressive to everyone (except presumably the vehicle's owner). "Come on, you guys are getting out of hand," Arnold scolded. "We gotta go before the bobbies come. Let's go eat."

There was a relentlessly methodical quality to Arnold's training, and his work in the gym was only part of it. Soon after he won the Mr. Universe title, he cabled Reg Park, telling him about his victory and expressing the hope that the bodybuilder would keep his promise to invite him to South Africa. Park was as good as his word; he cabled back the financial arrangements, and Arnold flew off to Africa in December 1967.

As a guest of the Parks, Arnold spent Christmas in Johannesburg, an experience that had a deep emotional impact on him. The young bodybuilder was hungry not only for fame and money but for a father figure and family. Bodybuilders often do not reach their peak development until their thirties, and forty-year-old Park had a formidable physique that had not dramatically diminished, even though he no longer competed. As the two men walked down the beach, they looked more like two brothers than a father and a son.

As much as Arnold had appreciated his time with the Gerstls, in the Parks he found a model of what he wanted his own life and family to be. "We would sit down to dinner in a very civilized way," Park said, "and we would discuss the day. He wasn't accustomed to that. His relationship with his father was not of that caliber. He favored the eldest son. He was always putting Arnold down, saying, 'Why are you doing this and why are you doing that?' And so at our house, he had freedom."

Marion Park was a beautiful woman, who at the age of nineteen had been in an automobile accident serious enough to end her promising career as a ballerina. Soon after, she met Reg, who had arrived from England on his bodybuilding tour of South Africa, and fell in love. They married and had two children. "Marion was an incredible woman, very feminine and mothering, and made me food and fruit salads and drove me around," said Arnold. "I just totally loved her. I said to Reg, 'She's the perfect woman.'"

"Arnold fell in love with my wife," said Reg. "He really did. She was what he wanted. She was a housemaker. She's a mummy." Marion happened to be Jewish, and though that had nothing do with Arnold's deep affection for her, it is further evidence that he is far from anti-Semitic. "I considered theirs the most perfect marriage," Arnold said later. "There was still the sort of relationship where the female does not compete with the man. He is boss, and that's the way it is." In later years Arnold would learn to keep his anti-feminist attitudes to himself or to temper them, but he continued to look with dismay at the American woman who, as he saw it, "feels inferior if she has to prepare her husband's dinner."

Reg lived in an exquisite house and ran five health clubs. Arnold was impressed with the whole symmetry of the man's life and the generous way that the Parks treated him during the six weeks he stayed with the family. "Arnold could hardly speak a word of English," recalled the Parks' son, Jon Jon. "He was very Teutonic in his whole appearance and dress. He wore sandals and socks. He'd part his hair on the side, kind of a Brylcreem look."

Arnold's English was still rudimentary, but the Parks took the time to understand him. Of all the gifts he might have given Reg that Christmas, the best was his dreams. He had never really opened up to anyone before about his ambitions, but he showed the Parks a sheet of paper on which had written his goals.

"I want to win the Mr. Universe many times like Reg," he said proudly. "I want to go into films like Reg. I want to be a billionaire. And then I want to go into politics."

Arnold knew that almost everything he wanted lay in America, and he began planning to get there. He understood that what others called luck was often nothing but good timing, and to be too early was as foolish as to be too late. With his victory in the amateur Mr. Universe contest, his value had increased to such a point that he could legitimately start making plans to go to the United States.

Arnold would have ended up in the United States eventually, but the way, time, and place it happened was due to his own calculation and careful preparation, as well as the press of events. Arnold had a friend in Munich who had gotten him involved in a business deal that not only was turning sour but involved illegalities. He had not known about the dealings, but he might have been indicted. "I almost made myself thrown out," Arnold said. "I got in trouble with the police. Little troubles. I created a situation that forced me to leave. Somebody told me—'Split. Now you *have* to go to America.'"

As an amateur, Arnold had no money to bankroll himself in America, and he needed some kind of sponsorship. There were two major competing body-building groups in the United States. The older organization was centered in York, Pennsylvania, where Bob Hoffman ran the York Barbell Company. York sold most of the barbells in America, and his publications were devoted more to weight lifting than bodybuilding.

Hoffman's nemesis, Joe Weider, was a full-fledged proponent of body-building. He took what the York man had begun and copied it, expanded it, opened it up, marketed it, and professionalized it. He started his own International Federation of Bodybuilders (IFBB), run by his brother, Ben Weider. Joe's magazines, including *Muscle Builder/Power* and *Mr. America,* had pizzazz and energy, while the Hoffman publications *Strength & Health* and *Muscular Development* projected a staid, gentlemanly understatement.

Arnold was already on the cover of *Muscular Development* in July 1967. Even before he arrived in the United States, he had a series of articles with his by-line in the York magazine that Busek believes were lifted from his German bodybuilding publication. Arnold may have appeared like a muscle-bound naïf, but he was sophisticated about bodybuilding, the only thing about which he cared deeply. "I was talking to three camps, York, Weider, and Dan Lurie [president of the World Body Building Guild]. There were three organizations, but most didn't have ties to business. Weider was the one known for picking up the guys, and grooming them in his magazines, and building this whole fantasy around you."

Arnold pursued his York contacts and tried to dangle that possibility in front of Weider. "He told Joe, 'Hoffman wants me to go to York,' and Joe went crazy," said Columbu. Weider was perfectly tuned into the small world of bodybuilding and had a sense of Arnold's potential. Weider was creating an empire that would one day reputedly make him close to a billionaire. It was a fortune built on developing bodybuilding stars with images exciting enough that readers would buy the nutrition supplements, pamphlets, books, barbells, and other equipment that he sold in the magazines.

Arnold was not a phenomenon who could be forgotten for long. Eventually Joe invited Arnold to the 1968 IFBB Mr. Olympia contest in New York City. This was the premier competition in bodybuilding. In exchange for plane fare and expenses, Arnold agreed to compete with the greatest bodybuilders in the world.

To prepare his readers for the arrival of the great new champion, Weider put Arnold on the cover of the July 1968 *Muscle Builder/Power*, looking superhuman, his upper chest bulging out like giant parabolic metal plates. The following month Rick Wayne wrote the first profile of Arnold. In that same issue, Ben Weider wrote a preview of the September contest in which Arnold's arrival is written about before it happens: "He's wearing dark glasses and an immense overcoat to cloak his enormous body. But the disguise does little good as his flaming blond hair gives him away. He's halfway up the steps when someone screamed: 'That's Arnold Schwarzenegger!' "

Beyond the hair color, there was at least one other major problem with the scenario. Although Arnold said that "his all-consuming dream, ambition, and goal [was] to beat Sergio [Oliva]," he realized that the Cuban American had a better physique and Arnold had no intention of getting beaten.

Arnold flew to London in September 1968, where he won the National Amateur Bodybuilders Association (NABBA) professional Mr. Universe title that he had so long coveted. All that was left for his next triumph was to take an American championship. Arnold told Weider's European representative, Ludwig Shusterich, at the last minute that he would compete in the IFBB Mr. Universe competition in Miami that was to take place immediately after the IFBB Mr. Olympia competition. There he would face lesser competition than he would have in New York. Shusterich's teenage son Kurt recalled driving to the London airport with his father and Arnold, who was clutching a gym bag as his only luggage. "Arnold was definitely excited," recalled Kurt Shusterich. "His goal and mission was to storm America in his chosen sport and field and to be a success and to be as big as he could be in the sport."

CHAPTER EIGHT

Joe Weider's Greatest Creation

W hen Arnold walked off the plane in Miami in late September, he was the physically biggest bodybuilder anyone had ever seen, and he had every reason to believe that the 1968 IFBB Mr. Universe title would be his. At twenty-one, Arnold appeared to have an arrogant certitude that matched his swaggering walk. Rick Wayne felt that Arnold "seemed damned sure of himself, full of Aryan contempt. You could tell by his stage manner, his pigeon-toed strut, the way he carried his enormous chest, that privately he held himself above the other Mr. Universe contestants."

At 250 pounds, Arnold was heavier than he should have been for the competition, but he believed that bigger was better. By that criterion, most of his opponents on the stage for the prejudging hardly belonged up there with him. One of them, Frank Zane, was three inches shorter and sixty-five pounds lighter—by Arnold's reasoning, a little man on a stage where big men triumphed. Zane had an elegantly perfected body, nothing overwrought or exaggerated. His was a classic form, a template. As for Zane, he was hardly in awe of the pudgy Austrian. A friend who had been in London had told him: "Don't worry about Arnold. He's not even in shape. He's big and smooth and looks like a white marshmallow." While Arnold looked pasty white, Zane had a Florida tan as perfect as if he had been turned on a rotisserie.

In the finals, Arnold finished second to Zane and saw that the world was not what he thought it was. Later that same evening, he stood on the side of the stage, watching instead of exhibiting his physique, as the emcee announced in a posing exhibition, "The one and only unchallenged king of bodybuilding—Sergio Oliva." In New York City the Cuban American had just won the top title in bodybuilding, Mr. Olympia, for the second year in a row, this latest time with no one daring to compete against him.

Oliva had a form that seemed to deny every law of human physiology. It did not appear possible that a man could have a dancer's waist and litheness as well as enormous twenty-inch slabs for thighs and huge arms that appeared to have been fused from some other giant creature. There should have been a sheer incongruity to his body, but it all came together in an absolute harmony that made Oliva a bodybuilder for the ages.

Arnold went back to his hotel that evening and cried himself to sleep. In Miami Beach he was alone, without the protective entourage of German-speaking friends. Everything about the city was foreign to him, exotic, impossible to understand. He had brought no clothes with him, because he had no intention of staying there. He told Wayne, "The idea was to just wipe everyone out and return home as king of the bodybuilders." Despite the cloud hanging over him in Munich, he still had shares in a thriving gym in the Bavarian capital. He hungered for constant companionship, and he had a world of comrades there. In Miami he knew nobody and could not even talk to people.

Arnold had had a dream of coming to America, but it was a poor man's dream, a dream of a man who had nothing to lose. Arnold had a good life in Munich, and a part of him was simply not ready or willing to give it up and walk away. Yet as he lay in that hotel bed crying, he was confronted by a new dilemma. He could not envision returning to Munich a loser. Whatever the cost, he would have to stay in America for a while. At first, he thought his defeat had been terribly unfair, but he had slowly begun to realize that size was not everything and that if he wanted to be the greatest bodybuilder in the world, he had much to learn.

When Arnold talked to Weider the next day, he was not the arrogant know-it-all he might have been had he won. He was a supplicant. Weider had seen Arnold looking at the winner's trophy with yearning eyes—and only Weider could make that happen. If Arnold had won in Miami, Weider would have celebrated his victory in the pages of his magazines but would not have had the story line he needed. "Even if he had won the title, he still had to come to us," said Weider. "Because he had no other real place to go to be idolized, promoted, and so forth."

Altruism was not Weider's primary motive. He said that the circulation of his magazines was declining, as was the sport itself in terms of popularity. If he could make Arnold Schwarzenegger the greatest bodybuilder of his time, not only would Weider have his greatest achievement as a kingmaker, but his magazines and business empire would benefit immeasurably.

Weider was in the business of taking bodybuilders and turning them into gigantic images onto which he could graft his products. "I sensed that this man would be a great idol for our sport," Weider said. "This is what brings a sport together and makes it accessible. I thought that he would be that man, because he was taller than most people, he was big, and he was very charming, and people liked him. Even his competitors liked him."

It remained only to convince Arnold—who, humbled by his defeat in Miami, was all ears. "I said, 'If you want to really know how the guys train to be champions, why don't I send you to California, and I'll get you a ticket to go there?' " Weider recalled saying. " 'You can become a member [of the gym] there, and I'll set it up for you. And I'll see that you have an apartment and you'll have a car and you'll have some food. I'll interview you, and I'll promote you to the whole world.' "

Weider had never before financed a bodybuilder the way he was offering to back Arnold. He was promising not only to dramatically elevate Arnold's physical being but to create a mythic image for Arnold every bit as huge as his frame. Arnold beamed, and his very chest seemed to expand at the prospect. "Oh, boy," he confessed, "that's my dream, to go to California and train and be on the beach with all the girls and all the champions. And I'll see how the champions train."

Several days later Arnold arrived in Los Angeles, clutching his second-place trophy, to be met by Dick Tyler, a Weider editor, and Art Zeller, a leading bodybuilding photographer. Arnold told his hosts that he intended to return to Munich after he had learned the newest bodybuilding techniques. "I hope it will be a year," he said. "I want to get as much training, sun, and supplements into me as I can." This was Weider's thinking at the time, too. Arnold would stay long enough to improve himself, then go back to Germany and open an office and do business there as Joe's European representative.

Los Angeles was a meat market, a struggle for survival. Arnold saw bodybuilders living in their cars, hustling their bodies, selling steroids, doing whatever they had to do to get by. Fortunately or unfortunately, Arnold was able to share an apartment in Studio City with an Australian bodybuilder named Paul Graham.

On December 9 and 10, 1968, two automobiles were stolen in Los Angeles, only to reappear in the Antipodes. In January 1969 the Justice Department filed a complaint asserting that Paul Graham had "transported two stolen Mustangs, a 1965 Ford Mustang and a 1966 Ford Mustang, in foreign commerce from Los Angeles, California, to Sydney, Australia."

Arnold danced a sinuous waltz to stay away from various illegal activities that bodybuilders used to make money. Arnold was close enough to Graham that in 1969 they were staying together in a hotel in Hawaii for a bodybuilding exhibition. "He said that he had some legal problems, and one day he left the hotel," said Arnold. "The next thing I knew, I was getting a phone call to visit him in some institution down in Long Beach. He and I never talked about it. I was very far removed and never saw him take any cars. It was a sensitive thing."

Arnold's association with Graham did not end as a result. "He always has been a fantastic friend and a great human being," said Arnold. Graham left the United States and returned to Australia, where he became the top executive in the bodybuilding federation controlled by the Weiders. Arnold invited the Australian to his wedding and was best man at Graham's. Several of Arnold's old friends believe that as a foreigner himself, he was fortunate not to have been drawn into Graham's legal problems. "I spoke to Arnold and he said no, he had nothing to do with it," said Weider. "I don't think Arnold is that kind of a guy." However, he was the kind of guy who would not abandon his friend, even though that led to unfair rumors that Graham had taken the rap for both of them.

Arnold now moved into an apartment supplied by Weider and started living on his weekly stipend. "I knew Arnold was a penny-pincher from way back," said Weider. "He pinches every penny. Gets milk out of everything. So I told the guys at my office to give him what he really needed to get by on. I knew he wouldn't take advantage of that, and that's what he did."

Twice a day Arnold worked out, in the morning down the street at Vince's Gym, in the evening at the home of Don Peters, a wealthy bodybuilder and fan. Within a few months Arnold moved to an apartment in Venice near Muscle Beach and began going daily to the nearby Gold's Gym.

"Arnold, anything you want, it's yours," Arnold recalled the feisty Joe Gold, a former Merchant Marine, telling his new patron the first day he entered the gym. Gold waited a moment until Arnold had fully breathed in the compliment. "You're just a stupid farmer from Austria, and you got a balloon belly!" Gold yelled. "It will take us a year to work on that." Arnold had just arrived, and Gold had already given him a nickname—"Balloon Belly."

As a young man, Gold had hung out at Muscle Beach when the term *beach bum* was a high compliment. He took his interest in bodybuilding and built Gold's Gym in Santa Monica, the legendary temple of the sport. The original

Gold's Gym has little to do with the modern franchised emporiums of health that bear the name across America. Gold's was smaller than contemporary gyms, about 5,000 square feet, taking up no more space than a typical store, and it was a rudimentary place. Most of the equipment Gold had built himself out of scrap metal.

"If you got up on the second-floor balcony and looked down, you'd think you were looking at hell, at Dante's Inferno," recalled bodybuilding journalist Dick Tyler. "The steam literally coming off the floor from the sweat and yelling and clanking plates. All of these guys training and the screaming. 'One more set!' 'One more set, you faggot!'"

In the middle of it, as often as not, stood Arnold. Although he could hardly communicate when he arrived, within a year he was fluent in his own peculiar brand of English. All around the room were mirrors, and Arnold and the others continually glanced at their reflected images and those of the others. Arnold was training around men who would be his opponents. Within the camaraderie, there was an element of one-upmanship as they psyched one another out.

Arnold drew people to him like no other leading bodybuilder. He was younger than most of his colleagues, but some of the older bodybuilders called him "mother." He was a font of advice, cautions, taunts, admonitions, and athletic axioms. There was in bodybuilding a peculiar rhythm, a slow, methodical pace broken by brief, intense bursts of activity, a rhythm that took over his entire life. He was soon nicknamed "the Austrian Oak," and the Austrian Oak did things fast, but he was not a man to rush or be rushed.

Arnold was lucky in many things, one being that he had arrived in the United States in time to be part of the end of bodybuilding's age of innocence. Innocence comes easier when there is little money at stake, and the rewards were so paltry that the term *professional* was almost an honorific. Men did not spend endless hours in the gym inspired by dreams of getting rich but rather of taking home a trophy and the honor it represented. They took steroids to help them bulk up, but the drugs were neither as dangerous nor as powerful as they would soon become. These men were outsiders, perceived as freaks of nature in an aberrant subculture, but that did not matter, either. Nothing mattered except the days in the gym and their clanking, collegial world.

"Oh, it was just wonderful," said author Charles Gaines, who became Arnold's friend and most eloquent chronicler. "It was not only the salad days of those individual men, but the salad days of bodybuilding. It was still outside the culture enough so that you felt like you could act with a sort of banditlike freedom. And it was just great, because you were having a ball. You're getting all that exercise, and you're high on endorphins all the time. You just feel so good, and you look so good. You work out in the gym and then you go out and hang out on the beach and then you go eat these gigantic meals and then you go party and there are girls always around them. It couldn't have been better."

Only one thing was missing, and that was Arnold's friend Franco. There was an element of joy in Arnold's young life that was lacking unless his Sardinian mate was lifting weights next to him, joining him in meeting young lovelies on Venice Beach, and sharing an apartment. "Arnold told me, 'Joe, this bodybuilder Franco, he's a buddy of mine, I miss him, I'm lonely for him. Will you do me a favor and bring him over, give him a job?'" said Weider. "You know, I try to please Arnold, so I said, 'Okay.'" It was a generous act on Weider's part, but Columbu was a formidable bodybuilder in his own right, who, despite his small size, would go on to win all the major titles. His story and personality were as unique as Arnold's. When the Sardinian's picture was on the cover of a Weider publication, it sold almost as well as Arnold's.

Arriving in Los Angeles, Franco moved with Arnold into a small two-bedroom apartment on the Strand along the boardwalk in Santa Monica. "Once every thousand years you will find two guys in one sport who click like that," said Columbu of their partnership. They had their wild and crazy times, but neither man was self-indulgent or prone to excess. They were both exceedingly neat, Arnold folding his clothes by rolling them up in the way he had learned in the Austrian army.

Their apartment became a social center for the bodybuilding world. The two friends shared a hustling, entrepreneurial spirit, and they figured out how to make money even from some of their parties. When they asked Weider for more money, he told them that they should write articles about their fellow bodybuilders. Neither man had the time or the inclination, so they decided simply to tape conversations with the other bodybuilders that Weider's writers could use as the basis for their articles. They invited the guys over. Arnold grilled steaks and opened a bottle of wine while Franco asked training questions with the tape recorder running.

As soon as they had accumulated five or six tapes, they drove over to Weider's office, where Arnold negotiated with the impresario. "Here, Joe, give us the money, fifteen hundred dollars," Arnold said. "Fifteen hundred dollars?" Weider replied incredulously. "Fifteen hundred? You guys just made the tapes. No, maybe a thousand."

The two friends left with a thousand dollars, laughing at how well they had scored. They were being paid by the tape, and after several times doing a series of interviews, they asked themselves why they let the confounded tapes run so long. They could change the tapes after ten or twenty minutes, and voilà, one tape became five. This worked blissfully well for about six months, until they showed up at headquarters and were shown into Weider's office, where an unhappy publisher sat waiting for them.

"You know, I give you an opportunity to become champions and big stars," Weider sputtered in an accent as thick as Arnold's. "I put you on the cover. And then I get these tapes and they're short and the tapes don't talk about training, they talk about how much wine you guys are drinking and how much . . ."

"Yeah, because we need to know the personality of the guys so the writers can write about them," Arnold said. No one was a better salesman than Arnold, but he had a product that morning even he couldn't move. The two friends left with no money and no more taping.

Frank Zane went out to Los Angeles to be part of those good times at Gold's Gym. He was the champion, not Arnold, but Joe Weider did not give him a stipend. Zane ended up teaching math in a Venice junior high school and working out beside Arnold. "Arnold was different," recalled Zane. "You could tell the guy had something going on, that he was special. Nothing bothered him. He was totally focused on winning and achieving his goals."

Zane and most of the leading bodybuilders trained together at Gold's each morning. "It seemed like all the other guys wanted to train when I trained," Arnold said four decades later. "If I switched my time to train at seven, they trained at seven. If I switched to nine, they'd switch. They weren't being sycophants. I think they got a certain energy from being around me when I worked out. I was always making noise and laughing about the pump and urging them. 'Forget thirty-five sets for back, today we're doing forty. Come on, sissy man, there is no such thing as pain, let's go for it.' So I think, and I hope, I brought this energy and joy to the workouts."

Bill Grant, an African-American bodybuilder, brought his three kids along with him to Gold's one day before he realized he had an important meeting. He looked around the gym and decided that he would have to ask Arnold to take care of his children. Two hours later a worried Grant returned to the gym. "My kids told me, 'Dad, Arnold was the nicest, sweetest guy,'" Grant said. "'He took us to the beach, to McDonald's, for ice cream, he played with us.' My kids have their own kids now and they *still* talk about it."

Arnold might have appeared to be living a frolicking, carefree life, but he was deadly serious. There were endless women, endless good times, but where he believed it mattered, he lived a disciplined life. He controlled his body in ways most people could hardly grasp. "Mentally most people have no connection with their muscles," he reflected. "Therefore they totally relax the stomach and it hangs out—mentally they have no control of these muscles."

When he worked out, Arnold used a technique of visualization. He saw in his mind's eye what his muscle should look like, basing the picture on another bodybuilder, an image he had seen somewhere else, or an exaggerated version of his own reality. And then he worked until he had turned that vision into a precise, physical reality. He did this first of all with bodybuilding, but it was the essential technique he applied to all aspects of his life.

Arnold had acclimated quickly to Los Angeles. He had a little apartment, a Volkswagen, a modest stipend, and no obligations except to work out regularly, be photographed, get interviewed, and give information that could be written up for bylined articles. The greatest prize in bodybuilding was only a thousand dollars, and no one made a living at the sport—no one, that is, except for Arnold and Franco. Sergio Oliva, the greatest of them all, worked all day in a Chicago foundry while Arnold was hanging out at the beach between workouts.

Arnold was the rarest of personality types, a true extrovert. He came to life around other people, and if he couldn't be around his friends, he would settle for someone else. To be alone meant to be dark and half dead. "If he ever went to the gym by himself, which was unusual, he would wait until he found somebody to work out with," said Frank Zane. "He went out to eat all the time, and he would buy somebody a meal to go out with him. Or he'd have somebody take him out, but never alone. He was always around people, always. Just couldn't be alone."

Arnold had no use for the false modesty that he saw all around him, an ersatz humility that is affected primarily to impress others. He knew his own value, and he was ready to tell you about it. As soon as Arnold had learned the rudiments of English, he started taking classes. He enrolled in general-education classes at Santa Monica City College to get an associate's degree, and Zane tutored him in algebra. Arnold was not much of a mathematician. He was not much of a reader, either, almost totally dependent on the lectures. Arnold had only a visitor's visa, so he could not enroll full-time anywhere. He attended classes at other schools, including business courses at UCLA and art classes at West Los Angeles College.

Arnold had sought a kind of freedom in bodybuilding, a sport in which he would not have to share acclaim with any teammates and in which there was no coach to define his day and workouts. He and his friends appeared free from all the tedious bureaucratic imperatives of the modern world. The reality was that they were part of a feudal empire overseen by Weider and his brother, Ben. If the two men had exercised similar control over baseball, they would by the same token have owned all the teams, most of the companies making bats and balls and other equipment, and the leading sports pages and sports magazines and run the umpires union, the Players Association, and the World Series.

Most of the leading bodybuilders struggled to make a living. Several of them were upset when Arnold arrived in their midst as Weider's new hero. "Some of the bodybuilders were a little intimidated by Arnold," said Betty Weider, a beautiful model married to Joe Weider. "Dave Draper was the big star then, and he sensed that Arnold was the future and he seemed a little depressed."

Arnold realized immediately that Weider "had two personalities . . . the warm, beautiful human Joe Weider in his private life, and the shrewd businessman at the office." Weider had grown up in Montreal, where he had begun building up his body to protect himself against French Canadian kids who enjoyed picking on a little Jewish boy with a heavy accent. He started his empire with a mimeographed sheet distributed in Canada. As he grew his fortune, he was the greatest, most enthusiastic, most genuine of fans. He gushed over bodybuilders, and he would have given anything to have been a champion himself. He had no greater honor than to be in their presence, and he created an image of himself as their noblest benefactor and friend. In the pages of his magazines, Weider promoted no one or no product as much as himself.

When Weider was negotiating a deal, hiring writers, or lining up bodybuilders for testimonials, Weider the fan was nowhere to be seen. What others considered a fair wage or an honest deal, he fancied little short of ransom, and ransoms he did not pay. As he made his great fortune, he carried almost no one with him except his brother; no editor was given equity in the company, no adviser made a partner. It was all his, and he had no doubt that that was the way it was supposed to be. Yet he says to this day that he was never concerned with money and makes a compelling case that he struggled on the edge for years before his empire began to grow.

Certainly, other than Arnold, no one has had such an impact on modern bodybuilding. This raw, self-educated man had brilliant perceptions into the modern male psyche. Bodybuilding comprised endless repetitions of a limited series of activities, a highly unlikely activity for a popular magazine. But Weider let the reader enter into what appeared to be the intimate lives of the bodybuilders. He embedded the technical information in casual profiles of the major bodybuilders, giving them personality and character.

Weider's publications were not traditional sports magazines, but a subtle, sophisticated life vision full of the hyperbole and exaggeration that is the central idiom of the sport. It was no more possible to detach the truth from the half-truth than to pour back the cream from a cup of coffee, and that was not why subscribers read the magazines anyway.

Weider was a bodybuilding version of Hugh Hefner. In the pages of *Playboy,* Hefner featured idealized nude playmates supposedly accessible to "playboys" with the affluence and style attainable by reading the magazine and acting on its ideas. In the pages of his magazines, Weider featured idealized, seminude bodybuilders, whose images appealed to his readers and whose forms could supposedly be copied by buying the products in its pages and practicing ideas set forth in its articles. Both Hefner and Weider, in their ways, had a profound influence on popular American culture and the ideals of manhood in the last third of the twentieth century.

Politically, the two men's agendas were poles apart. Hefner proffered what was a liberal political agenda; bodybuilding was largely a conservative's sport. Arnold and his bodybuilder friends were instinctive conservatives, at odds with the prevailing social culture of young America.

Although Weider boasted in the pages of his magazines that he was Arnold's trainer, Weider lived on the East Coast in those years. Even when he visited California, he was far from a regular at Gold's. "Joe's a promoter, a self-promoter," said Arnold. "It bothered other guys when he talked about the Weider principles. There was nobody but me who was training two or three times a day. He started calling it the 'Weider split routine.' That was okay with me as long as I got what I wanted. I got the exposure in the magazines. He believed in me and my future. He gave me a little bit of money. That's what I needed."

If Weider exaggerated his direct influence on Arnold, he underestimated his power of example—and Arnold's spongelike ability to learn by example. Arnold was an astute observer of almost everyone, and Joe had many lessons to impart. Weider became, as he proudly asserts, "a second father to Arnold," a man who taught Arnold much about the world.

Both men have massive egos, and over the years they squabbled about money, acknowledgment, business deals, the future of bodybuilding, and almost everything else they touched. "But the very fact that he brought me to America was like a pass for everything else." Arnold said. "He was my sponsor, so psychologically you feel you're going to a place where you'll have a home, and you'll be set up in a gymnasium where you can train with all the champions and you'll have a chance to work and go to school. So he became a kind of father image to me."

"Weider was very instrumental," said Arnold. "I learned a lot about business and deal making. He took me on trips overseas. He took me to art auctions. He taught me about bidding, how to get the best deals."

Arnold learned best and deepest not when people were consciously instructing him but when he made his own observations. He was an astute student of Weider's life. The publishing impresario had taken the marginalized sport of bodybuilding and created a great machine that was changing American culture and amassing a fortune and power for him.

These magazines that had first inspired Arnold when he was a teenager in Austria were not magazines at all, but brilliantly conceived catalogs. The articles themselves were showcases to sell Weider's products. The goods were touted in the articles themselves, infomercials that were probably more effective in moving merchandise than the overt ads. Weider was selling a lifestyle that could be fully achieved only by buying his products, and in Arnold he had found his ultimate centerfold. Every single ad was for a Weider product or those of bodybuilders associated with Weider. It was a compelling, irresistible vision to many young men who accepted as literal truth what was largely fantasy.

"I saw the Joe Weider magazines with all these fantasy articles," Arnold reflected in 1997 when he saw the world of bodybuilding straight on. "I read how Joe trained this champion and that champion, that they were given all these supplements and sent to the Weider Research Clinic. I thought the clinic was a huge research center somewhere in America connected to the movie industry and full of guys wanting to be Hercules. As a teenager, you have all these strange dreams and visions. Didn't matter that they were [wrong], it motivated me to get to America."

The famed Weider Research Clinic existed only in the pages of the magazines. Those around Weider soon learned that there was a mythic reality proffered in the pages of the magazines and there was what the uninitiated would call the truth, and they often had little to do with each other. Joe was constantly inventing new products to promote in the magazines with the heartfelt testimonials from the stars of bodybuilding. And the money came pouring in. One of his editors, Gene Mozee, recalls that on one memorable day in the early 1970s, over $90,000 arrived in cash and checks, some of it for products that did not even exist yet.

Arnold might get irritated at the way he felt Joe sometimes took advantage of him, but for the most part he set out to learn what he could from the master. Arnold may not have been an original thinker, but he had a brilliant ability to extrapolate the ideas of others, incorporate them into his own thinking, and apply them in new places, eventually in his movie and political careers. "He lit a candle." Arnold said. "I would be sitting in his office and I saw how you design a magazine. I saw why it's important to have great headlines and to use a language for sixteen-year-old kids rather than the twenty-five-year-olds. He would write headlines like HOW TO CREATE A CHEST LIKE A FORTRESS, not HOW TO BUILD YOUR CHEST. There always had to be a strong name, 'Cannon Ball Biceps' or 'Herculean Legs,' always adding something that made it more snappy. Hanging around him, I picked up all sorts of things."

Weider had other bodybuilding stars in and out of his office, but nobody learned the way Arnold did. "He saw how I had started with nothing, how I began building my magazines, and how I began building the sport and how I began to make statues and pictures and trophies and everything else," Weider said.

Bodybuilders made fun of the way Weider endlessly promoted himself, emblazoning his name on the cover of his magazines, having his photo and name throughout the publications, even his statue in the company headquarters. Puzzled, Arnold asked Weider about it. "'Why are you making a statue of yourself?'" Weider recalled the young Schwarzenegger demanding. To which Weider confided: "People think if you got a statue, you're something special.'"

It was a key insight. Beyond the narrow nucleus of the elite bodybuilding world, people across America were sending in their cash and checks. They revered Joe and thought him a mighty figure. And a mighty figure he was, an engine of self-promotion, a self-created myth, a contrived legend as famous as any of the bodybuilders. These were all things that Arnold observed and took on as part of his own being.

Weider had risen to fortune and power by the constant recitation of simple messages and simple images. He kept beating away at the public consciousness, and as he succeeded, tens of thousands of dollars started flowing into his headquarters every day, a tribute to him and his daring. Now all of his energy, ambition, and focus was on creating a gigantic image of an Arnold whom Weider considered his greatest creation and in truth was his greatest student.

CHAPTER NINE

The "Wow" with the "Pow"

In the sexually liberated sixties, Weider pushed forward the erotic promise of bodybuilding, and he used Arnold as his primary vehicle. In March 1969 Weider announced the debut of the first issue of the newly titled *Mr. America: The Fitness Magazine for Virile Men*. The magazine reached beyond the hardcore bodybuilder and promised not only information on training but "what current fashions appropriately set off a muscular physique, what hairstyle will enable him to look his best, how to plan for the future, and—last but not least—how to come on strong with the groovy gals." It would feature advice on "how to find, win, and keep the beauty of your choice" and "how to make people like and respect you."

Mr. America had become a lifestyle magazine, and Arnold was perfect for carrying forth its ideology. It was essentially Arnold's magazine: almost every issue featured him if not on the cover, then in major articles. He was prominent not only in pictures and articles but in advertising and promoting an endless array of Weider products: Vitatone, the high-potency iron/vitamin B tonic; the secret M.D. XR7 weight-loss plan; the Roller Slim and Slim Gard; Vitamin-Mineral 100 tablets.

The magazine told the story of Weider's meeting a saddened, defeated Arnold in Miami, where he poured out insecurities that resonated with the youthful readers. Weider commiserated with Arnold not only about his disappointing second-place finish in the Mr. Universe competition but also about his failures with women. "Well, I've not made the scene with girls quite as frequently as I used to," Arnold supposedly told the bodybuilding impresario. "Perhaps so much bulk overpowers them and makes them feel vaguely uncomfortable—the li'l dolls. Maybe it keeps me from really swinging. I'm still only twenty, and I certainly don't want to miss out on my jollies yet!"

"And you won't have to, Arnold," Weider is quoted as saying. "The principal need right now is to translate that tremendous leg size into dynamic muscularity so that your entire body is the sum of all its parts, so that it's not just a breathtaking chest, or arms, or back . . . but a totally breathtaking *you*. What is needed are new tools with which to work—new techniques—and to 'terror bomb' your legs in a totally different way than when you worked for size and bulk alone. Wanna know how?"

"Sock it to me, baby," Arnold said, immediately fluent in the American idiom. "I'm two hundred forty pounds of putty-in-your-hands."

Weider transformed Arnold, beginning with his hairstyle. "When he came to California, Arnold wore his hair in a raffish, any-old-way fashion that really dated him," the magazine noted. "Joe suggested that he put himself in the hands of a Hollywood hairstylist like [Jay] Sebring, who works on movie stars like George Hamilton, physique stars like Dave Draper, Don Peters and John Tristram, and on famous models like Mark Nixon."

Weider added the word *power* to the title of his other major publication, *Muscle Builder/Power*. That hard-core bodybuilding magazine also chronicled the virile pursuits of Arnold. "In the months ahead and for years to come . . . you're going to read and see a lot of Arnold Schwarzenegger in the Weider magazines," the editors announced, "because Joe Weider is busy making another immortal."

Arnold was younger than most of the other bodybuilders featured and a natural role model for the young readers. The magazines chronicled behavior that bordered on the misogynistic but was celebrated as the very model of how a man should act. In less than a year, using Weider's techniques, Arnold had supposedly transformed himself not only physically but sexually. He had become Weider's leading expert on male sexuality with insights such as "the laboring class still produce the most babies and are by all accounts the grooviest, sex-wise!" His smiling photo graced an article celebrating the virtues of masturbation, which stated that "masturbation is nature's way of keeping millions of healthy, virile young men from becoming savage rapists."

"He's [Arnold's] turned on like he never was before," the photographer Zeller told the readers of *Mr. America*, "and when we go out to the beach the girls flock over to him from Handsome Whoever-it-was, like bees to flowers, leaving their dates biting their nails and cursing the very word 'muscles.' He's so muscular and so streamlined and so sexy. When he goes into a malt shop or restaurant the girls take one look, then lay odds on who's gonna swing with him next (generally all of them win ... it takes a little time but Arnold doesn't play favorites!). ... Guys drop knives and forks right and left, and waitresses skid giddily over the floor with trays of food that will be spilled any second! The gals will be swinging from his biceps like a Maypole. He's the 'wow' with the 'pow,' and they're never gonna be the same again."

The idea was to have sex with a woman and then move on. "His [Arnold's] sex appeal is so terrific he never has to date the same girl twice," noted *Muscle Builder/Power*. "That's what muscles and mo-o-o will do for you!"

Arnold could be brutally hurtful to women whom he found unattractive or unworthy of his momentary pursuit. Usually Arnold's capacity for emotional cruelty was not chronicled, but this was so much a part of him that occasionally it made the pages of the magazines. "You are so lovely, my dear," he flattered a waitress, as reported by bodybuilding journalist Dick Tyler. When she turned to place the orders, Arnold's eyes followed her, and he told Tyler: "Her legs are bad." Arnold was endlessly amused at the gullibility and vanity of much of the human race.

When the waitress brought them their meals, he complimented her again: "Did anyone ever tell you that you have good legs?" The woman was not used to receiving such praise, and as she floated away, all smiling and happy, she did not hear Arnold's whispered aside: "Well, no one ever will." The happy waitress returned to take their dessert orders, and then walked toward the kitchen. As Arnold watched her retreating, he said: "Her skirt was up higher than when she first came. She thinks she has good legs, because I mentioned it, so she raised her skirt. This is so funny."

Gene Mozee, for many years a top Weider editor, told another story for the readers of *Mr. America* in June 1969. "Arnold wanted to stop for a strawberry milkshake, so we went into this place, and he sees this good-looking girl with some guy sitting at a table," Mozee said. "Well, he just goes over there and sits with them. In Germany and Austria this is the custom. You should have seen the look on the guy's face! He didn't know what to do. He asked the guy if it was okay, and the guy gulped and said, 'Sure.' By this time, we're nearly out with laughter! You see, in Austria if the guy looks at you, you say: 'What are you looking at?' Then you take his girl.'"

Not all of Arnold's sexual adventures were tales to inspire the readers of *Mr. America*. Arnold took pleasure in asserting his superiority not only against true competitors for trophies of bronze but over those who in no way challenged him. Don Peters was a movie-star-handsome bodybuilder who had won several regional titles in the sixties. He was a generous friend of the sport who opened up his home to Arnold to train and introduced his guest to his beautiful girlfriend. On one occasion the couple had a fight, and the young woman drove over to Arnold's apartment, a journey that presumably would not have taken place if there had not already been the beginnings of a flirtation. Later that evening Arnold asked the young woman if she would reschedule an appointment for him with his lawyer. Arnold dialed the number, and as soon as the woman realized the voice on the phone was Peters's, he grabbed the handset and, according to Mozee, shouted: "I just fucked her. I just fucked her."

Mozee recalled that he had his own problems with Arnold's sexual aggression, with both his wife and his secretary. "Not many people had the guts to confront Arnold on anything," Mozee said. "He would try to pick up your girlfriend. He made a move on my wife one time, and when she told me about it, I told him that was not only totally unacceptable, but I'd have to deal with it if it ever came up again. Another time, I brought my secretary, Sharon, over to Gold's Gym. Arnold walked over in his workout gear with his cutoff T-shirt. He gets up real close and starts to reach for her breast. And I said, 'Arnold, don't do that.' I mean, I don't know whether he was actually going to touch her breast or it was just kind of an intimidation, but that's the trouble."

Weider may have bragged in his magazines that his methods had created this new sexually vibrant Arnold, but he learned to his dismay that it was a spigot that could not easily be turned off. When Arnold went to visit the Weiders at the apartment they were renting on their L.A. visits, he took one look at Betty, Joe's gorgeous model wife, exclaimed, "Wow," and began flirting with her. Weider informed his protégé of the obvious: "Arnold, she's my wife."

Arnold backed off. "He looked so sad," Weider said. "He really, really liked her. Arnold said of all the women he knew and met and couldn't go to bed with, my wife was the only one [that he regretted]."

In most other circumstances, an employee hitting on his boss's wife would have found himself an ex-employee, but Arnold's sense of humor and wit were an amulet that he cast over his most untoward behavior, and suddenly it was all right. As Arnold's friends look back on those years, they privately make a defense that he never could publicly. They assert that women were constantly coming on to him, propositioning him, grabbing his body, and that as often as not, he was not the aggressor. Franco was as much a swordsman, and Arnold and he shared common experiences. "Sometimes people would bring these girls up to the apartment," said Tyler. "And they [Arnold and Franco] would be asleep, and they'd open the door and throw these girls in. They wouldn't know who they were. And the girls would just jump on top of them."

Arnold could reach out and touch a woman inappropriately or make a crude remark that would have merited a slap in the face for anyone else, but he did not consciously intimidate women with his physical strength. Betty Weider posed with Arnold in many photo sessions for the Weider publications and also handled the stable of models who appeared in the magazines. "There were some bodybuilders that the models didn't want to work with," said Betty Weider. "They didn't feel comfortable. Arnold was never on that list. He always did things in a kidding, playful, light way, never in a manipulative way."

When Arnold went on a bodybuilding exhibition tour to Hawaii, *Mr. America* noted that he had "leis upon leis . . . leis everywhere!" There was still a modicum of innocence in Arnold, still worlds he had not yet seen. "The restaurant had plenty of beautiful women," he wrote of one evening. "One had one of the most beautiful figures I had ever seen. She kept looking over, and I gave her the sign to join us. Ahh, what a lovely creature. We sat making eyes at each other and plans to be alone." Only afterward did his friends tell him that his prospective date was a female impersonator.

As much as Arnold was touted as bodybuilding's ultimate sex symbol, there were certain matters that were left largely unspoken. "And don't worry about your 'lonely Austrian boy,'" wrote Tyler in *Muscle Builder/Power* in June 1969. "Not only is he booked solid with girls, but he has a whole group of 'slaves.' I've found that every champion is usually surrounded by several 'satellites' and 'strangeloves.' The 'strangeloves' are those who are a little fruity about their hero and the 'satellites' are those young bodybuilders who tag along and follow, and drive and open doors for the champion."

Gays are a crucial component of bodybuilding. "The economic connection between bodybuilders and gays is clear," writes Alan M. Klein in *Little Big Men*, a study of the elite California bodybuilding world in the eighties. "Segments of the gay community have been bankrolling aspiring bodybuilders in the West for decades, either through their role as procurers of sexual services or through their position as entrepreneurs, contest judges, gym owners, seller of steroids, and the like."

The sport struggled to put down the idea that bodybuilding gyms were often little more than gay camps. Youthful bodybuilders were often insecure about their sexual identity. They were hardly likely to have swamped the gyms if they thought they were likely to be accosted there by gay bodybuilders. The supramasculinity personified by Arnold in Weider's magazines and the chronicles of his wild sexual adventures were offered as an antidote, driving the gay world of bodybuilding farther back into the closet.

"I remember in Gold's Gym there were a couple of bodybuilders who did porno movies," said bodybuilding journalist Bill Dobbins, "and I knew a bunch of others who would do these wrestling sessions, and these private posing sessions that didn't necessarily involve actual sex."

Bud Parker, the editor of *Muscle Builder*, was aware enough of the lucrative gay underworld that he quit Weider to publish *Queen's Quarterly*, a subscription-only publication forthrightly celebrating manly love for the physical form. His successor at *Muscle Builder*, Rick Wayne, learned that he must stay out of the private lives of the bodybuilding heroes, or he would end up destroying the illusions that Weider had spent decades creating. "How the champs met their rent and their enormous food bills, how they paid for their vital food supplements and steroids when the majority had no visible means of support was strictly their business," writes Wayne. "When the cops nabbed a Mr. Universe winner for pimping and operating several brothels, the story made headlines on both coasts—but not in *Muscle Builder*. And while at least a dozen of the West Coast's adulated hunks had sugar daddies, you'd never know it by reading their life stories in *Muscle Builder*, where every word aimed at 'glorifying the guys.'"

The fact was that bodybuilding appealed to gays, with their love and appreciation of the male body. Bodybuilders preened in front of mirrors, shaved their body hair, oiled their bodies, and studied their craft by reading magazines full of photos of nearly nude men. In the fifties bodybuilders often posed nude. For the mainstream bodybuilding magazines, a pouch was airbrushed over the genitals, while an underground gay audience bought copies of the original photograph. There was a whole series of pamphlet-size "bodybuilding" magazines that were largely meant for a gay audience.

Klein's sources told him that among elite bodybuilders "30 to 80 percent of the men used to or currently did hustle." Arnold had been introduced to that world when he turned down Putziger's entreaties in 1966 in Munich. In the years since, he had been propositioned at other times and in other ways. Wealthy gay aficionados of bodybuilding were willing to pay lavishly for the sexual services of bodybuilders. It was a savage irony: the hypermasculinity of bodybuilding and a hustler's fate. It was the one quick way to make money, and many of the bodybuilders did it. For the most part, they allowed their clients to perform oral sex on them. That way they could rationalize that they were not gay but were merely passive recipients.

Arnold was friendly with several wealthy gay fans of bodybuilding and even stayed in their homes. He inevitably became the subject of rumor and speculation about his sexual conduct. One biographer tried diligently to prove that Arnold had hustled gay men, but her most likely candidate told the journalist that Arnold was a "good tease." That is an unkind spin on what probably was his conduct, accepting the hospitality and largesse of wealthy gays, even on occasion being photographed nude, but unwilling to service them or to be serviced.

Arnold was far from homophobic. Two of his first important interviews in major publications were to *After Dark* and *Interview,* magazines that in the seventies were considered to have a large gay audience. He also posed for the celebrity photographer Francesco Scavullo, wearing only a few soap bubbles for what was originally supposed to be a *Cosmopolitan* centerfold.

The young titan was in many ways indeed a flirt, surrounded by fans and admirers, darting away when they pressed too closely. Yet another category of devotees was Arnold's "wall-to-wall satellites," fans willing to do whatever service, large or small, to be around their hero. Bodybuilding is a hierarchical sport, in which the elite are at times disdainful of weak fumblers who attempt to lift the same weights and perform the same exercises as the mighty. Their most important role is to stand back, observe, and applaud, rarely risking a word with the true elite bodybuilders. One of those on the fringes was the journalist Bill Dobbins. "I was sort of skittering around the equipment, trying to use it and stay out of their way," he recalled. "Nobody cut you much slack. As long as I stayed out of their way, they didn't mind. I did an article called 'Excuse me, Arnold, mind if I work in?' which is about what that feeling was like."

Such adulation, only a year after arriving in Los Angeles and still barely twenty-two, was a heady wine. Arnold had a claque and an entourage wherever he went. In his limited bodybuilding world, he was living with fame beyond most celebrities. And as Arnold saw the future, it was only the beginning.

CHAPTER TEN

Mr. Olympia

Arnold created the illusion that whatever he was doing, he was at play. But even when he was at play, he was usually working. When he put in his five-hour workouts at Gold's, he seemed to be goofing around a lot of the time, relaxing between exercises, but the focus was always there. He used whatever and whomever he could to ratchet up his program to another level, looking in the mirror when he was lifting massive weights as though he were observing someone else, motivating himself with the shouts and encouragements of his partner, varying his routine in stimulating ways. Now that he was in California, he ate the food and vitamins that Weider recommended. Within a year he had dropped twenty-five pounds and gained steely muscle and definition. "In Europe I had limited information on how to train, on equipment, limited information on food supplements, and what was available," he said. "I wanted to learn. I wanted to catch up. I was way behind. It was pure will."

Arnold also took steroids, but he did not suffer obviously bad consequences. "Some of the guys would come in, complaining to me that they had taken so many steroids that their nose would start to bleed," said Dick Tyler, who became a chiropractor with many bodybuilder patients. "And they would start to develop tumors in their bodies, things like that. It was awful stuff, but if a guy was smart and used it judiciously, he'd have a particular time when he needed it to put on a little extra strength, and Arnold was one that I think skated that very fine balance."

And while Arnold was building up his body, Weider's magazines were building up his image as a heroic figure of physical and sexual strength. Arnold did not complain if the facts were misleading, as long as the great myth was propagated. That was the way he made his money. He and Weider were perfect partners.

But none of the endless promotion or ceaseless workouts would matter unless he won Mr. Olympia, the highest prize in bodybuilding. In September 1969 both the less-prestigious Mr. Universe and the Mr. Olympia contests were held at the same time at the Brooklyn Academy of Music. Arnold handily won the Mr. Universe title. However, his competition with Oliva for Mr. Olympia was so close that the two contestants were called back twice to pose together. Arnold had built up his calves magnificently in the past twelve months and he had none of the husky bulk of the Miami contest, and Oliva was in equally exquisite form. As the judges conferred, the New York crowd full of blacks and Hispanics chanted Oliva's name.

Arnold never talked about what it was like to stand backstage and hear the deafening roar of his opponent's name, but it was a fearsome sound. If Arnold had won that evening, those shouts would have turned into boos and screams of dismay, and some thought that the dejected Oliva fans might have reacted violently. Arnold did not win. The moment Oliva's name was announced, Arnold walked over and embraced him. It was a brilliant gesture, leaving Oliva's fans with an image of a generous loser. It was done through calculation, not sentiment. "I knew the fans would remember how I took defeat," Arnold said later.

Arnold then flew to Great Britain, where he won the NABBA pro Mr. Universe for the second year in a row. "Things are great here in London," he wrote Weider. "I am treated like a god, but then I am a god! I stay with the Bennetts who provide me with everything, but *everything* I desire—and you know how and what I desire—5 hours of solid training, good food, sound sleep, and all the women I can handle—and that's a whole lot of women! As you prophesied, I made all the other contestants look like scrawny, underdeveloped chickens. All London talks of the superman S. They have never seen anything like me and won't again until I return."

Arnold was full of grandiosity even beyond the enormous images of Weider's magazines. He bragged publicly about the women he needed, not mentioning that he had started dating a young woman back in California. Arnold had met Barbara Outland, a hostess at his Santa Monica hangout Zucky's, in July 1969. "You're so sexy," he told the nineteen-year-old senior at San Diego State. "I want to ask you out on a date." That was an expurgated version of his usual come-on, an indication that he sensed that Outland was not quite like most of the other women he had met in his first nine months or so in America.

For his photo shoots, Arnold was around gorgeous models, and the Venice seashore was full of sensational nymphets ready for a romp with the king of the beach. Outland was pretty but not with the sensational double-take good looks of the archetypal Southern Californian girl. She was, as Arnold soon discovered, a virginal college girl from a good family. She was a Kappa Alpha Theta at San Diego State. Like most of her sorority sisters, she intended to get married after college to a wonderful man with whom she would raise a wonderful family and live happily ever after.

Arnold represented what was a daring adventure for Outland. "I don't know if it was rebellion, but there was just enough little spark of 'I want to be different, too,' so I can handle this guy for being so different," she reflected. "And I loved that aspect of it." Barbara's initial hesitation at even being seen with Arnold was hardly unexpected in a well-brought-up young woman. Arnold was living in a cul-de-sac of American culture among people thought of by many as aberrant freaks of nature. Arnold may have looked stunning in Weider's photos, but in person he sometimes appeared a socially inept vulgarian limited to a few catchphrases of English, as often as not laced with profanity, the import of which he may not have fully understood.

"He had poor table manners and had little understanding of polite society," Barbara Outland (now Barbara Outland Baker) said. "When I first met him, I found him a turn-off. At the beginning, it was humiliating to be seen with him in public. He was just too bizarre looking. I was from a wealthy, conservative background. How could I be seeing someone with all those creepy muscles?"

"So there was a rough diamond there to mold. And Arnold just wasn't very willing to let himself be molded until later. He lived in gym shorts and T-shirts, and on our first date his hair was unstylishly short.

"In some ways he was older than his years, and in some ways younger. It was an interesting combination. He was already the king of bodybuilding. So he already knew what it was like to have groupies and people fawning all over him, and yet it was normal even if it was a subculture."

Arnold's romance was an amalgam of the most sentimental emotions and social aspirations. Barbara Outland was a young woman of pristine morality, a political and social conservative totally removed from the youth revolution of America in the sixties. Like his mother or Marion Park, she was a woman whose highest aspiration was to be a good wife and mother, but she had other strong professional interests as well. "He saw in me that you can be around a really bright, capable, intelligent woman who loves the home and experimenting with gourmet cooking and is also academic," said Outland Baker.

Barbara was also a woman from a class far above his who would teach him how to behave in this new American world of which he had seen so little. "It was funny to hear him speak," Outland Baker recalled. "He had a very thick accent, poor grammar, and few words. I had to talk slowly. It was so unusual to be with somebody with whom you had to use charades, but he was willing to just go 'I'm open. Teach me anything, correct me.' Some friends said, 'Isn't that kind of rude? You're correcting him.' 'No, he wants me to correct [him].'

"My girlfriends, with their lawyer and doctor husbands, frowned on him. 'What do they know, they are just traditional,' he said. 'I am going to be famous beyond anything they know.'"

Arnold was not a seducer who spent time wooing women. Sex was food, and he would no more play endless games of romance than he would stand in line for a table in a restaurant. His romance with Barbara was different. He showed a tender, nourishing side he had not displayed before. "I was an old-fashioned, virginal schoolgirl," Outland Baker said. "I was 'no, no, no,' and I think it was the challenge that grabbed him. That and, I believe, my intelligence."

She returned to San Diego that fall to finish her senior year, assuming that her short-lived romance with Arnold was over. He began calling her at the sorority house. While her sorority sisters spent their weekends at college parties, she flew up to L.A. to be with her bodybuilder boyfriend. "I finally thought, 'You know what? He really does care for me,'" said Outland Baker. "All of his behavior manifested it, and so I just felt the commitment through the behavior and the words, so then we started a full-scale intimate relationship."

When Barbara graduated, most of her sorority sisters headed off to the altar while she moved to L.A. for a menial clerical job and a romance with Arnold. She wanted to get married, too, and considered her main problem not to be her free-spirited boyfriend but his roommate, Franco. The two Europeans were perfectly bonded. They were the most buoyant, exuberant spirit, at Gold's and on the beach, topping each other's jokes, ranking each other, challenging each other. Barbara knew if things were going to work out with Arnold, somehow she had to wean him off Columbu. "It was much easier to blame Franco than it was to blame Arnold," said Barbara. "So there was a period of a good year, I think, when we just tried not to speak to each other."

Columbu symbolized the free, unchallenged bodybuilder's life, a European sensibility that Barbara could never fully grasp. "Every time Arnold said something in German, Barbara thought we were talking about her," said Columbu. "Not necessarily true." For months there was a difficult, subtle, and largely unspoken negotiation going on between Arnold and Barbara. In the end, she agreed to a compromise that challenged all the values she had been brought up with. She had already given up her virginity to the cause, and now she agreed that if Arnold would give up sharing an apartment with Franco, she would live with him without the bonds of matrimony until he was ready to marry. The couple moved in together, first to an apartment on Sixth Street in Santa Monica and then to a six-unit apartment building.

Barbara describes her five years with Arnold as a relationship directly challenging much of the playboy image that Weider and Arnold were concocting in the pages of *Muscle Builder/Power* and *Mr. America*. He did not have to be carousing every night, roaming the boardwalk in Venice, prowling for good times. He was a busy man, but he was also a homebody. He learned from Barbara. He not only loved her, he liked her and appreciated her company. He liked her parents, and they came to like him. "He was straight," she recalled. "He didn't really drink. I mean, he'd have a beer. Much is made of the marijuana, but he never would have thought about doing that on his own."

Arnold had thoughtful qualities that had nothing to do with advancing himself in the world. He had gotten to know Reg Park's son in South Africa, and when the teenage Jon Jon arrived in Long Beach to spend eighteen months in America, Arnold watched out for him. "I spent a great deal of time with him on weekends in the spare bedroom," Jon Jon Park recalled. "He'd sometimes drive down and take me for dinners, pick me up, bring me back to L.A. You know, he treated me kind of like a kid brother. As fierce as he is as a competitor, a lot of people ask, 'What's he like?' They hear he can be arrogant or abrasive or sarcastic and, yes, he can be all those things, but if you know him and he likes you and he respects you, then he only shows you warmth."

Arnold was a man who wanted everything, and "everything" to him meant a warm, grounded home, a life of daring adventure and discovery, and a gigantic image as a wild, unfettered being. "I mean, he wanted that image for sure," Outland Baker said. "He eventually admitted to me that he had cheated on me, so I'm not being naive here. But a lot of it was just that that's what he wanted people to see."

For the most part, Arnold was a machine of learning, imbibing vast quantities of human experience, disgorging the inutile, and making whatever was true and useful part of his own being. A word. An idea. An opportunity. It all became part of him. "I think Joe Weider and I both gave him an imprint of logical thinking patterns," said Outland Baker. "I could see that a lot. And, of course, Arnold learned how to negotiate, because Joe was a hard driver."

When Barbara met Arnold, he could hardly speak a sentence of English without grammatical errors. She not only corrected his English but helped him with his writing. He became a masterful communicator, writing and rewriting his letters until they often had a subtle grace to them, qualities rare in the letters of even most native speakers of English. "We tried letter writing different ways," recalled Outland Baker. "Sometimes he would give me the idea. I'd write the letter. He'd reject it, because it wasn't his words. He'd write it all over again. Other times he would dictate, and I would transcribe and clean up the grammar. But it always had to be his essence, his wording; he was always very clear what he wanted to say."

A decade later, when he married Maria Shriver, some observers would suggest that the Kennedy family had strapped a social consciousness onto Arnold's unformed, narrow soul. Already in these years he was visiting prisons and thinking about how he could improve his beloved sport of bodybuilding. When Barbara talked about going back to school to become a teacher, seeking a secondary-school certificate and a master's degree, he enthusiastically supported her. "You know what?" he told her. "You're meant to be a teacher. You're a born teacher. Go to school and get your teaching credential." Arnold helped pay her tuition. During their last year together, when she drove each day to East L.A. to teach English to immigrant children, he was proud of her, and proud that he had helped her get her certification.

Every time Arnold went to the main post office in Santa Monica and picked up the mail from his box, he had proof that celebrity was one of the greatest products in America. There were scores of letters, most of them responding to the half-page ads Weider was running in his magazines that read "AT LAST!! THE 'AUSTRIAN OAK' REVEALS HIS TRAINING SECRETS." Weider had promised to write and print the training pamphlets, but he procrastinated with anything that cost him money or time, and month after month they were not ready.

Weider's staff finally wrote the material, but he had not printed the seven little pamphlets that were to be sold for two dollars apiece. "Please let me remind you about the training courses to make them ready as soon as possible; otherwise I get too many complaints," Arnold wrote Joe in October 1970 after he had been in America for two years. He was already thinking big. "Please print enough so I can sell 7,000 to England and 7,000 to South America. I have to get $15,000 as soon as possible so we can pay 30,000 dollars for an apartment building. I save every penny I can save."

Arnold's anger over Weider's broken promise was his first major blowup with his bodybuilding mentor, and he took over printing the pamphlets himself. This was Arnold's first entrepreneurial venture, and he oversaw every detail, seeking out the best price for envelopes and suing the printer when he failed to deliver what he had promised. Arnold proved a highly litigious businessman, going against anyone who did not come through as Arnold believed he had promised or anyone who sought to exploit his name unfairly.

When Arnold came home to his apartment, he went through the stack of mail, holding each envelope up to the light to see if there was a check or cash. If there was money, he put the letter in a stack on the table. If it appeared to be nothing but fan mail, several of Arnold's friends say that he dumped the letter into the wastebasket. Photographer George Butler says Arnold not only threw the letters away but bragged about it. It was not a scene that fit into the hagiographic image Weider was creating for Arnold, but it was a realistic, if cynical, appraisal of Arnold's own reality.

Arnold was his own product, and he was not going to give it away. Arnold, however, insists that this is not true, a view seconded by Barbara Outland Baker. "We separated it out, because I wanted to make sure that we would fill the orders right away," he said. "I wanted to be fast with the mail. Then on the weekend, I took the fan mail and read it. Many times we sent photographs."

In the end, the pamphlets sold extremely well, and thousands of dollars started pouring into Arnold's post office box. It was modern alchemy, turning an image into gold. Joe had been glad to run the ads, but he was not about to make Arnold rich without getting his slice. "Every once in a while Joe would get on his high horse and send Arnold a bill for the ads," said bodybuilding journalist Bill Dobbins. "And Arnold would say, 'Okay, if that's the way you want to play.' And he'd turn around and send Joe a bill for his appearances, and nothing got paid." In the end, Arnold was the one bodybuilder who clearly got far more from Weider than Weider got from him.

CHAPTER ELEVEN

Hercules in New York

As part of his continuing crusade for Arnold, Weider pushed for Arnold to play the lead in a small-budget feature film, *Hercules in New York*. This was the kind of film that leading bodybuilders had performed in for two decades, an exploitation picture that would have its greatest moments on Italian television. Since the producers were planning to dub the dialogue, they were not worried about Arnold's heavy accent. They were concerned about whether he could act. Weider tried to assuage those doubts by telling the producers that Arnold had been a Shakespearean actor in Vienna.

Arnold was amazed that after so little time in America he could be starring in a film. His salary was hardly worthy of a star, and during the shooting he shared a room at the Henry Hudson Hotel in New York with Franco Columbu. One evening the two friends went to Weider's apartment. Weider was a collector not only of bodybuilders but of art and historical memorabilia, and he displayed some of his prized possessions, including Hitler and Mussolini artifacts, paintings by some of the masters, and an exquisite chair from the Napoleonic era. Weider was proud that he had been able to acquire such rare objects.

Arnold followed Weider's description of each object with great interest. When it was all over, he plopped his enormous body down in the precious chair. If Arnold had set out to destroy the antique with a buzz saw, he could not have done more damage. It looked as if it had exploded into scores of little pieces littering the floor.

"Ohhh, my God, this is an original!" Weider lamented in a voice halfway between a scream and a whine. "A museum is looking for that chair."

Arnold picked up a few of the pieces. "Joe," he said in a philosophical tone worthy of Socrates as he looked at the scraps of wood.

"What? Ohhh, noooo," Weider whimpered, hardly able to compose a sentence.

"Joe," Arnold began again. "You're rich. You have a lot of money. Why are you so upset about the chair?"

Weider stared down at the chair and then looked up at the man he considered his greatest creation. "You're right, Arnold," Joe said. If Franco or anyone else had destroyed the chair, he would have wanted them disemboweled, with their ashes strewn to the four winds.

Hercules in New York was supposed to be a campy romp, as Zeus, Hercules' father, dumps his prodigal son into the mortal world of America. Hercules is decked out in what appear to be giant Pampers and a sheet, and speaks in pidgin English.

To call Arnold's performance "wooden" would be to risk a libel suit from the lumber industry. Arnold had none of the magical aura of a great undiscovered star shining through this most dismal of projects. What he did project was an immense likability, a gentle giant driving his chariot through Times Square, and a subtle, ironic distance—both crucial aspects of his eventual screen persona.

Weider had not only gotten Arnold the part but had given him a new screen name, Arnold Strong, using it in the pages of his magazines as well. To the bodybuilding audience, he was still Arnold Schwarzenegger, and Arnold rejected his new name. The movie had been a lark, but Arnold had a deep sense of his own destiny and the natural progression of his life. He knew that this was the year, 1970, he must be crowned as the undisputed champion of bodybuilding, or his opportunity might pass him by forever. Bodybuilding was the world onto which Arnold was pressing his will, and there was no way he could achieve his goals unless he was crowned Mr. Olympia, wresting the title from Sergio Oliva in September.

In the weeks just before the NABBA Mr. Universe competition in London, to be followed by the IFBB Mr. Olympia in New York, Arnold's intense eyes stared out at the readers of *Muscle Builder/Power* with his accusatory finger pointing at them. "We European bodybuilders have little respect for the American bodybuilder!" he said. "He is an unsporting, big-talking, no-action coward." This was incendiary rhetoric unheard-of in bodybuilding. The article appeared to be a defense of Oliva, whose competitors had often backed out of contests in which he would have defeated them, but the words were more Arnold shouting up his own courage. "And the fact that not one of those so-called 'greats' has had the GUTS to show up against him proves how deserving he is of his Mr. Olympia title," Arnold asserted. "Of course, now that little Schwarzenegger is here, there are going to be some changes!"

Arnold was only twenty-three years old and had been in the United States for a mere two years and he was doing something that almost anyone else would have considered almost mad. He was consciously, willfully turning himself into a figure of controversy. "I did this interview where I said American bodybuilders are all f—ing chicken s—. They don't want to compete against me," he recalled in 2000. "People were furious. The letters came in, including hate mail. One guy said he wanted to meet me in a dark alley to f—k me up. The American fans went nuts."

And Arnold loved it. In the *Muscle Builder/Power* article, Arnold also criticized a writer named Robert Kennedy who had called Reg Park the greatest bodybuilder of all time. It was a debatable assertion, but if anyone should have applauded such a sentiment, it was Arnold. Yet it rankled him that Kennedy would write what he considered nonsense. "Look at this junk!" Arnold said. "What makes a guy write this sort of thing? Everybody knows Park was the greatest *fifteen* years ago."

That was more controversy, and Arnold basked in it and anything else that shone an even brighter spotlight on him. He knew he could make people like him, but these comments gave an edge to his personality. Arnold's words had a haunting resonance. When he flew into London for the Mr. Universe contest, he learned that Park would be competing against him. Arnold wrote later that he had said to himself that he had two choices: "'One is to beat Reg, and you most likely will, and destroy your idol; and the other is to leave London and not compete at all.' I decided that leaving was stupid. It would be good for my ego and good for publicity to compete against Reg, to destroy my idol and win."

If Arnold had refused to compete at the last moment, it would have been seen as a transparent gesture that would have honored neither him nor Park, but that did not mean he had to grind his bodybuilding mentor into the dust. Park was forty-two years old, twice Arnold's age, and had not competed for half a decade. A loss to Arnold would not have destroyed him.

Arnold had a friend's knowledge of Reg's psyche, and he surely must have guessed the insecurity that Park would have felt, competing after so long at the end of a great career. Rick Wayne reported that backstage Park pumped himself up while Arnold dawdled in street clothes, gossiping with his mentor. It may have seemed the most innocent of conversations, but at such moments nothing is innocent.

"Damn it, Arnold!" the genial Park yelled. "Will you can the bullshit till after the contest?"

"What contest?" Arnold supposedly said, driving his shiv into Park's heart.

After losing that evening, Park did not speak to Arnold, but their friendship soon resumed, and the bodybuilder remembers only the good. "I was shit," Park said. "He deserved to win, end of story. When he was announced as the winner, he walked up and said, 'Reg, it was a great pleasure to compete against you.' I had nothing to complain about. I'm happy for the kid."

Arnold was brutal in combat but generous to those who bowed their heads and acknowledged his sovereignty. He had not set out to best Park, but when the South African dared challenge him, Arnold had defeated his mentor, driving him back into retirement.

Arnold had only one competitor left now who mattered to him, and that was Oliva. Arnold flew from London to Columbus, Ohio, to compete for a new title, Mr. World. Oliva showed up at the last minute on his own from Chicago. He thought that the judging panel would not be controlled by Weider and he would get a fair verdict. Afterward, when Arnold beat him hands down, Oliva promptly claimed that he had only reluctantly competed, as he was not quite yet in top form.

Arnold's triumph was only a skirmish before the Mr. Olympia contest, and Arnold used the occasion to plant what he hoped would be the seeds of Oliva's defeat in New York. He gently suggested to Oliva that to be at his prime, he needed to gain some weight before their next meeting. "To make sure I would have an even easier time in New York, I suggested you pack on twelve pounds for the Mr. Olympia contest," Arnold said later. "I told you you lost in Ohio because you were too light, and you were foolish enough to believe me. Do you really believe I would tell you how to beat me?" Arnold was saying that he was so persuasive, so cunning, that no matter how many times he misled his opponents, they still believed him and followed his dubious strategy to their doom.

Arnold had a chance in Columbus to talk extensively to James J. Lorimer, one of the promoters. Lorimer was a former FBI agent and an executive at Nationwide Mutual Insurance, the leading company in the Ohio city. He had done a superb job producing an event that had begun as the world weightlifting championship and added the bodybuilding competition to draw a bigger crowd. He had sold out Veterans Memorial Auditorium and saw to it that Arnold and the other competitors were treated with respect and deference.

Arnold was a man of instinctive judgment. That did not mean he was rash, intemperate, or mindlessly spontaneous. For the most part, he listened to his instincts and then rationally acted upon them. "One really strong thing about him is the way he reads people," said Lorimer, who has been a friend now for three decades. "Whenever he says to me, 'You know, Jim, my gut tells me so and so,' I listen. I haven't seen his gut miscommunicate."

Most of Arnold's mistakes have come when he went against his instincts and deferred to others or to his own rationalization. His life comes down to people, and his crucial judgments are about people. If he feels a rapport with you, that is enough, and it is enough because it is an emotional wisdom, based on everything he has learned about people over the years.

Arnold felt that rapport with Lorimer. He had first talked to the Ohio man when Lorimer had called him at Gold's Gym to ask him to take part in the Mr. World competition, telling him that there was a five-hundred-dollar top prize and that the competition would be shown on ABC's *Wide World of Sports*. On Arnold's visit to Columbus, the executive was every bit as loquacious as Arnold, full of tales of his FBI days when he had investigated the Muslim Cult of Islam and had arrested leading American communists. He loved sports and was a natural promoter. He had enthusiasm, endless energy, attention to detail, and a shrewd business head.

"When I'm done competing in the sport of bodybuilding, I want to go into the promotion of the sport and try to raise the level of the sport," Arnold said. "I want to raise the top prize from a thousand to ten thousand dollars and within three years to a hundred thousand. And I'd like you to be my partner."

This was by any measure ludicrous. Arnold had not even won the top prize in bodybuilding, and even if he did, so what? It was unthinkable that Arnold could muscle his way into the top ranks of promoting and then so outrageously increase the prize money. It was the kind of reverie that bodybuilders might have chatting among themselves, but any promoter would have told Arnold it was absurd.

Lorimer did not know whether Arnold was serious or fantasizing. He did not expect a call anytime soon, and yet there was something about the man that suggested it might be more than just another slice of pie in the sky. "His eyes were as clear, as bright and penetrating as they could be," said Lorimer. "And you could just see the health and the vitality just coming out at you. And he's looking right at you, too, so you know he's with you. I was impressed."

Weider wanted Arnold to win the Mr. Olympia title almost as much as Arnold did. Oliva was not the kind of champion who was going to advance the fortunes of bodybuilding in the broader world. He was an exotic dark Latin dandy decked out in diamond rings and gold chains, elevated on shoes with three-inch heels. He might appear a flamboyant Cuban American, but he had a subdued manner incongruous with his dress and body. He was never going to be the salesman for the sport that Arnold had already become. For a multitude of reasons both personal and professional, Weider desperately wanted Arnold crowned as the new Mr. Olympia, the undisputed champion.

Arnold's embrace of Oliva the previous year and his paeans of praise to the Cuban's greatness were ways to quell his competitive fires and to quiet Oliva's vociferous fans. While other bodybuilders were out lifting a few beers, Arnold was in his apartment, reviewing films of Oliva's posing, the way a football coach goes over an opponent's previous games. Nobody else bothered to do that. He knew what poses Oliva made and in what order, and he knew how he could choreograph his own moves to show him up.

One of the axioms Arnold lived by as a bodybuilder was that "no matter how great you are on the posing platform, if you have a small fault people say: 'If only he did not have this fault.'" That is true of life itself, people always look for some weakness to tear you down, but it is at the heart of bodybuilding competition. Through hours of training, you try to bulk up a weak leg or add definition to your chest. On the day of the competition you have to create the illusion that you are perfect. You pose in such a way that as hard as the judges look, they can find no muscle that is weak, no skin that is not taut, nothing but physical perfection.

Oliva had his new manager with him backstage at Manhattan's Town Hall for the final competition, but the man knew nothing of the nuances of competition. Arnold had Franco. Earlier in the evening, his closest friend had won the Mr. Universe title, the second-highest honor in bodybuilding. Instead of strutting a victor's march, Columbu turned his energy and attention to helping Arnold. Franco oiled Arnold up, checked him out, and voiced encouragement and pointers.

Weider was the great impresario of bodybuilding and the promoter of that evening's contest, and for both reasons he should have affected a semblance of neutrality. He cared so much about the outcome that he simply could not do so. Weider watched as Oliva began pumping up before he went out onstage, and Arnold joined him. "Don't pump, Arnold. It's no good," Weider recalled telling Arnold. "That guy is pumping, pumping, pumping, by the time he stops and goes onstage, he'll deflate. You just do a little, and when you go onstage, you're going to have your muscles full of blood, because you didn't overpump."

The time-honored tradition is that the holder of the title poses last, but Weider suggested a coin toss. Oliva would not hear of it, and in the end Arnold walked out onstage first. Unlike the ambivalent reception he had received the previous year, Arnold was greeted with booming applause. In his prime Arnold was an awesome physical specimen. From his fifty-seven-inch chest to his thirty-four-inch waist, from his twenty-inch calves to his twenty-two-inch arms, he was a massive, exquisitely sculptured human being walking out onto the stage. And that was only the beginning of it.

There has never been a bodybuilder, other than perhaps Sandow himself, as masterful at the public presentation of his body as Arnold. He had an intuitive grasp of the audience, and he played with the crowd, thrilling them with various takes on his manly form. Arnold turned and pirouetted, and it did not appear that he was calculating to expose only the best parts of his body but that he was turning and twisting so that everything was on view. With each move, the crowd became even more ecstatic.

There were more Oliva partisans in the audience than believers in Arnold. Even though they were applauding and shouting, too, for the most part these fans were awaiting their champion. At the highest level, bodybuilding is the aesthetic appreciation of the human body at its most physically developed. The sophisticated audience knows that behind each pose are hours and hours of relentless effort.

Aficionados will argue forever who represented the higher standard, Arnold or Oliva. Although Oliva received ovations, he was not at his best that evening. In the two weeks since Columbus, he had gained just enough weight to obscure his extraordinary form. Oliva's partisans saw their hero in his greatness, and as he walked offstage, they were convinced that he would be the winner.

While the judges conferred, the crowd shouted and hooted for their two champions to return for a final pose down. The crucial verdict had largely been made in the prejudging, and the posing earlier in the evening had validated what had already been decided. Arnold learned afterward that he was already a point or two ahead. This encore, then, had no major impact on the final decision, but Arnold and Sergio did not know that.

For the audience, this was in some ways the most memorable moment of all. It was like an animalistic ritual from thousands of years ago, two naked beasts in a clearing, strutting and spouting, each attempting to intimidate the other, driving his adversary back into the jungle.

For every pose that Oliva struck, Arnold hit two or three. The crowd screamed their adulation of the two champions, and again and again they struck new poses. It went on and on to ever rising waves of applause. At one point, Arnold suggested to his competitor that they leave the stage. Franco, who understands Arnold's bodybuilding psychology better than anyone, in part because he has so often been its victim, believes that Arnold made the suggestion because he thought that he was safely ahead.

The audience had no idea that Arnold told his opponent that it was time to leave the stage and that Oliva should lead the way. There had been no boos yet this evening, but now they fell upon the departing Oliva, mixed with renewed cheers for Arnold. When he heard the fans screaming his name, Arnold thought "there's a little meat on this chicken." The shouts and boos mingled together, and Arnold realized that the Cuban's departure had seemed a coward's retreat. And so Arnold stood onstage and posed alone. And the audience screamed and pounded on the wooden floors, an avalanche of sound so monumental that few judges would have dared deny the crowd its verdict.

The judges crowned a new king that evening, and a new crown prince as well. When the two friends left by the stage door, they were greeted by several thousand gesticulating, excited fans. Arnold and Franco signed autographs as they walked the eighteen blocks to the Henry Hudson Hotel surrounded by hundreds of adoring supporters. So many fans entered the lobby and sought to follow their heroes upstairs that the police had to be called to force them to leave.

Upstairs, Weider was so much a partisan of Arnold and Columbu that he was sharing a suite with them. At two in the morning, when they were talking endlessly about their triumphs, Oliva called from downstairs, saying he had nowhere to sleep. At times, Oliva seemed a threatening presence and Weider was reluctant to let him enter the suite. "Invite him up," Arnold said, no more threatened by Oliva in victory than in preparation for victory. A sullen Sergio arrived in the suite and fell asleep within a few minutes.

When Arnold slept, he was as dead to the world as if he had been given anesthesia. As for Columbu, he was still so high from his victory that he slept only fitfully. At about six o'clock, he heard a strange sound. He got out of bed and looked into Oliva's bedroom where the Cuban American was doing triceps exercises. Columbu could not believe it. After a big competition, bodybuilders always took a few weeks off, grossed out on steaks and desserts, and just relaxed.

Columbu shook Arnold awake, not the easiest of tasks. "Why are you waking me up?" Arnold asked as he sat on the side of the bed.

"You've got to see this. Sergio's doing triceps. He's training for next year."

"He's already lost," a drowsy Arnold said, and then went back to sleep.

Oliva never again won a major title. Arnold was proud of himself as a trickster and considered it one of his major contributions to bodybuilding. "It's very clear signals what I did to all my competitors," Arnold said. "I improvised those things. It was my doing, and it was kind of unique in the sport. I've seen it with Ali, I've seen it with other sports, but in bodybuilding it was unique."

After his victory Arnold had to brag about it, noting how he "tricked" Oliva and made the fans believe that Oliva had accepted Arnold's superiority. He continued in an open letter to Oliva published in *Muscle Builder/Power*, "Their boos, while they must have affected what little self-confidence you might have had, were like sweet soul music to my ears. I knew then that there could be no return for you, Sergio."

It was not enough for Arnold to defeat his opponent, he had to taunt and denigrate him until there was little left but bad memories. In his open letter, he concluded with a short poem mentioning Oliva's wife, who would shoot her husband in 1986:

> *Sergio, I'm so sorry you had to lose,*
> *'Cause now you might turn to*
> *Sin and booze.*
> *If you do, watch out for your wife—*
> *I hear she packs a knife!*

CHAPTER TWELVE

The Greatest

In two weeks Arnold had won three top competitions, something that no one in bodybuilding had ever done before. He may not have been the "the greatest bodybuilder of all time," as he boasted, but at an age when most competitors are only entering their prime, twenty-three-year-old Arnold was the undisputed king of bodybuilding. And he was already aspiring to a world beyond.

Arnold had a perceptive awareness of not only how to succeed in America but how to multiply that success. Unlike most young men in their early twenties, he saw life far into the future and realized the exponential benefit of saving and investing. He treated the economic realities of his life the same way he treated the bodybuilding realities, acting as if Arnold Schwarzenegger were a third person who needed to be subjected to discipline.

He began saving money when he had almost nothing. He was forever figuring out ways not only to make more money but to put more away. Even when he was having sex, he was often thinking about money. "But, y'know, the more your mind is complex, the less you can focus on sex," Arnold said. "Many times, while I was getting laid, in my head I was doing a business deal."

As Arnold saw it, California was still the American frontier, and a man with daring and initiative could do practically anything. To those who understood, even misfortune was the bearer of good tidings. The 1971 Sylmar earthquake left sixty-five dead and caused more than $500 million in damage, but there was money to be made for those who moved quickly. Arnold knew nothing about bricklaying, but Columbu had just started a company called

European Brick Works and had a card from the carpenters union that allowed him to work.

Columbu and Arnold had recently moved to a larger third-floor apartment on Fifteenth Street in Santa Monica. They had been jolted awake at dawn by the earthquake, and later in the morning the phone started ringing off the hook from victims of the quake looking for brick repairs. One of the callers was a woman in Santa Monica whose chimney was so precarious that safety inspectors had warned her that it had to be taken down immediately. "I called this guy, and he said, 'I have to bring a scaffold,' " she told Columbu when the partners met with her. "It costs five thousand bucks. I don't want to spend five thousand. Can't you just push it down?"

"We can do it in one day," Columbu promised. "It'll cost five hundred dollars."

Arnold countered: "Eight hundred."

"I'll give you a thousand if you do it now."

"We'll do it now," Columbu enthused.

A decade later, when Arnold reminisced about his short-lived career as a bricklayer to Johnny Carson on *The Tonight Show*, he made it sound as if he and Franco had been a step above con artists. "Franco climbed up on the roof to check the chimney—and he is very strong guy and a lifter, he pushed all the chimneys over so they fell down. So these people come and say, 'Oh, thank you for helping us. They could have fallen on somebody's' head.' " "Oh, what a racket," Carson exclaimed. "You go and push chimneys down and then rebuild them."

Even when Arnold appeared to be doing nothing but hustling customers, he was observing and taking in the American scene. "We were going into homes people would remodel and sell for twice the money," he recalled in 1986. "Right away, I learned that real estate was the place to be."

Weider advised him that it was the best, safest way to make money. "After a while, he said to me, 'Joe, what should I do with my money? What business should I invest it in?' I said, 'Forget about investing in businesses. Just buy real estate in the best area that you can find. And that's the best for you, because you don't have to like the business. You don't have to think, worry about double-crossing, all this stuff. You just sit back, and you can train. Your mind will be free to do what you want, and you can study and everything. And your money will work for you and so forth.' He thought it was a good idea, and since that time, he invested in real estate."

Arnold had all the qualities of a sound real estate investor. He was cautious. He had an insatiable curiosity. He was an excellent judge of people. He chose good partners. And when the time came, he was ready to pounce. For the most part, he had a Midas touch when it came to particular properties. He knew how to translate his optimism about the American future into picking real estate that lay on the fault line of the future.

After two years in America, Arnold had amassed $28,000 in savings, more than his father ever had in his life. In Hollywood, appearance is often the highest reality, and a man dreaming of stardom had best live in a neighborhood where movie stars lived, and drive a car a celebrity would drive. Arnold thought differently. Instead of plunking down a down payment for a place in the Hollywood Hills, he borrowed $10,000 more from Weider to purchase a six-unit apartment house in Santa Monica and lived in one of the apartments with Barbara Outland.

Arnold was a man of radical frugality, living not only within his means but far below them. Each investment became a means to a bigger investment. "The first money he got from shows he invested," said Columbu. "Once he did about five shows in South Africa and then I joined him and we did another five. He said, 'I'm not going to touch any of this money; I'll put it all away.' We came back, and he put every penny of it in an apartment building. Two years later, he bought a bigger one."

Arnold was proud of saying, then as now, that everything he knew he had learned from bodybuilding. It had given him "confidence and pride and an unlimited positive attitude." That was true, but he could have made almost any sport or endeavor the vehicle of his self-discovery. Others lifted those same weights and trained many of the same hours, but they took little away from those efforts except for larger muscle. That was his way, to suck every ounce of meaning out of a given situation, be it a person or a form of human endeavor. He was the greatest exemplar of the sport since Sandow, in part because he had taken so much from it.

Arnold did not make a dramatic decision to stay in the United States for good. The longer he stayed, the more America felt increasingly right, and he had fewer reasons to return to Europe. That was especially true after his brother, Meinhard, died in 1971 in a drunken car accident. Meinhard had once had a life of such promise, but every step he took dissipated his prospects. He was irresistible to women, and he endlessly and carelessly indulged himself. One result was three-year-old Patrick, his child born out of wedlock to a woman he said he loved. He had promised to marry the mother, Erika Knapp, but he was a man of empty promises. He had an easy charm and would have made a stellar salesman, but instead he conned people. At the time of his death, he was probably about to be indicted for one of his heartless scams.

Arnold did not attend the funeral, and he rarely talked about his elder brother. He walked away from pain, and his brother's life was nothing but pain. If Arnold sought to memorialize him, it was largely in living a different kind of life and in taking over the financial support of Patrick, eventually paying his way through college and law school in Los Angeles. Arnold gave his nephew more than money. He provided him with emotional support and a true family.

Arnold's father had been emotionally erratic for a number of years, so much so that years afterward Arnold wondered whether he had suffered from a brain tumor. The death of his beloved son pushed him even further into a disoriented despair. The next year Gustav died.

Arnold did not return to Austria for the burial and did not appear deeply affected by the deaths. "If he'd been thirty-five or forty, he probably would have acted quite differently," Outland Baker conjectured. "But at the time, he was so removed from family that it was just a sad conversation."

Barbara had had her own difficulties with her parents, but she saw how crucial it was that Arnold change his attitude. "You know, I think you really need to pay attention to your mom," she told him. "She's alone." Whether it was her prodding or Arnold's own instincts, he invited Aurelia to California to spend the next Christmas with him. "It was like 'Wow, what have I missed?'" Outland Baker recalled. "'My mother's really this wonderful, sweet, loving, kind, incredible person that I was just not seeing when I grew up.'"

Arnold took it on as a major responsibility to make the rest of his widowed mother's life as good as it could be. "From then on, each time I made a move forward, I wanted her to have part of it," Arnold said. "The more I grew up, the more I got it, the more it meant to me to spend time with her. I had the urge and the need to give back for the unbelievable effort she made and the selflessness that she displayed all the time, and it just felt like it was time to celebrate and to have the best life. I sent money to her every month and I paid for her condominium over there and sent her gifts and I tried to make her life wonderful."

As much as Aurelia was impressed by her son's success, she had the mentality that one should not reach too far or stand too tall, or one would fall. "When I saw what he had done, I thought he had gone as far as he could, he'd done everything," she said. It was said with a mother's love, but it was another part of Arnold's reality—a brother who had died an abject failure, a father who had died after a debilitating psychological decline, and a mother who feared that her son had gone far enough.

Not only did his mother worry about her surviving son reaching beyond his station, but she had a relentlessly downbeat or cautionary spin on almost everything. "When I made a phone call home, my mother's opening line was a lot of times, 'Where's the check?'" said Arnold. "I mean, it would always be like 'Oh, Arnold, I read this in the paper. That's terrible. Oh, I have to be so embarrassed about you when . . . ' So it was always a negative, but that was Austrian. That was her. That was just the way it is over there, and then she would turn it into something positive."

Arnold had nothing of his mother's negativity, and he set out to establish himself as a great bodybuilding champion, defeating any who dared challenge him. By all rights, the 1971 Mr. Olympia should have been a classic competition between Arnold and Sergio, the new champion and the old, but the Cuban was not allowed to participate. He had entered a non-IFBB event the previous year, and Weider suspended him for a year on the eve of the event. "He used any kind of trick," said Oliva. Weider may have had his legitimate reasons, but to Sergio it looked as if Weider would do anything to protect Arnold.

Arnold easily held on to his title, but the 1972 contest was a different matter. Oliva planned to participate, and he was in superb form. By his own admission, Arnold was three pounds overweight and not in the best shape of his career. Oliva was the only competitor who rightfully could have broken Arnold's string of victories.

The contest, held in Essen, Germany, had a makeshift quality to it, so much so that at the last minute the promoters were still deciding where to hold the prejudging. Arnold suggested that it take place in the warm-up room.

Oliva, who two years before had walked off the stage at Arnold's suggestion, had no objection. He and the other top contender, Serge Nubret, were black, their skin color blending in against the dark wall, while Arnold's white body stood out. "To this day I believe that was how I got the edge," Arnold said. "In a nutshell, the judges saw more than I actually had that day in Germany."

Sergio was tightly focused on what he considered the contest; but whatever he considered it to be, Arnold made it into something else. Arnold probably was not correct that the color of the wall determined the outcome, but it was a way of asserting himself as the master of competition. Arnold bragged about his trick afterward, a further act of gamesmanship. Arnold made the maddening assertion that he had swooped down and wrested the Mr. Olympia trophy out of Oliva's hands and the Cuban American was too slow to catch him. Next time Oliva would be looking upward to catch Arnold at his game, and Arnold would attack him from someplace new.

"Certainly Sergio was great enough in Germany to take the Mr. Olympia title," Arnold reflected afterward. "And let me tell you that had he been awarded the number one spot, I would have been the very first to congratulate him. I will go further and admit that had I been a judge in Germany, I would have voted in favor of Oliva over me."

Arnold put forth himself as a magnanimous champion, making Oliva's defeat even more bitter. Arnold was Weider's golden boy, fully cooperative with the paternalistic system that the bodybuilding impresario had perfected, while Oliva fitfully attempted to live outside it. Oliva believed that he had lost because the system was set up for him to lose, and there was no way the judges would name him the winner. "They call him [Weider] the 'Master,' but I don't know the master of what," reflected Oliva. "Maybe the master of breaking your back and your brains."

Arnold had studied well at Weider's feet. He turned each year's competition into a dramatic narrative in which great matters were at stake. "I want all to know I have recovered my old drive, and I am raring to go," Arnold said, anticipating the 1973 Mr. Olympia competition.

Several times a year Arnold flew overseas for exhibitions that brought in much of his annual income. He was the greatest star of bodybuilding, but outside that world he was not well known and bodybuilding itself remained a marginalized sport in much of the world. On his tour of South Africa late in 1972, he arrived at one venue to find that there was no posing platform that he could stand on above the crowd. Arnold had no entourage traveling with him. Many performers would have fumed at the lack of a proper stage, but Arnold went ahead and built the platform himself.

Whether he worked too fast or did not know quite what he was doing, in the midst of his exhibition, the platform collapsed and Arnold fell among the splintered lumber. The damage was serious—a broken knee, torn cartilage, and a kneecap twisted out of place. Arnold was fixed up on crutches to continue the tour, and was operated upon as soon as he returned to the United States. The accident would have ended the career of some athletes, but Arnold returned to the gym and built himself up to his previous form.

Few bodybuilders have the emotional might to match their physical strength, and Oliva appeared increasingly distraught. He did not even enter the Mr. Olympia contest in the fall of 1973 but instead won the Mr. International title in Mexico. Arnold was in the audience that day, and Oliva taunted Arnold, daring him to come onstage to see who the true champion was. "Arnold was going to go onstage and compete with him," said Weider, who was sitting next to him that day. "I told Arnold, 'Stop it.' They planned it, you know, months ago, and that guy, Sergio, was in his best shape. I told Arnold, 'You're going to be trapped, you're going to lose.' "

Arnold refused that day, and he refused later when Oliva challenged Arnold to a weight-lifting contest on *The Tomorrow Show* with Tom Snyder. That was Oliva's attempt at upstaging Arnold, tricking him into a competition that he would surely lose, but Arnold was not about to be goaded into dubious battle. "I have never claimed to be a weight lifting champion like Sergio," he said. 'Only that I have the better body. That is why I am Mr. Olympia and Sergio is not!"

CHAPTER THIRTEEN

Games Arnold Played

In September 1972, the morning after the Mr. America contest in New York City, Arnold had breakfast with Charles Gaines, a writer, and George Butler, a photographer, who were doing a magazine piece on bodybuilding. Butler sensed that Arnold was suspicious, but he eventually came to trust the two men. They were unlike any journalists Arnold had ever met. He liked to be around people who looked good, and they were tall, handsome men full of self-confidence. They had the patina of the American upper class, yet were clearly men of their time and generation, able to talk articulately about the broadest reaches of American culture, from the Vietnam antiwar movement to the latest gossip from the salons of the Upper East Side.

Butler had an aristocratic persona as well as a photographer's sense of just where and whom to hustle. He had befriended John Kerry during their college years. Kerry had returned from Vietnam a war hero and was now an antiwar activist. While Butler was exploring Arnold with his camera, he was also focusing on Kerry with an eye that sensed these images would one day be known by millions.

Gaines was a highly talented young writer and an outdoorsman who liked to ride and hunt. He had worked on a mango farm in Florida and a ranch in Wyoming. He said that he was "from old, well-off Southern stock" and that he had "always enjoyed that fact unreservedly."

Gaines had just written a well-received first novel, *Stay Hungry*, that placed him firmly in the manly tradition of Ernest Hemingway. The main protagonist in the novel is the bodybuilder Santo. The man may appear uneducated, but he is not a semi-illiterate noble savage, but rather a sensitive, self-aware, self-educated man. Santo seeks the life of the physical senses, not because that is his only choice but because that is where freedom lies, and he will sacrifice anything to be free. Santo compares the athletic life to the paintings of Cézannne. "Well when you ski or shoot rapids you do to country what he [Cézanne] did to it with paintings. . . . You discover with your whole body the breaks and rises of terrain: cornice, rill, coulee, bowl, ridge. You learn the intimate things about earth that a mole knows, say, or a snake. It's well, it's almost like making love. And on a river, on a good river you find how water *flows*. You feel through the skin of your boat that falling, shaping force, and that is a joy J-O-Y, joy."

Santo is equally eloquent when talking about bodybuilding. "The thing that inspired Michelangelo, Rodin, guys like that, was the human body. You take [Steve] Reeves or [John] Grimek or [Reg] Park—those guys are walking art work. The fact that they don't know it or care doesn't make any difference. In a way a bodybuilder is like the simplest kind of artist. He takes the only thing he really owns and develops it as far as it'll go. He's kind of a sculptor of himself."

As Gaines began spending time with Arnold, he thought he was seeing a reincarnation of Santo. Like Gaines's fictional character, Arnold held a philosophy that could have been summarized in the book's title, *Stay Hungry*. Gaines had invented a character, Santo, in whom he had dramatized and exaggerated traits he had observed in life. Yet here was a man even more dramatic, even larger physically and spiritually, than the novelist could have imagined. There were differences. Santo valued nothing more than freedom, and he walked away from everything—financial security, love, stability, friends, everything—so that he could travel that lonely road. Arnold sought to have it all, to have a freedom and joy that few men ever had, yet all the awards that society had to offer, money and fame and adoration.

Arnold called Gaines "one of my heroes," and Gaines would have said the same of a man who became his lifelong friend. Arnold admired Gaines, in part because the novelist heard the poetry of bodybuilding and transcribed its music onto the page, but it was also that this man lived his own life and had confidence in his own being. And with this new friend, Arnold could walk into a world he had not yet encountered.

"There was a lot of pulling and tugging on the raw material of Arnold," said Gaines. "Arnold always was this fabulous one-of-a-kind creature, but there was a lot of rock obscuring the sculpture. And so it was really just a question of trying to bring out all of those things that all of us saw in Arnold."

Arnold was a listener, and he picked up on many of the ideas that the author proffered, and made them his own, melding in aspects of the Santo character. "I was able to say a few things to Arnold that were just unarticulated thoughts or beliefs of his own," said Gaines. "For example, the business about bodybuilders being sculptors themselves. Being like Michelangelo. That was an idea that I brought to my first or second meeting with Arnold. That had never really been brought into the forefront of his mind, and once it was, it just fascinated him."

Arnold appropriated some of the very language Santo spoke in the novel. "The bodybuilder is the sculptor of his own body," he told *Newsweek* in 1975. "Whatever Michelangelo, Rodin or da Vinci imagined in their minds and put together on stone or marble, this is what the bodybuilder makes possible in reality."

Gaines and Butler were so impressed with Arnold that they set out to write a nonfiction book about the marginalized, often-despised world of bodybuilding. Gaines was an amateur bodybuilder himself, and for him it was a way to write about bodybuilding as the central focus of his mind and spirit. It was a way to sit with Arnold for hours and listen to him.

Many people who read *Pumping Iron* when it came out in 1974 will tell you that it is about Arnold and that his photo is on the cover, but Arnold is only one character and it is another bodybuilder, Ed Corney, who poses on the front of the book. And yet Arnold does dominate the pages, as the highest exemplar of this hidden world. Gaines's prose and Butler's photos brilliantly complement each other, and *Pumping Iron* gave bodybuilding a dignity it had never had before—and in many respects, would never have again.

Gaines and Butler helped elevate Arnold to a unique place, not only in bodybuilding but in American popular culture. Gaines was a robust heterosexual who wrote about Arnold's body with unembarrassed loving, lyrical prose. He declared flatly that Arnold was "very possibly the most perfectly developed man in the history of the world" with "the perfect balance of everything—of biceps to calves, shoulders to waist, thighs to chest—and the detail and clarity of every part." Not only was he the physical epitome of the male species but he was "one of the most magnetic men in the Western world today." Butler's photographs were a luminous evocation of Gaines's provocative themes, mythic celebrations of the body reminiscent of Leni Riefenstahl's film of the 1936 Olympics in Berlin.

In Gaines and Butler's world of bodybuilding—and it was the first time that most readers of this unlikely bestseller had encountered the sport—there is no stench of sweat, no foul epithets, no gay hustlers, no steroid dealers, no diuretics, and no sore losers. The book is a classic of sports journalism, but as much as it purports to be the truth about bodybuilding, the words and photos are an ideal that the sport has rarely achieved. And above it all stands Arnold.

Gaines and Butler exalt Arnold's body as the most exquisite triumph of the human form, but that is a wildly subjective judgment. Others would have praised Reg Park, Sergio Oliva, or Frank Zane in the same terms before happily pointing out the weaknesses in Arnold's "perfect" body. "Everybody has weak points," said Zane. "Arnold's waistline was small, but he did not have great abdominal tone. His thighs weren't real big. Straight-on poses, his hips were rather wide and his shoulders weren't real narrow, but when he posed, everything came together."

That was the crucial point. Nobody posed better. No bodybuilder was better at creating the illusion of physical perfection.

The two men invited their new friend to Elaine's, an Upper East Side restaurant that was the bistro of choice for many of New York's most celebrated literati. Arnold fit in perfectly—or more accurately, he did not fit in at all, he overwhelmed the place. Elaine Kaufman was a doorkeeper who relegated cultural hangers-on to the bar or the back room, but Arnold was greeted like a regular. If he could eat next to the likes of Woody Allen at Elaine's, he was moving beyond the confines of bodybuilding.

One evening he sat next to Rudolf Nureyev, the most legendary ballet dancer of his time. Arnold did not know who he was but managed to have a conversation. "When was the last time you went back to Russia?" Arnold asked.

Nureyev looked in painful disbelief at the ignorant giant sitting next to him. "I don't go back to Russia anymore," he said almost curtly, leaving it unsaid that if he did, he would be thrown in prison.

"You must never give up your Russian background," Arnold lectured. "You should go."

Gaines and Butler brought Arnold to Andy Warhol's famous Factory, another stop on the happening tour of America in the seventies. Gaines took him hunting and fishing and down to his family home in Alabama. "I introduced Arnold to a lot of aspects of life that he might not have gotten around to had it not been for me," said Gaines. "And it was great fun to do."

"Arnold was definitely our Pygmalion," said Butler. "Arnold was so green in those days. He didn't know how to do anything that was socially graceful, yet he was enormously engaging."

Every valuable experience Arnold had in America he used as a beachhead from which he never retreated. When Gaines met Arnold, he was still making money building brick walls, hardly a job likely to impress the cultural elite in

New York. Yet Arnold was not intimidated by the cliquish gathering at Elaine's or by Gaines's and Butler's friends. For the most part, he made himself the center of the social gatherings with his wit and repartee.

At one café society event, Arnold was surrounded by debutantes and socialites taking inordinate delight in pinching his muscles to ascertain if they were as big and as steely as they appeared. This went on and on, as if Arnold were the evening's freak show, a part of the entertainment. The one man standing watching this was author Burton Hersh, one of Gaines's friends. Hersh was athletic himself, but Arnold picked him up like Raggedy Andy and set him in his lap. "Here's my lover boy," he said to the women. "Leave me alone."

There were plans to make a movie of *Stay Hungry*. Despite director Bob Rafelson's doubts, the young novelist pushed to have his friend Arnold play Santo. Early in 1975, to prepare Arnold for his first serious acting, Rafelson set him up with nine weeks of private lessons with Eric Morris, a highly regarded acting coach. Morris is an intense, wiry man who teaches his students to take an event in their own lives and to affix that emotional reality onto the scene they are playing. Morris considers the most agonizing, secret moments in a person's life an actor's greatest capital. Thus, the students have to plumb their lives for their most painful episodes. If they cannot reach down into the well of the past, then they can pretend but they cannot act. Reaching for these moments is a dangerous business, and Morris is adept at plunging into the students' emotional innards. He can be soothingly conciliatory, but he can also be brutal, and not all aspiring actors can walk through that gauntlet of fire.

Arnold believed in walking away from emotional pain. He was the most unlikely of students to accept Morris's approach, and yet from the moment Arnold got out of his silver BMW, put out his big hand, and said, "I'm Arnold," the two men hit it off. They were both men who made penetrating judgments of others. "Probably he told me more than he's ever told anybody else, because I was working with him," said Morris. "And we liked each other a lot. It was very, very obvious that we had a connection.

"The one thing about Arnold I have to tell you, if he likes you, he'll do anything for you," reflected Morris. "He's a good, loyal friend. But if he doesn't like you, look out. He's got a tongue that's sharp on both sides." As much as Arnold wanted to play Santo in *Stay Hungry*, if he had not liked Morris, he probably would have either walked out or given nothing of himself.

These long sessions with Morris were the one time in his adult life that Arnold focused with intensity and introspection on his emotional life. In an attempt to find episodes and people in Arnold's life that he could use as mirrors for scenes and characters in *Stay Hungry*, Morris led Arnold through much of his past. Arnold talked about his mother and about serving in the army and about his friendship with Columbu. Morris was not a therapist, but an acting coach, and though he found it curious, he said nothing about the fact that Arnold would not talk about his late father. "Arnold never expressed hatred or dislike," said Morris. "But he really kind of avoided talking about him. He never really brought him up."

Arnold was not about to reach down into the emotional pain that his father's name evoked, even if that was the route to greatness as an actor.

Arnold took far more from most people than they took from him. It was not so much that he exploited others as that he made those around him the vehicle of his learning. In his five years with Barbara Outland, Arnold had learned many things. With her, Arnold lived an orderly life. She prepared good, nutritious meals, and by example she taught him manners that he simply had not had before. Outland Baker was a serious young woman who was teaching in a school in the Latino ghetto of East L.A., not simply mouthing the words of virtue but living them.

All these years Outland Baker had been waiting for Arnold to end his obsessive career in bodybuilding, to ask her to marry him and settle down into what most people would consider a normal life. "Arnold would say, 'You know, we have such a perfect life. Why should we change this?'" Outland Baker said. "And I would say, 'Because I want to.' It's a typical woman thing. You just want your nest. I could have left him at any time, but I just didn't want to, until finally I decided I'm never going to get my dream here. I've got to find it.'"

Barbara reluctantly realized that the man was not going to change, that he would be as consumed with his new career as an actor or whatever else he chose to do as he was with his life as a bodybuilder. She loved Arnold, but she loved the idea of a life with family and children and home even more. When Arnold flew off to Birmingham, Alabama, to film *Stay Hungry* in April 1975, she packed up and left their apartment for good. And Outland Baker, who so much wanted one husband and many children, has had four marriages and no children. Arnold moved on.

Arnold had not discarded Outland Baker when he moved onto a new life. He could not live the life she wanted him to, but he needed and wanted her. After always having had her there for him, it was not easy to be alone in a strange Southern city, acting in an important film. Arnold was not easily intimidated, but everyone else on the set had credentials that made his amateur status even more obvious. Rafelson had directed the well-regarded, edgy *Five Easy Pieces*, and there was every expectation that *Stay Hungry* would be an important cutting-edge film. Jeff Bridges, who played the Southern aristocrat Craig Blake, was a fine young actor, as was Sally Field, who played the lover of both men.

Since Arnold was incapable of doing a Southern accent, Santo had been transformed into an Austrian living in Birmingham. The Arnold on the set and around Birmingham was a far larger character than the Santo on the screen. He stayed at a friend's house and enjoyed his company during the day and the pleasure of the family's nanny at night. He enjoyed the camaraderie of the film set, especially the climactic scene in the film, which takes place at a Mr. Universe competition in Birmingham. That was a world he knew, and many leading bodybuilders had been hired as extras.

The crew and cast were hanging out around the pool at their hotel when one of the bodybuilders appeared on the roof of the ten-story building. "I'm going to jump into the pool," he announced. It was no more unlikely than many of the scenes in the film, and one of the filmmakers ran to get a camera to film it. Most of the others stood or sat, mortified. The pool was set so far back from the building that the man probably would end up splattered on the concrete.

Arnold rose up from his chaise with leisurely nonchalance, as if he found the whole matter tedious, holding him back from the serious business of improving his suntan. "You can do it if you want," Arnold said slowly. "But I got to tell you. I'm retiring from bodybuilding, and you'll be the new Mr. Olympia."

"Are you serious?" the bodybuilder asked. "You're retiring?"

"Yeah, nobody knows."

"And you think it'll be me?"

"Of course," Arnold said with a shrug. "But do what you want."

The man's head disappeared from the rooftop, and Arnold went back to his tan.

CHAPTER FOURTEEN

Pumping Iron

Even when Barbara Outland was living there, Arnold's apartment had been a bachelor's pad, largely without a woman's touch. He was a meticulous man, and everything was in order, from the sets of bodybuilding pamphlets for his mail-order business to the juices lined up in the refrigerator to the paintings on the wall.

Wherever Arnold went in the world, he was often given gifts or brought back mementos. Arnold loved to show first-time visitors his artwork, ticking off all the places he had visited. There was a painting of flowers from Holland, a tourist painting from Hawaii, a Don Quixote statue from Spain, a wooden statute from Rio, a copy of the statue *The Kiss* obtained in New York, and a statue of lovers brought back from Puerto Rico.

When Arnold rolled up to the doors of Gold's Gym, visitors saw him as a demigod, a legend whose stories his peers enjoyed telling and retelling. He could have endlessly played the star, but he did not like doing so around his friends. He divided the world into fans and non-fans, and he didn't like hanging out with people who too obviously sucked up to him. It was a measure of masculine self-confidence that he was proud of being a nurturing figure. He tried to help out his buddies. He hired several bodybuilders to work on his new apartment, including Columbu for the cement work, Eddie Giuliani for electrical installation, Roger Callard for carpentry, and Dave Draper to build furniture using wood from the old Santa Monica Pier.

Arnold had begun talking about taking on a role as a protector and promoter of bodybuilding. It was something that a great athlete at his peak rarely did, but Arnold announced publicly that he hoped to improve the lives of professional bodybuilders. The bodybuilding prizes were by any measure pathetic, and Arnold sought to increase them five-, ten-, or twenty-fivefold, to amounts that could truly change a person's life. He knew the unsavory backstage conditions in many contests, and he sought decent dressing rooms and showers and wanted to limit the number of visitors backstage. And he wanted serious bodybuilding to be the center of the finals, not gussied up with dancers and vaudeville sideshows.

The five-time Mr. Olympia had little more to win and much to lose if he retired after a loss. Arnold was financially well-off, and if he never posed again or took another movie role, he could have lived moderately well off his investments, or more likely become a major California businessman, riding the expansion of the economy into millions of dollars.

Arnold was only twenty-eight years old, mere adolescence for a champion bodybuilder. Yet he was the old man of the sport, blocking the way of ambitious athletes, many of whom were actually older than Arnold. He contemplated retiring after the 1974 competition, but George Butler had come to him to tell him that he and Charles Gaines planned to make a movie about bodybuilding. The film would have the same title as the book, *Pumping Iron*, but it would be based on a whole different series of events. The movie would be the story of a group of bodybuilders preparing and vying for the 1975 Mr. Olympia title. If Arnold did not compete, he would find himself out of the film. Since Arnold hoped for a major career in Hollywood, he could hardly allow another bodybuilder to be the star of the film, and he agreed to hold off on retirement.

That Arnold's personal friends were making a documentary starring Arnold irritated some of his competitors. "Why don't you call it *Pumping Arnold*?" Frank Zane told Gaines. "It's not about the iron game."

Although other bodybuilders are featured, the filmmakers decided to make the central focus of *Pumping Iron* a dramatic confrontation between Arnold and Lou Ferrigno, who had placed second in the heavyweight division in the 1974 Mr. Olympia. At six feet five inches and 280 pounds, Lou was the biggest bodybuilder ever, overshadowing even Arnold. That did not threaten Arnold as much as it stimulated him. As Arnold learned from Weider, fans wanted dramatic conflict, and Schwarzenegger vs. Ferrigno had all the makings of a classic. Arnold began hawking it like a carnival barker. "There is no doubt in my mind that Lou Ferrigno will be the most dangerous bodybuilding challenger I have ever faced!" Arnold told the readers of *Muscle Builder/Power*. "I have to completely reevaluate my whole training plan for my coming battle with this modern Colossus!"

Arnold was in some measure merely toying with Lou. Arnold could see at a glance how burdened Ferrigno was by his life. As a baby, Lou had suffered an ear infection that left him partially deaf. He headed off to kindergarten wearing a hearing aid. He learned to read lips. His father, Matty, was a lieutenant in the New York City Police Department. When Matty came home at night, wearing his blue uniform, he expected dinner on the table and all to be right with the world. And all was not right with the world when his son could not hear and spoke with mumbling uncertainty. As the boy grew bigger, his ineptness grew, too, or so it seemed to Matty. Lou was still a kid when his father sent him off to work in a sheet-metal factory.

Even now when Ferrigno talks about his childhood, he says that his younger brother was "perfect." "I wanted to prove myself perfect like my brother, who was perfect," Lou said. "I wanted to prove it so my father would love me. I thought he would love and respect me if I got into bodybuilding. But the relationship didn't improve at all."

The teenage Lou had been standing outside with the crowds at New York's Town Hall in 1970 when Arnold won his first Mr. Olympia. The new champion exited holding his trophy in his arm with a look of radiant happiness. Lou had never had a smile like that on his lips, and he thought that in bodybuilding he might one day find it. What he did have, the one thing on which he could build his life, was that bodybuilding was *his*. Nobody else was lifting those 500-pound weights. Nobody else was heading to the gym on those cold Brooklyn mornings.

Ferrigno identified with Arnold not only as the greatest champion of bodybuilding but as a man with whom he had much in common. "That's why I tried to emulate him," Ferrigno said. "We had similar backgrounds." Arnold's father had been a police officer. Arnold's father had favored his brother. Arnold had been a sickly kid.

The filmmakers had drama in the competition between Arnold and Lou, but that by itself was unlikely to hold a general audience in their seats. Butler and Gaines needed to raise the emotional ante. The audience might think they were seeing a documentary, but Butler was making what he called a docudrama. To him that meant he could create characters and stage scenes. He came to Lou and said that for dramatic purposes, the filmmakers would like Matty to play Lou's coach. As sound a dramatic device as it was, it was equally a brutal psychological assault on everything Lou was trying to become. Matty took over his son's life, overwhelming Lou with his constant counsel. The filmmakers went to Brooklyn and shot Matty invoking Arnold's name so much that Lou screamed his archrival's name as he worked out. Day after day, Lou lifted weights in a cold, dark gym among flabby civilians while

Arnold hung out at sunny Gold's among his peers. Lou wanted to fly west and work out at Gold's, too, but that would have destroyed the drama, and he was told to stay where he was in gray old Brooklyn.

Arnold was a connoisseur of competition, structuring his life so he could have mini-competitions every day, from going at his partner in training to breaking away first at a traffic light. Defeating twenty-three-year-old Lou was a sure thing. It was a sure thing because Arnold had the tough, impregnable core of a victor, while Lou was a loser—and both men realized it. "I think that Arnold was playing tricks, but the reality was I wasn't ready, and he knew it," said Ferrigno. "The camera was on me and my father even though I was beaten down. I think Arnold knew what I was going through. I'll tell you one thing, if I had been ready, Arnold wouldn't have been so cocky and arrogant. If he knew he was going to lose, it would have been frightening. But he knew I wasn't at my best, and he was going to win easily."

The greatest competition for Arnold was not the Mr. Olympia title as much as the film itself. Arnold enjoyed playing himself more than any other role, and in *Pumping Iron* he plays himself exceedingly well. There is not a moment when he is in the film that he does not overwhelm everyone else. He is at ease with himself, whether working out at Gold's, sleeping on the beach, or musing about the competition. "I knew the more outrageous I was, the more screen time I would get, and the more I would be remembered by the audience," Arnold recalled three decades later.

Arnold not only spoke English fluently but had his own bold idiom, witty and revealing, peppered with vulgarity. He had a level of candor that would have been mindlessly reckless in many public figures, whether a politician or a television star.

Butler chose not to include many of Arnold's most provocative comments. Arnold saw the world with the sensibility of a bodybuilder. The gym is not a place to sing hymns to the glorious equality of human beings. In the weight room, the stark inequalities of men are on view. Only a determined few have the will, strength, and discipline to lift the heaviest of weights.

Arnold sought power, and the physical power of bodybuilding was only the beginning, the first training ground. When he stepped outside the gym, he saw the world no differently than when inside. "My relationship to power and authority is that I'm all for it," Arnold told Butler. "People need somebody to watch over them and tell them what to do. Ninety-five percent of the people in the world need to be told what to do and how to behave."

Arnold admired such leaders as Charlemagne and Napoléon, who could take the inert, passive masses and forge them into a force to make history. As an Austrian, he had learned how Hitler had mesmerized the Austrian and German peoples. "I admired Hitler, for instance, because he came from being a little man with almost no formal education, up to power," Arnold said. "And I admire him for being such a good public speaker and his way of getting to the people and so on. But I didn't admire him for what he did with it."

Arnold had parsed Hitler down the middle, celebrating the messianic skills and energy that brought him to power and detesting his abuse of that power. That may have been morally obtuse, but he was not the only ambitious, power-seeking young man fascinated by the Führer. "You can easily understand how that within a few years Hitler will emerge from the hatred that surrounds him now as one of the most significant figures who ever lived," wrote John F. Kennedy, one of Arnold's authentic heroes, in his diary after World War II. "He had boundless ambition for his country which rendered him a menace to the peace of the world. He had in him the stuff of which legends are made."

Arnold had an almost authoritarian sense of power. What some called liberty, he deemed anarchy. "I feel, if you want to create a strong nation and a strong country, you cannot let everybody be an individual, because everybody has his own opinions and you can't just stick together as a strong nation," he said. "Then you have to tell people what to do, and you can't just let them float away. In Germany there was a lot of unity. The German solders were the best, and with the police force and everything."

Arnold believed that what America needed was a great leader with all the messianic skills of Hitler but for good, not evil. "There's only one thing I don't like here and that is that people go on their own little trips too much," he said. "The unity isn't there anymore. And I don't think it's too much the people's fault. I think it's because we don't have a strong leader here."

Arnold used his fascination with Hitler as a way to startle people with humor that many would have considered far beyond the pale. Douglas Kent Hall, his collaborator on *Arnold: The Education of a Bodybuilder*, recalls Arnold's humorous imitations of the German leader. The author has a picture of Arnold playing Hitler in a barbershop, turning a comb into a mustache and raising his fist to the camera. Butler remembers how Arnold played "Nazi marching songs from long-playing records in his collection at home" and that he "frequently clicked his heels and pretended to be an S.S. officer."

None of his Hitler antics got into the film, but there was plenty of room for Arnold to take certain traits and blow them up into caricature. "Pumping is better than coming," Arnold said in what is perhaps the most memorable line of the film. The idea that flexing your muscles with such intensity that they fill with blood and expand far beyond their normal size is more pleasurable than an orgasm is absurd, but Arnold had long ago learned that if a statement is outrageous enough, it takes on its own truth. "Is a pump better than coming?" Arnold asked rhetorically years later. "No. It feels good to pump up, but how can you compare those two things? I made those things up, because I felt that was the way you get attention. I felt that the more outrageous things you said, the more you get in the paper, and the more the sport of bodybuilding benefitted."

In Pretoria, South Africa, at the 1975 Mr. Olympia competition, Arnold hardly had to reach into his grab bag of tricks. Ferrigno had found it devastating to compete not only against Arnold but against his father's oppressive presence. He came in third behind the Frenchman Serge Nubret in the Big Men's competition. Ferrigno would never again finish even that high, and his professional career was largely over. Arnold's real battle was with Columbu, who won the Short Man's title and competed against his closest friend in the finals. Franco's attitude was that "if Arnold wins, it's almost the same as I'm winning." That was not an attitude that his friend shared. Arnold won his sixth straight Mr. Olympia title. Clutching his victory trophy, he announced his retirement from the sport that he said had given him everything.

CHAPTER FIFTEEN

The Promoter

On his way back from South Africa, Arnold stopped in Columbus, Ohio, to visit Jim Lorimer at the Holiday Inn. The two men had hit it off five years before, and Arnold had promised that when he retired from bodybuilding he would return to promote jointly a major annual bodybuilding competition.

"I'm done competing," Arnold said. "The most I've ever won was a thousand dollars. If you're willing, next year we'll have a contest here where we're going to raise the cash prizes to ten thousand the first year. We'll have it up to a hundred thousand within four years. And you handle the details of the weekend itself, I'll work on athletes and sponsors, and we'll be partners."

Arnold could have tried to elbow his way into promoting with the Weiders, but they were not interested in dramatically increasing the prize money. Lorimer was different, and a handshake was the only agreement Arnold ever had with him. They began by running the most important bodybuilding competition, Mr. Olympia, from Columbus. That they could do so was a measure of what a good relationship Arnold had with the Weiders and how marginal bodybuilding was in American life.

The first year the event was held at Veterans Memorial Auditorium and was a raging success, creating a kind of excitement in the American heartland that it rarely achieved in New York. The four-thousand-seat venue was sold out. Afterward, Arnold went to the insurance company executive's house to count the money on a card table in the living room. The two men had ended up with a ten-thousand-dollar profit. The partners were ecstatic at what they had pulled off, holding the cold cash in their hands. Arnold tucked his $5,000 into his cowboy boots and headed back to Los Angeles.

For some in bodybuilding, it was simply too much that Arnold could move from winning Mr. Olympia one year to promoting the contest the next. Arnold and Lorimer were handing out ten times the prize money as before, and still Arnold found himself criticized for exploiting bodybuilding by making money off the sport. It was true that Arnold did nothing that did not benefit him in some measure. Yet as Arnold saw it, he was trying to give something back. The sheer jealousy of so many of his former competitors rankled him, whispering behind his back that he was out for a quick buck. It was the kind of pettiness that he had fled from in Austria, and it was disconcerting to find it alive and well in America. He had the soul of an entrepreneur. He admired businesspeople who put up their own money to put on an event, and he despised those who merely lounged on the sidelines, complaining.

Arnold flung back the same criticisms that had been made of him, accusing other bodybuilders of being greedy themselves. "Too many bodybuilders, let's face it, are content to be bums and parasites," Arnold charged. "Just take a walk along Venice Beach on any sunny day, and you'll see the numbers of muscle guys who are unemployed. They have to live. But instead of going out and getting some kind of job, they lie on the hot sand and dream up ways of making easy money."

Each year before the competition, many of the top bodybuilders went to Arnold to try out their posing routines and to get his authoritative criticism. He had astute suggestions for most of them and almost always the same wonderful praise: "If I had your body, I would win." When the bodybuilders compared notes, they were upset at Arnold's disingenuous compliment that he passed out so promiscuously. Only Frank Zane, the most intellectual of them all, got the essential point. "The fact is that Arnold could have won the Olympia with a number of different bodies because of his attitude," said Zane. "It was all his attitude."

Arnold was leaving professional bodybuilding in the midst of great upheaval in which the sport was being subsumed by far larger social movements. In the post-Vietnam era, Americans had turned inward, preoccupied with themselves and their health and appearance. Weider's magazines and equipment were selling extraordinarily well. Gyms were opening across America. Nautilus was no longer primarily the name of a submarine, but of exercise equipment. Until now, few movie and TV stars worked out seriously. George Reeves, who played Superman on television, looked more muscular dressed in his suit and tie than in his cape and tights, but Sylvester Stallone in the celebrated new film *Rocky* was not embarrassed to show his body. Robert De

Niro was working out to play boxer Jake La Motta. And Arnold didn't look so extreme anymore.

In order to raise the visibility of his *Pumping Iron* film project and attract more investors, George Butler set up a special evening at the prestigious Whitney Art Museum on Manhattan's East Side at which Arnold, Frank Zane, and Ed Corney posed in front of an audience of art lovers. In the seventies, modern art often seemed to the uninitiated to be whatever anyone said it was, but even given that mind-set, the evening risked being seen as a ridiculous farce. Butler thought they would be lucky to get a crowd of three hundred, but more than 2,500 New Yorkers jammed into the space.

Arnold walked to the platform in his posing briefs as if it were his outfit of choice at art museums. The refined audience heard nothing of the clang of steel or the rank oaths at Gold's and smelled nothing of the odors of exertion. While Arnold was rotated slowly on a bodybuilder-size lazy Susan, the young actress Candice Bergen lay on the floor photographing him. It was a heady evening, but it was as close as bodybuilding would get to the social acceptance it had had when kings and queens saw the great Sandow.

Bodybuilding may have retreated from the haute regions of New York, but Arnold did not. Without a major movie career or recognition in a premier sport, Arnold had managed to become a celebrity in a way he was not in Los Angeles. He was a person who brought cachet to high-profile events.

Arnold's sheer physicality had turned him into a generic name for muscle, size, and strength. Writer Molly Haskell described as an "Arnold Schwarzenegger type" a "muscle-bound male bimbo" who "removes his unguents and applies his body toner before going to bed at night." Arnold was easy material for satire. *New York Times* humor columnist Russell Baker wrote: "Arnold may look like he's all rock, but deep down is an old softie who cries shamelessly every time he sees *Imitation of Life*." Arnold had not even arrived yet, and the cultural mavens were already starting to yawn. *The Washington Post* included Arnold's name on a list of BORING THINGS THAT ARE SORT OF FUN.

Arnold had broken out of the bodybuilding ghetto, but he still had a kind of amorphous celebrity that was not leading him to the movie career he sought. His optimism was rock-solid. He did not squander his time worrying about the might-have-beens of life. If he had, he would have found ample room in the critical and popular reception of *Stay Hungry* when it opened in the spring of 1976. Several of the critics reviewed the film as a glorious mess, bemoaning what might have been. Arnold had played the bodybuilder protagonist Santo, but it captured neither the extraordinary character of the novel nor Arnold's own extraordinary personality. Arnold was given neither dialogue to elucidate the ecstasy of bodybuilding nor scenes that show him working out with pleasured intensity. Arnold does a workmanlike job, but the movie rarely captures the powerful character with his belief in the spiritual life of the body, largely because of the failures of the script. The film barely hints at why a person could rightfully find bodybuilding a valuable endeavor. The movie makes it seem part of an aberrant subculture, hardly worthy even of two hours' time in a movie theater.

To some people, Arnold's body was a physical provocation. They did not see him or react to the person. They saw his body, and they immediately disliked him and thought him stupid or unworthy. One of those was the studiously acerbic critic John Simon, who assumed that a big body meant a small mind and said so in his review of *Stay Hungry*. "It is one thing to make a movie about bodybuilders, the ambiguous Mr. Americas or Mr. Worlds who muscle it on certain beaches where, like beached whales, they become objects of mingled awe and ridicule," Simon opined, "but it is quite another to make these fanatics of the superhealthy body with no room in it for a mind, healthy or otherwise, into a symbol of noble striving, a grand alternative to commercialism and greed."

Public relations is the great engine of contemporary celebrity, and as the opening of *Pumping Iron* approached, Arnold had an opportunity to study the craft at the foot of a master. In September 1976 the producers hired Bobby Zarem to work the film. Zarem is a phenomenon almost extinct from the cultural landscape now, an independent publicist. As a Yale graduate with an aristocratic Southerner's easy charm, he can mingle comfortably with anyone, but what has made him successful is the passion he brings to his projects. He is partially the model for the role Al Pacino played in the overlooked 2002 film *People I Know*. When Zarem called, it was often to promote something at the cutting edge of popular culture: the rock opera *Tommy*, the movie *Saturday Night Fever*, and *Pumping Iron*.

"Arnold got a lot of his knowledge and savvy from me," said Zarem. "He learned from me. He wanted to be accepted on a higher level. He wanted people to be educated to what he was. So much of that is instinct. He learned from the moment he met me that I understood what a phenomenon he was. It was instant communication. He knew that I knew what I was doing."

Zarem treated the press like a friend with a mercurial temperament: at times cheerily civil, at others an irritable, demanding patron. In either case, the press had to be carefully fed in bite-size, easily digestible morsels. No detail was too small for the publicist. He did not crank out mimeographed releases. He hand sold each person. He wrote letters, personal notes, made phone calls, did favors, sent gifts, followed up. He was being paid to promote the movie, but he was selling Arnold, and it was a perfect fit, the irrepressible Zarem selling the irrepressible Schwarzenegger. He got Arnold in everywhere, all the New York dailies, the newsmagazines, the television networks, and even to Jamie Wyeth, painter of Presidents, with Arnold as his subject.

Shortly before the opening of *Pumping Iron*, Zarem staged a luncheon honoring Arnold at Elaine's. At the various tables sat Andy Warhol, the very definition of happening; Paulette Goddard, the aging star; George Plimpton, the author and man about town; and the greatest trophy of them all, Jacqueline Onassis, an editor at Viking Press. These people came not simply because Zarem had so assiduously importuned them but because they felt that something was happening, and they wanted to be there to see it, whatever it was. This was where Arnold's broader stardom began, not with fans shouting his name in the street but with celebrities adjusting their schedule to meet him, and such people as the gossip columnist Liz Smith and the celebrity interviewer Barbara Walters talking about him.

If Walters was impressed with how soft Arnold's arm was when she touched it, other women found him an offputting, threatening figure. Arnold experienced that directly when he appeared on a New York television program, *Midday Live!* The other guests were the ten women named by *Esquire* magazine as the top young professional women of the year. They were not women who hung around bodybuilders, and several watched with squeamish distaste when Arnold took off his shirt and posed.

Afterward the male host asked the women what they thought of Arnold. They seemed to take it as a sign of solidarity to profess distaste at such an unseemly display of muscles. One of the women said that she preferred the host's parabolic chest to that of the overwrought Mr. Olympia.

"What do you think of that?" the host asked Arnold, presumably unaware that Arnold enjoyed the verbal equivalent of throwing firecrackers into a garden party.

"Look where it comes from," Arnold said, shaking his head at the woman, whose homeliness would have gone unacknowledged except for his remark. "I have twenty beautiful women a day chasing me at the Park Lane Hotel for sex. Do you think if this woman moved into the Park Lane that twenty men would chase *her* every day?"

In the space of a minute, Arnold had violated two fundamental precepts of proper conduct in the modern urban male: trashing a woman's looks and bragging about his own sexual conquests. And he wasn't finished. "I think some of these women are afraid to admire my body, because their ugly husbands are at home watching them on TV," Arnold continued, managing the unlikely feat of insulting the husbands as well as the wives. "Remember, unfeminine women are uncomfortable around masculine men, and some of these women are abnormally career oriented."

Unlike the bland public personalities of the television age, Arnold was studiously provocative, always ready to rile up at least part of his audience, carrying them to the edge of disliking him before he pulled back. He was willing to take chances that few others would, then shrug his shoulders at the risk involved. He wanted an audience to know and remember him, and he would say and do whatever necessary to ensure that that happened.

It was only four degrees above zero on the January 1977 evening of the premiere of *Pumping Iron*, but the Plaza Theater was filled with an eclectic group of stars, celebrities, journalists, and others. Arnold did not know singers Paul Simon, Carly Simon, and James Taylor; actors Tony Perkins and Sylvia Miles; and fashion maven Diana Vreeland, but they knew enough about him to be there that evening. Arnold had brought two escorts for the evening, the stunning Delfina Rattazzi, an Italian heiress who worked as Jacqueline Onassis's assistant, and his mother, whom he had flown over from Austria.

The evening included not only a screening of the film but posing bodybuilders, capped by Franco holding a steel bar in his teeth and twisting it like a paper clip. At the dinner afterward at the New York Steak House, twenty-nine-year-old Arnold worked the crowd, practicing his meet and greet on the elite of New York. When it was all over and the last of the notables wandered out of the Time-Life Building, Arnold sat sipping a cup of coffee, still resplendent in black tie. "At least fifteen women propositioned me tonight," he said, "but I told them all I was too busy. The intellectual world of New York is falling on its knees in front of me."

To promote *Pumping Iron*, Arnold went to a radio studio to do an interview with Joy Browne. Browne's advice program is now nationally syndicated, but then she was a young journalist. Browne says that during the interview, Arnold reached under the table and massaged her legs. He left his Gold American Express card behind and asked that she return it to him in his hotel room. When she arrived with her little daughter in tow, he was wearing no shirt and asked if her daughter could "take a walk for a while." Browne gave Arnold his card and left. Looking back on the incident, the psychologist says that Arnold's advances "were a lot about power, not about sex for him."

Arnold went on a short promotional tour, including a trip to Boston. There he had an interview in a radio station housed in the penthouse of a downtown office building. The station had its own elevator, and a pretty young woman was waiting in the lobby to escort Arnold along with a photographer accompanying him. As the elevator door shut and the elevator headed upward, Arnold reached under the woman's dress, grabbed her by the crotch, and picked her up. "How's this for a lift?" he asked.

Arnold asserted his sovereignty over women in one way and over men in another. He felt it his right to reach out and touch and feel whatever he felt like touching and feeling. "Arnold used to love to shock people," said Bill Dobbins, a bodybuilding journalist who co-authored three of Arnold's books. "I would always assume that something like these groping stories was Arnold teasing people and acting out and showing that he was the big cheese and could get away with stuff. Arnold is not a sexual predator. Whatever he was doing was not a sexual act. Arnold likes to bully and tease and make fun of people."

Arnold and his European friends treated sex very differently from their American counterparts, and they were at times frustrated and puzzled by American conduct. When a European is asked, "What are your morals?" he will typically discourse on many matters, from ethics to questions of faith and politics. When an American is asked the same question, he often gives a lengthy discourse on his sexual mores.

To Arnold, sex was no big deal, but he was no longer living in the raunchy, unrestrained sexual world of Venice Beach, and he took that conduct with him. As with everything else in his life, Arnold was so disarmingly charming that he received a free pass on conduct that would have had serious consequences for almost anyone else.

By the time the elevator reached the penthouse, Arnold had removed his hand and set the woman back down and she had managed to compose herself. The doors opened and Arnold walked into the radio station. He was his own engaging self, and nothing was said or made of the incident in the elevator.

Zarem did such a spectacular and extravagant job publicizing *Pumping Iron* that Cinema 5 decided to spend almost no money on advertising. Arnold, Zarem, and Butler tried to convince the distributor otherwise, but it was too late. Whether that was the reason, or it was simply too esoteric a subject for a general audience, *Pumping Iron* did not reach beyond a limited art theater audience.

For Arnold, though, it was a singular success. He was now a star—a star without portfolio, but still a star. Beyond that, he received what proved to be some of the best reviews of his career. One of the critics, Gary Arnold of *The Washington Post*, grasped Arnold's potential the way no one had before:

> *Schwarzenegger is the first personality since Bruce Lee who might become a unique and credible physical star, idolized in particular by kids but enjoyed and admired by a vast cross section of the public. In its own way his physical self-possession seems as remarkable as Lee's, or Fred Astaire's. Like them, Schwarzenegger can make unusual physical attributes appear to be the most natural thing in the world. He doesn't disarm only his competitors. He carries that phenomenal physique so nonchalantly that one can't help feeling charmed and reassured. It is difficult to foresee what direction Schwarzenegger's movie career might take. One could imagine Schwarzenegger as Superman if his accent were slightly more subdued and Clark Kent were less of a straight arrow. He would be wasted on conventional muscleman heroics of the sort that made Steve Reeves a hit for a while. One would need to devise a format that accommodated Schwarzenegger's obvious intelligence and wittiness.*

Two weeks after the premier of *Pumping Iron*, Arnold attended the annual Golden Globe Awards at the Beverly Hilton Hotel. He entered the ballroom with his mother and moved slowly toward his table near that of Sylvester Stallone. Arnold had been nominated for *Stay Hungry* as the Best Motion Picture Debut in a Motion Picture—Male. Though there were many people who wanted to congratulate him, it was nothing compared with the greetings Stallone received. Stallone had not only starred in the celebrated inspirational hit *Rocky* but had written the script, and now he could do pretty much what he wanted in Hollywood. Even Joe Weider's *Muscle Builder/Power*, practically a house organ for Arnold's career, called Stallone "a bodybuilder of sorts," and Arnold knew the emphasis was definitely on "of sorts."

When the host, Harry Belafonte, announced that Arnold had won as the outstanding male newcomer, no one applauded louder than Stallone—indeed "Rocky" came up to Arnold's table and told him that he had a great part for him in a script Stallone had just written called *Hell's Kitchen*.

For Arnold it was a glorious achievement, but his moment of recognition was short-lived, forgotten in the triumphant procession to the podium of major stars winning major awards. At the end of the evening, the most important prize for Best Picture was given to *Rocky*. Leaping from his seat at the table, Stallone ripped the centerpiece apart, threw the flowers high in the air, and kissed every female within reach before going up to receive his trophy.

That's what it meant to be a Hollywood star. For all his gleaming muscles and the adulation he enjoyed at the gym, Arnold was barely in the same room with Stallone.

CHAPTER SIXTEEN

The Maria Factor

In August 1977 Bobby Zarem called Arnold and invited him to play at the Robert F. Kennedy pro-am celebrity tennis tournament only a few days before the event. Another celebrity, James Caan, had been unable to make it, and Zarem had suggested that Arnold take his place. The annual charity event, held just before the U.S. Open and hosted by Ethel Kennedy, had become one of the megacelebrity gatherings of the time. That Arnold did not play tennis and was going to have to play the game in front of thousands of New Yorkers did not dissuade him.

Arnold had just acquired his first Hollywood agents, Lawrence Kubik and Craig Rumar, and he figured that this was a matter for their expertise. "He asked, had I ever heard of the tournament," said Kubik. "I said that I had, and I took him up to the Malibu Tennis Club to teach him some tennis. The balls were flying everywhere. When we finished, he asked, 'What am I going to do?'"

By the time Arnold arrived in New York a few days later, he had learned the rudiments of the sport. The spectators in the Forest Hills Stadium watched an array of games, everything from comedian Buddy Hackett doing his pratfalls after a bad shot to Senator Edward Kennedy and Vice President Walter Mondale taking on two television journalists, Tom Brokaw and David Hartman. But *The New York Times* described "the highlight of the day" as the massive doubles duo of Arnold and retired football player Roosevelt Grier against a couple of sprightly kids. Arnold and Grier were big hams like Hackett. After losing their first game to the two determined boys, they ripped off their shirts and proceeded to defeat their youthful opponents.

Arnold had plenty of time to talk to others at the event. He had never been taken much by the romance of the Kennedys, but they were the first family of American politics and had an undeniable energy that appealed to him. There were three generations running around the grounds, including a large array of Shrivers, almost all of them excellent tennis players. Arnold had already met Bobby Shriver, a gadfly who was working as a reporter for the *Los Angeles Herald Examiner*, and that day he met others, including Bobby's younger sister, twenty-one-year-old Maria.

Maria was intrigued enough by thirty-year-old Arnold to invite him to Hyannis Port, Massachusetts, the summer home of the Kennedy clan. Arnold did not fly northward full of social ambition, out to make his way in the world by latching on to a Kennedy. That was simply not the way he looked at women. For the most part, Arnold did not date women to advance himself. It was one of the oldest gambits of Hollywood publicists to set up young stars with faux romances that got their names in the gossip columns. If that had been Arnold's pleasure, he could have dated a stream of publicity-seeking starlets mixed in with socially prominent single women, but he did not do that, either.

Arnold did not like women who were emotionally troublesome, and the famous and rich and the highborn all immediately qualified. He was living now with Sue Moray, a warm, feisty, pretty young woman who was a hairdresser. He had set out the parameters of the relationship. When he was in town, he was loyal to her. When he was away, he did what he wanted, and so could she.

Arnold considered the actress Candice Bergen his womanly ideal. She was as beautiful as any model, but if you thought that meant she was stupid, she immediately disabused you of that notion with her intimidating intellect. Arnold said that he was looking for a woman "that's brighter than I . . . an aggressive woman who can talk and is not always in the background." That may have been what Arnold was looking for, or more likely what he liked to think he was looking for, a drop-dead gorgeous woman who royally trumped him in intelligence. He never sought such women out but preferred someone like Moray as long as he could sweeten his evenings out of town with an endless array of others.

Arnold proudly called himself a "butt man" and could lovingly talk about that part of a woman's anatomy the way a wine lover discusses vintages. Maria was a lush beauty with Reubenesque thighs. She was five feet, seven inches tall and weighed as much as 150 pounds. "When Arnold first met Maria, she was entirely different," recalled Kubik. "She was a young girl, her body was different, she was certainly enamored with Arnold, and I thought he likes big girls."

Maria's parents were one of the most extraordinary political couples in

America. Her father, Sargent Shriver, came from an old Maryland family that had lost its wealth. He had graduated from Yale, flown a navy plane in World War II, gone to work for Joseph P. Kennedy, and married his daughter Eunice. He was the first director of the Peace Corps, led the War on Poverty, ran for Vice President on the ticket with Senator George McGovern in 1972, and ran for the Democratic presidential nomination four years later. Maria adored her father, and the lover or husband who inherited that love would find it intense, passionate, and almost overwhelming.

Among the many gifts her father gave Maria was her initial fascination with journalism. In 1972 she had traveled in the back of the plane with the journalists covering the McGovern-Shriver campaign for the presidency. It was hardly the most desired assignment of the campaign, but doom brings out the best in journalists, and they had many weeks to practice gallows humor. There were no other sixteen-year-olds among the scribes, and Maria enjoyed being "part of this pack of intense and highly competitive professionals." She had found her métier. To her it was politics without the pain.

Maria's love for her mother was just as intense, but far more complicated. Some people thought that Eunice Kennedy Shriver was a saint, but they had not worked for her. She was a woman to whom any mountaintop was only a momentary plateau. She founded the Special Olympics and worked to develop it into a worldwide institution that helped change the way the developmentally disabled are viewed. She was not a name-on-the-letterhead kind of person, but an in-the-muck, in-your-face perfectionist. That was also true of the way she brought up her children, especially her only daughter. She wanted to make sure that Maria, the second of her five children, knew that the world was as wide-open and free for her as it was for her brothers.

"Growing up, people would come up and say to my mother, 'Oh, your daughter is so pretty,'" Maria recalled. "My mother would always say, 'Stop it. Stop it.' Then she would turn to me and say, 'Don't you pay any attention to that. It's your mind, your mind!' I was always saying to myself, 'Oh, she's so weird.' She was always pushing me to do boys' activities, you know, to speak up when the boys were there. My father would say, 'I'm going to the baseball game.' She'd go, 'Maria is going.' And she'd push me right along like I came to believe I was a boy or one of the boys. She never emphasized anything feminine with me."

Maria, like her brothers, was brought up with a constant diet of stories of the greatness of her family, reinforced by pictures of the various Kennedys all over the Shriver house in Maryland. Although she was close to her three younger brothers, Timothy, Mark, and Anthony, she was closest to her elder brother, Bobby. She was inculcated with the idea that she had blessed and sacred blood in her veins, that family mattered more than anything, and that her family mattered more than any other. And yet it was not a lazy entitlement that her mother handed to her. She wanted her children tested and challenged. It was fine to go to live in Paris, where Sarge Shriver served as ambassador in the last years of the Johnson administration, but she pushed Maria out to test herself, to live on a kibbutz in Israel and in a village in Africa, experiences suitable perhaps for young adults, but not so obviously for young teenagers.

When she was a little girl, her parents had in her estimation "traveled and worked an excessive amount," leaving Maria and Bobby in the care of nannies and aides. That hurt her, especially when she contrasted it to how often her parents were with her when she was older, and what a constant presence they were in the lives of her younger siblings. "I can remember staying overnight at Maria's house when we were growing up," said Theo Hayes, one of her closest friends. "And I could hear Mrs. Shriver up on the third floor, sitting in the hallway in between the two doors of the boys' bedrooms at ten o'clock at night, and she's reading stories to Maria's younger brothers, putting them to bed. Maria never had that."

Maria had been old enough to have known and felt the deaths of her uncles Jack and Bobby and seen how the tragedies emotionally ravaged her family. That was a price that she did not intend to pay, yet she was intellectually and emotionally drawn to politics, not simply by the drama of it but by how politics could change things and how people used politics for purposes good and bad.

Maria was hungry to test herself in the world, but as neither a Kennedy nor a Shriver. She was not about to get involved in politics, but she wanted to come to it as a professional observer reporting on the great public events of her time. "I always had a desire to go against the flow, so I wanted to pick something different," she said. "Yet I wanted to use what I had been brought up to believe in and work in—in a different field."

She wanted to be a television journalist and to be able to state that she had made it on her own. "I think I was obsessive about that," she said. It was an inheritor's greatest burden, to be able to believe that your accomplishments are not based largely on the fact that your name and wealth has positioned you far in front of those you consider your competitors. She ended up signing on as an intern at KYW-TV in Philadelphia for twelve thousand dollars a year.

For all Eunice's concern that Maria not be defined by her sex, she found it unacceptable for her daughter to be so chunky. It never quite occurred to her that one reason Maria was so heavy is that when the Shrivers returned from Paris, Eunice brought a French chef with her who filled the dinner table with heavy, rich foods that the teenage Maria found irresistible. Eunice was constantly lecturing her daughter to lose weight.

This obsession with weight had been common among the Kennedy women for at least three generations. In turn-of-the-century Boston, where girth marked one as having peasant origins, Maria's great-grandmother Josephine Fitzgerald was proud of her wineglass figure. Maria's grandmother Rose took pills and obsessively dieted to stay thin, boasting that she wore the same gown to her son's inauguration that twenty-three years before she had worn to be presented to the king and queen in Great Britain. Eunice was railthin. Maria was a robust, healthy young woman, and this fixation with weight was a malady that the women in the family passed on like recipes or childrearing advice.

Maria's brother Anthony was there that weekend in Hyannis Port, and he watched the mating dance. He had the sense that several of Maria's cousins were intrigued by Arnold, too. "Maria didn't necessarily have the physique she has now," Anthony said. "And he saw in her qualities. It wasn't about getting the Kennedy thing going. Caroline was there, and all those other people were there, so he got it on with Maria, and he figured it out that she was the star."

Nothing Maria had done in her life was as daring as dating Arnold. Many young heirs are under the illusion that if you marry a person equally wealthy, you are not marrying that person for his or her money. Yet, up until that point, she had generally dated men of her own class or social background, including Larry Lucchino, an ambitious young attorney who would end up as CEO of the Boston Red Sox. She had been trained to have a subtle social caution. There were people out there who wanted to use her and her family, people who wanted to get to her family through her, and part of her job was not to let that happen.

Arnold was precisely the kind of man that a well-brought-up Kennedy woman was taught to avoid. He was not even a movie or television star, but a freak celebrity. He had already had his moment of notoriety, and odds were that he would soon turn to flab and obscurity. He was, by all accounts, a man of dangerous sexuality who flaunted his promiscuous lifestyle. He may have played tennis with Sarge and spoken German with Grandmother Rose, an action more impressive on the Kennedy matriarch's part than Arnold's, but that he was partially housebroken did not mean that he should be invited regularly into one's home.

Arnold had supped at Elaine's, but he had not fully learned the social graces that came naturally to the Kennedys and their associates. Everything was a little off, from his hair to his shoes. Maria's girlfriends were struck by how bad Arnold smelled. He gave off what they called a peculiarly European odor, which they felt came from unfamiliarity with deodorants. That probably was not true, but rather a projection of how threatening they found Arnold and how wrong for their friend. He did give off an odor of danger, and they were appalled that their beloved friend should be seeing such a man. Theo Hayes was so upset at this untoward intrusion that a few weeks later she refused to allow Maria to bring Arnold to her wedding.

"Everybody had problems with Arnold," Maria said. "I don't know one person who thought he was a good idea. People around him would say, 'What the hell is that?' They had never met anybody like him. And everybody around me said the same. So I was on a pretty lonely island there."

Maria's friends were for the most part good Catholic girls, and none of them had ever seen anything like Arnold. He was someone you ran from, the very model of the kind of man the nuns told you to avoid. "Sex was the great compelling force of the relationship," said another friend. There was a gloriously lustful center to their love. A measure of that was that two and a half decades later, Maria is still talking about her sexuality in a way that was unthinkable for a Kennedy woman. "I wish I'd known how creative, crucial, and consistent sex would have to be," Maria wrote. "And I certainly never knew I'd wind up talking about it so much."

It was almost unheard-of for a Kennedy woman to have such an openly randy relationship. Maria came from a family in which most of the men sought their sexual entertainment outside marriage, and many of their wives came to consider sex one of the onerous obligations of marriage. Maria's aunt Pat crossed herself before having sex with her husband, Peter Lawford. Maria's own mother, Eunice, was so ignorant about birth control that she thought that men with a sexual gleam in their eye strapped on condoms before leaving the house. Even if these women found pleasure in having sex with their husbands, marriage was too important a matter to be left to such fickle, transient matters as sexual attraction.

Arnold and Maria talked to each other about myriad subjects, either in person or on the phone, but unquestionably the sexual component was key. Arnold flew to Washington to attend the Special Olympics and other social events, and Maria made her trips to California, too. Distance allowed their affair to continue. Arnold simply was not ready for a relationship that was intense and monogamous.

The couple had gone out only once or twice when they headed out with Joe and Betty Weider for a weekend of antiquing in the Pennsylvania countryside, to be followed by a bodybuilding show. The foursome arrived so late at the Philadelphia airport that they missed the plane to the exhibition. Arnold wanted to rent a private plane so that he could make his scheduled appearance. The only one available was an ancient craft that Betty thought might have flown in World War I, with an ancient pilot who might have flown it. Anyone with a modicum of caution would have walked away—anyone but Arnold. "I was in shock and I think Maria was in shock, and at first Joe said, 'I'm not going,' " said Betty Weider. "Arnold figured if the man had flown for sixty years, he could fly." They had not reckoned on Arnold's persistence, and off they flew into the Pennsylvania sky. The old man buzzed the urban skyline before heading out over the countryside. Betty kept asking the pilot questions about how he flew the plane. She wanted to be ready in case he died of a heart attack before they landed and she had to take over the controls.

Arnold was not good at saying no, and he was no good at endings. His love affair with Moray ended in tortured convulsions. Arnold was full of gentle duplicities that he used to cushion unpleasantness. He kept telling Moray that Maria was terribly young and that his relationship with her was platonic. Moray became obsessed with Maria, full of paranoia and jealousy. Tired of Arnold's fibbing, she walked out of the house, only to return. "I found him there, crying," she said. "I've never seen a man cry so hard. He was just like a baby, crying and crying."

Arnold liked routine, be it in bodybuilding or romance, and he did not want Moray to leave. Maria was matchless as a weekend or vacation partner, but theirs was not the casual, comfortable relationship Arnold had with Moray. It was not until a year after Arnold met Maria that Sue finally left, and she says their sexual relationship continued for a while even after that.

Arnold was a man of limitless ambition, but he was not obsessed with his career in the same way Maria was. He could let go and think of other things, while she put no limit on the hours she would work or the commitments she would make. She was a woman of exhausting intensity, obsessed by succeeding in broadcasting. She had moved to a producer's slot in Baltimore at WJZ. When she said she worked night and day, she was not indulging in hyperbole. She never found time even to unpack the boxes she had shipped from Philadelphia. Despite the endless work, Maria was passionately in love with Arnold. He was a man of special occasions and splendid good times. With her compulsive work schedule, it was the perfect romance.

Arnold brought Franco Columbu with him to the Shriver home for

Thanksgiving their first year together. "Come in the kitchen, Franco," Maria said to Arnold's closest friend. Columbu hardly knew Maria, and he was appreciative of her immediate warmth. "This is a carrot cake," she told him. "It smells funny," Franco replied. "It's a burnt cake."

"Smell it," Maria commanded. As Columbu leaned over the cake, Maria shoved his face into it. He had hardly stood up to begin to wipe the frosting off his face when another Shriver entered the kitchen and threw a cake in Maria's face. Columbu had known Arnold's previous girlfriends, but nobody like Maria and no family like the Shrivers.

Arnold did not know quite what to make of this unpredictable young woman. "She always says that the first time she met me she really liked me, and it was like love at first sight," he said. "I'm slower about these things, I don't jump. As time went on, the more I talked to her and the more I saw her, I started to love her."

He brought to romance all the skills of a diplomat, giving her the illusion that she was the only woman in his life. He was proud of her, and he appeared proud that she was a Kennedy and that she was in love with him. He detailed her physical attributes to his bodybuilding buddies while they worked out. She was energetic and fun to be with, but she was a wearing, emotionally demanding person. Anybody's bet was that the affair would not last. Maria had one quality she shared with Arnold that was crucial to the longevity of their affair. She was growing and learning and changing, and so was he.

"People have always written that Arnold went and got himself a Kennedy," reflected Maria. "No. He and I fell in love. He wasn't finished growing and he saw in me someone who could grow with him and could help. I was saying, 'You can do more. We can go together.' He had found someone unlike his mother who believed he could go further. And nobody felt that he could go further but the two of us. And everybody laughed at his dreams. People were mad at me, because I was supposedly taking him further away. That's where Arnold wanted to go. You can't take a guy like Arnold somewhere where he doesn't want to go."

The Shrivers might be Democrats when it came time to vote, but they were snobs when it came to their only daughter, and they could hardly envision that this hulk might be their future son-in-law. Nevertheless, Eunice involved anyone within shouting radius in the Special Olympics, and Arnold immediately and enthusiastically took part. It meant little to fly into Washington to attend a $500-a-ticket benefit with Maria that coincided with the premiere of *Superman* in December 1978. It meant a little more to be there that same weekend for a sports clinic for the Special Olympics. And it meant a lot more to become the weight-lifting adviser to the organization and to work to make it an important sport. Arnold was a wonderfully sensitive coach, never patronizing, his enthusiasm perfectly fitted to his task.

Arnold loomed large not only as a figure in the bodybuilding world but as a guru in the whole fitness revolution. His 1978 book, *Arnold: The Education of a Bodybuilder*, was a bestseller. Written with Douglas Kent Hall, it was half autobiography and half a program on how to get in shape. Many celebrities publish ghostwritten books for which they have made minimal contributions and which they sometimes have not even read. That was not the case with this book. *Arnold* was worthwhile and solid, a further indication that Arnold saw himself as a product that could be merchandised in many different ways as long as full value was delivered.

Arnold promoted the semi-autobiography as avidly as he would a movie. It was a mark of his persistence, perseverance, and marketing vision that he did so. When Simon & Schuster put together a five-city tour for the first-time author, he told them that it was not enough, it was hardly a beginning.

"I said, 'No, I want to go to at least thirty cities,'" Arnold recalled with pleasure. "And they looked at me like I was totally out of my mind. They had never even been in touch with anyone in those cities, so they had no contacts and had to hire some outside consultants. I wanted to go out and do something unique and different and not just do the traditional way of marketing. They got out my book into sporting-goods stores, which never happened before, and I went to thirty cities and we made our book a bestseller, which has never happened before with any bodybuilding book. So that was like a huge victory."

This was the first of a series of bodybuilding books and videos bearing Arnold's name that were released during the next two decades. They were a lucrative sideline, and Arnold perceived them as part of his legacy and as a mark of his serious commitment to bodybuilding. The books delivered fully upon their promise. "He wanted everything to be perfect and went over every line with me," recalled co-author Bill Dobbins. "He would generally add a lot of very personal stuff about his own training in Austria and elsewhere."

When Arnold was in Washington on the book tour, he had a chance to see Maria for Halloween. She was a pleasant diversion, but the relationship was neither compelling nor deep. "She picked me up in the hotel lobby," he recalled. "She was dressed up all goofy as some kind of gypsy, wearing a lot of weird earrings and stuff, and I thought, 'God, this girl is just too much.' I loved that. She was also so witty, so 'on' that night. I went to Europe then and thought about her a lot. I had a feeling it was reciprocal."

CHAPTER SEVENTEEN

"Part of the Entertaining Show"

Maria was a pleasant enough diversion, but his Golden Globe for *Stay Hungry* was leading him nowhere and Arnold was consumed with making it in Hollywood. Arnold returned to study under Eric Morris in a weekly class with other students. Like everyone else in the room, he said that he was looking for the right role. The idea of playing the Swede in Ernest Hemingway's short story "The Killers" attracted him. It would have been film noir, a dark little tale of a man who has double-crossed people he should not have. The Swede knows he is going to be murdered. He does not think there is anything he can do to stop it. "If there's one thing I should do, it's the unexpected," Arnold argued. "Whether it's 'The Killers' or something else, I probably should play the victim."

That was the thinking of a man who wanted to be a serious actor. That was what Morris's acting class was all about. For a year or so Arnold went every week when he was in town and went through what everybody else was going through. The students took their places in chairs that formed a horseshoe around a small stage, where they took turns performing. Morris sat on the side, watching the students and making comments. The teacher was an adept reader of faces, and one evening he saw that Arnold was distracted and full of contained rage.

"Get up there, Arnold," Morris commanded. Arnold slowly rose and stood before the twenty or so students.

"Okay, it's obvious you're upset. What's the matter?"

"I'm pissed off! It's bullshit! They don't like my name, they don't like my accent, they don't like my body, but fuck them! I'm going to be a superstar!"

"Okay, I'm with you. What's going on?"

"I see agents. They say, 'Your accent is too heavy. You're too big. What can you play?'"

"Arnold, you're charismatic. Everybody in this room is pinned and nailed, glued to you. I mean, that is something you can't teach somebody. If you've got it, you've got it. If you ain't got it, you ain't got it. So, I mean, you've got it. You've just got to be patient."

That was just about the last time Arnold went to the class. He did not talk much anymore about becoming a serious actor. He talked about being a star, the greatest star in the world. And he talked about it in a way that was either mindlessly boastful or perfectly confident. "I love to entertain," Arnold said. "I want to entertain more people than any actor ever has. But I will stay away from serious shows. I want to be part of the entertaining show, make people laugh and have a good time."

Arnold turned away from whatever was negative, and acting as such had become an onerous, unpleasant business. "I don't care if I ever become an actor, I'm going to become a star, and everyone is going to know the name Schwarzenegger," he told Betty Weider, who sensed the driven nature of the man. "I know how to become a star. Maybe I don't have the talent to become an actor, but I'll become a star."

Arnold did not want to plumb whatever darkness he had in his own soul and lay out that darkness before the world. He understood himself, not some fantasy of what he might have been, not some ideal that other people wanted him to be, but what he was. "You have to think positive and program yourself to be a winner," he said. "I am simply not programmed to think bad thoughts. Successful people have the ability to take a risk and make a tough decision, no matter what everyone around them says."

To become a movie star, Arnold had to overcome the most merciless stereotypes. "The first movies that were offered to me were Nazi movies, play a Nazi officer and all that stuff," remembered Arnold. "So, I think people always look whether he's from Germany or from Austria, and say, 'Oh, he's a Nazi.' I remember when I walked into World Gym and the people called, 'Oh, the Boy from Brazil,' all those kind of things. If you have a German accent, that's what you get."

Arnold's first agent, Craig Rumar, does not remember how he and Lawrence Kubik got their new client, but there was no great competition to represent him. Hollywood is a place where people spend their days trying to find ways to say no, and in Arnold's case it was just too easy. He had a foreign accent.

That was bad enough, but it was also a German accent, and in what was largely a Jewish industry, that was a further reason to turn him away. He was also a conservative Republican. "It's not like you can go to Nat and Al's deli in Beverly Hills in the morning for breakfast and sit in the Republican section," said Rumar. "You can't do it. That was a huge element for Arnold to overcome. You do not know the vile hatred that they had for him."

Rumar had a number of famous clients, but he had never had anyone who impressed him in so many ways. "He oozed charm and confidence," said Rumar. "But it wasn't Hollywood phony. He was sort of like a young messiah who could come in and do anything he wanted to. For whatever reason, he chose acting. He could have gone into business and been one of the great tycoons in the world."

Acting was Arnold's first choice as a profession, but it was perhaps not the choice for which he was best suited. Other than *Pumping Iron*, Arnold did not radiate stardom in his early film work. In a secondary role in *The Villain*, starring Kirk Douglas and Ann-Margret, Arnold was so boring and leaden that he seemed an anti-star "more of a weight on the movie than even *he* might be able to lift," as *The New York Times* sniffed. He was adequate as Jayne Mansfield's lover Mickey Hargitay in the 1980 TV movie *The Jayne Mansfield Story* but displayed nothing of the charisma and excitement needed to succeed even on the small screen.

Arnold's first chance at a role custom fit to him was to play Conan the Cimmerian, in a film based on the fantasy adventure stories by the late Robert E. Howard. In the Great Depression, these stories led teenage boys away from the uncertainty of their daily existence into a brutal, mythic world where might was right and revenge the noblest of motives. Howard set out an irresistibly compelling vision of a barbarian world: "Between the years when the oceans drank Atlantis and the gleaming cities . . . there was an Age undreamed of, when shining kingdoms lay spread across the world like blue mantles beneath the stars. . . . Hither came Conan, the Cimmerian, blackhaired, sullen-eyed, sword in hand . . . to tread the jeweled thorns of the Earth under his sandaled feet."

The role of such a hero seemed tailor-made for Arnold Schwarzenegger, world-conquering bodybuilder with his own mythic dreams. The producer Edward Pressman purchased the film rights to Conan and signed Arnold to do a whole series. Pressman subsequently sold the project to Dino De Laurentiis, the Italian producer. The diminutive De Laurentiis was not a highbrow artiste but a shrewd entrepreneur who was as happy to roll the dice with *Conan the Barbarian* or *Barbarella* as such legendary films of his as *La Strada* or

Nights of Cabiria. De Laurentiis gave Arnold a higher education in the machinations of Hollywood, where few plots are as complicated or as full of potential betrayal and disappointment as in the making of the film.

When Arnold and Kubik went in to see De Laurentiis in his Hollywood office, the producer sat behind a desk so large that practically only his head was visible. The producer got up and walked out from behind the desk. "Why does a man so small need such a big desk?" Arnold asked him. The meeting ended shortly thereafter. Out in the hall, Arnold's agent berated him. "You destroyed your career!" he railed.

"No, I made it," Arnold replied.

Kubik recalled saying ironically, "Well, you handled that well."

No other young actor would have been so bold or foolish as to make such a comment, but Arnold did not care that he had spoken so rudely. The agents had already negotiated a tiered deal that Rumar said totaled $5 million for five films. De Laurentiis did not have to make the films, but if he did, Arnold earned increasing amounts that could earn him a fortune.

Arnold not only had limited acting skills, but he was sometimes hard to understand. "His accent was much thicker than it is today," said Kubik. "He worked very hard over the years to lessen his accent." His voice would be dubbed in other languages and perhaps even in English, and thus in his first major film the accent was not a concern. It was all about business, in any case, and it was business that saved Arnold.

De Laurentiis recalled that he flew to London to meet the director Ridley Scott to sign him up for the film. "Dino, I'd love to do it," Scott said, "but I need an actor. I cannot do it with Arnold Schwarzenegger."

"If I have to choose between you and Arnold, I choose Arnold," said De Laurentiis.

That Arnold was legally tied to the project was a technicality that the producer's lawyers could probably have voided. Arnold brought something else that most Hollywood film studios had not yet fully grasped: the significance of the worldwide market. Arnold was famous in much of the world as a bodybuilder, and De Laurentiis envisioned *Conan the Barbarian* as a movie that would make its profit by being successful in scores of countries. De Laurentiis was going through one of his periodic downtimes, and he needed to sell those foreign rights if he was going to get the film into production.

Kubik had ample opportunity to observe Arnold before he made his first important film. "I saw the terrific discipline and confidence that he had," said the agent. "There were no limits on his ambition. He exerts a tremendous amount of control. He had a vision, and he knew he could turn it into reality. In his mind, whatever he's doing is like a film getting made."

Making a film involves a great deal of waiting around, and the least of it is on the set. In Arnold's case, from the time he first heard about the project, he waited almost half a decade for shooting to begin. He was in his early thirties, already an unlikely age to become a major star. He could hardly afford to sit around, but there was one delay after another.

The talented young screenwriter Oliver Stone wrote the first screenplay of *Conan the Barbarian*. It was a wild fantastical adventure that would have been prohibitively expensive to shoot. When Pressman sold the project to De Laurentiis, the Italian producer brought in another prominent young screenwriter, John Milius, to write a script that could be shot economically. If Milius did that, he would be given the opportunity to direct the film.

Milius was a rudely spoken, vulgar, literate, obsessive, burly, bearded, proud, gun-toting anachronism. He had cowritten what was probably the greatest screenplay of the epoch, *Apocalypse Now*, a dark, operatic saga of Vietnam. In writing the Conan script, Milius poured all his fierce anger and artistic energy not only into a grand vision but into exquisite details and evocative descriptions. Although he shared the screenplay credit with Stone, it is unquestionably Milius's story, a compelling, evocative piece of work grounded in his darkly romantic view of history. The script follows the life of Conan from the childhood day his father is run through with a sword and disemboweled by dogs in front of his son, his mother is decapitated as the boy stands next to her holding her hand, and young Conan is pressed into slavery.

At the beginning of his screenplay, Milius places an epigram from Nietzsche: "That which does not destroy us, makes us stronger." It was perfect not only for Conan but for Arnold. There is a persistent theme in Arnold's life and the lives of many of those with whom he has been artistically associated: out of weakness grows strength. Out of the forthright admission of one's frailties and the determined commitment to go on comes a laminated strength powerful enough to overcome those who have not made such a struggle.

Howard, the author of the Conan stories, was a weak little boy pummeled by the town bully. He turned to bodybuilding so that he could defend himself. And he turned to his Conan stories to create a mythic man who would ride through a blood-tinged barbaric world, meting out vengeful justice with a fierce and certain sword. It was a world uniquely appealing to teenage boys, who fancied themselves living in their own barbaric, adult-controlled universe and dreamed of their own revenge. Milius himself had been so weak and sickly that he was turned down by the military service he so admired, and had become a troubadour of lost traditional manhood.

There is an atavistic, self-consciously primitive quality expressed in much of Milius's work, as if only by stripping away the shoddy veneer of civilization can the manly life be reborn. Milius and Howard share a dramatic world in which men head out into danger, seeking certain truths. If these are truths that only teenage boys understand, the fault lies not in the youths but in their spiritually anesthetized elders.

Arnold's own life resonated with many of these same themes, though he largely disguised what Milius proudly proclaimed. Arnold was a man from Styria, a land whose glories were in the past, in years of brave struggle holding back the hated Ottomans from their assault on the West. Even today the armory museum in Graz is the largest in the world, with rooms full of body armor, spikes, muskets, and guns, relics of a time when a man proved his mettle against fire and sword. Arnold hungered for heroism, and he loved tales of great men and their deeds. He was the man to play Conan, and his physical form was only part of the reason.

When Milius went to Arnold's office to discuss the script, he noticed a photograph that convinced him that Arnold could convey the essence of Conan. "It was a picture of him on his back, grotesquely lifting this bent curling bar with these giant fucking dumbbells on it, and he had this thing around his waist so that he wouldn't burst or something from the strain," Milius said. "It was just horrible, the strain on his muscles, and all the veins were stressed, everything. And he has this expression on his face of Zen bliss, combined with the look of the lion. I said to Arnold, 'Whenever you kill someone, that's the way you should be. That's who you are. This is more than pleasure. This is you doing what you do, this is what you can't help but do. And Conan must always be thus, instead of ever yelling in rage or anything like that, Conan must always be cool.'"

Arnold, who had arguably created the greatest physique in the history of bodybuilding, devoted most of his effort to creating the physical presence of Conan. From the moment he heard about the Conan role, he began to develop the on-screen presence. "One of the first things I did was to look up the character and see what he did well," said Arnold. "That turned out to be swordfighting, climbing, and horseback riding. So I felt that, on my own, before they even selected a director, I should go out and train for those things. I also started to do athletic things like running and climbing." In months of preparation, he developed his own aggressive style of swordplay, his own manner of running and fighting, and his own set of expressions.

In preparing to play Conan, Arnold had gained the same control over his physical gestures and movements that he sought over all the externals of his life. His public presence and every gesture and nuance of it had become as calculated for effect as the rhetoric in a speech. It was a change observed by George Butler, who for several years had photographed his countenance. "In the early days, when I photographed Arnold, before he had acted in movies, his facial expressions were natural," he said. "I began to notice that he was thinking about his expressions. I doubt he will ever have that natural expressiveness again that we captured in the film [*Pumping Iron*]."

Milius was inordinately proud of his image as a wild man, and he told Arnold that if he wanted to understand Conan, he should hang out with the Hell's Angels, the outlaw biker gang. Arnold, like Milius, liked to drive his Harley in the winding hills, and he had run into his fair share of Angels. "I always find that they are basically wonderful characters and great human beings," Arnold said. "The only thing is, they prefer a freer life than the law allows today."

That was Arnold speaking, not Conan, and it was hardly an objective view of an often violent, drug-riddled subculture. Arnold may have been prepping himself to play a movie role, but in doing so he reinforced his own political beliefs. His natural sympathies were with those living on the wild fringes of American life. He fancied that these self-conscious outlaws were the torchbearers of a kind of liberty that those in corporate/bureaucratic America had long forgotten or considered mere indulgence. He was a skeet-shooting hunting control. He had, by his count, about fifteen guns in his house, including not only shotguns and pistols but an Uzi.

Arnold was preparing for his role not only by taking fencing and riding lessons but by working to keep his name in the forefront of the public consciousness. Arnold was still featured in the Weider publications, but there was no longer the buzz there had been when *Pumping Iron* came out. The most certain way to get major publicity was to win another bodybuilding title, but he had been out of competition for five years. Although Arnold was still in good shape, he was hardly in the form to walk back into the highest reaches of the sport. He decided that it would help promote his movie if he competed and won the 1980 Mr. Olympia.

For the past four years, Arnold and Lorimer had put on the Mr. Olympia contest in Columbus. It had been a raging success, and the Weiders had taken it back, saying that they wanted to stage the premier contest in bodybuilding around the world. They arranged for the 1980 event to take place in Sydney, Australia.

Arnold had other reasons to win that great prize an unprecedented seventh time. The year before, Arnold had been working as a commentator for CBS on its live coverage of the 1979 Mr. Olympia finals in Columbus. When Frank Zane won the title for the third time, Arnold asked him how it felt. "Great, Arnold," Zane said. "Almost as good as the time I beat you in '68."

Nobody humiliated Arnold on national television. He called Zane afterward, raging at him for his audacious insult. "Yeah, Arnold, you've got a good sense of humor if the joke's not on you," Zane said. "You do this all the time to other people. Somebody does it to you, it's not so funny." Arnold said nothing more, but he envisioned the sweetest revenge of all, ripping the trophy out of Zane's hands in Australia.

Another top bodybuilder, Mike Mentzer, represented far more of a threat to Arnold than Zane. The Washington, D.C., area resident had won the 1978 Mr. Universe title with a perfect score and finished second to Zane in the 1979 Mr. Olympia. He had ample reason to believe that he was primed to wear the crown this year. Mentzer might never win as many championships as Arnold, but he represented another kind of challenge. Arnold fancied himself not only the greatest champion of all time but the great philosopher of bodybuilding, He was the proudest product of the Weider system, who supposedly represented what could happen if you used Weider equipment, took Weider vitamins and supplements, and followed the rigorous Weider workout routines.

Mentzer was a direct confrontation of everything Arnold represented. He was the most intellectual of any of the bodybuilders, a onetime premed student who would as likely as not quote Jung, Freud, or Ayn Rand when he talked about training. His Heavy Duty training system was an extrapolation and elaboration of the ideas of Arthur Jones, the developer of the Nautilus fitness equipment. Mentzer said that the way to build one's body was to work out intensely and properly, but not to overexercise. Bodybuilders who worked out five or six hours a day were not giving their muscles time to recover and were hurting themselves.

Weider had condemned the Nautilus machines in the pages of his magazines, but the equipment had taken over much of the space in health clubs across America. If Mentzer won Mr. Olympia, his victory would be equally for a system that risked rendering suspect almost everything Weider did—from a workout philosophy so brilliantly exemplified in Arnold's efforts and the equipment he sold to the magazines. Weider was too powerful a figure to be seriously diminished by the mere victory of one man, but Mentzer did represent a new kind of threat to Arnold. Arnold did not read books and rarely peppered his remarks with historical or philosophical allusions. He was part of an aural tradition of learning. If he was insightful and wise about bodybuilding, there was a limit to his knowledge. Mentzer sounded far more erudite and

Except for a modern new church, the bucolic village of Thal, Austria, looks much the same as it did when Arnold Schwarzenegger was born here in 1947. (Laurence Leamer)

RIGHT: Sixteen-year-old Arnold with two friends, Karl Gerstl (right) and Willi Richter, at the lake in Thal in the summer of 1963. (Alfred Gerstl)

LEFT: Schwarzenegger and his Austrian mentor, eighty-one-year-old Alfred Gerstl, in the governor's Sacramento office in January 2005. (Alfred Gerstl)

No other bodybuilder did Arnold admire as much as the South African champion Reg Park. (Jon Jon Park)

ABOVE: Arnold with his bodybuilding mentor Joe Weider at the Mr. Olympia contest in October 2003. (AP/Wide World)

BELOW: Arnold and Joe Gold bear-hug at the legendary Gold's Gym in Santa Monica, California. (Photograph © George Butler/Contact Press Images)

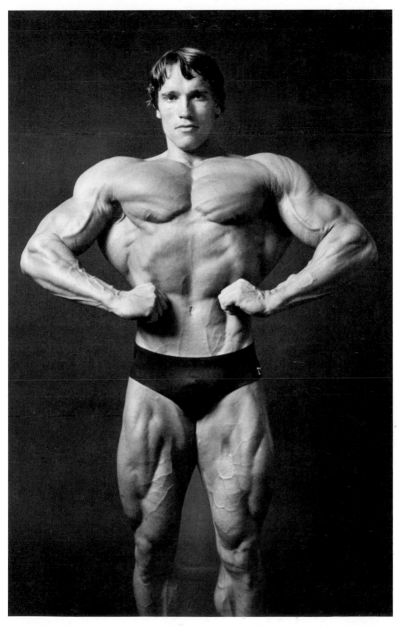

Arnold Schwarzenegger developed himself into what author Charles Gaines called "very possibly the most perfectly developed man in the history of the world." (Photograph © George Butler/Contact Press Images)

Arnold took steroids, but the key to his greatness was that he worked out harder than any other bodybuilder. (Photograph © George Butler/Contact Press Images)

Arnold found joy in every aspect of bodybuilding. (Photograph © George Butler/Contact Press Images)

It took endless workouts to develop Arnold's twenty-two-inch arms. (Photograph © George Butler/Contact Press Images)

Arnold was a showman who knew how to display his body better than any of his competitors. (Photograph © George Butler/Contact Press Images)

Arnold's legs are the last part of his body that he fully developed. (Photograph © George Butler/Contact Press Images)

In his classes at Santa Monica College, Arnold was not just another student. (Photograph © George Butler/ Contact Press Images)

Arnold fell in love with Barbara Outland and lived with her for five years in the early 1970s. (Barbara Outland Baker)

Arnold met Maria Shriver at the 1977 Robert F. Kennedy Pro-Celebrity Tennis Tournament, where he played tennis with football great Rosie Grier. (AP/Wide World)

If Maria Shriver introduced Arnold to a world he had never seen, he introduced her to a world new to her as well. (Photograph © George Butler/Contact Press Images)

Maria accompanied Arnold when he became an American citizen on September 16, 1983.
(AP/Wide World)

scientific than Arnold. With victory, Mentzer would have the public platform that he sought.

Three months before the Sydney competition, Arnold gave an interview in *Muscle Mag International* in which he said that Mentzer did not have a "world-class physique" and would never win the Mr. Olympia title. It was an inappropriate thing to say, especially since Arnold was then scheduled to be one of the judges.

Several months before the October competition, Arnold began training seriously. Arnold worked out with other bodybuilders and it took shrewd deception to hide what he was doing. When Arnold prepared for a major competition, he focused on his major opponents, figuring out their strengths and weaknesses. It was crucial to any bodybuilder's training, and around the world elite bodybuilders were planning and strategizing with no idea that Arnold would be posing on that stage beside them.

"Arnold, I had this injury, and what would you do if you were me?" Frank Zane asked Arnold one day.

"I would go to Australia and defend your title."

"Are you going to compete?"

"No, I'm just getting in shape for the *Conan* movie. I'm going to go to Australia to do commentary for CBS."

Arnold told a different tale to George Butler, whom he telephoned in September and invited to fly to Australia to photograph him. "Actually, I just start my training now," he told his friend. "But don't worry. I still fuck everyone else up. I am working on Mike Mentzer."

A month later Butler flew to L.A. to catch Arnold's last week of training before flying off with him and Maria to Australia. "I win," Arnold boasted as he worked out. "Don't worry. I don't need to control the judges. I control the bodybuilders. Already Mike Mentzer has left the gym this morning. I said: 'Mike, what is wrong?' He said, 'Arnold, stop smiling!' I said, 'Why?' He said, 'You're driving me crazy with that smile.'

"So this afternoon he misses training to see a shrink," Arnold continued as he stood surveying the other bodybuilders working out. "And he pays him to analyze me! He should remember that another Austrian was King of the Shrinks. I could advise him for free." Then Arnold returned to the next set of what he called his "savage training program."

When Arnold arrived in Sydney and entered the contest, it was a jolting shock to his competitors. That by itself was a giant step toward victory. As always, Arnold had Columbu at his side, watching over every moment. Bodybuilding competitors did not generally insult one another verbally, but Arnold could not resist turning a group meeting into an assault on his most dangerous challenger. In the midst of a discussion of a different matter, Arnold said, "Mike Mentzer, we all know Zane beat you last year because you have a big stomach."

Mentzer was still fuming because he believed the rules had been changed so Arnold could enter at the last minute, and now he had to listen to his insults. Mentzer rushed Arnold. Franco wanted to "let them fight a little bit, because I love to see fights." His thinking was that if Arnold was trouncing Mentzer, he would let them fight; if Arnold was losing, the former boxing champion would get in a few licks himself. But he did not have a chance, for others separated the two heavyweights before the battle began.

Arnold was always posing, putting forth his most positive features on view while hiding his weaker aspects. He created a wondrously compelling image of himself as a man who through rigorous training had taken his body to a place not only of unprecedented beauty but of unprecedented health. He did not talk about the steroids he introduced into his system, and he did not talk about the other things he did to create that illusion.

Before heading to Australia, Arnold injected cortisone to dull the pain from a shoulder injury. The medication worked but increased his fluid retention. That is always a problem before a competition and the reason many bodybuilders use diuretics. Arnold tried to sweat it out, wearing a heavy suit while he did his posing routine fifty times or more.

He was not the only one trying to get rid of fluids so his body would appear perfectly muscled, without a hint of fat. Mentzer had fixed up his own sauna in the kitchen of his hotel suite, where he sat popping potassium pills in front of the open oven, wearing a jogging suit and a rubber suit on top of that, the water pouring off of him. Shortly after one of the other bodybuilders, Samir Bannout, took the diuretic Lactix, his heart started beating irregularly. A quick dose of potassium pills settled him down, and he too continued preparing for the competition.

These elite bodybuilders did whatever necessary so that when they walked onto the stage that evening at the Sydney Opera House, they would present the fantasy of physical perfection. As the contestants posed on the stage, Columbu sat in the front row among the thousands of excited spectators looking up at the final competition.

Columbu realized that the opera lighting on the left side of the stage was far better and that Arnold was standing on the right side. He shouted in German to Arnold to move to the other side of the stage. Perhaps the words were lost in the tumult of applause and screams, but more likely Arnold was not listening. "Arnold has a tendency, when you have a friend so long, so good best friends, that a lot of times, he doesn't pay attention to me," said Columbu. "I've seen that a million times with him, so I'm used to it. And he's not paying attention."

Columbu knew that Arnold had no right to move to another position. But Columbu bolted out of his seat, hurried backstage, grabbed a towel, and ran onstage. He came up behind Arnold, who was facing the audience, grabbed him by the shoulder, and said in a loud voice, "Here is the towel! You're sweating!" Then in German he whispered to his friend: "You cannot be there. You have to move to the area of number four and number five and number six. There's no light here. You understand?" Arnold took the towel from Franco, wiped his neck, and then raised his friend's arm into the sky and shouted: "Mr. Olympia! Franco Columbu!"

Although Columbu had won the coveted title the year after Arnold retired, that was hardly a reason for him to be up there now. The Australian crowd cheered and applauded as if they were being given a special treat, seeing one of the other immortals of bodybuilding in person. As the applause died down, Columbu walked offstage with the towel in his hand. Arnold moved to the other side of the stage and pushed himself between two of his competitors.

This unprecedented interruption focused the audience even more on Arnold and visibly upset the other contestants, causing several of them to seem to shrink. Before they had gone onstage, they had engorged their muscles in order to display themselves to full advantage. But with all the distractions, some of them were no longer able to hold their pump. In the end, Mentzer came in an unthinkable fifth and Arnold won the title. It was the trickster Arnold who won, the trickster who had kept secret his intention to compete, and with Columbu's help had played another game. He won, but this time the cost he paid was exorbitant.

When the 1980 Mr. Olympia was announced, the great auditorium resonated not only with clapping but with boos as powerful and interminable as the applause Arnold had received in other victories. It was a measure of Arnold that he did not hear the derision or, if he heard, does not remember. "You know the applause was very clearly overwhelming for me," he said. "There were maybe some boos there, but I mean, I cannot even remember those as far as that goes." That was Arnold. At midnight in a bed of nettles, he could find a single rose.

The boos eventually died down that evening, but they did not die down within the bodybuilding community. Mentzer said that the event had been fixed, a libelous accusation if untrue, while judges such as Arnold's friend Albert Busek are adamant that the victory was fair. Although Butler does not call the results rigged, he says that Arnold's status was such that "as long as he was in respectable shape he would win."

Like Sergio Oliva and Lou Ferrigno before him, the defeat was so devastating to Mentzer that it effectively ended his professional career. He continued to write and speak out about bodybuilding, but he was no longer heir to Arnold's throne, and he was increasingly disturbed and troubled.

Zane was so angry that he boycotted not only the next year's contest promoted by Arnold and Lorimer but another event that he had promised Arnold he would attend. For breaking that pledge, Arnold sued him. Eventually Arnold dropped the lawsuit and the two men made up over breakfast.

It still rankled Zane that Arnold had coaxed him into competing and misled him about not competing himself. Zane told Arnold as much, but Arnold is not a man to say, "I'm sorry."

"If Jimmy Carter goes to Ronald Reagan and says to him, 'Reagan, this is how I plan to win the presidency,' and he tells him exactly how he's going to do it, Reagan would be a fool not to take advantage of that and use it to win," Arnold said. "Just like I did in the Olympia. Competition is not about friendship, it's about strategy."

PART THREE

PART THREE

The Star

CHAPTER EIGHTEEN

Arnold the Barbarian

During the many months of delay in production on *Conan the Barbarian*, Milius sometimes drove over to Venice, where Arnold was studying swordplay techniques under a master. Arnold was learning to fight like a samurai, but that did not change the fact that Milius thought Arnold was "a terrible actor." When Arnold stopped his vigorous training long enough to ask the director what acting approach they would be using, Milius told him: "We're going to use the dog-training technique. We're going to do it again and again and again until it is yours, and then you can do it without thinking. It's the Pavlov technique. It's not a movie where there's a lot of dialogue. This movie is supposed to be more like a ballet, a very simple story of revenge and redemption."

Milius's sense of the dramatic neither began nor ended on the screen. He was so nonplussed by having a novice as the star of this $19 million picture that as costar to play Valeria, Queen of Thieves, he signed Sandahl Bergman, a dancer who had been featured in *All That Jazz*, Bob Fosse's musical about dancers. As Conan's sidekick Subotai, Milius hired Gerry Lopez, a surfing champion and friend, who had no acting experience at all. Bergman referred to the trio as "the three stooges: a bodybuilder, a dancer, and a surfer." Milius balanced this team of amateurs with two great contemporary actors: James Earl Jones, playing the evil Thulsa Doom, and Max von Sydow as King Osric.

When Arnold arrived in Spain around Thanksgiving in 1980 for filming that did not begin until early January, Maria was with him and they had a glorious few weeks, riding horses in the countryside. Arnold looked like the personification of the mythic hero. He had learned to wield a great sword and ride a bold horse, and he had inculcated much of the spiritual aura of Conan.

In Spain, Milius created a psychological and physical ambience in which the film and the world around it blended seamlessly into each other. The palaces, dungeons, and villages did not seem so much like temporary sets as a different universe. A group of eleven enormous Danes, who looked as if they had been left over from the Vikings, contributed significantly to the atmosphere. One of them, Sven-Ole Thorsen, had met Arnold when he had gone to Copenhagen to promote *Pumping Iron*. Sven was the king of bodybuilding in Denmark. At nearly six and a half feet tall and 330 pounds, he was not a king to be casually provoked. Arnold had a marvelous time in the Danish capital and returned several times, and Sven visited California.

On one of his trips to Los Angeles, Sven met Milius. The director took one look at him and hired him to play one of the villains, then asked him to invite his friends to play other evil characters and be stuntmen. Milius called them the "Great Danes" and said later that they acted like "naughty puppies." Everyone else called them "the animals," an appellation that they worked diligently to deserve.

At meals the cast sat together dressed in their costumes, as if at a banquet in an ancient mead hall. Milius told the cast and crew to throw away their eating utensils and rip their meat off the bones with their hands. "It should be very tribal," he said. "Whenever we're shooting at night, we must have a bonfire so that people can sit around and tell stories or eat, stick stuff in the bonfire." He told them, "If you want to fight, if you have an argument with somebody, make sure you fight in front of everyone so that we may enjoy the pleasure of mutual combat." He said that the women of Spain were worthy conquests for the cast and crew. They did not pillage the neighborhoods and rape the choicer specimens among the fifteen hundred extras as they would have if they had lived out the film literally, but they still played conquerors indulging themselves and moving on.

"When you're dressed like a barbarian and you're fourteen hours a day wearing a barbarian outfit, I'm sure some part of you becomes a little barbaric," Sven recalled fondly. "This movie was the most fun for Arnold, for John, for all of us. When you're a kid, this is what you imagine a barbarian would be like. The horses, the swords, the women. So, we felt we were kind of conquering Spain, because we had about seventeen locations all over the country. I actually got divorced based on that, because I was gone from home for six months."

The very first day of shooting set the tenor for the entire five months. Arnold was to be attacked by four wolves as he climbed up a rock wall. He was a moment late in finding his foothold on the Styrofoam rock, and the wolf-like dogs were released a moment too early. The dogs went overenthusiastically at the meat-scented cloth on Arnold's buttocks. Arnold fell down and suffered a large enough wound to require stitches.

"The wolf almost got my ass!" he exclaimed in amazement. That accident would have caused many directors to call in a stuntman for further dangerous shots rather than risk injuring the star of the film. The idea never occurred to Milius. The next day Arnold was out there being run down by twenty horses. "I fall!" Arnold recalled. "But I get up again. You cannot imagine the joy of not feeling afraid. I don't care if I'm wounded physically. I am inspired by not being afraid of fearful things."

That was one of the essential philosophical lessons that Milius sought to impart in the film, and in Arnold he had found the perfect person to convey it. It did not matter that Arnold was not a real actor; he communicated that truth, because he felt it so deeply. Arnold had brought an entire gym with him, and he worked out before filming and sometimes afterward. He convinced one crew member, a hollow-chested cineast whose heaviest exercise was lifting film books, that he'd better get in shape. That was almost a command, and the young man obeyed, gaining almost twenty pounds by the time the film finished production.

Bergman was the only actress on the set regularly. "Sandahl, take off your shirt, show us your breasts," Arnold shouted. Bergman took it as just a raunchy joke and often threw herself in his lap, just one of the boys.

The cast and crew traveled from the cities to the mountains to the coast. There was snow and rain and cold and heat and bugs, and almost nobody complained. Milius seemed to be turning the film set into as close an approximation of a battlefield as he could devise. Bergman had her finger half cut off in a swordfighting scene, and her long wig caught on fire in another scene.

Arnold rolled down a mountainside and lay crumbled among the rocks. "Look. Real blood! I'm cut up," he exclaimed, more in surprise than apprehension. "Don't touch it," Milius said. "It looks great."

Looking down at his wounded star, Milius decided that more than bandages, Arnold needed the balm of his philosophy. "Pain is momentary, film is eternal," Milius said. Arnold remembered Milius's pithy epigram, and for years repeated it whenever there was difficulty on a set.

When one actor said that he could not put up with the cold any longer, Arnold said nothing but retreated to his trailer. When the disgruntled actor passed by with Milius on their way to the set, Arnold was sitting outside the trailer. He was naked from the waist up, with windblown snow on his head, and was reading a magazine. "What are you doing?" Milius asked. "I'm learning not to shiver," Arnold replied. The two men walked on, and the actor complained no more.

It was fun at the beginning, but as the months went by, tempers flared and there was an irritable sensibility on the set at times—all except for Arnold. "At the end he was in as good a mood as at the beginning," said Lopez.

"You know, I love making movies," Arnold told Thorsen at a time when other cast members were having their doubts. "It's like being in the military. They wake you up in the morning. They feed you. And all day long they tell you what to do. Then you go home, and you feel good, because you've worked hard and you can focus on yourself. I love that."

When Maria arrived for her long visits, everything changed. She was intimidating to some of the other cast members, this elegant, well-spoken woman who seemed uncomfortable with the often vulgar repartee of the movie set. "You can talk about opposites attract," recalled Bergman. "Like sort of a gym rat and sort of an aristocratic background. And at that point in time, he was totally physically obsessed and Maria wasn't at all. She was more zaftig."

Arnold enjoyed having Maria with him, but he was different when she was in Spain, more cautious in what he said, more reserved. He was one person on the movie set, one person with Sven and Franco and the rest of his gang, one person hanging out in Santa Monica, and somebody else around Maria.

That became one of the persistent themes of their life together. Maria had a foul enough mouth to merit membership in the Teamsters, and having grown up with four brothers, she was not easily shocked by male vulgarity. Yet many people were intimidated, almost frightened around her, and at times she became the convenient receptacle for complaints that rightfully should have been directed against him.

Maria happened to be in Spain the day Milius shot the love scene between Arnold and Bergman. One of the many reasons *Conan the Barbarian* is the archetypal Arnold film is that there is so little sex, and most of that is unpleasant. Early in the film the slave Conan is used as a stud, made to mate a comely maiden in front of an interested crowd. The atmosphere on the set was such that the largely naked woman was terrified, as if she felt she were about to be ravished in front of the entire crew. Later in the film Conan accepts the entreaties of a beautiful woman who in his embrace turns into a wolf witch. In another scene he turns down the blandishments of whores. There is also a scene in which a gay priest attempts to seduce him. He takes the man out in the desert, smites him with one blow, and steals his robe.

The scene with Bergman is different, as tender a love scene as Arnold would ever film. The five-foot, ten-inch-tall Bergman was the perfect physical match for Arnold. She was not only beautiful, statuesque, and athletic but still had something of the small-town Kansas girl in her. In Spain she had gotten involved with Terry Leonard, the second unit director/stunt coordinator. "I remember Arnold and I chatting about the scene," Bergman recalled. "It was so strange, because he and I were friendly, but the love scenes are so awkward when you don't have that emotionality about it. So I remember him saying, 'Isn't this weird that Maria's here visiting at this particular time? And your new guy now is the stunt coordinator, probably going to beat the living daylights out of me.'"

Arnold was not comfortable playing emotional scenes, and it was just as well that he had so little dialogue. He was playing a comic-book hero, and he recited part of the dialogue as if reading words on a balloon over his head. And yet the sheer physicality of the man was so extraordinary and the energy and enthusiasm he brought so enormous that he truly became Conan.

The Conan that Arnold helped create is a giant by all measures, not just his size and strength but his spirit and will. There had been other movies starring bodybuilders, but they had largely starred their bodies, showing them half draped, focusing on their muscles. In *Conan the Barbarian*, it is the story of Conan's journey that drives the movie.

There had rarely been a Hollywood film intended for a youthful audience with so much bloody mayhem as *Conan the Barbarian*. In that way, too, it is the archetypal Schwarzenegger film. Toward the end of the movie, Conan is crucified on a gnarled, barren tree that could have been painted by Goya. Conan has been nailed there for endless hours and is close to death. A vulture lands on his shoulder and starts to pick away at his wounds. Conan reaches out and bites the vulture, killing it. No matter how close to death, no matter how impossible the circumstance, Conan destroys those who seek to hurt him.

At the end of the film, having destroyed all his enemies except for the evil Thulsa Doom, Conan stands confronting his ultimate nemesis, ready to kill him. "I am the wellspring from which you flow," Thulsa Doom says. "What would you be without me?" For Arnold as well as for Conan, it is the struggle that is the essence, for with victory comes emptiness. Conan thinks for a long moment and then with a single stroke of his great sword lops off Thulsa Doom's head, just as his enemy had decapitated his mother.

On the way back to the States, Arnold, Milius, and Lopez stopped in Maui for a few days. Milius and Lopez went up into the hills and shot a wild hog and brought it back to prepare a luau in Arnold's honor. Before the feast, they insisted that he go out beyond the breakwater to surf with them. Lopez was a great surfer and Milius a good one, and they doubted that Arnold would even think of joining them. But he paddled out on a board. When they were far out at the beginning of the great waves, Arnold let his board go and said that he would bodysurf. And so he did, and when they reached the beach, the three friends had their great repast.

"Everyone in Hollywood is an assassin," said Rumar. "They don't want you to succeed for whatever reason. Working with Dino made Arnold legitimate. He beat the system, and everybody in Hollywood hates somebody who beats the system."

Arnold had enough confidence in how *Conan the Barbarian* would do that he decided to drop his agents and to move up to somebody more prestigious. It was not a particularly admirable part of the business of stardom, but what set Arnold apart was not that he did it but that he did it before most actors would have dared walk away from the agents who got them their first deal. "Our contract had come to an end, and he was pressured by his then attorney to make a move and he did," said Kubik. "There was no hard feeling."

Arnold invited his new agent, Lou Pitt of ICM, a Hollywood powerhouse, to his office to discuss his future. They did not discuss art or craft. They discussed business. Arnold led Pitt into the back room that looked like a full-fledged store full of mail-order Arnold merchandise, from T-shirts to pamphlets to books, piles of goods all neatly laid out. "I know how to merchandise, and I can merchandise myself," Arnold said. "I know how to do that. Give me the opportunity, and I'll do that." Pitt was a major agent with big clients, but he had never had anyone talk to him quite that way about his career.

"He's always been the master of his own destiny," said Pitt. "When he walks into a room, no matter what anybody wants to talk about or what anybody's agenda is, his thought process was, 'That may be your agenda, but it's not my agenda. So, what I'm going to do is, I'm going to share with you what I want to share with you.'"

It was only right that Conan should narrate his own tale, but Arnold's accent bothered De Laurentiis so much that he insisted on someone else telling the story. "My father always disliked that film," said Raffaella De Laurentiis, one of the film's producers. "He never understood it. Never, never, never got it." Although Milius agreed to another narrator, he fought Dino De Laurentiis's intention to dub the dialogue as best he could and got the producer to agree to wait until the first screening in Las Vegas to see how the audience reacted.

The studio had booked one of the three theaters in a multiplex in March 1982. By the time De Laurentiis, his daughter, and the studio brass arrived, the theater was full and there was a line around the block, and in the line were a gang of bikers, who did not like waiting in lines. They said that if there were not more screenings, they would tear up the theater, and by the way they looked, no one doubted them. So a second theater was added, and then a third, and the reels were carried back and forth. In every theater the reaction was the same. The audience cheered the first time they saw Arnold on-screen, pushing the wheel of pain, and from then on they loved the film. By the time the evening was over, even De Laurentiis realized that they had a hit on their hands and that Arnold was a star.

"I became swept up in this incredible machinery," Arnold said, machinery that he learned to ride and guide as have few others. He was just a fledgling star who should have been happy just to be along for the ride, but already he sought to sit behind the wheel and drive the machine precisely where he wanted it to go. He nagged the marketing people in a way that even his agent would not have done. "We should have gone to Cannes," he told them, though he had not an iota of experience in marketing a film. "We should go to the places where the press is from all over the world, and Cannes is the place. Why aren't they organizing anything? We should be way ahead of the game before we even come out with the movie and have the Conan cover on all the muscle magazines all over the world."

To those who did not want to hear his message, Arnold was a relentless pest. He pushed and he pushed and he pushed. At a time when many stars would not have thought of leaving the United States to promote a film, he insisted that he be sent to countries around the world. He headed out with enthusiasm, energy, and joy and he talked to anyone and everyone who would stop long enough to hear his tale of the making of *Conan the Barbarian*.

"There's not one actor in the U.S. who is as good as Arnold in promoting a movie," reflected De Laurentiis. "That's true both because of his ability at promoting and his willingness to go out there. There's nobody like that who would go out internationally and really push the movie. He really knew how to sell the movie so people would really want to go out and see it."

CHAPTER NINETEEN

Paying the Price

In October 1983 Arnold was down in Samalayuca, Mexico, filming the sequel to *Conan the Barbarian*. He was staying at the Plaza Juarez Hotel, hanging out at a table around the pool with members of the cast and crew on a Sunday evening. Arnold was glad to be doing another Conan film, though it did not seem right that Milius was not directing. He was busy with other projects, and Milius and De Laurentiis simply did not get along. So instead, the producer brought in Richard Fleischer, a director who could work in many different styles and for many different masters.

The critics had thrown caldrons of abuse on Arnold's performance in *Conan the Barbarian*. *Time* noted "the flatness of Schwarzenegger's performance, the dullness of his odyssey." *Newsweek* called Arnold's Conan "a dull clod with a sharp sword, a human collage of pectorals and latissimi who's got less style and wit than Lassie." That is only a small sampling of the savagery. The reviews would have devastated many actors, but to Arnold they did not merit even a shrug. He remained focused on his goal, which was to be the biggest star in the world, and *Conan the Barbarian* was a great start. It was one of the hits of the summer of 1982, displaced from its top spot only by *E.T. the Extra-Terrestrial*, one of the biggest films of all time. Almost half of the $69 million the film took in came from outside the United States, evidence that Arnold was on his way to becoming a global star.

Arnold might not have cared about reviews, but he did care immensely about the image he projected to the world. He had learned much from Weider, and he put forth a precise image that he allowed nothing or no one to disturb.

As Arnold was sitting, having dinner with his associates, Alicia Figueroa, a society reporter from the *Diario de Juarez*, came up to the table and asked to take his picture. He wanted his image out there his way, and a photo of the group was decidedly not his way. He told the woman no pictures. She stepped back and took photos of the others at the table. Arnold did not say anything, but when one of the men took off his bathing suit to swim naked, Arnold told the reporter in what Figueroa called "a forceful voice" to give him her camera. He took the camera, pulled out the film, and returned it empty. The Juarez Press Association was so upset that it tried to have Arnold thrown out of the country, but nothing was done and the matter was largely forgotten.

In almost every respect, Arnold was finding the second Conan film a very different experience. De Laurentiis had been astounded that *Conan the Barbarian* was such a hit. The sequel took what seemed to be a shrewd tact, cutting down on the violence so *Conan the Destroyer* would receive a PG rating, purging the script of Milius's pretentious philosophical underpinnings, stripping Arnold down literally to his crowd-pleasing bare-chested, bodybuilder essence, and adding a touch of humor to the main character.

Conan's task is to lead Princess Jehnna (Olivia d'Abo), a movie virgin with deep cleavage exposing her budding breasts, to find the sacred Heart of Ahriman, a gem with magical powers that looked like a gigantic phallus. He is helped by Bombaata (Wilt Chamberlain), who intends to betray him once the jewel is found. On the journey they meet Akiro (Mako) and Zula (Grace Jones). The other actors were congenial, but there was nothing of the camaraderie of Spain, or the sense of an epic adventure whose journey is almost as important as the final film.

Sven Thorsen had once again been hired to play one of the villains, but he was there largely because Arnold liked to have his friend around. Arnold slept little, no more than five hours a night plus two or three tiny power naps during the day that revitalized him. The naps were not fitful attempts at rest, but seemingly deep sleep. "He's gone," said Sven. "Like you cannot wake him up."

Arnold loved his life not simply abstractly or in the great moments, but in its details, and he was hungry for as much of it as he could have. At thirty-six, his hair was already turning gray. He was beginning to feel pain in his body at an earlier age than those who have not so dramatically challenged their bodies. "After years of pounding my knees and shoulders with heavy weights, I'm paying the price," Arnold said. "These days it hurts like hell to do a respectable squat or press behind the neck. Bench presses are murder!"

Arnold had daily intimations of his own mortality. By sleeping so little, he had essentially an extra day a week. "We were living in this big hacienda during much of the filming," Sven said. "Our gym was put up in a church. There was only candlelight. So, four o'clock in the morning, we leave our fucking hacienda and hit our gym and work out with candlelight."

Maria decided to visit during shooting in the middle of the jungle. When Arnold drove to the airport to pick her up, Sven collected dozens of frogs and put them in Arnold's bathtub. A few hours later Sven heard Maria's scream through the walls as she entered a bedroom full of frogs.

"Sven, how could you do that?" Arnold asked. He could do it because Arnold liked this boyish pranksters' world in which you never knew who would get you next. He was not so much mad as figuring out a way to get even.

When Arnold was still in Mexico on the set of *Conan the Destroyer*, he was already thinking about promoting the film. For two years he had been represented by the Hollywood public relations firm Rogers & Cowan, and he was not happy with the job that his publicist, Paul Bloch, was doing. Without any warning, Arnold received a phone call from someone else at the prestigious agency saying that she was representing the film. He blew up.

Arnold did not waste a moment on social niceties. "What's the matter with you people?" he yelled at Charlotte Parker. The young woman was a relative newcomer at the firm, and she loved the kind of films Arnold was making. Most of the other account executives there liked to work with big-budget, classy films that might win Academy Awards, not sword-and-sorcery knock-offs, and no one was interested in working on Arnold's film. That was the reason Parker was given *Conan the Destroyer* as her first film. She had called to talk about publicity.

"Hey, I'm new," Parker said. "Stop yelling at me. What do you want? Stop yelling so I can find out what you want."

"Don't you know anything?" Arnold sputtered. "Can't you do anything?"

"Just tell me what you want," Parker implored.

"I want European covers."

"Fine, no problem."

There probably was not another star in Hollywood fuming and fretting because his face was not on the cover of European movie magazines. It was a mark of how aware Arnold was of his own marketing that he grasped the significance of something that other stars would have dismissed as irrelevant or unworthy of their time. Parker had helped create the international division of Rogers & Cowan, and she had her own special awareness of the world market.

In the next two decades, the foreign movie money would steadily increase, eventually overtaking the domestic box office. Few people in Hollywood grasped that trend earlier than Arnold. On most of his films, the international receipts far outpaced the American ticket sales. "Being from Austria, I knew that America wasn't the world," said Arnold. "Coming from an athletic back-ground where the world is your stage, I felt that ought to be with everything. I saw it in bodybuilding firsthand that the people's interest was the same all around the world. It was just a matter of publicizing and promoting it the right way. It was the same with any product."

Arnold worked these markets assiduously before most stars were willing to have their passports stamped. The result was that as big an American star as he became, he was in some ways bigger outside the country, becoming a world cultural figure of the same type though not quite the magnitude of Muhammad Ali.

Arnold and Parker did not meet until the first screening of the film in Los Angeles. Afterward, Arnold announced in his abrupt way that he wanted to have dinner with his publicist. Parker made a U-turn on Santa Monica Boulevard and followed him to the Palm, where they spent the evening discussing Arnold's future.

Arnold was at a point in his career where people were still comfortable telling him the truth. He was not the intimidating public persona that he would soon become; equally important, in those years Arnold signaled to those around him that he wanted to be spoken to frankly. And he heard the truth even if it was lightly sweetened to his taste. Parker had not liked the film at all, so when Arnold asked her what she thought, she praised his performance as well as those of Chamberlain and Jones. Arnold surely understood that what was not said was as important as what was said.

Parker was young, impressionable, ambitious, and focused, and she had found in Arnold's career the perfect vehicle for her aspirations. She had wanted to be a poet or a short-story writer and had almost gone to the well-regarded writers program at the University of Iowa. She decided against it and poured all her creativity and energy into Arnold's career. She had not fallen in love with Arnold, but with the idea of Arnold, with the immense iconic image of him. Serendipitously for Parker, Arnold was equally in love with that image.

Parker had seen what was within Arnold, and she grasped not only what Arnold was but what he could be. It was something not even the film critic Gary Arnold or the filmmakers Butler and Gaines had perceived. That was the Arnold she began talking about to reporters.

"I sat, and I had dinner with the reporters and I told them the story of Arnold and enrolled them in my Arnold point of view," Parker said. "And by the time they got to Arnold, they already loved him!"

Parker also talked with the tabloids, aware how much, in the increasingly celebrity-led world of media, they could help create the image she wanted for Arnold. "I think I was in the forefront of trying to deal with them," Parker reflected. "You know, if they had something, I would try to explain to them that it wasn't right or whatever." She did not just put them right, though, she rewarded them. As she added, smiling: "And then later, we'd give them a nice story."

When *Conan the Destroyer* was first in theaters in June 1984, it was next to impossible to avoid seeing Arnold out there somewhere promoting his film. Parker worked with feverish diligence, getting Arnold so much publicity that the loose-leaf media notebook was as thick as a Tom Wolfe novel. Within the agency, it became a model of how a publicity campaign should be run. Arnold was ubiquitous, giving interviews not only to major media—AP, UPI, David Letterman, and *The Tonight Show*—but to small outlets such as *SoHo Arts Weekly*, *Waikiki Beach Press*, *Woman's Own* magazine, and *Starfix* magazine that most stars considered beneath them. He did the same in the international market, traveling wherever the film was opening, promoting from morning till the last evening interview.

When the extensive tour was over, Arnold asked Parker, who had been responsible for setting up the media, to become his personal publicist. The two of them began what became one of the crucial professional relationships of Arnold's life. He has transcended reviews, personal attacks, even the success and failure of individual films, and it was Arnold and Parker together who made it happen.

Conan the Destroyer did far less business in the United States than the original, but about as well overseas, and much of the film's success had to do with Arnold's relentless promotion. Although some of the critics were kind to him, others were no happier with this version than the first one. If bad reviews stung like scorpions, Arnold would have been in constant pain. "It's neither a man nor a bird, but it could be a moose wearing a sweatband," wrote Vincent Canby in *The New York Times*. "Actually, it's large-jawed, Austrian-born Arnold Schwarzenegger."

Arnold said that he was not angry at such reviews but enjoyed them "if they are witty." That was not only shrewdly disarming but deeply insightful of the positive impact that even negative reviews could have on his career. It was not simply that Arnold was review-proof but that even the ugliest of these attacks advanced him as a gigantic icon. He was becoming a metaphor and an organic part of American popular culture. "The U.S. dollar is the Arnold Schwarzenegger of major world currencies right now," wrote *Industry Week* in September 1984, and the readers of that trade publication did not have to be told that that meant the dollar was extremely strong.

Arnold had a full career as an action-movie hero, but that was only part of his life. He continued to manage a series of books that others wrote in his name, and developed workout videos and other products that he could sell with his name on them. He turned down many opportunities to endorse products, though when he became a top star he pitched a select group of products on Japanese television.

Most of Arnold's business interests were in a wide range of increasingly sophisticated real estate investments. "Schwarzenegger has acquired a reputation in the last two decades as a razor-sharp entrepreneur and as one of the most prosperous real estate developers in Southern California," wrote *California Business* in 1986. As with everything else in his life, business began and ended with people. In his Santa Monica deals, he partnered with a major real estate developer, Al Ehringer, who may have been drawn to Arnold by his celebrity and capital but soon learned that his cohort was a shrewd, detail-oriented businessman. The two men developed a 39,000-square-foot complex on the then-marginal end of Santa Monica's Main Street, just where it becomes the beginning of the more downscale Venice. The high-tech industrial look was perfectly fitted for the area, anchoring an enlarged and vital area of stores, restaurants, and offices. Arnold set up his own offices in the old gas company building across the street.

The Santa Monica project was enormously profitable, but only part of his real estate holdings in the small seaside town. When he bragged that "90 percent of my investments have been very, very profitable," he was speaking of startling yields. Even when something did not work out that well, like a condominium conversion in San Francisco, he was generally able to get out with a profit that would have pleased many investors.

The Conan films established Arnold as a leading adventure hero. He was in his mid-thirties and had what by any measure was a good life. It was a doubly good life because he knew it and appreciated it every day. As much as he enjoyed the endless perks of newfound wealth and stardom, things did not define him.

Arnold enjoyed his many good times with Maria, but he was not consumed by her. He had his friends, his work, and his bodybuilding, each a crucial part of his life as his long-term, faraway girlfriend. After helping out on her uncle Ted's failed campaign for the Democratic presidential nomination in 1980, Maria decided that she wanted to be an on-air correspondent. She had as many obstacles to a career on television as Arnold had to Hollywood stardom. She went to one of the top agents in the business and was told that if he was going to represent her, she would have to lose twenty-five pounds and do something about her nasal voice.

After she got through crying and calling her parents, who condemned the agent for his merciless untruths, she set out to do precisely what he suggested. She lost the weight and more, and she added to her other anxieties a deepened obsession with weight. Most others saw only her svelte form, so perfect for the body-hugging styles of the time, or admired her looks on television, where the camera added five pounds to her overly thin form, but her friends knew the psychological cost of maintaining that image.

A voice coach worked with her, but the problem was not so much her voice as the fact that she did not have the chipper, ingratiating personality that appealed to television audiences. There was often an unrelieved harshness about her on camera as she stuck the microphone in someone's face. She developed into a stunning public speaker and was more the natural politician than any of her brothers. Yet for reasons more psychological than political, she did not consider doing what she would have done best.

Maria was able to latch onto a position as a Los Angeles correspondent for *PM Magazine*, a chatty, lightweight show produced by Westinghouse. "When Maria was in New York, Arnold would play around so much that she knew she had to be there in Los Angeles," said one close friend. In deference to the Shrivers' moral sensitivities, Maria supposedly was living with her brother Bobby—but if you called her number, it rang at both homes.

Arnold immensely enjoyed his time with Maria, but he did not back off from friendships unusual in number and intensity for a celebrity. There were Franco and Sven and the guys down at World Gym, and he was unusual, too, in the way he picked up friends along the route of his life and did not drop them. Milius was in that group, along with several others.

While *Conan the Barbarian* was still in the theaters, Milius invited Arnold to go down to Edwards Air Force Base, south of Los Angeles. It would not sell that many tickets, but Arnold was ready to do it as long as the air force let him fly in one of its jets. Even when that did not work out, he still agreed to go, bringing Columbu with him.

Arnold gave a speech and then attended the high-school senior prom in the evening, dancing with about twenty-five delighted teenagers. "Of course, he's having a great time, because they're good-looking, and he's flirting with them and joking and he takes one and dances with her and passes her on and dances with the next one," Milius recalled with Falstaffian relish. "And he comes back and he says, 'I thought I was going to get to fly on a jet. Instead, I have to go to the senior prom.' We were staying in special officers quarters, and he and Franco short-sheeted my bed. He had to remind me that he thought we were going to get the jet ride. Now, you know, it was great, and those people never forgot that. And he had a really good time. Somebody else might have sat there and said, 'I don't want to do this.' Whatever it was, he was going to do it and do it well."

When Arnold was sworn in with several hundred others as a new citizen on September 16, 1983, at the Shrine Auditorium in Los Angeles, it was a perfect American mesh of patriotism and self-promotion. He arrived wearing a red tie, white shirt, and blue suit. Duly notified by Rogers & Cowan, the media were out in full force to chronicle Arnold's taking the oath while Maria looked on. "Now I want to embody the whole American ideal," he announced, "have the privilege of calling myself an American and travel the world as an American."

As much as Arnold loved America, he loved his homeland, too, and was still an Austrian. His closest friends in America were mainly Europeans. He went back to Austria often, and he invited his mother to Los Angeles for a lengthy visit every year. He still called his old comrades back in Graz and Thal. He went to his dear friend and mentor Alfred Gerstl, who had become an important Austrian politician. Gerstl arranged it so that Arnold could keep his Austrian citizenship. He would be an American but he would remain European, too, both legally and emotionally.

CHAPTER TWENTY

The Terminator

Arnold's proximity to Maria did not change his politics one iota. He was not a Kennedy clone, something he made clear in 1984 when he attended the Republican National Convention. The week was not only a celebration of President Ronald Reagan but a paean of patriotism, a flag-waving, boot-stomping celebration. The campaign film shown to the delegates was no tedious recitation of administration accomplishments but rather an irresistible celebration of a largely lost America: small towns, bright white faces, picket fences, church spires. The Republicans had picked up what in the post-Vietnam era had become the underused symbols of patriotism and nationalism and turned them into party possessions. Arnold was there to watch them do it. He had his own secret political ambitions, and those days were a brilliant primer on how to motivate people emotionally.

Reagan had given his own deeply moving speech to close the convention. It was well after midnight when Arnold finally got his chance to meet the seventy-three-year-old President. "I was already tired and I'm thirty-seven," Arnold said. "But he was right there, fast, quick with his answers—full of energy. He appears fifteen years younger than he is. God, when I'm his age, I hope I'm still alive. He's remarkable."

There was no figure in public life whom Arnold admired as much as Reagan. It was not just the President's politics, though Arnold stood fully square with him there, but also his style and charisma. As Arnold saw it, the President was the model not only of how it could be done but of how it should be done. The two men had something else in common. Reagan had a deeply troubled, drunken father who had shamed him and his family, and the President's buoyant optimism was in part his thrusting upward out of darkness.

Just like Reagan during most of his long film career, Arnold was far down on the list of actors considered suitable to star in a good movie. In fact, he was not even on the list at all. The young director James Cameron had already found someone to play the villain in his new science-fiction project, *The Terminator*, and now he needed a hero.

Cameron's script begins in Los Angeles in 2029. Nuclear war has leveled the city, and in the rubble the remnants of humanity are fighting a desperate guerrilla war against the intelligent machines of Cyberdyne Systems. In this world it is possible to go back in time, and Cyberdyne Systems sends back Cyberdyne Systems Model 101, "the Terminator," to 1984 to kill a woman, Sarah Connor, before she gives birth to the son who will grow up to lead humanity in its war against the machines. The humans send back one of their kind, Kyle Reese, to find the Terminator and try to destroy him before he kills the woman who unknowingly holds the future of the human race in her womb.

Cameron did not require a Shakespearean thespian to play the hero Kyle Reese, but the director wanted at least what he considered an actor, and he definitely did not want Arnold. Cameron's problem was that thanks to the success of *Conan*, Arnold was considered bankable and Orion Pictures had sent Arnold the script. If he signed on for the film, the studio would probably make it a go, but even so, Cameron did not want him.

Cameron understood the prickly egos of actors. All it would take would be a few subtle digs, and he would irritate Arnold enough that he would walk away from the project without anyone knowing Cameron had sabotaged Arnold's involvement. "Looks like I gotta go pick a fight with Conan," Cameron said to his roommate as he headed off for lunch with Arnold.

As the two men sat together, Arnold articulated in great detail his conception of the film. "Mike Medavoy, the studio head, told me that O.J. Simpson had been hired to play the Terminator and I should play Reese, the hero," Arnold recalled. "When I first met with Cameron, for half an hour I told him how the Terminator should act."

Despite his ambitions, Cameron was just another wannabe living in a modest apartment in Sacramento Valley. He could hardly believe that Arnold had actually read his script and was commenting intelligently on the intricacies of the screenplay. Cameron thought, "Well, there goes this 'Blow This Up Over Creative Differences' scenario." Cameron envisioned Reese as a lean, highly verbal character, and sitting there across from Arnold, he just couldn't see him playing the part. He couldn't see him playing the Terminator, either, whom Cameron had written almost as a cipher, an anonymous character who could flow out of the crowd for his moment of mayhem, and then flow back again, lost until his next savage act.

As engrossed as he was he was with Arnold's explication of the character, Cameron found himself inexplicably drawn to the idea of Arnold playing the dark title character. Cameron almost stopped listening to Arnold and sat there staring at the iconic reality of Arnold, the incredible bone structure, the powerful features, the whole demeanor. It was like a curtain opening and there stood the man on the screen. In an instant, the whole concept of the movie radically changed. Arnold was an irresistible force, a relentless pile driver. "You have to be the Terminator, with your voice and body, that's for you," Cameron said with intense conviction.

Arnold was irresistibly drawn to Cyberdyne Systems Model 101, the Terminator. Arnold was not a character actor. He was a star whose own persona was his only capital. Why play a villain and risk tainting yourself with such negativity that the audience might no longer believe in you as an action hero? Yet Arnold was, once again, one step ahead of the conventional thinking in the film industry. Arnold had a game plan, and playing Cyberdyne Systems Model 101 fit it perfectly. "I chose to play the villain both as a personal move and as a career move," Arnold explained his strange yet intriguing decision. "I figured it would be a good career move after establishing that my fans like to see me in heroic terms. On a personal level, I felt it would be a challenge."

After the lunch, Arnold called Lou Pitt, his new agent. Pitt made a point of counting the number of words of dialogue for Arnold in scripts offered to his client. This did not require higher math, but the *Terminator* script was an extreme—only seventy-four words. Pitt pointed that out to Arnold, but he was adamant about wanting the part.

Arnold was not an actor as much as he was a performer who played various versions of his idealized self on-screen. His largest limitation was his inability to express painful emotions. Instead of trying to make a living as an emotionally cramped-up, self-contained actor, he had forged himself into a suprahuman character who appeared beyond emotion. He joked that his only love scenes were with guns, but surely it was a kind of artistic impotence that his characters are incapable of making love. Love scenes were shot in several of his films but generally not used. They just did not work with Arnold.

Arnold was comfortable as a character without feelings. The Terminator was supposed to be the most anonymous of characters, a cipher appearing in and out of the shadows. Arnold could not possibly play the character that way. Since Arnold's aura was as large as his physical size, he had to create a totally different character. "The thing that I learned from my acting teacher, Eric Morris, was not to act, but to be," said Arnold. "So, I had to work hard over a period of months, learning to to be a machine. In reading the script over and over, I envisioned the character and what his moves will be. For instance, it was important when the Terminator reloaded his gun that he never looked down. There are certain gestures where you can sell the idea that you're different."

Just as in the first *Conan* film, Arnold spent much time thinking about and developing the physical presence of the character. Cyberdyne Systems Model 101 is a robot. Instead of affecting a kind of mechanical abruptness, Arnold played the Terminator with smooth efficiency. He never squanders any movement and always moves directly toward his goal by the shortest route, leaving mayhem and gore in his wake. In one scene, the Terminator's eyes move toward their prey like the turret on a tank, the head then follows.

The Terminator does not run. That was one of Arnold's essential insights into projecting a strong image. He almost never runs or hurries on-screen in this or any other film. He applied this principle to his image off-screen as well, always striding purposefully onward, but never rushing, never scurrying in or out of an event.

Making a film means living a compressed life, and the key for Arnold was living it with a director he completely trusts. Arnold thrives on difficulty, and in the months of shooting *The Terminator*, his plate was full. It was a demanding physical feat of filmmaking. Through it all, Arnold was ready to lance tension on the set with wry asides.

The film was shot on location in Los Angeles, but the emotional reality was as if they were off in a remote country. Most of *The Terminator* was shot at night in the grittier precincts of Los Angeles. Cameron directed the film on the limited budget of $6.5 million, which necessarily tempered his perfectionism. The film was nothing but one relentless action shot after action shot, one difficult physical moment after another.

Arnold, like most of his peers in the action-hero business, suggested that he did many or even most of his own stunts. A studio would never risk a multimillion-dollar production when there were trained stuntmen ready to do the dangerous scenes. Arnold was proud that on *The Terminator*, he did one major stunt. "I was lying on the hood of this car and they lit me on fire," he recalled. "The car took off backwards and I was supposed to be punching my fist through the windshield. Luckily, they had everything timed and situated just right, and they jumped on me and put the flames out as soon as each shot was over. A hydraulic arm was used for the close-up of the fist breaking through the glass."

Arnold had no sympathy for actors who complained, and he dismissed them with what he considered his cruelest epithet—accusing them of being sissies. "I have to just smile at those other girly-men that are around who do the whimpering and the suffering and the complaining because they have to shoot at night and work sixteen hours," he said. "They come in and say, 'I cannot take it anymore, I have to call my agent: I've had it!' I say, '*You morons!* What did you *have*? What about being in the war somewhere or being in the SEALs and going through that kind of training with no food or anything?' "

When Arnold attended one of the first prescreenings, he was startled to hear the audience cheering the Terminator. He had not tried to make the character sympathetic. If anything, he had done just the opposite, playing the role without even a suspicion of human feelings or motivation. In a strange way, the denatured violence of his character was almost refreshing, and the audience took pleasure in the havoc. Early on in the film the Terminator walks into a police station and utters what has become one of the most famous lines in cinema history: "I'll be back." The line captured the nightmarish quality of a villain who cannot be killed, but it also resonated with Arnold's own personal characteristics, his relentless, unyielding pursuit of whatever he wanted.

The film is full of outstanding performances, including Linda Hamilton as Sarah Connor and Michael Biehn as Kyle Reese, but it is Arnold's movie. In this low-budget, supposedly B movie, he creates a new kind of villain. Cameron and producer Gale Anne Hurd had written a strong script, and Cameron directed the film with aplomb, but it is Arnold's stunning performance that turns *The Terminator* into a memorable film.

When Charlotte Parker saw *The Terminator* for the first time, she bolted out of her seat and called *Time* and told them that she had just seen a classic of the genre that far transcended its B-movie origins. It was, but the film might well have come and gone, remembered largely by science-fiction buffs, had it not been for the determined efforts of Parker. Orion Pictures focused its attention on *Amadeus*, a big-budget, serious film that looked certain to win several Academy Awards. The studio was so indifferent about *The Terminator* that it intended to run only a half-page ad in the Calendar section of the *Los Angeles Times*. Ads are placed not only to fill theaters but to impress the industry, and a half-page ad said that Orion didn't think much of the film's prospects.

Parker was so upset that she convinced Arnold that they should go to see Orion cofounder Mike Medavoy. Stars and publicists did not march into a studio to discuss the minutia of publicity with the top executive. Arnold was impressed and amused by Parker's concern, and mostly sat there and watched the publicist overwhelm the powerful executive with her arguments. Arnold did not talk as much as Parker, but his was the voice of authority. He was not somebody you wanted to see if he wanted something from you and you planned to turn him down. Orion ended up running full-page ads for two weeks straight and supporting the film in a much stronger manner.

When the film came out in the fall of 1984, Arnold received the best reviews of his career, and *Time* magazine named *The Terminator* one of the ten best films of the year. It was an influential film affecting a whole generation of darkly hued science fiction, and it was one of Arnold's best performances.

The Terminator did decently at the box office, grossing $30 million domestically, but if Arnold was to use the film as the springboard to bigger movies—and bigger-budget sequels—it was imperative that it be seen in Hollywood as a far bigger, more successful film than it was commercially. This was Parker's contribution to the *perception* of the film in the City of Dreams. "I talked about how big the box office was," Parker recalled, "how Arnold was a big international star. When I got through with it, you thought it was a huge hit."

Not the reality but the public perception of reality had become the higher truth. Hollywood is not only a creator of myth but a consumer of it. Parker had helped give Arnold the opportunity to fashion his own mystique on an even higher plane. From now on, he would be the producer, director, and screenwriter of his own career.

Chasing Sly

In 1984 Arnold attended a fund-raising dinner for the Wiesenthal Center in Los Angeles. Within a few years it would become de rigueur for a star to be identified with a charity, but in the mid-eighties only a few performers were so involved. It was his publicist Parker's idea that Arnold attend the event to raise money for a Museum of Tolerance—and Arnold took up the cause with alacrity.

Part of the attraction was the personality of the director and fund-raiser, Rabbi Marvin Hier. Los Angeles is a city of entrepreneurs, in religion as in everything else, and Hier was an ambitious man. After arriving from Vancouver, British Columbia, where he headed a conservative synagogue, he had begun aggressively turning the Wiesenthal Center into an important, much-publicized institution.

The Hollywood figures who contributed heavily were mainly Jewish studio executives. Although there were few Christians involved, Parker—who knew Rabbi Hier personally—thought it would be valuable for Arnold to join the group. She knew nothing of the comments Arnold had made about Hitler's abilities as a speaker or his penchant for playing Nazi marches. "I would have walked away from Arnold if I thought he was in any way anti-Semitic," she said, and there is no reason to doubt her, especially since she was born in Austria to parents who were Holocaust survivors.

Almost no one in America knew that Arnold's father had been a Nazi, but simply the fact of Arnold's Austrian birth and his Catholic faith were enough to make his presence at the event unusual. It was even more singular that Arnold did not limit his involvement to an occasional charity event. He became friendly with Hier, who was appreciative and astounded when Arnold started giving fifty thousand dollars every time he starred in a film, making him the single largest Hollywood contributor other than the top studio executives.

Arnold attended many fund-raising dinners. The emotional high point of the events was always survivors coming forward to tell their stories. It would be a wrenching experience for anyone; for Arnold, who could not stand to look at the pain of his past, it was unique—this son of Austria hearing in appalling detail what his countrymen had perpetrated.

Hier was by necessity an astute judge of humans and their venalities, and he sensed that there was some other purpose behind the donations. For the first five years Arnold gave his gifts without requesting to be acknowledged publicly. That was unusual for him, as it would be for most philanthropists. His gesture suggests either a selfless generosity or some other, hidden motive. "How many Austrians do we have that are interested in wanting to come forward?" asked Hier "So, I knew that there was something that was driving him to be involved with this, but for a number of years I didn't know what it was."

In 1989 Arnold made his involvement public when he took a seat on the dais for a fund-raising dinner at the Century Plaza Hotel in which Yitzhak Shamir, prime minister of Israel, gave the keynote speech. Whatever motivated Arnold, it was unlikely that he was anticipating one day being accused of pro-Nazi views or feared that his antics filming *Pumping Iron* might come to light. As he viewed matters, it was inconceivable that he could be accused of anti-Semitism. Yes, he had been insensitive, gross, and mindlessly vulgar at times, but the two greatest mentors in his young life had been Jewish—Gerstl and Weider—and his third mentor, Reg Park, had a Jewish wife. His agent was Jewish. His publicist was Jewish. Most of the people he worked with on films were Jewish. If he was anti-Semitic, then he was a pathetic ingrate denying his own life.

The truth was much more personal. Each survivor's story was a reminder of what had not been addressed in his childhood, either in his community or within his own family. Arnold could not deal with the emotions he felt over his father, and if his contributions were in part guilt or penance, they were also markers of a search for greater understanding and knowledge. "He understood very much what the Holocaust was, and he was ashamed that Austrians did not want to confront it in reality," said Hier. "It was never spoken about in Austrian homes; he was very negative about his Austrian educational experience."

Meanwhile, Parker was constantly trying to position Arnold by placing him every way she could alongside the greatest stars and figures in Hollywood.

He was naturally linked with a series of action heroes, including Sylvester Stallone, Clint Eastwood, Chuck Norris, and Charles Bronson. Whenever she sent out press releases, pitched him to television programs, or briefed journalists before their interviews, she mentioned him in the company of the biggest names, usually Stallone and Eastwood. When Arnold went to a premiere or a big Hollywood party, she asked him to stand only with stars more famous than he was and not allow himself to be photographed with a minor star or starlet. One person she advised avoiding was the forthrightly conservative Charlton Heston, who since *The Ten Commandments* had brought Moseslike authority to his political convictions. While Arnold's political ideas weren't that different from Heston's, and it would have seemed natural for the two conservative stars to stand arm in arm, Parker's protective instinct was to keep Arnold away from the National Rifle Association's (NRA's) Hollywood poster child. If Heston appeared at the same event, Parker insisted, Arnold must never allow himself to be photographed with Heston, or, she warned, he would become marked as a right-wing ideologue.

Parker's protective caution was found at every level. She interviewed every journalist before he or she talked to Arnold. At premieres, she showed up early and walked the rope line, talking to reporters, selecting the ones Arnold would just happen to stop and talk to as he walked into the theater— the actor and his publicist in perfect harmony. "It was all so effortless. I would give him the reporter's first name, and he would look at me, knowing that I would guide him. It was an unspoken thing," Parker recalled, marveling at the way Arnold would pick up his cue and apply his charismatic charm.

As Arnold was relentlessly promoted by Parker and giving his all to each movie, his legendary luck held true. Just as he had ridden the crest of bodybuilding to what would be seen as its golden days, his movie career now coincided with the golden days of the fantasy action films—the very genre that was his forte. In another era, he might not have become a superstar, but the Reagan years seemed tailor-made for his brand of superhero. No longer a time for self-doubting, introspective protagonists, the new epoch called for savage heroes operating outside the pristine parameters of law and civilization. It was a time when black was black and white was white and gray was a coward's color. Against the background of Reagan's battle between America and the Evil Empire of communism, audiences throughout the world flocked to watch mighty heroes slay their enemies by the score, walking through flame and flood, eternally invincible.

Arnold was not alone, of course, in rising to the cinematic challenge of his age. Sylvester Stallone had imprinted his image on a generation of Americans in his Rocky sagas. Stallone was bound to be Arnold's major competitor. In his way, Stallone had as compelling and inspiring a life story as Arnold. A facial nerve was severed at birth, affecting the left side of his face. He had been kicked out of school after school for his disruptive behavior.

The stars, however, were such different types that they would not have gotten along no matter where they encountered each other—on the school playground, the athletic field, the corporate world, or Hollywood. Stallone was at his best playing the archetypal little guy who overcomes adversity, a role Arnold could not even think of playing. Stallone had the face of a palooka, but he was viewed as a Hollywood Renaissance man who could not only act but write scripts and direct.

"I said to myself, 'Hey, this is the guy that I have to pass if I want to be the top-paying action star,'" Arnold remembered his feeling being at the time. "And so for me, that was the motivation. Because he was the action guy when I came onto the scene, I always had Sly in front of me. I was chasing him. If he is not around, and if I wouldn't have felt about him the way I did, then I would not have been as motivated."

His competitive adrenaline rising, Arnold played the same sort of games on Stallone that he had played on Sergio Oliva and Lou Ferrigno. He understood the emotional vulnerabilities of the man. Nothing was worse for Stallone than to be called cowardly or unmanly. In statements he made publicly, Arnold suggested that he was bolder, more daring in his career choices than Stallone was. After all, Arnold had played the villain in *The Terminator*, while Stallone could not move beyond his role as Rocky Balboa, constantly wrapping himself in the red, white, and blue. "All that flag waving is a lot of bull—we're all in the entertainment business," Arnold said in a 1985 interview. Stallone was trying to move beyond his Rocky image, and Arnold came close to suggesting that Stallone was copying him. "I see him working out in the gym all the time lately—working out very seriously, because he wants to be in shape for this [new] picture," he told *GQ* in 1986.

Arnold's complacency was rudely shattered when one of the films he was sniffing at became *Rambo: First Blood Part II*, the 1985 epic of a rampaging folk hero whose triumph was matched that same year by *Rocky IV*. "Stallone's ingenious comic-strip artistry has zapped them all," wrote *Newsweek*, pointedly including Arnold among those who had been zapped. Stallone's "success with two series at once, and with two grunt heroes, is unprecedented in the industry."

Arnold was less than happy about the achievement. He had a predator's proprietary sense of his own turf, and Stallone was stepping into what Arnold considered his territory. Stallone's Rambo was a larger-than-life superhero, a modern-day Conan who returns to Vietnam to wreak his revenge.

What made things worse for Arnold was that he had signed what once had looked like a wonderful deal for a series of Conan films. That now felt like bondage. Arnold had all kinds of exciting projects being offered to him that might have helped him overtake Stallone in the popular mind, but he had obligations to De Laurentiis. He therefore agreed to do a cameo in *Red Sonja*, a film based on a Howard character who was a female Conan. De Laurentiis saw it as a way to create a second lucrative Conan franchise. He brought back not only Arnold but Sandhal Bergman, who played the evil Queen Gedren. And then, as Sonja herself, a magnificent physical specimen with a body that in its sensuous, voluptuous way was the female counterpart of Arnold's: Brigitte Nielsen.

Red Sonja

Almost from the day Arnold arrived on the set of *Red Sonja* in Italy, there were persistent rumors linking him with costar Brigitte Nielsen. Six-foot, one-inch-tall Nielsen was a Danish model, performing in her first film. Twenty-one years old, she was already a divorcée with a baby at home. Some of those who knew Arnold assumed that it would be extraordinary if he were not attracted to her. Even Maria had heard the rumors and tried to learn if they were true.

If Maria could have known more about her boyfriend's travels, she would have been even more worried. Arnold and Nielsen were spotted traveling together from Rome to Vienna, where they stayed at the Hilton Vienna. They went to a party together, where they were photographed, and they were seen together on their way to Munich, and from there to a ski resort in Austria.

Arnold reflected later that Nielsen had cast him as her next husband. "She said, 'I want to move to America and be your wife or woman,'" Arnold recalled. "I said, 'I have a girlfriend that I'm very serious about. I am committed to Maria.' She said, 'I am unbeatable.' I said to her, 'I can guarantee you that I will not change my mind. But there are a lot of guys over there in America.'"

Nielsen was almost an irresistible force, so once he returned to the United States, Arnold sought to deflect her attentions elsewhere. "Here, go to Warren Beatty, Stallone, or Jack Nicholson, there are many of those guys out there if you want to marry a star," he told her. "You've met my lawyer, Jake Bloom, when he came to visit in Rome and we did the movie. So, he's the guy; he's your contact."

Arnold said that Bloom invited Stallone and Nielsen to dinner and "he was immediately smitten crazy about her." As with most Hollywood romances, the story would be told in different ways. Both Stallone and Nielsen tell how she first met Stallone by sending him a nude photo, but even if that story is to be believed, Arnold bequeathed Nielsen to Stallone in the aftermath of *Red Sonja*. It proved to be an unfortunate gift. The actor married Nielsen, but they had barely returned from their honeymoon before the tabloids starting writing about Nielsen's alleged lesbian affair with her assistant, and Nielsen denied that, charging that it was her husband, Stallone, who was cheating.

The marriage lasted less than two years. Stallone was a far more emotional person than Arnold. Though it is impossible to gauge the price he paid for his time with Nielsen, it was enormous. Stallone drew on his emotions and his instincts for almost all his creativity. He had written *Rocky* in three feverish days. No move script emerged from the nightmare with Nielsen. Arnold was not responsible for the failure of Stallone's marriage, but it was a stark lesson in what might have happened had he allowed himself to fall in love with Nielsen.

To Arnold, Nielsen brought bad luck, and bad karma. When Arnold saw the ads for *Red Sonja,* he felt that De Laurentiis had tricked him. He was portrayed as the primary star. "I felt I should do a favor to Dino De Laurentiis," Arnold said, "to participate and do a cameo, and he ended up using every foot of film that I did."

Arnold had the kind of optimism that could turn a can of Spam into Spanish ham, but even he was confounded with this dreadful film. "We were at a screening, and I was with my agent," recalled Sandahl Bergman. "And after the movie, Maria and I turned to each other and went 'Oh, this is just terrible.' And he was very disappointed because *The Terminator* had come out and sort of really jumped him over the top." The film disappeared into the cavernous earth, taking Nielsen's career with it. For Arnold there was nothing to do but laugh at life's vagaries. He salvaged the matter by turning *Red Sonja* into a running joke, a film so awful that it became a badge of honor that he had survived it and gone on.

There were lessons to be learned here, too. For Arnold, making a film was all about choosing—the right script, the right producer, the right director, and the right deal. *Red Sonja* reinforced his determination never to accept an offer, a commission, a project, or an appearance without embracing it 100 percent. He could be impossible when he was in the midst of this process, second-guessing himself and everyone around him. His agent Pitt was in the center of all of this decision making. Arnold had a way of emotionally entwining those who worked for him. Lou was a friend Arnold could call in the middle of the night or ask for advice on matters that had nothing to do with the movies. On matters such as choosing Arnold's next project, they went back and forth, often with Maria as a third participant, working through each step, until he was sure.

They certainly did not sit around discussing the scripts on Arnold's desk, searching for the one that might win him an Academy Award as Best Actor, or at least give him wider respect as a thespian. Rather, they tried to figure out which movie would have the biggest audience, and how they could tinker with the script so that ever more people would walk into the theater. It was not unlike a populist politician looking at the polls and figuring just what position he could take to achieve the highest popularity.

"We talked about how you expand a career," Pitt said. The answer lay in the market for Arnold's films. "We talked about expanding it by ten percent. He was very clever, and it was very systematic. I remember us talking about this a lot, actually. We've got young males, let's make sure we don't lose the young males. How do we get the young girls? How do we get the older females? How do we get the older males, you know?"

And once Arnold had signed on, all doubt was forgotten, and he was there completely. Arnold always had several projects in front of him. As usual, to help him decide what to do, he asked Parker to read the scripts. That is not something that publicists generally do, and if they do, they are expected to concur with conventional wisdom. Parker was appalled at the film he was ready to do, a shoddy knockoff of the Mel Gibson hit *The Road Warrior*. "I'm not knocking myself out for you to do such pathetic crap," Parker told him. "This is the one you should do, *Commando*, the right kind of studio film." Parker got called into her bosses' office and reamed out for second-guessing Arnold's agent, but she was so concerned with Arnold's future that she did not care.

In the end, however, Arnold did decide that for his next film he would play Colonel John Matrix in *Commando*. John Matrix is a legendary Delta Force commando who has retired to a rural retreat with his eleven-year-old daughter, Jenny. The first part of the film gives Arnold his first opportunity to do what in Arnold's case is called "acting," which is largely the empathic portrayal of a character in a way that appeals to women. Arnold is surprisingly good at playing a brave man whose skills are no longer needed or much appreciated and who has taken up a pastoral life.

When his daughter is kidnapped by men loyal to a Latin American dictator deposed in part by Matrix's task force, the colonel reverts to his former self and journeys to the fictional country of Val Verde to rescue his daughter. The script is peppered with one-line wit appealing to men, but what the film's largest audience of young males is waiting for is Matrix's bloody quest to find his daughter. Matrix weaves and jumps his way around bullets as he single-handedly kills scores of the enemy. He shoots them, stabs them, and pummels them to death. There is a rude acrobatic ballet to his movements. He knows how to use guns in a realistic enough way to pass muster as a combat veteran.

Arnold kills so many people in *Commando* that at one point the film becomes an endless slaughter. The more than a hundred deaths were sufficient for *Premiere* to give the film the dubious honor of being the most violent film of all time. *Commando* is to violence what pornography is to sex, nothing but numbing anonymity. Much of the film is a circus of violence, a thrilling catharsis to the audience, and it succeeds superbly on its own terms. Moreover, it is a film made to garner a huge audience—with Arnold being paid a huge salary. "It was a pivotal film for him," recalled Pitt. "And it was a breakthrough in terms of money."

At the premiere, various luminaries praised *Commando* as a milestone in the history of cinema in which Arnold's greatness was immortalized. It was not the truth, but it was pleasant to the ear and nothing more than Hollywood's standard garish hyperbole. When all the major players had their say, Arnold called up Thorsen to say a few words. Sven had just moved to Los Angeles and had never been to a premiere. He thought of it as nothing but a big friendly party for his buddy Arnold. "Yeah, it's a good movie," Thorsen said, relishing the moment. "Congratulations! But let's be honest. Isn't it only a seven?"

Afterward, Arnold got his friend alone. "Sven, what the fuck is wrong with you?" he asked.

"What do you mean?" Sven said. "I was honest."

"Yeah, but, you know, this is the movie business."

To Arnold, movies were above everything else a business, and if you were a star, you had to deliver. *Commando* proved a big hit when it opened in October 1985, and made a great deal of money for 20th Century-Fox—which augured well for Arnold's next work.

There was a troubling irritant pestering Arnold—and its name was Stallone. As successful as it was, *Commando* did not come close to the formidable receipts that *Rambo* had amassed. By 1985 Stallone had become the biggest film star in the world. *Parade* reported that he earned far more than anyone else—$12 million a film, compared with $3 million for Arnold.

Such a comparison was difficult enough for Arnold to take, but there was something even worse: he was criticized for starring in a film that was a cynical knockoff of the Stallone film—and the rivalry between the two men rose to new heights.

Arnold could not stand the idea of anyone's imagining that he would stoop to copy Stallone. "I'd be angry at hearing my name mentioned in the same breath as Stallone's," he snorted, though for the past couple of years much of his publicity and positioning campaign had linked him with Stallone. The reality was that Parker's plan had worked brilliantly, and it was not simply positioning any longer. Arnold had become Stallone's powerful new competitor. It was crunch time. "Watch out, Rambo! Matrix—in the mountainous form of Arnold Schwarzenegger—is stealing your thunder," wrote the *Daily News*.

From this point on, it was not a case of being placed alongside Stallone in publicity, but being placed in opposition. Arnold told a reporter that Stallone used "body doubles for some of the close-ups in his movies. I don't." He was essentially accusing Stallone of cowardice and delivering false goods.

Arnold had a superb grasp of Stallone's vulnerabilities, and he probed them mercilessly. "I think Stallone, as far as I know him, is extremely intense all the time, even when he comes to the gym," he said, picking at Stallone's psyche in an interview with *GQ*'s Jean Vallely in July 1986. "He's obsessed, and that carries through in the way he dresses, how hard he tries to belong to a charity organization," he said with contempt. "It's all Rocky."

Arnold charged that Stallone's feelings did not come from the heart. "There's no love there," he asserted. "And people see that. You can fake your way through for a year, but for ten years, that's hard. Eventually it catches up to you. I think that's the difference between him and me."

Arnold loved to stick it to people, to play practical jokes that sometimes seemed gratuitously mean, or to make fun of a person's vulnerabilities, but he almost never did so publicly, or if he did, it was for a purpose. Had he slipped one time and made a demeaning comment about Stallone, it might be seen as a mistake, or a momentary excess, but those who knew Arnold from his bodybuilding past realized that there was a method behind such repeated needling. Arnold kept at it enough that it became clear he was playing with Stallone's head.

If it was to be a reprise of Arnold's bodybuilding ways, he would work toward a final victory that would devastate his opponent. He would look back and tell with disarming humor how he had tricked poor Stallone and led him down a path that carried him from the peak of stardom—a peak where now only Arnold resided.

The Good Life

Arnold continued to squirrel away great amounts of money, but he was doing so well now that he lived in a Spanish-style house on a quiet street in Santa Monica with lithographs by Warhol, Wyeth, Dalí, and Chagall on the walls, serious books on the shelves, and a swimming pool and a hot tub. He had brought almost nothing from his old apartment, none of the kitschy art from around the world and almost none of the overwrought furniture. He had assumed all the accoutrements of a Hollywood aristocrat, from his designer suits to his Tony Lama cowboy boots. He acted to the manner born, comfortable with an entourage of people who served him and made his life easy. There was often a hubbub in the home, people tearing in or out on one mission or another, Arnold sitting at the dining-room table with a speech expert, pronouncing English words.

In the mornings, when he did not have to be on the set, he drove to World Gym. Joe Gold had long since sold his gym, and though it bore his name, it was no longer the same. After a stint in the Merchant Marines, Gold had come back and started another gym, and Arnold had happily made the transition to his friend's new one. World was a fancy, high-tech place, nothing like the old legendary Gold's Gym that had been Arnold's second home. The new gym was a testament to the democratization of bodybuilding into fitness workouts for the millions, a social change to which Arnold had contributed as much as anyone.

There, as almost everywhere he went, life coalesced around Arnold. "Most of the people only knew him as the icon," said Neal Nordlinger, a close friend since the late seventies. "So they would treat him with incredible reverence.

And then there were the guys who were, like, he's still just Arnold, like they knew him when he was some stupid farm boy from Austria. And so it was really fun."

People were often startled to see that in person Arnold did not look like a bodybuilding giant. At 220 pounds, he was below his competition weight, and so was not bulked up. In a more important sense, he was bigger than ever. The aura of fame that he had first won as a bodybuilder had grown. People took pleasure in simply seeing him. He was only a movie hero, but the derring-do on the screen had become part of his persona, and wherever he went there were often awe and wonder. Few people have tasted the power of fame the way he did. He made sure that he felt it wherever he went, nodding his head at passersby when they recognized him, dropping a word or two, letting people touch him (but just barely) before he moved on. It was as if he had to make sure that his megacelebrity was still there, like someone constantly touching his wallet to check that it hadn't been stolen.

After working out, Arnold often drove up the Pacific Coast Highway to Patrick's Roadhouse for breakfast. Hollywood's idea of a power place to breakfast is the Polo Lounge at the Beverly Hills Hotel, but this lime green old diner is where Arnold liked to go. His presence helped make it the hip place for the younger stars and studio executives to eat. Most of them had modest breakfasts, not the "Schwarzenegger special" or "Bauernfrühstück," a gigantic meal of breakfast foods, which was Arnold's favorite. He was the only customer with his own special table, a tradition that Arnold understood and appreciated from his days in Thal.

If Arnold was not working on a film, he would go to his office in Venice after breakfast. Arnold had a team of people watching out for him, starting with his devoted agent and publicist. Many stars keep an office to deal with fan mail and movie business, but Arnold had a real office. He had constant real estate deals and other investments. He watched over his properties in great detail. He spent more money on his apartment buildings than was necessary, replacing carpets every two years, keeping the walls freshly painted, making sure the property values held. He had a mail-order business that he did not regard as a big profit center but as a way to keep kids interested in him, kids who sent in for a T-shirt, an autographed photo, or a gym bag. He and Jim Lorimer had an annual bodybuilding event to produce in Columbus, Ohio.

When he arrived in America, Arnold had been an abysmal dresser. He now understood how clothes projected one's image to the world. He cringed when he saw bodybuilders in cutoff sweatshirts or rolled-up T-shirts, flaunting their muscularity. He dressed to hide his muscles, not emphasize them. He liked a preppy look and was partial to casual clothes from L. L. Bean. He had tailors in New York and Los Angeles who styled conservative suits that downplayed his shoulders and slimmed his torso. Those were the outfits he wore to business meetings and dinners at the exclusive Regency Club in Westwood, where he hobnobbed with the magnate David Murdock, a man he called one of his "idols."

Arnold had the same interest in the dollar that Weider had recognized when he arrived in the United States. He was inordinately proud that his salary as a star was doubling year after year, yet he wanted to keep that to himself as much as possible, for it would only make people jealous to hear that he was earning $3 million or $6 million a picture, and jealousy did no one any good. He was being offered all kinds of big-money, multi-picture deals, but he always said no because he wanted to have control over each film project.

Even though Arnold appeared comfortable at the highest reaches of society, he had the soul of a poor boy, a quality he considered an attribute, not the shameful psychological baggage of his past. He knew that he understood the value of things the way no one born to wealth could. When a button came off a shirt, he often sewed a new one on himself, and did the same for Maria's dresses. When he went out on his expansive lawn for a game of touch football, he put on an old sweater whereas Maria wore whatever she happened to have on. His favorite car was an old Jeep, and he vowed wrongly that he would never be found driving a car that too flamboyantly advertised his wealth.

He believed, too, that he loved America in a way that no one blessed with being born here could. American liberty was a fresh breeze in his face, not the air that he had always lived in. American opportunity was a precious new gift, not a birthright he took for granted.

Arnold had turned his intense pleasure in life, his laserlike focus, and his endless dreaming about his own future into a philosophy that had not changed since he was a teenager. "I set a goal," he said, "visualized it very clearly, and created the drive, the hunger, for turning it into reality. There's a kind of joy in that kind of ambition, in having a vision in front of you. With that kind of joy, discipline isn't difficult, or negative, or grim. You love doing what you have to do—going to the gym, working hard on the set. Even when pain is part of reaching your goal—and it usually is—you can accept that, too."

Arnold is a man who knows what he knows and what he does not know. He knows how to learn and when to learn. How to learn is by listening to people, and when to learn is all the time. "A lot of people are very sensitive about what they don't know, but he's never been that way," said Jim Lorimer. "Right from the beginning, if you say something he doesn't understand, he'll say, 'What do you mean?' If he doesn't know it, he'll say, 'What is it?'"

The least introspective of men, unconcerned with the foibles and failures of the past, Arnold took what he needed from his earlier life and moved on. He deeply appreciated what he had been able to achieve in America. That was the wellspring of his patriotism and his conservative politics. He focused so completely on whatever lay before him that he seemed almost slow. He was full of pleasure no matter what he was doing, and yet he remained profoundly ambitious, having a game plan that would take him well into the future. He often talked about politics, about perhaps running for governor of California one day. Those who knew him best realized that he was not merely daydreaming, but vocalizing the blueprint of his future.

"What I am most happy about is that I can zero in on a vision of where I want to be in the future," Arnold said in 1986. "I can see it so clearly in front of me, when I daydream, that it's almost a reality. Then I get this easy feeling, and I don't have to be uptight to get there because I already feel like I'm there, that it's just a matter of time."

Arnold saw that celebrity risked walling him off from much of what most people called life. He wanted to experience life at its broadest and deepest reaches, and he could not do that with the self-conscious life of a full-time celebrity. He did not always have bodyguards around him. He did not live his life in the seclusion of limousines and private planes. He took them when he needed to, but when he wanted, he jumped on his Harley and roared off with his friends into the hills, or he drove over to Caffé Roma in Beverly Hills with its eclectic mix of European expatriates and locals, to hang out with Sven and Franco and make fun of the people strolling by. He liked to have parties at his house at which he talked on and on into the night, parties that weren't about business or deal making, but only about having a good time among good friends.

As much as Arnold was elated with the small moments of life as well as the large, he occasionally questioned the meaning of everything and anything he was doing. There were times when he felt that all the money he had and all the money he would earn in the future meant nothing. There were times that he felt that all of his obsessions with achieving the ultimate success in body-building meant nothing. There were times when he felt that his dream of becoming the greatest star in the world meant nothing.

"What does it mean?" he asked himself. "Nothing. Nothing. Nothing. If you'd look down on the world, you'd say 'What the fuck, these guys are crazy.' You know when I was standing up on the stage trying to win Mr. Universe? I said, 'Isn't this absolutely all funny and silly? Here you are trying to be the most muscular man in the world.' "

Arnold's friends knew that they were to be amusing and upbeat and not to burden him with their own petty woes and complaints. He did not like naysayers, and he banished anyone from his presence who reeked of negativity. By a few verbal incantations, he could take an obstacle as high as a wall and turn it into a mere bump in the road as thrilling as a carnival ride. Everything was fantastic, and if it was not, by his mere incantation, it became so. And damn anyone who said otherwise.

Most of Arnold's friends exuded an ultramacho quality, but it was not that alone which brought these men together. Although they rarely exposed it, each man had a sensitivity grounded in painful experience. His Munich friend Albert Busek lost a son to cancer and a wife to a decade-long struggle with multiple sclerosis, yet he remained full of the most compelling optimism about life. Franco had struggled up from the most modest of circumstances in Sardinia, without money, education, or prospects, and he, too, was bullish on life. Sven had a police officer father who thought his son a worthless oaf. Much of his life was a struggle to win an approval that would never come. Arnold and his friends did not sit around endlessly pawing through the dead embers of the past, but the past was in them and it helped to make them lifelong friends.

As big a star as he became, Arnold was there for his friends. When Busek's wife died, the first call he made was to Arnold on location, and his friend was there as long as he wanted to talk. Sven had moved to the United States and was a fixture in Arnold's movies. Franco had advanced much further in the world than he ever would have without Arnold, and now had a new career as a chiropractor.

That said, there was an emotional stinginess to Arnold. He complained privately to his friends about how cheap Maria and her family were, but he was hardly generous when it came to helping some of his friends advance in the world. He cared for his buddies but could have done so much more for them at almost no cost to himself. He could have helped Franco when he tried to have his own movie career. He could have pushed Sven. But he did not, and they knew if they wanted to stay his friends, they should not ask.

There was inevitably a one-sided quality to these friendships that went far beyond the massive difference in wealth. His friends waited for Arnold.

Arnold did not wait for them. As irreverent and rowdy as they could be with him, each of these men was in awe of Arnold.

"Arnold used to say when he went to the gym on a rainy day, the sun was shining around the gym only," said Sven. "He can walk in the rain, he used to say, and it pours, and he's dry. Just like a spotlight of no rain is around him. I get goose bumps when he says that, because I've seen it. I've seen it so many times. He's bulletproof. I don't know what it is. It's something you can't even describe with words. He's chosen. I mean, it's a little tough to use that word. But he's chosen. They don't come around too often."

Since the late seventies, Arnold had changed his agent, his house, his dress style, and his social ambience—everything but Maria. "When I was traveling back and forth, and going here and there, people used to say, 'I can't believe Arnold lets you do that,'" said Maria. "My whole example was my father, a man who not only let my mother 'do it' but encouraged her to do it. As I became kind of more aware, I realized that that wasn't really the norm. Most husbands didn't want their wives out conquering the world."

Arnold had always wanted a traditional, stay-at-home wife, but his girlfriend was an ambitious, driven woman who cared about her career as much as he cared about his. What he gained was her sophisticated sense of the world of power and politics and just how things worked in the world. In that respect, Maria was far wiser than Arnold. As shrewdly as he had learned to disguise it, he still had not shaken free of his provincial roots. Maria, just like her mother, could be a merciless goad, picking away at Arnold's supposed foibles. But it was Eunice who, as Arnold saw it, was one of the keys to predicting how Maria would be as a wife and mother. He saw the emotional energy that Eunice put into her children, and he figured that Maria would do the same.

As the years went by, Maria's career and work schedule had only increased, and she was gone much of the time. She had moved on from *PM Magazine* to become a junior reporter for the low-rated *CBS Morning News* and by the spring of 1985 occasionally flew back to New York to cohost the troubled program. There was even talk that if the much-derided Phyllis George left the show, Maria might have a shot at being a regular host.

For years Arnold had said privately that he would marry Maria one day, but that day had always been out there far in the future. "Maria fell for him and was in love with him," said one close observer. "She was getting older, and she couldn't be in that position forever. He went out and saw other people. I think he valued her. He appreciated where she came from. He had to make a decision. Am I going to have this or not?"

Maria says that Arnold asked her twice to marry him before she said yes. In the late spring of 1985, Lorimer was visiting Arnold in Los Angeles. It was about midnight and the two friends were relaxing in the Jacuzzi. Lorimer was twenty years older than thirty-seven-year-old Arnold. His friend was a man whose judgment Arnold trusted on all sorts of levels.

"Arnold, you've been going with this girl now for eight years," Lorimer said. "The relationship has stood the test of time. She has a career, you have a career; you're very successful, and nobody could accuse you of marrying the girl for her money. You don't need anybody's money. You don't have to work for the rest of your life. But you've got to experience all of life's processes. And that means marriage, stable home, children, and grandchildren. You've got to make the move and ask her to marry you."

"Yeah, yeah, thanks," Arnold said, and they went on to talk of other things, as if he had dismissed his friend's advice. However, Lorimer had approached the matter in the only way that would have caught Arnold's attention. It was not about being fair to Maria and all the years she had been waiting for him. It was not about looking like a solid citizen, especially if he intended to run for office one day. It was about Arnold's experiencing life to its fullest. His fear had always been that marriage would wall in his life and close down his future, and here Lorimer was telling him just the opposite. If he wanted to live life at its deepest, he had to get married.

In August, Arnold and Maria flew to Austria to visit his native village. Going back to Thal was a way to place his boots solidly on the earth, to sense not only how far he had gone but how much he remained. He rented one of the boats on the shore of the tiny Thalersee and rowed out into the middle of the lake. And there he asked Maria to marry him, and there she said yes.

The couple had barely returned to the United States when CBS offered Maria the coveted position of cohosting *CBS Morning News* with Forrest Sawyer. Her professional dream was to be the cohost of a network morning show, but her personal dream was to marry Arnold. Accepting the CBS position would mean that she would have to move to New York City. "I had to make a wrenching decision," she told *The New York Times*. "It was the job I'd always wanted. But I had worked a long time at that relationship, and I had just finally gotten it where I wanted it, and all of a sudden, I was faced with moving 3,000 miles away and pursuing a very demanding job. But I knew that if I didn't take it, there were other people who would."

What Maria did not tell the *Times* was how difficult it was to be away from Arnold when she feared that there were other women approaching her fiancé.

It did not matter that they were engaged. "Girls were always chasing him," said her friend Theo Hayes. "I went to restaurants with them where girls would walk by the table and slip a piece of paper under his hand while Maria was sitting there with a big engagement ring on. I'm telling you, these women were throwing themselves at him. I can remember we were walking in Georgetown one night. My husband and Arnold were in front, and Maria and I were five steps behind, and it had just happened in this restaurant. This woman had heaved her bosoms in his face while we're eating and gave Arnold her card. And I said to Maria, 'How do you handle it?' She goes, 'What can I do?' "

As much as she disguised it, Maria had been more the pursuer than the pursued with Arnold. She had waited close to a decade for him to ask for her hand. Arnold encouraged her to accept the CBS offer even though it meant he would see her primarily only on weekends. Her program was a distant third in the ratings, under extreme pressure to do better. She lived in a hotel room, and during the week practically all she did was work. She had almost no social life in New York.

"Shriver does not look like she cares about the answers to any questions except, 'What time will Arnold be home?' and 'Where's my brush?' " the acerbic Tom Shales wrote in *The Washington Post*. "She sucks in her cheeks and deflates her face, looking a little like one of those cartoon characters who got slipped a dose of alum." If anything, Maria cared too much and was trying too hard.

Maria was cohosting the program at a time when women had to prove that they were as serious as their male colleagues. When she was criticized for posing for the cover of *Harper's Bazaar* with her colleague Meredith Viera, she said that she had done so to please the CBS publicity department. There had been no criticism when ABC's Peter Jennings and NBC's Tom Brokaw appeared on the cover of *GQ*. Maria's impending marriage to Arnold was an almost irresistible opportunity to promote herself and give a jolt to the anemic ratings, but she refused to talk on air about Arnold. Off air, she enthusiastically threw herself into planning a large wedding, fully in the Kennedy family tradition. On her last Friday as a single woman, she told the audience, "I'll be taking a few days off."

Previous generations of the Kennedy men had married women who were socially their superiors and would advance them in the world. The women had generally married men who tied themselves to the fortunes of the family. Maria's father had been employed by Joseph P. Kennedy when he met Eunice. The closest parallel to Maria's own marriage was that of her aunt Patricia. She had married the British-born actor Peter Lawford, who introduced his brother-in-law Senator John F. Kennedy to the Hollywood world. Lawford had largely dissipated himself with drugs and alcohol before the couple became the first of many Kennedys to divorce.

Arnold was not subordinating himself to the fortunes of the Kennedys or the Shrivers. He neither needed nor wanted the family imprimatur to make his way in the world. Nor was Maria consciously subordinating herself and her fortunes to those of her husband. She planned to keep her last name, and she considered the proud Shriver heritage the essence of her being. She insisted that the marriage vows be changed from "man and wife" to "husband and wife," signifying that in her mind the bonds that united her with Arnold were the same that united Arnold with her.

For all their concern for the poor and the needy, the Shrivers had a sense of social order and class worthy of the Windsors. They consciously used people for their various causes and charities, and they had their own ever-changing hierarchy, the pinnacle of which was formed by those who sat closest to them and contributed greatest to their advance. Many of Arnold's friends and other wedding guests got a rude introduction to that reality when they discovered that there was a wedding party beforehand at the Shrivers' Hyannis Port home to which they were not invited.

The five-hundred-person guest list itself included the close friends of the bride and the groom, but it was also full of media people who would prove extremely helpful to the couple in the years that followed. Oprah Winfrey, Maria's former colleague in Baltimore, had her own talk show and had been nominated for an Academy Award as Best Supporting Actress for her role in *The Color Purple*. She was emerging as a most influential person, and Maria was one of her closest friends. Other guests from the media included Tom Brokaw, Diane Sawyer, and Barbara Walters, whose paths would cross again and again with Arnold and Maria's.

Maria's bridesmaids included several of her cousins and close friends: Renée Schink, Charlotte Soames Hambro, Theo Hayes, Wanda McDaniel Ruddy, and Roberta Hollander. As Arnold already knew, these women were as close to Maria as his bodybuilding buddies were to him. She talked to them all the time and confided to her girlfriends the way he rarely did to anyone.

As Arnold stood in front of the St. Francis Xavier Church in Hyannis on April 26, 1986, he was with the two people in the world who mattered the most to him, his bride and his mother. Maria was her mother's daughter in that often she did not care how she looked. She had learned to pay attention to her dress, because she had to if she wanted to succeed in the world. A wedding dress was something else, and like her mother before her, she took great care to have an exquisite dress. The designer of the gown, Marc Bohan, was a guest at the wedding so that he could appreciate his elaborate handiwork of white silk and lace.

Arnold's mother had originally not been happy with her son's choice of a bride. Since his father's death, Arnold had made sure that his mother had a life of ease and comfort, and she may have worried about losing that. She may also not have felt comfortable with Maria, who neither spoke her language nor had the convivial warmth of so many Styrian women. There was another reason his mother blanched when he told her of the engagement. "She felt originally that she may lose the attention that I've given her," said Arnold.

Aurelia was an uneducated village woman, but she had a natural grace and dignity. She looked a match for any of the Kennedy ladies in her elegant violet dress, pearls, pink shoes, and mink coat. As proud as she appeared and as apprehensive as she probably felt, she was Arnold's mother and deserved to be treated with the highest respect. Jackie Onassis, whose sense of manners did not end at the dinner table, invited Arnold's mother to her Hyannis Port house. "It's amazing how nice she is, and how nice they were to me," she told Arnold afterward. "And Teddy was the one that helped me out of the church and offered his arm."

What Aurelia did not tell her son, and several of the guests had noticed, was how rudely some members of the Kennedy family treated her, not even granting her the minimal courtesy of greeting the mother of the groom. Arnold did not notice and even now finds it hard to believe, but his friends observed and remembered. Maria is equally adamant that her mother-in-law was royally treated. "I don't know if you're talking about three or four people who might have seen her alone for two minutes with no one to talk to who could have said that? Yes. If she had to wait for five minutes to get a car, could that have happened? Yes. But you know, I've never seen in my lifetime a woman treated as a queen as that woman was. From the minute I met her to the minute she was buried, she was a queen."

The guest who was the most discussed was one who was not there, former secretary-general of the United Nations Kurt Waldheim, who was in the last days of his campaign for the Austrian presidency. When Arnold invited Waldheim, he did not know that within a few weeks the World Jewish Congress would expose that Waldheim had been posted to a unit that had been involved in numerous atrocities in the Balkans during World War II. In his official appraisal of the charges, Austrian President Rudolf Kirchschlaeger said that although Lieutenant Waldheim did not appear guilty of war crimes, he surely had knowledge of the "reprisal actions against the partisans."

Waldheim had sent a gift that was reason alone for him to be much discussed, a life-size papier-mâché statue of Arnold and Maria in native Austrian dress. Except for the prominence of the subjects and the overwhelming size, the statue looked like something bought in a souvenir shop. The guests at the reception grew strangely quiet when the Austrian contingent unveiled the bizarre sculpture. "Maria looked like Gloria Swanson in 'Sunset Boulevard,'" one of the guests told the *Chicago Tribune*. No one probably would have even commented on the Waldheim gift if Arnold had not made such a point of it during the reception. "My friends don't want me to mention Kurt's name, because of all the recent Nazi stuff and the U.N. controversy," said Arnold, as Andy Warhol recorded the words in his diary, "but I love him and Maria does too, and so thank you, Kurt."

Arnold is a loyal friend, a virtue that allows him to forgive what should not be forgiven, and cast his eyes away from matters that should be faced. He is not a man who believes in apologies, and he has never publicly regretted his defense of Waldheim.

Arnold's sense of loyalty was also displayed at its best that wedding weekend. His guest list was not jammed with studio executives and others invited because it might advance his career. His list was full of old friends and relatives. Franco Columbu, was his best man. Paul Graham, who ten years before had left California after spending time in prison, flew in from Australia. Not only did Albert Busek arrive from Munich, but he brought his wife with him. Mrs. Busek was in the advanced stages of multiple sclerosis. She was in a wheelchair and had a difficult time holding down her food, but Arnold insisted that she be at his wedding. Although George Butler was invited, Arnold had grown suspicious enough of the man whose photography had helped make him celebrated that he had his camera confiscated. "That was a caddish thing to do," said Butler. "It was Arnold at his worst."

Other cronies were invited and played prominent roles. "I'm having Jim Lorimer do the reading for me, because he's the only one of my friends who can read," Arnold joked to his friends. Sven Thorsen was an usher. After his impromptu speech at the *Commando* premiere, Arnold might have retired him from the speaker's platform, but a friend was always a friend. Sven had his say. "In Denmark, and my wife here is my witness, the household for a man needs three things—a vacuum cleaner, a dishwasher, and a woman," Sven said, in his foghorn voice. "And in that order."

"Who the fuck is your friend?" Senator Edward Kennedy asked after the laughter died down. "Ah, he's from Denmark," Arnold replied. "He's a comedian. I don't like him."

Maria had broken her toe in her New York apartment, so she put on sneakers to dance with her husband. Neither the bride nor the groom knew how to waltz, and they had taken private lessons to be ready for the day. They moved gracefully around the heated tent to the music of Peter Duchin. The newlyweds exuded happiness, Arnold as much as his bride.

Raw Deals

In the summer of 1986, the newlyweds moved into a splendid $4 million house on Sunset Boulevard in Pacific Palisades eminently suitable for one of the greatest of Hollywood stars. The seven-bathroom, seven-bedroom home had an open, airy feeling; and spacious grounds with a swimming pool, a fountain, and a tennis court adjacent to Will Rogers Park. For the first few months, Arnold enjoyed the new house with his bride primarily on weekends, since Maria was back in New York cohosting *CBS Morning News*.

Arnold rationalized that "it's only a temporary thing, but she should do it, because she'll be happy the rest of her life because she's done it." Certainly Arnold tried to make the best of it. "We fly back and forth as much as possible, and we run up thousands of dollars in phone bills," Arnold told Boston television station WBZ. "We have over-the-phone sex, but there's no way we can have children with her on the East Coast and me on the West Coast."

Arnold had married a formidable woman with her own agenda, but he had done so in his own time and in his own way. He was not going to change his habits and his pleasures. If he did, it would only be after the shrewdest, most concerted effort on Maria's part.

In most successful marriages, one partner makes a greater commitment to the marriage and expends far more emotional energy in making the relationship work. If this celebrity marriage did not suffer the common fate of most first celebrity marriages, it would be primarily because of Maria. Maria was a possessive woman. For close to a decade, she had held those feelings in check until Arnold finally asked for her hand. Given how much she wanted the marriage to work, it was a mark of her ambition that she was willing to be apart from her new husband. She knew her husband and the risk she was taking, but she wanted to play out her aspirations on the highest scale.

Maria was initially devastated when she was fired from *CBS Morning News* on August 1. But she soon chalked it up to experience and returned to Los Angeles, to be hired by NBC. It was a fortunate move. Within three years, she was working on magazine shows during the week, anchoring *NBC Nightly News* on Saturday evening from New York City, and hosting *Sunday Today* from Washington, D.C., the next morning. For a woman who was far from a natural for television, it was an extraordinary achievement. She had become one of the top women in the business, poised for even higher positions, perhaps one day even anchoring *NBC Nightly News* full-time or having her own program.

"Maria worked the same hours everybody else did," said Sandy Gleysteen, her longtime NBC producer and close friend. "Around the clock, really hard." Maria tried to maintain her Shriver family ideals by agreeing to do celebrity-oriented stories as long as she could report on important social issues as well.

Some husbands would have found it intolerable to have their bride jetting across the country each weekend and working endless hours during the week, but for Arnold it was fine. He was often flying off somewhere, too, or busy on the set or elsewhere. When the couple were together, there was a special intensity.

Arnold had a well-deserved reputation for managing every last detail of his career, but compared with his wife, he was self-indulgent. "Maria is so nervous and she's the most controlling of people," said one close observer. "It's basically one control freak married to another."

Maria's mother had taught her only daughter that whatever she did was only a beginning and that nothing was ever quite good enough. Maria applied this rule most harshly to herself, but to those around her as well, especially her husband. She could be critical of Arnold in a way no one ever had been before. It could be his dress, his language, or his choice of film roles, but she was direct and forceful in her opinions.

Arnold projected onto the world an image of himself that was far more sophisticated than the reality. He had managed to obtain a business degree from the University of Wisconsin at Superior largely by correspondence, but it was far from the kind of education he would have received if he had spent significant time in the classroom. He was almost totally self-educated. Like someone who only marginally speaks a foreign language and smiles knowingly when he doesn't understand, Arnold was often in a world where he fooled people into thinking he understood more than he did.

Having grown up as a Kennedy and a Shriver, Maria had a more intuitive awareness of the world of power and wealth in America than most people. Her family used their name and position every day to do what they considered good and to advance themselves economically and politically. Arnold learned how to grasp those levers that moved American society at its highest levels. He learned to do good and to do well and to see no contradiction between the two.

Arnold was not only the great love of Maria's life but her great project. She taught him more than anyone he had ever met. "Maria took a kid and turned him into a man," said Betty Weider. "She helped him to mature. She took a rock and made him into a gem, polished him. He had the ability to learn and to be part of her. She's been like a miracle to him."

As much good as Maria did for Arnold, she also turned her hypercriticism on her husband. As much as her advice helped Arnold, it resulted in an uncertainty about himself that was not there before.

That Maria loved her husband did not mean that she had to love his friends, and she found several of them worthless hangers-on. To her mind, they brought out the vulgar, self-indulgent part of Arnold that squandered time and energy. She knew the history several of these men had with Arnold and the endless women who were adjuncts to their lives. That was the part of her husband's life that she wanted only in the forgotten past. As long as these men were around him, so also was that part of Arnold's life.

As soon as he moved into their new house, Arnold invited his close friends over for an evening. "This is our house, boys," Arnold said. At least one of them took him literally, showing up and using the pool whenever the whim hit him, but most of them thought it meant simply that they were always welcome. A couple of months later, when Maria was back in town, he invited them all over again. It was boys' night out and they were sitting out back, smoking cigars, drinking, telling dirty jokes, and using language that the Sacred Heart nuns, who educated Maria, had never heard.

In the middle of the joshing camaraderie, Maria appeared and stood before them, holding a cigarette in a long cigarette holder. "Hey, would you guys light me?" she said, and then added: "Yeah, I want to sit here, smoking, and be tough and full of myself."

Arnold looked up at her and set down his cigar. He had his time with his friends and nothing was going to change that, not even his wife. "Hey, sweetheart," he said, looking up. "Go inside."

Maria went inside.

———

Arnold had done everything he could to reassure his mother that even with his new marriage, his concern for her would be undiminished. Arnold had the European attitude that his mother was welcome for as long as she wanted to stay. Every winter he invited Aurelia to Los Angeles, where she usually spent three months. When Maria invited her mother, Eunice usually came only for a few days and she was always overscheduled, running from one Special Olympics event to another, visiting her son Bobby or other friends.

Friends of the couple assert that Maria found it hard having her mother-in-law there for all those months, and it became one of the difficulties of her marriage. Maria points out that she invited the mother-in-law she refers to as "Mrs. Schwarzenegger" to come and stay, had dinner with her every evening, and tried to make her welcome. Though she does not admit how onerous it was to have Arnold's mother in her house for such lengthy visits, her discomfort seeped out in measures large enough for her friends to observe.

Aurelia was not a sweet-tempered grandmother who spent her days spoiling her grandchildren. As she saw it, her son had married far beyond his station to a woman who did not speak German. Maria did not have the convivial demeanor of many Austrian women and never seemed fully to relax. Since Maria could not cook, Arnold's mother prepared the Austrian dishes her son loved. One of Arnold's fondest memories of his childhood was the Sunday dinner of schnitzel and steamed rice, which he anticipated all week long. In Los Angeles his mother cooked the dish for him as well as other Austrian favorites. She worried that he was too thin and tried to bulk him up and lectured her beloved Arnold that he should eat first before exercising.

When Arnold was gone for weeks on a movie set, Aurelia did not call her friends in Austria to complain about her son, but she did leave the impression that she was alone in this immense house with people who could not speak to her and did not seem to care. The reality was that Arnold was the most dutiful and loving of sons who did everything he could do to give his mother the ease, comfort, and pleasure in the last decades of her life that she had not had in her earlier years. Maria understood and respected the love that Arnold felt for his mother, and if she was incapable of the overwhelming hospitality that is the essence of the Austrian villager, she went beyond what most American women would have put up with from an often difficult mother-in-law.

Maria asserted herself in her marriage, but equality had its limits, and Arnold insisted that when they went out with him, both Maria and his mother never wear pants. That was a sticking point with him. If women started wearing pants literally, they would wear them figuratively as well, and he did not like either. Women should neither dress like men nor act like them.

Maria began to make her presence felt in Arnold's professional life as well, commenting on his film scripts, attending meetings, making suggestions, criticizing those who worked with and for him. Arnold's other advisers tiptoed around her, not daring to risk riling her. They knew that the one thing they could never say was that they valued Maria's judgment less than her husband did.

"She is extremely smart and feels much more comfortable and happier to help me than to help herself," Arnold said five years after their marriage. "Reading movie scripts: 'You should talk to the director about this page.' 'I think you are wasting your time with this [scene].' Things like that. She is right there. When we have a rough-cut screening, the director will say, 'What are the things you didn't like?' I'll say, 'I'm just seeing it the first time.' But my wife is handing him a two-page written list of comments."

Arnold's life was in place. He had the house he might well live in for the rest of his life and the wife who would live with him there. His career was equally set. It was not about grand artistic vision, but about marketing. His films were brilliantly conceived products on which he placed his mark from their very inception. "When people come to me with a script or concept, I tell them, 'Before we shoot the first frame, we have to shoot the poster,'" he told the *Los Angeles Times*. "What is the image? What are we trying to sell here? Say in one sentence what the movie is about. You can't? Then how are you going to sell the movie? So forget that. Next project."

Arnold's film that summer of 1986, *Raw Deal*, could easily be encapsulated in a single sentence: A disgraced FBI agent redeems himself as an undercover cop by single-handedly destroying a Chicago mob. The film systematically incorporated all the elements of a Schwarzenegger movie: the hero's brawn and wit, an unconsummated love affair, and a regular diet of violence, leading up to a banquet of death and gore. As Arnold's character dresses in black for that cathartic bloody buffet, he checks himself out in the mirror and then heads out to the music of the Rolling Stones' "(I Can't Get No) Satisfaction," proving the song wrong by wiping out a Chicago mob. In ninety-seven minutes of film, he kills forty-two people.

Raw Deal failed at the box office that summer, as did its main competitor, Stallone's *Cobra*. As bad as the reviews were for *Raw Deal*, they were better than those meted out to *Cobra*. SCHWARZENEGGER BEATS SLIMY SLY AT HIS OWN GAME, headlined the *Toronto Star*. Stallone received brutal criticism for the mindless violence of his films, but Arnold was able to sidestep such judgments partially because his characters leavened their bloodshed with humor, but mostly because of Arnold's manipulation of the entertainment media.

Arnold had moved beyond the days when he reached out for every scrap of publicity, giving whatever outrageous quote would garner the most attention. He still did far more publicity than any other star of his magnitude. Now that he was established as a brand name, he and Parker rigorously controlled his message. He had no romantic illusions about the entertainment media being part of a glorious free press. He was his own product and he did not like others making money off him. He considered the media a poster on which to emblazon his message.

He was the product. If people were going to make money, sell magazines, and get ratings using this product, then he would exploit that product on his own terms. With the Weider publications, he had already been educated in controlling an image, but he was operating at a far higher level.

"There were many times we would be walking through a hotel and a gorgeous girl would come up and want a photo with him, and he wisely said no," recalled Joel Parker, partner with his wife, Charlotte, in a public relations firm. "There was a beauty queen from Russia and he said, 'Keep her away from me.' He's someone who understands the game at a very advanced level."

Arnold was so successful that he developed an almost proprietary attitude toward the media over the years. Journalists had their own professional hierarchy in which entertainment media stood in the lowest quadrant. Arnold had his hierarchy, too. At the top were the media and journalists who did what he wanted them to do, at the bottom those who did not.

Before the star talked to a magazine, Parker attempted to negotiate a guaranteed cover. She next met with the reporter and tried to understand him or her well enough to advise Arnold on how to handle the interview. In most cases, she limited the interview to a short session. That way, Arnold projected an aura of spontaneity as he rigorously monitored what he said. "Arnold is absolutely brilliant at how to project his own image while making the reporter feel very valued and important," said Parker.

What the star and the publicist were doing became common practice in the next few years among stars and their publicists, but Arnold and Parker were among the first to do it. The movie community is small, jealous, and constantly observant of one another's prerogatives. His control of the entertainment media was as if Arnold had negotiated an extraordinary new clause in his contracts.

In exchange for access, entertainment journalists and media essentially gave up part of their freedom in an almost formalized way. Although most reporters easily went along, some of them blanched at what they thought were intolerable limits. Parker bore the brunt of whatever anger and dissatisfaction the journalist may have felt. "People were jealous of her position," said Arnold. "I always said to Charlotte, 'It's jealousy you have to earn. Obviously people think that you're good, and that's why they're upset.'"

Arnold grasped early on that he was not an actor like Dustin Hoffman or Robert De Niro who could achieve a long, successful career through the variety and quality of the roles he selected. He was the product, and if the public did not like him, he was finished. For the most part, the late-night and morning talk shows and much of the other entertainment media were places where an endless array of celebrity peddlers came forward to sell their wares. "I hate to do interviews and talk shows when I don't have a reason for it," Arnold said. "But when I have a film out, then I'm very excited, especially if I have a film I think is great."

When it came Arnold's turn to leave the green room to have his moment on television, he was professionally charming and witty, but never did he forget that he was out there to sell his film. He understood the rhythm of celebrity. He wanted to come crashing into the public consciousness like a great wave, then retreat until his next film, and then come crashing into awareness again. At times, he held back publicity if it wouldn't effectively promote what or when he wanted.

Arnold was obsessed with getting his face on magazine covers because his face was his visual signature. He could control his photographic image like no other aspect of his publicity. The words inside were decidedly secondary. In her office, Parker started tacking up each cover. That wall became a chronology of Arnold's career. On one side, there were almost exclusively bodybuilding magazines. Then movie magazines were added to the mix, and farther along business periodicals, and finally all sorts of general-interest magazines. Nothing just happened. As Arnold evolved, Parker went out and pushed publicity for each developing part of his career and life. He had grown to justify the words that had been written about him.

When he was out promoting a movie, he was not about to share a cover with Maria. It was not a competitive issue. He had a movie to sell, and the best way to do so was to have his focused image out there. Beyond that, he was his own story and it rankled him to be bundled up and trundled off into another episode of the ongoing Kennedy saga. "I don't want them to sell the Kennedy shit," he said while he was a rising star.

As much as Arnold controlled his image, it was perhaps inevitable that he would at some point slip up. Arnold did almost no media without Parker prepping him—and usually sitting in on the interview. But one day Arnold agreed to an interview for *Playboy* with Joan Goodman, a well-regarded freelance writer, without first telling Parker.

Parker thought of Arnold as her media creation, and was infuriated that he would end-around her. "It was the one and only time that happened," recalled Parker. "I told Arnold, 'Don't do this.' I told him, 'I don't have a good feeling about this girl.' I was just so angry that she went around me and I was angry at everybody because of the fact that here I was, left with this big mess. I told Arnold how pissed I was."

Parker had always set the terms of the interview, but this time Arnold did it himself. "There's one condition under which I will do this interview," Arnold told Goodman, "that Brigitte Nielsen's name not be mentioned, even her initials. Nothing about her will appear."

"I can agree to this, and I will ask *Playboy*. But can you tell me why?"

"Maria is not a difficult woman," Arnold said. "She's a Kennedy, and she understands the film business, but the one person who troubles her is Brigitte Nielsen."

Goodman flew to the set of *Red Heat* in Chicago. The subject of a *Playboy* interview usually sits with the interviewer so many hours that the celebrity inevitably says things he would not in a single session. During their first evening together with a group from the film, one of Arnold's friends alluded to Nielsen, and Arnold made a gesture as if relieved that the whole business was over.

During the many times Arnold talked to Goodman, he frequently discussed Nielsen—Stallone's ex-wife. As Goodman listened to Arnold's obsessive talk, she concluded that Arnold had been looking at the female version of himself. "She had ambition and ego equally to his and persistence in bettering herself socially, financially, in every way that was precisely the same," said Goodman. "Arnold was ambivalent about her, and it was quite raw."

Arnold explained how Nielsen pursued him, how he and Jake Bloom had gotten rid of her by setting her up with Stallone. Arnold happened to run into the newlyweds in a store in New York. "She said, 'Don't buy that jacket, it doesn't look good on you, let's go to another store,'" Arnold recalled. "She had everything under her control. I felt sorry for the poor guy."

Arnold savaged Stallone in his talks with Goodman, but he did so after asking that his remarks be off the record. The first time Arnold talked about Stallone with Goodman was just before the trip to Chicago. He specifically said, "This is off the record." Later, while once again discussing Stallone, Arnold said, "This is not for the story," and Goodman said, "Of course."

When Arnold learned beforehand what would be appearing in the January 1988 interview, he realized he had made the largest media mistake of his career. It was not simply that Arnold said things that would dog him from then on but also that it was almost unprecedented for one star to unload on another the way he savaged Stallone.

Goodman claimed that the material Arnold declared off the record quoted word for word in the interview was repeated later on the record. If true, there is no evidence of it in the transcripts of the interviews. She also says that she and the *Playboy* lawyers decided that by "this is not for the story," Arnold meant merely that he considered it irrelevant and that if Arnold had wanted it off the record, he would have said so specifically.

"He [Stallone] is not my friend," Arnold said in the published interview. "He just hits me the wrong way. I make every effort that is humanly possible to be friendly to the guy, but he just gives off the wrong vibrations. Listen, he hired the best publicity agents in the world and they couldn't straighten out his act. There's nothing anyone can do out there to save his ass and his image." He went on to criticize Stallone's attitude toward women and even his dress, mocking his "white suit, trying to look slick and hip," and "that fucking fur coat when he directs."

Arnold was so upset that he called from Mexico, where he was on location, to talk to Barry Golson, one of the top *Playboy* editors. It was a call that should have been made by Parker, never by Arnold personally. "His beef was that he'd criticized Sly Stallone for his vanity in caustic terms and was now having second thoughts about it," recalled Golson. "Would I consent to delete those remarks? I asked why. He gave me a convoluted reason. I said I couldn't do that. He said he could offer me something much juicier at some future time. I said, No thanks. He then said that he would find some way of repaying me and *Playboy* for this lack of cooperation. Wound himself up into a real nasty snarl at the end."

Arnold had probably never given such a revealing interview in his life, and this man who learned from everything learned that he never again could fully trust a journalist. "Was what I said about Sly presumptuous?" Arnold asked. "Yes, it was, because he was definitely a bigger star than I was. But I had my opinions about things, and I said it, but not for publication. I thought she [Goodman] gives journalists a bad name, because I lost my trust in people.

"I was, at that point, still naive. And the sad story is that because there are some journalists who do not keep their promises, very rarely is there an interview where anyone says anything that is really on their mind. It's too bad, because the people never really get to know the real you."

As soon as the edition appeared on the newsstands, Arnold went on *Good Morning America* and explained that he had been misquoted. That was not true. He had been fairly and accurately quoted. *Playboy* replied that there were quotes that it did not use that were far more explosive. That was not true, either. *Playboy* had used the essence of almost all the off-the-record quotes in the published interview. And the German issue of the magazine published the off-the-record material about Nielsen. In the end, as Arnold realized, "what it created was him [Stallone] hating me and him feeling suspicious about me."

A few days after the *Playboy* issue appeared, British celebrity journalist Wendy Leigh says that Stallone invited her to the set of *Rambo III* in Yuma, Arizona. After no more than half an hour discussing his film, Stallone turned angrily to a discussion of Arnold. "We were sitting on these high chairs on the edge of the set, waiting for his call," Leigh recalled, "when he said, 'Arnold is a very bad guy.'" Once Stallone began, unmitigated rage poured out of him. "I never did anything to the f—er," Stallone said. "But he's always been out to get me. Now he's gone too far."

Stallone's best source for information on Arnold was his own ex-wife. "Brigitte was in Austria with him, met his mother, found out a lot about him," Stallone told Leigh. "I could give you a great story." Stallone said that Arnold's father had been a member of the Nazi Party. Arnold had even shown Brigitte Nielsen a picture of his father in a brown uniform of the Nazi SA.

Leigh says that over the next few weeks, Stallone told her a number of startling revelations. On February 19, 1988, she had a tape-recorded telephone conversation with the actor and told him that a story would be appearing on the front page of the British tabloid *News of the World* the following Sunday. Leigh also called Parker to tell her about some of the allegations. The publicist says she told Leigh that she was the child of Austrian Holocaust survivors, and if Arnold was in any way anti-Semitic or pro-Nazi, she would not be working for him.

The article headlined HOLLYWOOD STAR'S NAZI SECRET charged that Arnold was a "secret admirer of Adolph Hitler" who held "fervent Nazi and anti-Semitic views." The article alleged further that Arnold's father was not simply a Nazi but had personally directed the rounding up of Jews to be taken to concentration camps. Nowhere in the piece was there a word of Parker's denial of the charges. Leigh was given a joint byline on the story, though since she was living in America, she had nothing to do with writing it.

Arnold shrugged off bad reviews, but nothing was capable of angering him more than allegations that he was anti-Semitic or pro-Nazi. He immediately contacted Rupert Murdoch, the owner of *News of the World*, to complain. In an attempt to back up the story, Leigh got in touch again with Stallone, who according to Leigh provided her with even more scandalous material on Arnold that had nothing to do with the original story. When she told Stallone that she was thinking of expanding the material into a book, he immediately came to her hotel to persuade her to go ahead. "I'll get you an agent, an accountant, a publicist, twenty-four-hour-a-day bodyguards," she recalled him saying. "Anything you want."

Leigh went ahead with the book. Behind the scenes, she claims, Stallone orchestrated much of the project. He found her an agent and put her in touch with Arnold's former publicist Paul Bloch. He lined up three other sources to attest that Arnold had a relationship with Nielsen. He put the journalist in contact with Lacy H. Rich Jr., a gay aficionado of the bodybuilding world obsessed with hurting Arnold, and he became Leigh's crucial guide and confidant. Stallone also put Leigh in touch with a detective who led her to one of Arnold's former girlfriends. The star was obsessed with Arnold. "I think of Schwarzenegger every night before I go to sleep," Leigh recalled Stallone telling her.

Unauthorized biographers often receive their most revealing material from ex's and enemies. After the interviews, the author is left with the unenviable task of separating elements of the truth from the venom, vitriol, and willful exaggeration with which the material is frequently presented. Stallone was a fine source, but Leigh allowed him to become so close to her project that he even read the first draft of her manuscript. "Honey, reading this is better than getting four blow jobs," she remembered him telling her. The star had reason to feel that he would have his revenge with publication of the book.

Leigh was already in the midst of an expensive lawsuit, and she was playing a very dangerous game. Both Arnold's agent and publicist at the time say they knew nothing about Stallone's involvement, and Arnold probably did not yet realize the extent to which the hero of *Rocky* was responsible for the most offensive libels. He set out on several fronts to attempt to squelch the publication of the book, and when that failed, to bury it.

Leigh says that Arnold filed his lawsuit against the tabloid and her personally only after he learned about her book project. British libel laws are much tougher than in America. The newspaper had to prove not only that it believed the story was the truth but that it was indeed the truth and in the public interest that the truth be known. In December 1989 the British paper settled with Arnold for an undisclosed sum and publicly stated that there was no truth to any of the allegations and that they would not be repeated. The lawsuit against Leigh continued. The journalist was left in an unenviable position. Her publisher was not about to publish a book by a biographer whose primary credential was that she had libeled the subject. She was forced to defend herself when it would have been far easier to join with *News of the World* in a public mea culpa.

When Leigh's book was in production at Congdon & Weed, publisher Harvey Plotnick received two unusual phone calls. "Both were people I know and who know Schwarzenegger," said Plotnick. "We publish a lot of sports and bodybuilding books, so we know a lot of people in common. One call suggested that if I didn't publish the book and paid Wendy off, then this individual and Schwarzenegger would in return write a joint autobiography. I was also told Arnold Schwarzenegger had deep pockets and could put me out of business." The second call offered to pay Plotnick for buying the book but not publishing it.

In the spring of 1990, Plotnick went ahead with publication of *Arnold: An Unauthorized Biography*. Parker called television programs that had booked Leigh or were contemplating it. The publicist pointed out that Arnold was suing Leigh for libel. She suggested that if the author appeared, Arnold would bypass the program on his next publicity junket. Several programs dropped Leigh or stopped considering booking her. *Time*'s James Willwerth received what he called "urgent, demanding pleas" from Parker that he not mention Leigh's book in a profile on Arnold he was writing for the newsweekly. At the 1990 Cannes Film Festival, Parker asked reporters to sign an agreement that they would not ask Arnold questions about the book before they were admitted to a press conference. Stallone kept up the appearance of friendship with Arnold, even dancing with him at a party at the film festival that year.

In the end, Leigh was left not with a controversial bestseller but disappointing sales, heavy research expenses, a spurned media campaign, and an expensive lawsuit. Leigh says that she saw Stallone again on July 17, 1991, shortly before she gave a deposition in which she would be forced to admit that Stallone was the source for her charges about Arnold and Nazism. This was a few weeks before Stallone planned to announce that he had become associated with Arnold in Planet Hollywood, a theme restaurant chain. The partners were planning to hype the concept to a fever pitch and then go public. Arnold, Stallone, and Bruce Willis, the other star investor, were supposedly buddies who loved hanging out together—so why not at their own theme restaurant? It would be disastrous if Stallone's role in the *News of the World* story became public.

Leigh says that Stallone introduced her to a high-powered Washington attorney and offered to pay all further costs of her lawsuit as long as his man took over. The attorney guided the case in such a manner that Stallone's role never came out. In 1993 she settled out of court by paying Arnold substantial damages and legal costs, all of which Leigh says were paid by Stallone. She also publicly stated that there "was not a word of truth" in the article.

During the course of the lawsuit, Arnold learned that Stallone was supporting Leigh, and he realized that the whole train of deception, starting with *News of the World*, had been started by his fellow star. The slanderous assertion that he was pro-Nazi and anti-Semitic would haunt him for the rest of his days in public life, and he had every reason to hate Stallone. When asked about the matter for this book, Arnold only reluctantly confirmed the story.

"I felt somewhat responsible because I said the things about him, and therefore it made him so angry about it," said Arnold. "If she [Goodman] would have kept her word, this would have never been in the magazine. He was so furious, because he obviously was a sensitive guy, and so with the Planet Hollywood thing, luckily we could just literally go and make peace."

Arnold did not so much make peace as establish a truce. He embraced Stallone when the cameras were on, but he kept a wary, watchful distance from the man who had once been his greatest competitor.

"You Are What You Do"

Arnold and Stallone were natural competitors, many of their roles almost interchangeable. After Stallone starred in *Rocky IV* in 1985, Hollywood joked that he would have to fight an alien in *Rocky V*. That sounded like a splendid idea to screenwriters Jim and John Thomas, who wrote a script in which a creature from outer space arrives in the Central American jungle. The enormous reptilian biomechanoid has a moral sensitivity unknown to most earthbound villains. He wants to fight and destroy only an opponent of worthy stature. Once the script was purchased by Fox and given to *Commando* producer Joel Silver, that opponent turned out to be Arnold, not Stallone. Arnold did not like the idea of facing off against the monster alone for the whole length of the film, and he had the scriptwriters add a team of tough mercenaries, including Jesse Ventura, a professional wrestler and former Navy SEAL, and Carl Weathers, who had so convincingly played Apollo Creed in the *Rocky* films.

Most of *Predator* was shot in the jungles of Mexico, and it was Arnold's toughest filmmaking experience since *Conan the Barbarian*. There was 100-degree heat, then nearly freezing weather. Arnold stood baked in mud or stripped to his waist. Arnold not only refused to complain but was a singularly upbeat force on the set. Critics who tended to like action films generally praised *Predator,* while others panned it. The film opened in June 1987 to major box-office success, in the end doing about $70 million worth of business in the United States alone.

Arnold's second movie that year was *The Running Man*, based very loosely on a novel by Stephen King writing as Richard Bachman. The futuristic thriller, which grossed $38.1 million domestically, takes place in a totalitarian future akin to Orwell's *1984*. Every night, the subdued masses watch the world's most popular television program, *The Running Man*, in which criminals are chased down and killed by gladiators. The homeless watch the live, three-hour program on gigantic outdoor screens and bet on the outcome. This perverse game show is hosted by the egomaniacal, manipulative Damon Killian, played by Richard Dawson, the longtime host of TV's *Family Feud*, ratcheting up his own persona into a darkly brilliant performance.

The Dawson character throws a media bread and circus to the masses, a bloody, brutal game that the vast audience applauds and celebrates. They feel cheated when Ben Richards (Arnold) kills their heroes, Subzero (Toru Tanaka) and Buzzsaw (Gus Rethwisch), and again when he refuses to give them their expected denouement by killing a helpless third gladiator, Dynamo (Erland van Lidth). "Do it!" the audience screams. They want only victors. In the end, they applaud Richards's victory not because he represents freedom but because he is the winner.

The Running Man may be only a comic strip, but behind even the most politically denatured film about totalitarianism lies the Holocaust. In some of the early scenes Arnold is in a prison much like a Nazi concentration camp. During the filming, Arnold became friendly with George Linder, the coproducer. Linder introduced Arnold to his father, Bert Linder, who lost his wife and child but survived Auschwitz, Nordhausen-Dora, and Bergen-Belsen.

During the seven weeks Arnold spent on location at the Kaiser Steel Mill in Fontana, California, he had plenty of time for his friends. Linder, who was with him most of the time, says that he saw absolutely nothing of the untoward sexual conduct that would later be so well publicized.

Sven Thorsen had a role as the game-show host's massive bodyguard. During the shooting, Thorsen accompanied Arnold when he went shopping for a Porsche. "Arnold, give me a fucking break," Thorsen said after about the tenth trip.

"It's a thing you don't understand," Arnold said. "I want to stay hungry. I want to work to find the right car so I can deserve the car."

And so the two friends kept right on shopping. "We had seen forty fucking cars before he found his Porsche," recalled Thorsen. "He saved eight hundred bucks, and he was happy."

In June 1988 Thorsen was over at Arnold's house when he saw his friend sitting with a tear running down his cheek. He was holding an issue of *Variety* in his hands. Thorsen had seen his friend like this only once before. That was when fifty-four-year-old stunt coordinator Bennie Dobbins had died of a heart attack during production. "What the fuck is wrong?" Thorsen asked urgently.

"Fucking *Red Heat*," Arnold said. In his just-released movie, he plays a Russian homicide detective searching for a dangerous drug dealer in Chicago with a local cop (Jim Belushi). The early scenes shot in the Soviet Union were both cinematically powerful and unique footage, but once Moscow detective Ivan Danko arrives in the Midwest, as *The Washington Post* noted, "even though the Austrian-born star adopts a Russian accent for the role, the character is virtually indistinguishable from any other he has played." Audiences realized that they had seen all this before, and the film earned only $35 million in the United States, a disappointing total for a man set on becoming the number one star in the world.

"Come on," Sven said, realizing that his friend was down. "It's number two. Come on."

"You don't understand," Arnold said, shaking his head. "I want to be number one."

By any measure, Arnold was a major star, but he did not receive respect and recognition as an important actor. He was merely a moneymaker. He had done so for 20th Century-Fox, starring in two of the studio's hits, *Commando* (1985) and *Predator* (1987).

In December 1988, Arnold attended an elaborate party on the Fox lot after the premiere of *Working Girl*, starring Harrison Ford, Sigourney Weaver, and Melanie Griffith. The film directed by Mike Nichols was the kind of classy project that studios lived for. Studio head Barry Diller followed the Hollywood axiom that nothing impresses like excess. The "Christmas in New York in Los Angeles" theme party included ice skaters on real ice, roasting chestnuts, enough gourmet food for much of West L.A., elaborate entertainment, and decorations all along New York Street.

Arnold was impressed. "Hey, Barry," he called out. "Barry!" Diller walked over to Arnold. "Barry," Arnold said as he grasped Diller's hands and embraced him. "Why don't you give me one of these premieres?" Diller looked up at Arnold and, as he turned to walk away, made a passing aside: "Thanks to you, I can afford to give this one."

Arnold realized that in Hollywood you are only as good as your last movie. If it was a bomb, then so were you. He was consumed with starring in hit after hit until he, too, had his spectacular premieres.

After the disappointing box office of *Red Heat*, Arnold went on a tear, starring in three enormous hits in a row that propelled him to the top rank of stardom and made him more than $50 million. For the first of them, *Twins* (1988), the comedic director Ivan Reitman proposed to Arnold and Danny DeVito that they do a film together in which they would take small salaries but get a cut of the gross. The percentage that the two stars and the director took meant that for Universal Pictures to make a profit, *Twins* had to be an enormous hit. "The risk to the studio was tremendous," said Lou Pitt. "Here these three stars came together and said, 'Look, let's not take any cash, let's just take first-dollar gross together. We're all at risk but we'll keep the budget at a very low level, and if it works, we'll all get rich together, which is what happened."

As always, Thorsen had a small role in his friend's film. Afterward Arnold happened to be at Thorsen's cottage in Santa Monica on the very day he received a residual check for *Twins*. "Look at it, fifteen thousand dollars," Thorsen said excitedly, holding out the check to Arnold. "Thank you, Arnold. Thank you very much."

"Good for you," Arnold replied. "You know I never see my residual checks, and I don't recall just what I got from *Twins*, if it was fourteen or fifteen million."

Arnold received 17½ percent of the $110 million gross, or more than $20 million, at the time possibly the most money a star had ever made on a film. He also got his cut of the $104.7 million it made internationally. Within months other stars, from Jack Nicholson to Harrison Ford to Bill Murray, were cutting their own deals for a percentage of the gross, wresting money and power from the studios.

Twins was a breakthrough for Arnold in another sense, too. Arnold appeared for the first time in a comedy. He was the king of one-liners, but it was a daring stretch to build an entire movie around that part of him. Arnold played Julius Benedict, the result of a scientific experiment trying to breed the perfect human, blending the sperm of half a dozen brilliant men with a gorgeous young woman. The experiment went wrong when the mother had a second birth: a repository of genetic garbage, the bad, inferior Vincent Benedict (Danny DeVito). The audience was forgiving of a film that had far fewer laughs than an Arnold action film had killings, but Arnold carried it off perfectly as the sweet-tempered, gallant, virginal, innocent Julius.

The role resonated with something hidden within Arnold. When he was asked in August 2004 by NPR's Renée Montagne what roles had most exposed parts of his own self, he turned first to *Terminator*, the Arnold archetype, then mentioned his character in *Twins*, "like a kid that's funny, humorous, and lighthearted and all that. I'm both sides." Maria chimed in that Arnold was precisely right. He had long protected that boyish, impish self, sheltering it from adult reality, and finally in *Twins* he could expose it publicly.

Arnold had an eye focused on what he wanted and the most grasping of reaches. For years he had known about a screenplay called *Total Recall* by Ronald Shusett and Dan O'Bannon, best known for their work on *Alien* (1979). The story, based on a classic science-fiction short story by Philip K. Dick, takes place on that unguarded border between reality and fantasy, truth and paranoia. A construction worker in 2084 is so obsessed with Mars that he takes a so-called fantasy vacation to the distant planet. To do so, false memories are implanted into his brain so that he can travel without ever leaving Earth. Something goes terribly wrong, and he becomes lost in a world where he does not know what is real and what is fantasy. In the screenplay, he ends up traveling to Mars, where he frees the darkly totalitarian society from its oppressors. Or does he? Is it all just a dream? For years, the unfinished screenplay wandered from studio to studio, lost in the endless circles of development purgatory.

Shusett, who was locked into the project not only as writer but as producer, was consumed by the screenplay that had monopolized almost a decade of his life. He was acutely sensitive to anyone who might wrest even a modicum of control from him. In the mid-1980s, when Dino De Laurentiis owned the project, Arnold approached the Italian producer about starring in the film. Dino wanted to consider Arnold, but Shusett thought him so inappropriate that he initially avoided him, not even returning his phone calls. When the two finally met in a Santa Monica restaurant, the writer was startled at the insight Arnold had into his beloved screenplay and how he would play the role.

"If I'm going to do it, you've got to change certain things," Arnold said. "Some of this dialogue is wonderful, but English isn't my first language. You've got to make my speech less complicated. The people around me can say sophisticated, complex things, but my part has to be simpler. I don't want the audience to say, 'Here comes this big Austrian again.' I'm a presence, a persona, not an actor, but I'll make it a big hit. But you gotta play it differently. It's like after twenty minutes, when does Arnold go into the phone booth and become Superman?"

Shusett reluctantly conceded that Arnold might work, even if it turned the movie into more of a comic book. Arnold was not yet bankable on the big-budget level of this film, and Dino apparently was willing neither to pay the star his princely fee nor to give Arnold the control over the project that he considered only his due. After several false starts, De Laurentiis settled upon the latest sex sensation, Patrick Swayze, fresh from the hit *Dirty Dancing*, to be directed by Bruce Beresford.

In 1987 the film was in pre-production in Australia when De Laurentiis's company bottomed out. Arnold saw this as his opportunity, but he had to move quickly before Dino's company declared bankruptcy. Arnold called one of the big new players in the industry, Andrew Vajna of Carolco, and suggested that he buy the rights to *Total Recall*. Each time the project had changed hands, it carried new production and screenplay costs until it now carried a monumental price tag of about $7 million. Arnold, the real estate tycoon, knew that the best time to buy a property is when there is a scent of desperation in the air. "[Bleep] him," Arnold said. "He's lucky if he gets half of it." Dino settled for about $3 million.

By then, Arnold had become a big star. His agent and lawyer cut a $10 million deal, plus a cut of the profits, in which the star also had veto power over the producer, director, screenplay, costars, and promotion. A few other top stars negotiated similar clauses, but none of them used that power as thoroughly as Arnold did or was so involved in every aspect of a movie. Despite whatever names rolled across the screen, Arnold was the ultimate producer, and he did not have to thump on his chest to get his way.

Even as he was getting Carolco to buy the script, Arnold already had Paul Verhoeven in mind as director. A few months before, he had run into the Dutch director at Orlando Orsini's, a popular hangout for movie types near 20th Century-Fox. Verhoeven had directed the edgy, daring *RoboCop*, and Arnold figured this dark poet of violence was the ideal candidate. Arnold personally called Verhoeven and importuned him to make *Total Recall* his next project, but what convinced the director was that it was "an audacious script," even if there were still some problems.

Verhoeven read all forty-two versions of the screenplay and realized that no one had come up with a decent third act yet. So he brought in his own writer, Gary Goldman. That was threatening to Shusett. If he invoked his practical veto power over the script, Verhoeven would walk—and that might be the end of *Total Recall*. It was almost unheard-of for a star to step into a project to protect a mere writer, but Arnold did just that. "Arnold just told them he wanted me involved," Shusett said later. During the eight months of shooting in Mexico City, the two screenwriters and the director bonded, and Arnold's instincts were vindicated. Early on, when Carolco criticized Verhoeven for shooting too slowly, Arnold weighed in again.

Arnold brought his own chef and food with him to Mexico. He was practically the only American who did not get sick. "I was completely dehydrated one night and had to be on fluids basically for hours to recuperate because I couldn't even stand anymore," recalled Verhoeven. "So, it was a tough time and shooting the movie, yeah, probably went slower than they would have wished, but I don't know how it could have been faster because it was so fucking difficult."

Total Recall cost about $73 million, then one of the most expensive films of all time. Much of the money went into elaborate sets and special effects in a film that has one startling action sequence after another. Arnold had respect for the creative contributions of everyone on this huge, complex project, and he did not impose his will arbitrarily or unnecessarily. If you happened to have walked onto the set during moments of levity, you might have assumed that Arnold was a boyishly nonchalant actor unconcerned with anything beyond his trailer and the camera. You would have had no idea that he was the central figure on *Total Recall* in every sense, missing nothing of consequence but asserting himself only on crucial matters.

Arnold was always under control even when he seemed not to be. For a man who considered impatience his worst weakness, he seemed almost casual on the set. His endless joshing, pinching of women, and bawdy humor were in part a means to loosen things up, to lance the inevitable tension of weeks on a set, and to create an atmosphere in which a film could be created to advance Arnold's fortunes.

Verhoeven has a reputation as a brilliant, difficult man who makes few friends and leaves many enemies, and is devoid of false praise. He saw what Arnold was doing and ended up an unqualified admirer. "What impressed me was his ability to always be aware of other people and to be really listening to them, always ready to say, 'Okay, what can be done then even if it's not possible, what can be done?'" said the director. "How he would really bring people together. How we would sit together and say, 'Come on, guys, now let's go back to the beginning.' How he would handle the Mexican crew. And how he would be together in parties and in his speeches basically would bring people together, give them attention and embrace them in his kind of laconic and funny way. I mean, I've never seen that. So, basically for me, it was like, 'Wow, I wish I could do all that.'"

Part of the very conduct that Verhoeven and his peers thought so positive and so bonding was precisely what irritated and offended others. On the set Arnold amused himself by teasing a stuntwoman about the peculiar tilt of her breasts and by goading another woman to drink so much tequila that she threw up. One day he went to the home of the famous sculptor Francisco Zuñiga. Another guest recalled in an incident chronicled by Connie Bruck in *The New Yorker* how Arnold was seated next to a young woman who was dating the sculptor's son. "You know," he said as he touched the woman's arm, "the thing I love about Mexican women is how furry their pussies are." Such incidents were generally Arnold's schoolboy idea of fun, but in a world where an emerging political correctness sometimes trumped pleasure and spontaneity, Arnold was taking untoward risks with his reputation.

"There's certainly a mean-spirited part of Arnold, but that doesn't rule him in any way," said Pitt. The problem was, rather, that Arnold did not quite get the new rules of his adopted culture. "So whether he understands what pranks are palatable and acceptable and what aren't, he's clueless. His idea of saying something like 'girlie man,' which he used to use all the time, he thinks is cute."

Given the false memories in his brain, Arnold's character in *Total Recall* is unable to know what is real. Nothing is real: not his marriage, not his life, nothing. He asks himself, "If I'm not me, who the hell am I?" *Total Recall* has deeper emotional resonance than any of Arnold's previous films. His character had captured something truthful about contemporary life. With the relentless tempo of modern society and the endless intrusions of the media, like the character Quaid, we all ask ourselves, "Who the hell am I?" Quaid has his answer in a scene where he meets Kuato (Marshall Bell), the mutant leader of the rebels. "You are what you do," Kuato tells him. "A man is defined by his actions, not his memory." If that is Quaid's mantra, so was it Arnold's.

In one scene, Quaid confronts the reality that he cannot remember Melina (Rachel Ticotin), the woman he loves, and has to tell her that for him their life together does not exist any longer. It is the most vulnerable moment Arnold had ever had in a film, confronting the theft of his entire emotional life. He found it extremely difficult to evoke his feelings for the camera. This was the part of an actor's life that he had always sidestepped, detoured to avoid territory he did not want to risk traversing. He was not in an acting class, but on a film set with scores of people watching him trying to emote what he could not.

He kept saying the lines over and over, but they had no life. He knew it and everyone else knew it, too. "I have to tell you something, Melina," he said for the umpteenth time. "I don't remember you . . . I don't remember us . . . I don't remember Verhoeven. I don't remember Shusett . . . I don't remember . . ." Everyone on the set convulsed in laughter.

After that, Arnold felt better, and the problem vanished.

One close friend says that he has discussed with Arnold the fact that Quaid is the film character he most closely resembles. He did not think of himself as an actor. He was playing bits and pieces of this colossal persona he had built. He had willed into creation a public image that was like a billboard hovering above the world. Was he playing himself, or was there no difference between the character on the screen, his own public persona, and whatever he was in his private moments? Like Quaid, Arnold was not pretending to be some-

thing different from what he was or thought he was. In the character
played on-screen, he had not so much acted as projected parts of his own persona. On-screen at least he was a great, awe-inspiring wizard. But was that the
real Arnold? Of course there was a difference between what he played on-
screen and who he really was. But was he even capable of recognizing that
difference any longer? He and Hollywood had created a giant mythic Arnold
Schwarzenegger of such overwhelming force that at times even he did not
know where the character ended and the man began.

Three weeks before *Total Recall* was to be released in June 1990, Shusett
handed Arnold a tape of a television news show in which Martin Grove, a veteran Hollywood reporter, said that *Total Recall* had a low 40 percent public
recognition of the title. That was disastrous in a season of big-budget films,
and while it was a nervy act to involve the star himself, it wasn't half as nervy
as what Arnold did. After watching the clip, he went to Carolco and used his
clout and their desire to work with him in the future to push the company to
throw millions of dollars into new advertising. Hundreds of television ads began appearing across America, and there was almost universal awareness of
Total Recall on the day it premiered. *Total Recall* was a blockbuster, grossing
more than $119 million domestically and $142 million overseas, becoming
one of the signature films of Arnold's career.

The Sins of the Father

A rnold's second 1990 film was the comedy *Kindergarten Cop*, directed by Ivan Reitman, who had also directed *Twins*. Arnold plays Detective John Kimble, who goes from the streets of downtown L.A. to undercover duty as a schoolteacher in the charming seaside town of Astoria, Oregon. His task is to uncover the ex-wife of his nemesis, a vicious drug dealer and murderer. The first minutes in L.A. are brutal and bloody, an enjoyable romp through the familiar violent terrain of Arnold's most familiar screen persona. In Oregon we may be in a small town but these are not the streets of Frank Capra's America.

Beneath the sentimental veneer of the film, we are smack in the middle of dysfunctional, disoriented America of the nineties. Half the kids' parents seem to be divorced. One father abuses his son. Another has run off to live with his boyfriend. A mother is worried that her kindergartener may be gay. One little boy keeps uttering through the film, "Boys have a penis, girls have vaginas." And Kimble barges in on a couple of sixth-graders making out in an empty office.

This was the film you took your family to at Christmas in 1990, and Arnold made the film appear far more innocent than it is. He holds his own as an actor against the most merciless of scene-stealers, twenty-six absurdly cute kids. And he grows in vulnerability and humanity through the film.

This was a project in which Arnold and Reitman got big cuts of the gross, as with their previous collaboration. *Kindergarten Cop* grossed $91.5 million domestically and an astounding $110.5 million overseas for a comedy with very American themes. Arnold had done what no other action star had done before, transcended his own genre to become a worldwide star as a comedic actor.

Arnold may have had a special rapport with the children in *Kindergarten Cop* because in December 1989 Maria gave birth to their first daughter, Katherine Eunice. Arnold had long dreamed of a real family like Reg Park's, and his waiting all those years to marry did not make that dream any less important. If he was to do what Jim Lorimer said he must, to live life fully, then this was part of it.

He wanted to be there when Maria gave birth. "It's really great to be part of the delivery," he said afterward. "You really respect the woman more. The pain and the hours and hours of pure torture brought us even closer together."

He knew how the life of celebrity walled off a person from many human experiences. Having a child was a way of bringing him back into real life, and he relished it. Arnold considered it a sacrament of life to take his turn getting up in the middle of the night and give little Katherine her bottle. Of course, Arnold and Maria had a nanny, but they put Katherine's basinet in their bedroom. During the day Arnold delighted at every moment he could spend with his daughter. "When I'm at home with my kid, I don't need those masks," Arnold said perceptively. "I can be as silly as I like." That was Katherine's gift to her father, to give him back part of his childhood and a fathering experience that was the one of the truly selfless acts of his adulthood.

Maria was one of the I-can-have-it-all women. If she could not have it all, then no woman could. She went back to work, flying to the East Coast each weekend and working hard during the week as well. By now Maria had her own show, *First Person with Maria Shriver*, which aired several times a year on NBC. "We took Katherine with us on a couple stories for that first show," said producer Sandy Gleysteen. "We took her up to interview Sinéad O'Connor in Seattle. And so she had her own show but she had already decided, 'If I have a child, I can't work full-time.' The problem was she doesn't know about not working full-time. Her fervor and her commitment to what she does is always a hundred percent. And so suddenly there's a hundred percent going to work and then she's trying to also be a wife to Arnold, but Arnold was away shooting films a lot, so he wasn't pulling on her yet. She had to stifle her own instinct about working so hard and being so committed to work in order to fulfill her commitment to being a mom. And that was a real turnoff for her. Serious. I think when you grow up with parents who think your job is to change the world, that's what you think your job is."

In the end, Maria gave up her two anchoring positions and took on part-time assignments instead. "How lucky am I?" she has asked rhetorically. "*Very*. I had the financial ability to downsize my career, and I had employers who understood my priorities and were willing to work with me to maintain the strong and solid family life I wanted. Still, back when I made that choice, I felt so anxious and guilty."

The birth of Christina Maria Aurelia in 1991 and Patrick Arnold in 1993 made Maria's decision seem even more sound. Although she liked to view herself as a part-time journalist and full-time mom, she worked with the intensity and zeal of an ambitious young reporter. She was careful never to exploit her name or her marriage, but in some of the subjects she dealt with in *First Person with Maria Shriver* she confronted some of her own personal realities. She did a program, "Total Exposure: Privacy and the Press," in which she outlined her dilemma in being "as aggressive as the next reporter" while abhorring the unwanted attention she received "as a member of the Kennedy family and as the wife of a famous movie star" and a television personality. "You can send your tax-free contribution to Saving the Celebrities," wrote Walter Goodman in *The New York Times*, not alone in finding Maria's complaints either lame or exaggerated. In one of the most attention-grabbing programs, Maria interviewed former Oakland Raider football great Lyle Alzado, who said that he was dying of brain cancer caused by his use of steroids. Maria did not allude to her own husband, but many watching the program knew about Arnold's bodybuilding use of the drug.

Arnold admired the way Maria could manage many different activities while being a formidable mother. As paternity drew Arnold in one direction, another kind of excitement was pulling him in the opposite: power. Proximity is half the game in politics, as it is in Hollywood. It is access that makes it possible to make the pitch and to cut the deal. Arnold had attended the Republican National Convention in New Orleans and helped raise money for the party, and in the last days of the 1988 presidential campaign between Governor Michael Dukakis and Vice President George Herbert Walker Bush, he introduced the Republican candidate to an audience in Columbus, Ohio.

For someone who is politically ambitious, there are few moments that offer as much potential benefit as introducing a major candidate at a speech. The role requires that one must flatter without seeming to, and shine without outshining. Arnold understood precisely how it was done. And after introducing the Republican presidential candidate, he flew across the Midwest with George Bush, who talked to Arnold about possibly chairing the Council on Physical Fitness and Sports in the new administration.

Arnold was far from the only serious candidate for the position in the new administration. Stallone had his own idea of chairing the council, and he saw Arnold as his competition. "I've had people write to Bush and remind him that Arnold smoked pot in *Pumping Iron*," he confided to Wendy Leigh.

Arnold had stronger credentials than most, but he had not managed to cast off the cloak of controversy from his past completely. It was not just smoking marijuana in *Pumping Iron*, but also his history of taking steroids, as well as association with those who still did. At the 1989 Arnold Classic, for example, there had been a drug bust of Luiz Freitas, the 1987 Mr. Universe, for trafficking steroids. Regardless, his courtship of Bush paid off in January 1990, when the president officially appointed Arnold Schwarzenegger as the new chairman of the President's Council on Physical Fitness and Sports.

Arnold was ecstatic, taking what until then had been an honorary position and making it into an active one. Flying in his own jet and paying his own way, he visited all fifty states, meeting with the governors of all but Arkansas, where William Jefferson Clinton could not find the time. He staged the Great American Workout on the South Lawn of the White House and did a monumental job of publicizing the manifold benefits of exercise and sports. He made the position something it had not been before, and has not been since, a bully pulpit to get America off its flabby behind.

Arnold was sincerely trying to get millions of Americans to wake up to what a physically active life would do for them, while promoting his own potential political career. The chairmanship was like running for national office without any serious opponents and with nothing but endless applause and accolades. He was so active, so hands-on, that a few officials in Washington thought him overwhelming, but he motivated and excited most of those on the staff. Everything he did was a stepping-stone to something else, and the chairmanship was a shrewd choice for his first position in American political life. He was eminently suited for the job. He liked and admired President Bush, who was old enough to be his father, and was proud to be a part of his administration.

Arnold's newfound prominence as America's preeminent sports fitness cheerleader and his closeness to the Bush administration left him open to a constant string of people hitting him up for favors. One of the many supplicants was Danny Hernandez, who ran the Hollenbeck Youth Center in East Los Angeles. Hernandez was a pugnacious former Marine and Vietnam veteran who had built the center into a place where thousands of Latino children could learn to box and play basketball and other sports. He was a hustler, because if he did not hustle city officials, foundations, and business leaders, his kids wouldn't have their center.

"Arnold, man, I've got to talk to you, man," Danny told Arnold in his office at the old gasworks in Venice. "I want to make you Man of the Year. It's a big event, a fund-raiser for all our kids."

Such "honors" were, as Arnold knew, largely fund-raising devices, and if he was always skeptical, his staff was even more questioning. Nevertheless, he was impressed enough by Danny's presentation that he agreed to see him again. After fully vetting the operation, he agreed to be honored. That summer of 1991 he served as executive commissioner of the first Inner-City Games in which more than five thousand finalists participated in athletic events at Cal State.

That should have been it. Good deed done. Good publicity received. Another year. Another cause. Danny asked Arnold to be the executive commissioner for a second year. He received no response. Then in April 1992, after police officers involved in the beating of Rodney King were found not guilty, Los Angeles erupted in riots. The four days of turmoil caused $2 billion in damage and left fifty-five dead, along with a deeply troubled political and business establishment. There was a new urgency to help the inner city, and Arnold got Hernandez together with a group that included Maria, Bobby Shriver, and several Hollywood figures. They wanted to do something big and they wanted to do it immediately, and the Inner-City Games were an opportunity. They expanded the idea to include not just East L.A., but the entire city.

"Arnold committed to asking all of his celebrity friends to donate money, and we were able to raise $250,000," recalled Hernandez. The games that October took place at Cal State L.A., USC, and other institutions. They were such a success that not only did they become an important annual event but observers from other cities sought to replicate the games at home.

It had been Hernandez's idea, but Arnold was such an overwhelming force that he subsumed the Latino activist. The two men flew around the country in Arnold's jet to set up games in cities from Las Vegas to Miami. "Everywhere we went, there was support from celebrities, city officials, everyone," said Hernandez. "You see, we were two pure individuals saying, 'This can work. This is really happening.' I think that for this particular cause, it was something that came from love. And it shows. And we did our games."

Before quietly lobbying for the position with Bush, Arnold had taken care of another matter that could have haunted him. For all Arnold knew, the accusations about his father in *News of the World* might have been true. Gustav

Schwarzenegger rarely talked about his experiences during the war. The sins of the father are not rightfully vested on the son, but if Gustav was a war criminal, it could not help but taint Arnold. He decided that he had best learn the truth about his father, and he called Rabbi Hier to elicit his help. Arnold planned out much of his life years in advance. If he had not instigated a relationship with Hier and the Wiesenthal Center for precisely this purpose, he surely realized that it would help inoculate him against problems that his family background might create for him.

Hier says that Arnold called him and said bluntly: "Look, I'm in a sort of difficult situation. I'd like to know what my father did during the Second World War." Arnold told the rabbi that the subject had never been discussed in his home and that there were all kinds of rumors out there. He wanted to find out the truth, and he wanted to be sent the results directly.

Simon Wiesenthal was renowned for tracking down Nazi war criminals. Arnold could not have gone to a more authoritative place to learn the truth about his father. A number of weeks later Hier called Arnold to tell him the results. Hier told Arnold that his father had been a member of the Nazi Party, and they had found his party card. Beyond that, Heir said, there were no indications that Gustav Schwarzenegger had committed any war crimes.

The Simon Wiesenthal Center did not research far enough to learn that Arnold's father had joined the SA, the notorious "brownshirts," hardly something Gustav would have done unless he was a fervent Nazi. That may not have been an easy matter to find out, but certainly not as difficult as locating Nazi war criminals in South America.

It would not be until thirteen years later, when Arnold was running for governor, that the Wiesenthal Center reinvestigated Gustav's past—and then only after the *Los Angeles Times* had done its own investigative reporting and discovered in recently opened archives that Gustav had been a member of the notorious SA. The Wiesenthal Center went on to more fully document Schwarzenegger's war record as a sergeant in Unit 521 of the Feldgendarmerie, the military police. "We cannot say with absolute certainty that because . . . unit 521 has never been charged, that it did not participate in crimes against civilians," said Stefan Klemp, the historian who did the updated report. "My experience in research in Germany shows that often police units were never tried, sometimes not even investigated. However, what we have before us now shows no evidence of any crimes committed."

Although the new documents did not make Arnold's father a war criminal, they brought Gustav in direct proximity to some of the war's worst atrocities. That shadow in no way deserved to fall upon Arnold, who was born two years after the end of World War II. But in the heavily Jewish film industry such a revelation would have had an unsettling effect and probably revived some of the prejudices and suspicions that he had long since overcome.

There is no indication that Arnold was anything less than sincere in his request, and anything less than sincere in believing that Hier had come up with the full truth. With that unsettling matter seemingly resolved in Arnold's eyes, he began talking to the rabbi about growing up in Austria. Hier could tell that Arnold had been alienated from his father, and it troubled him that as a child he had learned almost nothing about the Nazi past, nothing about his father's war record, nothing about what his mother thought or felt, nothing in school, nothing.

If the Wiesenthal Center could find no records that Gustav had committed war crimes, it was unlikely that anyone else would, either. Arnold began taking a high-profile role within Hier's organization in Los Angeles. In 1991 he agreed to accept the Wiesenthal Center's National Leadership Award. This award for his humanitarian efforts was a watershed in his career. This was not given to honor Arnold simply because of his philanthropic concerns, but because he was a celebrity and a major drawing card. In agreeing to be honored, Arnold was equally agreeing to use his clout to make the dinner a success and to raise several million dollars.

Maria became the producer of the dinner, making sure that the elite of Hollywood were in full attendance at an event where President Bush would be an honored guest. She made sure that every aspect of the evening in the grand ballroom at the Century Plaza Hotel—from the table settings to the music—was first-class. Her goal was to make it an event that was almost as unthinkable of missing as the Academy Awards when you had a nomination. She was obsessed with details and did as good a job as any professional party planner.

There are endless fund-raising dinners in Hollywood, but few that are attended by the entirety of the film aristocracy. Almost every major studio head was there. The chairmen for the evening were Peter Guber of Sony and Jon Peters, formerly of Sony. The cochairs included the heads of MCA/Universal, Fox, Disney, Paramount, and Warner Brothers. The attendees were mainly Democrats but were there with President Bush and Arnold, paying up to $40,000 a table for the honor. Arnold and Maria had pulled it off, and the evening took him to an elevated place in the hierarchy of the American elite.

As Arnold basked in the warm glow of adulation from his Hollywood peers, he had a strange, determined foe obsessed with destroying him. His name was

Lacy H. Rich Jr. Though he made his living reproducing photos, his main goal was to bring down Arnold. He lived in a cluttered apartment in North Hollywood overrun with files, faxes, newspapers, dirty ashtrays, and unwashed dishes. Rich told some people that his hatred began when his friend Mike Mentzer was so devastated by his defeat in Sydney at the 1980 Mr. Olympia that he began a precipitous emotional decline. Rich managed the apartment building where the sadly diminished Mentzer lived, and Rich wanted to get even. But that is hardly enough to explain the depth of his hatred.

"We are talking today about a bodybuilder turned 'actor,' who potentially could become senator or governor, then President of the United States, if he could get the Constitution changed," Rich told Schwarzenegger biographer Nigel Andrews in an unattributed interview. "And with Arnold's track record I'm not sure he couldn't manage that. And I'm damned if I'm going to see this hypocrisy elected to public office in this country."

Rich did not like to be seen in person. He was a voice on the phone. He was a mysterious fax arriving in the middle of the night, pages and pages of material, everything from frontal nudes of Arnold to stills from porno movies involving Arnold's past associates to allegations of all kinds of excesses and crimes. Some revelations were true, more were partially true, and many were demonstrably false or had nothing to do with Arnold, all of them blended together in a venomous stew. He sought to bait Arnold and those who tried to protect him. He tried in every way to create a media confrontation.

Rich called Charlotte Parker and faxed her pages of the material that he was also sending to journalists and anyone else in the media. He said he went to see Joe Weider and tried to get to Arnold through him. He picketed the Weiders. "He hated everybody," Weider said. "He had a group walking in front of my house, saying that I hire illegals and create bodybuilders who are homosexuals and all that kind of crap."

Arnold ignored Rich's activities. "I paid absolutely no attention," he said. "He was no obstacle to my career, period. Absolutely none. He was just a lunatic that was sending around pictures of me in underwear and saying, 'Oh, Arnold had gay relationships.' You know, it was so ludicrous because everyone that knew me knew that this guy was totally out of whack. He was a sick guy and that was the end of that. Otherwise, I would have sued him if I would have felt that he was really doing anything to my career."

When the satire magazine *Spy* published a devastating article on Arnold in March 1992, Rich's name was not mentioned but he had played a role. The writer of the piece, Charles Fleming, says that Rich supplied a nude photo of Arnold that illustrated the story, but Rich's contributions probably went beyond that. Afterward, Rich talked about the piece as if he had almost written it, saying people had called to say that he "had a lot of courage to buck the system."

"Here was the star of these huge movies, making this huge amount of money, and yet there were these appalling things about him that nobody was willing to say," said Fleming. "Nobody was willing to discuss it, because of the way that he was wielding his Hollywood power—and that made him a target. Because he was behaving like such a bully, he was worth shooting at."

Spy was a witty magazine with an upscale audience, and the fact that it published the article suggested the distinction between the tabloids and the mainstream media was beginning to crumble—and anyone and anything was fair game. Much of the material was scurrilous and ugly and based almost exclusively on anonymous sources. "All right, so what if the rumors—confirmed for *Spy* by a businessman and longtime friend of Arnold's—that in the 1970s he enjoyed playing and giving away records of Hitler's speeches are true?" the article asked. "There's the journalist who mirthfully tells of the star's back lot misdeeds—how he surprised Arnold *in flagrante delicto* during the filming of one of his blockbusters and how Arnold said, 'Ve von't tell Maria about dis'—but who will never commit that story to print. And there's the movie executive who will tell you only in private, and never for attribution, about Arnold's occasional suggestions to the owner of a store where he shops that the two find some chicks who will perform an act Arnold calls 'polishing the helmet.' Arnold's rationalization, according to the store owner? 'It's not being unfaithful. It's only some plo-jobs.' Probably no one will ever quote the Hollywood producer who pals around with Arnold and says, 'He's an unstoppable womanizer, even worse than the Kennedys.'"

Fleming detailed in *Spy* how with Parker's help, Arnold controlled and manipulated his image, a task made easy by the symbiotic relationship between the entertainment reporters and Hollywood. The article stated that "by all accounts, he hopes to run for governor of California or the U.S. Senate" and "you can't help but wonder, for example, how campaign reporters would have treated the dinner at the Simon Wiesenthal Center. If Arnold were in the middle of a political campaign and were honored by a Holocaust philanthropy, some intrepid reporter would be digging into his past associations."

Fleming was one of the first reporters to write about Arnold's political ambition. He recalls how reporters came up to his desk at *Variety* after the article appeared, to "whisper things like 'Senator Schwarzenegger' and fall all over themselves laughing. And I just kept saying, 'Get off my back. I didn't say he was running for office. But you watch. You just watch. . . .'"

The *Spy* article had documented one of the essential problems of Arnold's putative political career. If Arnold decided to run for political office, these accusations and stories might spill over into the mainstream political media, irreparably sullying his reputation. Rich's efforts were a painful way for Arnold to see just how far these stories would go. Rich had already orchestrated a tabloid article alleging that Arnold had played Nazi music at a party in the early 1980s, and contributed to the *Spy* article.

In September 1992 Rich sent out yet another fax to a list of journalists and publicists, including Parker. "Coming in October will be the most complete outing Hollywood has ever seen. Thrill to week after week of gay outings of Hollywoods [sic] elite in words and picture. All the good ole boys that made Arnold possible. Yes they banded around him to cover his lies, now see if they band together to protect their own butts." Beneath the words was a full frontal nude of Arnold with the caption: "A Smoking Gun? Republican Moral Values? Bush sure can pick 'em!!"

October came and went without the media picking up on any of Rich's charges, and he continued his futile, doomed crusade. He wrote a pamphlet about his struggle against Arnold and in June 1995 placed several chapters on the Internet. Rich had become more and more marginalized, more and more possessed. In September he committed suicide. He and his obsession were gone, but his tales and accusations lived on as part of a whispered underground about Arnold's life.

Number One

In June 1990, while shooting parts of *Kindergarten Cop* in Oregon, Arnold saw a Hummer in a caravan of military vehicles. He thought the vehicle looked "ballsy" and decided he had to have one. "He just went ape for that machine," said his agent, Lou Pitt "I mean, it was big, it was unique, and it was something that was larger than him. He just loved the vehicle and what it could do and what it looked like and made him stand out in it and vice versa." Almost everything Arnold did was a subtle mixture of calculation and spontaneity. He immediately grasped what the Hummer could do for him and what he could do for the Hummer.

Arnold called the manufacturer, which had no interest in selling it to him. He called again. In the end, he convinced AMC that there would be a civilian market for the unlikely vehicle. He got one of the first Hummers, and he more than anyone else made it the macho man's choice of an SUV and one of the most unusual success stories in the automotive industry. He understood what he had done. He probably could have negotiated a massive promotional fee. Instead, when AMC sold Hummer to General Motors, he went to see Hummer general manager Mike DiGiovanni in Detroit in the summer of 1999. Arnold looked at a clay model of the new H2 and made substantive suggestions, particularly about the windshield, that were incorporated in the final vehicle.

That evening at a dinner with a group that included GM president Ron Zarrella, Arnold laid out plans for Hummer to sponsor the Inner-City Games that he was expanding into other cities. "He was thinking much bigger arrangements, very expensive, and there was no way we could afford it—we were two years away from production," said DiGiovanni. "I knew he was the foundation of the brand, but I couldn't afford it." The following spring, Arnold contacted the Hummer division again, with a more modest proposal. Hummer agreed to contribute $13 million over seven years. Hummer also became involved with awarding Hummers to the bodybuilding winners each year in Columbus.

In December 1990 Arnold made the cover of *Time* as "the movies' top star." In less than a decade, forty-three-year-old Arnold had made an astounding leap. Although he might have appeared little more than an oversize cartoon, he was a star who had intuitively grasped that America would sell ideas and images as its most important product. As with his Hummer, he was one of the torchbearers.

Arnold's horizons did not stop at the shores of America. "They see me as both American and European," he told *Time*. "And they know that I am not dealing with an American arrogance that says we are the kings. I go to Australia, even though there is no money there. If the Soviet Union would have a premiere of my film, I would go, because I know that *The Terminator* was the hottest tape on the black market. So my attitude is that you have to pay attention to the entire world. Everything is becoming very global, especially movies. Look what has happened overseas in the past five years with video and cable and TV. American companies are finally waking up and cleaning up. But they were not ahead of the game. Only because of demand are they waking up. We've got to look at everything as equally important."

That was an insight into the global economy that many economists and business leaders were just beginning to grasp, and it was only part of Arnold's understanding. Lou Pitt observed Arnold's own brilliant creation of a megaimage that led to his unique placement in modern popular culture. "When he got into the Hummer and cigars and sunglasses and his lifestyle, it was really about a branding of a lifestyle," said Pitt. "He went from being an icon to a life force in many ways because of his fitness program, his presence in that world, Hummer, his dress, the Hawaiian shirts, smoking cigars. His persona became so large, and he had such an extraordinary following that even people who didn't see his films or want to see his films fell in love with him because of that."

Since the earliest days of Hollywood, moviegoers have left theaters ready to emulate their favorite stars. In 1934, Clark Gable's taking off his shirt in *It Happened One Night* and revealing his bare chest is said to have led to a dramatic decline in sales of undershirts. Arnold's impact did not even always depend on a film.

In promoting bodybuilding, Arnold had learned that success can be the mother of failure. He and Lorimer had done such a great job handling the Mr. Olympia contest that the Weiders decided to take it away from them. They said that they wanted to move it around the world, helping to expand bodybuilding.

The two partners put on other contests during much of the eighties, but at the end of the decade Arnold had an ambitious idea. "I think that probably my image is now at the point where we ought to have a contest called the Arnold Classic," he told Lorimer. He talked about it as if discussing a kind of currency. "I think that's a great idea," said Lorimer, who had as solid an under-standing of Arnold's possibilities as anyone.

The first annual Arnold Classic took place in the spring of 1989. The event became not only the second-most-important title in bodybuilding but also the most innovative competition, fostering more aesthetic presentations. Vendors sold dietary supplements and workout equipment. Each year a growing number of other sports had their own contests, so that bodybuilding became only a small part of the celebratory weekend of athletic events.

Arnold also agreed to lend his name in partial exchange for equity in a new Columbus shopping center, the Easton Town Center, and he became increasingly a part of the Ohio world. In 1994, when Arnold wanted to purchase the army tank he had driven during his military service in Austria, the vehicle was literally dug up, refurbished, and shipped to America. The tank first sat at a Planet Hollywood at the upscale mall. When the restaurant closed for good, Arnold had the chance to drive the tank around the grounds. Then he loaned the military vehicle to the Motts Military Museum outside Columbus, where it sits today. He visits the tank periodically to show his kids what their dad used to do.

Arnold always had to be on the edge, testing the limits of his invincibility, but not when it came to the roles he played. Arnold was the biggest star in the world, and he chose films that he believed would help him stay on top. The only role he was interested in reprising was that of the Terminator, almost the emblem of his film career.

One morning Arnold was sitting in his Santa Monica restaurant Schatzi on Main discussing the project with Cameron. "All right, now here's the concept," Cameron said as Arnold listened intensely. "The Terminator comes back and he is going to protect John Connor and he doesn't kill anyone."

"But *I'm* the Terminator," Arnold said as if Cameron was trying to steal his birthright. "I have to terminate. That's what the audience wants to see, me kicking in the doors, machine-gunning everybody."

"But you don't do that in this film."

"But that's the character," Arnold insisted.

As he had done with *Total Recall,* he was the crucial person in helping bring together the various elements. First came Carolco, with the resources and daring to spend $94 million on the most expensive film in history to that point. The studio would not have made such a massive commitment without James Cameron once again directing. Linda Hamilton also returned as the female lead. In lieu of salary, Arnold took one of the baubles of a megastar's life, a $12 million Gulfstream GIII plane, plus a cut of the film's profits.

Terminator 2: Judgment Day begins in the ruins of L.A., leveled in a nuclear holocaust on August 29, 1997, that around the world killed 3 billion people. In the L.A. rubble live the remnants of free men and women, fighting a guerrilla war against computer-controlled machines that dominate the ravaged earth. The machines' greatest challenge is the rebel leader, John Connor. To thwart him, the machines send the robot Terminator T-1000 (Robert Patrick) back in time to 1994. T-1000 is a perfect image of a human being. Its mission is to kill the boy John Connor so that he will not grow up to become the machine's most dangerous enemy. The resistance sends back its own Terminator T-800 (Arnold) to protect the boy so that the tyranny will not inevitably triumph.

Early on, when T-800 in black leather jacket and sunglasses rides on a Harley-Davidson motorcycle along a California highway, we are seeing the ultimate manifestation of Arnold's film image. At the time of the 1990–91 filming, Arnold's awesome physicality was at its prime and there was iconic depth to his countenance. The Terminator is only a machine with a computer chip for a soul, but it is constantly learning. In its interactions with young John (Edward Furlong) and his mother, Sarah (Linda Hamilton), T-800 begins to understand what it means to be a human being and to have feelings and moral values.

Most of Arnold's films are wars against the dehumanized totalitarianism of the modern Western world. In *Total Recall* the despotic government controls the very air on Mars and cuts it off for those who fight against its hegemony. In *The Running Man* television itself is the great engine of enslavement. Even in the comedy *Twins,* the Arnold character and his brother are the products of the malevolent excesses of scientific experimentation funded by the U.S. government.

In film after film, Arnold's characters define themselves through forceful assertion against the antihuman forces of death and control. "Remember the message," Sarah's late husband tells her in a dream in *Terminator 2*. "The future is not set. There is no fate but what we make for ourselves." That is almost precisely what the wise mutant leader Kuato tells Arnold's character, Quaid, in *Total Recall*: "You are what you do. A man is defined by his actions, not his memory."

Arnold always learned from whatever he was doing, including these roles that literally involved years of his life. He incorporated them into his own political and cultural image of modern society. He, too, believed that individual man fashioned his individual fate, and that destiny is a creation of each of us in a free society.

In the end, the most deeply generously human in *Terminator 2* is the Terminator, who has no heart or soul. He is able to destroy not only his dark nemesis from the future but also the technology that brought with it nuclear fire and the tyranny of the machines. He is the only manifestation left of that technology. As long as he exists, others may use that technology for evil purposes. Thus, the Terminator makes the deeply moral, heroic decision to destroy himself. In the final scene, T-800 lets himself down into a boiling caldron of molten steel. Then in a voice-over, Sarah speaks the film's last words: "The unknown future rolls toward us, and I face it for the first time with a sense of hope. If a computer can learn the value of human life, maybe we can, too. . . ."

That those final words are so powerfully moving is a tribute to Arnold's performance. It is a subtle, nuanced piece of work, half lost behind the elaborate makeup, the brilliant special effects, the endless one-liners, and the spectacular action scenes. But his performance is nonetheless the heart of what is one of the best action films of all time. In terms of Arnold's highest goal of worldwide popularity, *Terminator 2: Judgment Day* proved his biggest film when it opened in the summer of 1991. It grossed $204 million in the United States and Canada and $312 million in the rest of the world, making it the thirty-fourth-biggest film of all time.

For a number of years, Arnold had talked to George Butler about buying all rights to *Pumping Iron*. Years before, Butler had hired a truck and driver to haul about 120 hours of outtakes from a New York City office to the cellar of his New Hampshire home. He knew that Arnold's soliloquies about Nazism could prove embarrassing; however, the photographer considered them "a lot of smoking Derringers, but no smoking guns."

Arnold was more concerned with unfortunate pictures from the past than any inappropriate remarks he might have made. Among the eight thousand or so photographs that Butler had taken, there was a series of nude photographs, including some with a woman bodybuilder that a regular reader of *Playboy* would have appreciated but were hardly images you wanted to become public if you had political ambitions.

Butler had the images appraised for a million dollars, a figure based not on their artistic merit but on the price the tabloids would likely have paid for them. Arnold agreed to pay $1.25 million for the film rights to *Pumping Iron* and the outtakes. The deal memorandum also gave Arnold's friend Neal Nordlinger the right to examine the photo collection and, with Butler's concurrence, "destroy any of such photographs and negatives of such photographs, as well as copies thereof, which in Nordlinger's opinion are either embarrassing to Schwarzenegger or in any way reflect negatively on Schwarzenegger's professional or private life." Butler knew just how litigious Arnold could be. Although Butler agreed to the destruction of what he says were forty-three photographs, he insisted that Arnold acknowledge that he owned and had the right to sell all of the other photographs.

Freed of the potential embarrassment of his early nude photos and with his film and protopolitical career burgeoning, Arnold had every right to feel good. By the early 1990s, in fact, Arnold was seen to be full of what one of his closest associates called "grandiosity and a feeling of omnipotence." Hubris was an occupational hazard for megastars. It was not unusual that Arnold had come down with the malady, only that it had taken so long and that he had such a bad case of it. Lou Pitt had a client looking for a surefire hit.

Weekends are the only time in Hollywood that much reading gets done, and on Friday afternoons, like every other major agent, Pitt went home with a bunch of scripts. "This is a weekend read around town, and I think it's going to go for a lot," a Columbia TriStar executive told Pitt one Friday in November 1991. "Would you read it and see if you think it's something for Arnold?"

Pitt read every page of the spec screenplay by twenty-three-year-old Zak Penn and twenty-four-year-old Adam Leff. It was a comedic thriller in which an alienated kid is sucked through a movie screen to join his favorite action hero to go on a merry, bloody romp. Pitt loved it. "I'm not telling you to buy it or not buy it," he told the exec Monday morning, "but I think this is a really terrific idea and if done right, it could be fantastic. But I'm not promising Arnold will read it, let alone do it. So you guys decide."

TriStar bought the script, and a few weeks later Pitt called the film executives to say that Arnold had read it and was interested. He was "interested" in half a dozen other potential films, too, a way to keep the studios off balance and to make sure he got the best deal. Even if he had a favorite project, he did not let anyone know. Arnold chose his projects with the instincts of a marketer, not a filmmaker, and his marketing began in the nature of the screenplay.

Arnold was a kind of populist cultural politician who judged himself not by the number of votes he received but by the number of tickets he sold. Arnold had his action-movie fans and his comedy fans, and he wanted to expand his audience even further. He was attuned to the popular consciousness as well as anyone in Hollywood, and he sensed a reaction against the ultraviolent films that were his forte. In some measure, the whole genre had become a cliché-ridden formula of blood and guts, with a large but ultimately limited audience. A new generation of parents wanted something different to see with their kids. Family-oriented films such as *Home Alone* and *Back to the Future Part III* were going gangbusters. If you wanted a shot at $100 million grosses, this is where the action was.

"I just feel we are at a time where people want to see less graphic violence, and I think if that's what people want, then that's what you ought to give them," Arnold told *The Boston Globe*'s Jay Carr in 1993. "People want to go much more as a whole family. I feel very much influenced by the public, because I want to do the movies for the public, not for me. So I listen and get a feeling for what works and what doesn't."

Everyone in Hollywood wanted to do business with the biggest star in the world, and hardly anyone cared what the project was as long as Arnold was in it. That was flattering, but it also made it very difficult for him to make good, unbiased decisions. In January, Peter Guber, chairman and CEO of Sony Pictures (including Columbia and TriStar), and other top executives paid deference to the star by driving from their offices in Culver City to Arnold's new restaurant, Schatzi on Main, in Santa Monica for lunch.

Arnold had no illusions that the row of top executives were sitting there across from him because they loved his saintly form. They sat there because he was money in the bank. Arnold explained that he liked the idea of the film, but not the screenplay. "Having a kid come into a movie awakened certain fantasies I had as a kid in Austria," he said. "What would it be like to sit on John Wayne's saddle, or have him come with this huge horse right out of the screen? The script had a great concept, but it wasn't executed professionally."

The screenplay was about what one would expect from two fledgling screenwriters. They had already been paid off to make way for some of the top talent in Hollywood to rewrite the script for Arnold. "The best thing would have been if we could have told Arnold, 'We have Jesus Christ rewriting this,'" one of the luncheon participants told Aljean Harmetz of *The New York Times*. Short of Him, there was no one they were not willing to attach to the project. They brought in a hot young writer, Shane Black, for a million dollars to rewrite what was now called *Last Action Hero*. Black brought in his friend David Arnott for $250,000. Arnold wasn't that happy with the results, so the studio brought in his choice of a director, John McTiernan. And yet Arnold still was not willing to commit to the film.

It was not only Arnold who was unhappy. Maria had become Arnold's most opinionated adviser. Many of the professionals around the star dreaded her input, feeling she had tin ears for the nuances of filmmaking. "Creatively, she's a complete wash," said one close observer. "And yet she inserts herself in a way that asserts, 'I know what I'm doing.' And she doesn't."

Not all of Arnold's close advisers felt that way. "I never got back from any of the meetings that Maria attended where she was a negative," said Jake Bloom, Arnold's longtime lawyer. "Arnold always made his own decisions on anything. If she was there, he wanted her there, but she didn't tell him what movies to do. There were a bunch of pictures she didn't want him to do that he did."

As much good as Maria did for Arnold, she also turned her hypercritical eye on her husband. Several of his associates felt her judgments resulted in a never-before-seen uncertainty about himself. Maria's defenders say that observation is totally wrong. She attended many of Arnold's meetings with his agent and producers, speaking up as if she were his manager. Some of the participants found Maria's contributions valuable and essential, while others felt that she was sitting where she did not belong, speaking with a boldness and certitude that her words scarcely merited.

Maria's presence made her a convenient target for criticism. "It's very easy to blame the woman," says Maria. "When Arnold didn't pick a certain movie, people used to say it's because I said no. I had nothing to do with it. Some of the times, I'd never even seen the script, but I would hear all the time, 'It's because she wants him to be in PG movies,' or, 'She wants him to be in movies that kids can go to.' That was a terrible accusation. I'm very clear about what I think I've done in Arnold's career and in his life, and I'm very comfortable with it."

Whatever her weaknesses, Maria was almost alone in confronting Arnold with the most forceful, definitive judgments. Maria did not like the whole idea of *Last Action Hero* and preferred that her husband do a comedy called *Sweet*

Tooth. Arnold's buddies started calling him "the Tooth Fairy," an appellation that hardly made the project more appealing.

Arnold finally agreed to do *Last Action Hero* if the studio would bring in the celebrated screenwriter William Goldman to add "emotion." Goldman went ahead, earning $750,000 for his four weeks of work. Arnold was the star and the coproducer, and he controlled practically everything about the film: a director he liked, the costars with whom he worked, the advertising, and the promotion. It was his film, and Columbia crowed about its coup at landing Arnold in what surely would be the biggest hit of the summer of 1993.

Last Action Hero

When Arnold flew to Nice to attend the Cannes Film Festival a month before the mid-June opening of *Last Action Hero*, he was met at the airport by a studio limousine from Sony/Columbia. The black sedan drove slowly through the narrow streets of the Mediterranean resort and along the fabled road in front of the beachfront hotels so that he could see the scores of banners with the words LAST ACTION HERO emblazoned on them. A few days later Stallone arrived at the airport to be picked up by a studio limousine from Columbia TriStar, which was producing his forthcoming film, *Cliffhanger*. The driver drove into Cannes and along the Croisette by a different route, one lined with banner after banner celebrating Stallone's summer film and almost nothing promoting his competitor's film.

Stallone might have had as many banners, but no one bested Arnold in promotion. He had already started touting *Last Action Hero*. Columbia had only twelve and a half minutes of footage to show the assembled journalists at Cannes, so the burden fell even more heavily on Arnold. At a lavish dinner at Hôtel du Cap, he told the three hundred VIP guests that *Last Action Hero* will be "huge, large. It's monstrous. It's gigantic." That week he bragged that he did fifty-four print and forty TV interviews in a single day, running the journalists through his suite one after another. Arnold's presence in Cannes had been amplified by a seventy-five-foot-tall, twenty-foot-wide gun-toting Arnold riding on a barge a mile offshore, looking like a lost balloon from the Macy's Thanksgiving Day Parade. When the photographers arrived for a sunset shoot, the monumental Arnold balloon deflated, as if tired of publicity. The other promotion that did not work out was Columbia's plan to pay $500,000 to splash the words *Last Action Hero* on a NASA rocket launched the same time as the premiere.

"Arnold was often extreme: let's do it bigger and better than anybody," said Sid Ganis, then Columbia's president of marketing and distribution. By the day that the film opened in theaters, Arnold made sure that he was everywhere, from television ads to billboards, from posters and *Last Action Hero* cups at Burger King to the aisles of Toys "R" Us, with hundreds of the new *Last Action Hero* Mattel figures personally approved by Arnold. When he was first shown the toys, he dismissed the Mattel executives and told Danny Simon, a licensing executive, "I hate the fucking line. There's all this violence and it's not explained. Fix it."

Even before the movie opened, there was bad buzz on the film. Arnold was still out shooting action shots and adding dialogue only a few weeks before *Last Action Hero* opened, which is generally not a good sign. He wrote off all the negative rumors to jealousy, the strongest emotion in Hollywood. "Everyone in this town is jealous of the next guy," Arnold said. "They're all a bunch of jealous bitches sitting around saying, 'I hope he takes a dive.'"

"What happens in Hollywood is every year they pick on someone and take someone down. They look for a crack and if they find the crack they will move in. Because I had had the number one box-office hit of the previous year, it was, 'Hey, where can we find a crack?'"

Although Arnold did not know it, much of the bad buzz had been orchestrated by an anonymous source who was feeding negative material about the studio to leading media outlets. Arnold had gone to Columbia only because it had cut the deal for the movie he wanted to make, but he found himself in the midst of a vicious internecine struggle to bring down the top executives. "Hollywood is a cannibal that loves to eat its young," said coproducer and friend Neal Nordlinger. "People had a lot of animus toward the executives Peter Guber and Mark Canton. And, of course, there was animus toward Arnold as well."

The studio had a "deep throat," a man who lied to reporters that he was a Columbia studio executive. In one of his first messages, the source tried peddling a story that *Last Action Hero* had done badly in a preview. Reporters at *The Hollywood Reporter* could not verify the account and refused to publish it. The story made it into print at the *Los Angeles Times* on June 6, a week and a half before the movie opened. Jeffrey Wells, a freelance writer, reported that numerous sources, including "actors, directors and film industry executives to social workers, body builders and dental technicians," confirmed that there had been a screening about two weeks earlier at Pasadena's UA Marketplace cinema. Columbia denied that the screening took place, and Wells concluded that the studio wanted to keep it quiet because the audience had so disliked the film. In Hollywood, the worst news is often the best news, and there was hardly anyone beyond the Columbia loyalists who believed the executives.

"We suffered, because the *L.A. Times* didn't care that day," said Ganis. "Journalism wasn't that important." The marketing president was so upset that he personally went downtown to the newspaper office to protest. When that got the studio nowhere, Ganis did what he in retrospect calls "a stupid thing." The week Arnold's film was opening, just when all the attention should have been on *Last Action Hero*, the studio revved up its fight with the *Los Angeles Times* by vowing to have nothing to do with California's premier paper unless it stopped carrying Wells's stories. The daily stood its ground, and the reporter justified himself to *The New York Times* by saying "that his article sought only to convey the rumors about a screening." That is not at all what he had conveyed to the media-savvy readers, including film critics who had reason to believe that *Last Action Hero* was a bomb. In reality, as Peter Bart reported in *Variety*, "a film was previewed in Pasadena, but it was *Rising Sun*, the upcoming Fox project, and this information never overtook the rumor."

On June 9, just days before *Last Action Hero* opened, twenty-seven-year-old Heidi Fleiss was arrested for sexual pandering, pimping, and narcotics. Soon afterward, the secret source called reporters, giving them detailed information about Fleiss's call-girl ring that serviced Hollywood executives and stars. Fleiss later claimed that one of *Last Action Hero*'s producers was a regular customer, and there were rumors of her girls appearing as extras in the film.

In the first days that Hollywood whispered fervidly about the ring, Charlotte Parker worked to make sure that Arnold's name was kept out of any stories of purported acts on the set of his latest film. That did not stop the eventual mention of allegations about activities on the set of *Last Action Hero*. "Sources close to alleged Hollywood madam Heidi Fleiss told *The Hollywood Reporter* that women who worked for her had been sent to the set and they believed that part of the payment may have been listed as 'masseuse' expenses," wrote Anita Busch in *The Hollywood Reporter* in August. The trade publication said that the studio was reportedly under investigation by the IRS for the misuse of corporate funds; nothing more was heard of the matter.

On the June morning when Arnold was about ready to begin the media marathon to coincide with the opening of *Last Action Hero*, Parker took him aside to tell him that earlier in the day she had read the first reviews, and some of them were devastating. She had seen bad reviews, but there had usually been some wit or generosity in the criticism. These were ugly, almost personal, as if the writers had been waiting for the opportunity to unload a decade's worth of venom. The publicist would have liked to drive around the reviews like an accident on the highway, but she knew that Arnold would be asked about them, and as tough as it was, she felt she had to tell him.

Variety called *Last Action Hero* "a joyless, soulless machine of a movie," while the *Los Angeles Daily News* said it was "the last big, loud, ugly thing of the summer, a case study of how intellectually ambitious material can be botched." For the *Los Angeles Times*, it was "an awkward mixture of overproduced action and underwhelming comedy, this ponderous joy ride is more notable for how strenuously it's been promoted than for how much pleasure it delivers."

When Arnold met the first group of writers in a suite at a Beverly Hills hotel, he pretended that all was right with the world, making eye contact with the five journalists, shaking their hands firmly, and sitting down as if ready to devour a banquet of life.

An Atlanta critic began by quoting from the current cover story of *Entertainment Weekly* that said Arnold's days were over, he was a symbol of the eighties, "as much an archetype of the decade as junk bonds, Republican presidents and Madonna."

Arnold almost never showed his irritation to interviewers, but he greeted the question with testy silence and a killer stare. "First of all I don't believe that eras fall into neat decades," he said. "Second of all, I'm not a product of any era. I'm a product of myself."

The critics were either so uninterested in his film or so negative that they asked no questions about *Last Action Hero*, only about Arnold's life. After their allotted time with the star, Parker entered the suite to take him to the next group. "This movie is the ultimate entertainment," Arnold asserted as he left, trying to stamp the group with his ersatz optimism. "People will love it. You'll see."

As the film dropped off dramatically and seemed poised to be one of the classic debacles, right alongside *Ishtar* and *Howard the Duck*, the attack went from the film to Arnold personally. The New York *Daily News* depicted Arnold as uncharitable. The *Los Angeles Times* suggested that Arnold liked dealing only with reporters happy to be "Schwarzeneggered." *USA Today*'s headline was something Arnold had never seen before: SCHWARZENEGGER'S STAR DIMMING.

There is no way to gauge the impact that the Wells story in the *Los Angeles Times* had on the film's reception, but it became a major focal point for all the anger over *Last Action Hero*'s disappointing reception. Arnold developed a highly justified suspicion of a *Los Angeles Times* that was willing to let such falsehood stand despite its pretensions to journalistic excellence.

Last Action Hero was a creative failure in part because the script had been written not for millions of moviegoers but for Arnold. The script had jagged bits and pieces of too many good ideas tearing into one another. In the film, Danny Madigan, a child of divorce played by Austin O'Brien, fantasizes about his favorite action hero, the megastar Jack Slater (Arnold). With the help of a magic ticket, the wildly imaginative youth projects himself through the screen of an old movie theater right into the middle of the latest Jack Slater film. He and his hero romp through scenes of a typical Arnold/Sly shoot-'em-up, with buckets of blood and arsenals of weapons.

The film is not that scary and it is not that funny. In trying to satirize the whole idea of action heroes and blood-tinged comic-book movies, *Last Action Hero* makes fun of Arnold himself and the millions of people who had bought tickets to his movies.

The film's failure became such a major topic in Hollywood that Peter Bart wrote a public memo about it in the trade publication *Variety*. "Part of the problem is of your own making," Bart wrote. "In your exuberance at achieving stardom, you've managed to develop some serious syndromes. At the preview of 'Last Action Hero,' did you really have to say, 'I've turned out another great movie and everyone seems to love it and the critics have already said that it's a great summer hit.' Chill out, Arnold. It's understandable that you want to pitch 'Last Action Hero,' but how many Planet Hollywoods can you open in one year? Most stars do an occasional magazine cover, but the newsstands these days present a sea of Schwarzenegger. Forget the bravado, the hard-sell aphorisms, the self-hype. Cool down. Relax. All of a sudden everyone will forget you're the bad guy of the moment and start loving you again."

Arnold had expected to go head-to-head with *Jurassic Park*, but Steven Spielberg's film demolished *Last Action Hero*, earning over half a billion dollars worldwide, one of the biggest films of all time. Arnold thought he had lapped Stallone for good, but *Cliffhanger* overwhelmed his film, too. *Last Action Hero* was not the total disaster everyone said it was. It cost about $120 million to make and market, and took in about the same amount worldwide, coming close to breaking even. Still, much of the media considered *Last Action Hero* one of the great failures of modern filmmaking.

The film failed in part because Arnold was Hollywood's golden cow of endless bounty. Columbia was so revved up for its Arnold film that the screenplay was okayed before it was ready, and the film was pushed through production far more quickly than it should have been. It had taken fifteen years to produce *Total Recall* because the script did not have a third act. Neither does this film, as Nordlinger admits. If Arnold had waited and let *Last Action Hero* simmer, he might have had a brilliant film to elevate his career to a level it had never been.

Both Pitt and Parker sensed that Arnold was upset by the poor reaction as never before and was depressed in a way they had never seen him. Parker had tried to do a professional job, to be honest with her client and temper the negative media. In the green room at *The Tonight Show*, a few hours after the publicist had first apprised Arnold of the negative reviews, Maria turned to Parker and said: "You upset Arnold. I never want you to upset Arnold again."

"Maria is unbelievably protective," said Arnold. "She will destroy if she feels someone is trying to do harm to me. She felt it was totally inexcusable to come to me, saying, 'Here are these disastrous reviews,' when she could have said, 'There are some good ones and some bad ones, but who cares?' I toned it down. I said, 'Maria, don't worry about it. We're going to move on with this.'"

As Arnold saw it, Charlotte Parker had violated one of his basic emotional tenets. "I have a support system around me with everything, and I have always despised when people came to me in the morning with bad news. In my office somebody would put down a bad *USA Today* review on my desk, and later in the day there would come in twenty great quotes from reviews, and I would go ballistic. I would say, 'What schmuck would put a bad review there when I walk into the office when we have twenty good reviews?' When you're successful, people take a certain joy looking you in the eye and giving you a bad review. I don't need that. I need always positive reinforcement and then face reality."

Parker knew that no one loved Arnold more than Maria did. If she was upset, it could only be that Arnold had been overwhelmingly affected by the reviews, in a way that even his longtime publicist had missed. There had been no good reviews to show Arnold, and Parker found Maria's comments unsettling. Although she continued to do her job the way she thought she had to, there was a new element of uncertainty and new demands. "I was a miracle worker as it was, but now there was no limit to what he felt should or could be done," said Parker. "That was the beginning of the end."

As she does whenever her husband is suffering or needy, Maria came forward to protect Arnold. "Maria means well, and her every waking breath is for him," said one close friend. "But I think she's the reason why during those years his decline happened so enormously. He kept losing more and more parts of himself. And she—always well-meaning—was taking away from him who he was. You know, knocking his legs out from under him, saying, 'You're going to look like an idiot.' She didn't like his friends, low-class, vulgar. She brought in more and more of her people and made them his."

"Arnold's friends could not be Maria's friends," says another close friend.

Arnold was not the same toward Pitt, either. "People like Maria and Arnold, they're not really good about publicly admitting mistakes," said one of their closest friends. "So, what do they do after *Last Action Hero* crashed? He fires Lou Pitt, who had been his agent and had been the most loyal person forever and ever. And then hires this guy, Robert Stein, just because his wife was friends with Maria. Maria encouraged Arnold to hire him, and he never really did much, either."

It was not until four years later that Arnold fired Pitt. The star considered loyalty one of the essential virtues, and if you were loyal to him and doing your job, he was going to try to be loyal to you. But several sources say that Maria's harping began to take hold of his judgment. Maria claims that she had nothing to do with Pitt and Parker's relationship with Arnold, another example of her being blamed for something that did not involve her. She says she was opposed to her husband hiring her friend's husband as his agent: "I said, 'Well, what will happen if in fact it doesn't work out? I don't want to lose my girlfriend.'"

Both Pitt and Parker had served Arnold well, and it would have been better for everyone if he had simply ended the relationships, but he could not bring himself to do so. Arnold takes issue with the idea that he blamed them for his professional difficulties. "Charlotte Parker was a hardworking woman who was killing herself for me, and Lou Pitt was a hardworking agent who was killing himself for me," he says. "That's the way it is. Everyone was trying to make winners, but you just can't make winners all the time."

Arnold distanced himself from Parker, made the publicist the convenient repository for his self-doubts, and blamed her for any less-than-stellar presentations in the media. In the early years, Parker had talked to Arnold almost every day, but now her phone calls were not always returned, and she often had to make decisions based on her own instincts. She was not getting his scripts to read any longer. He could be curt and mean to her, not only in private, but in situations in which others witnessed it.

Parker had been absolutely crucial to his rise to worldwide stardom. Together they had orchestrated a brilliant image campaign. He had paid her what any other public relations flack would have charged, but the salary she earned was hardly commensurate with all she had done for Arnold. Finally, after one rebuke too many, she left her longtime employer, staying loyal to him and his secrets. She continued in public relations, serving an impressive list of film and corporate clients.

As for Pitt, his company was earning 10 percent of Arnold's millions, and he hung in there. Pitt brought many valuable projects to his client, and it was not the agent's fault that Arnold passed on them. One of the most intriguing projects was *Crusades*, about the medieval European attempt to take back the Holy Land from the Muslims. It was an epic idea, with Arnold starring as an eleventh-century knight. Pitt went to New York City to talk to Martin Scorsese about taking on the mammoth project. The idea of putting together Arnold and Scorsese was a daring one, and Pitt was delighted that the director of *Taxi Driver* and *Raging Bull* responded so positively. The agent set up a meeting at a studio in Los Angeles for the two men to get together for the first time and discuss the project.

Arnold had impeccable manners for a movie star. In the hierarchy of show business, he and Scorsese were equals. It was no small statement when Arnold showed up many minutes late for their hour-long meeting. Pitt was upset, but the two men hit it off amazingly well, trading compliments and inside stories. The agent was delighted things were working out so well but disappointed that the two enjoyed musing about past films so much that they ended up talking little about *Crusades*.

Enough had been said that it was up to Arnold to take the next step, but it never happened. "I don't think Arnold believed in it," Pitt reflected. "I don't think he wanted to pursue it. And it was criminal that [it] didn't happen. One might think it had to do with Arnold's insecurities, but, you know, it's never about schedules. It's always about, does this make sense or is this a great idea? And for Arnold, it was an inspired idea, and the shame is that it never happened."

Pitt had other strong ideas, including putting Arnold together with Tom Clancy, but that did not work out, either. "I think Arnold's problem was that he had too much control," said John Milius. "I think that what happened in his movie career was that he tried to second-guess everything. When he was daring and just went out and made things and said, 'I'll just do this, I'll try something like this,' and he tried something different and more daring, then they really worked. When he tried to make Arnold movies, they failed."

The biological clock beats nowhere more loudly than in Hollywood, and Arnold was a forty-six-year-old action hero in a young man's business. He was not a star who could see himself evolving into character roles. And so, after the failure of *Last Action Hero*, for the most part he returned to what he believed would sell best, films that were little more than comfortable formulas.

Private Lives

In the predawn darkness of a winter's morning, Arnold's Gulfstream jet lifted out of Van Nuys Airport. Arnold's day had begun several hours before. He had already been at work at four A.M., sitting in front of the fireplace, smoking a cigar when Sven Thorsen arrived. Arnold continued making business calls to Europe and finishing up some paperwork with his secretary for another hour or so before the two friends headed off in the waiting limousine for a day of skiing at Mammoth, three hundred miles north of the city.

John Milius, another of Arnold's friends, believes that his life began to change when Arnold got his own jet, with its two pilots and stewardess. If there is a meaningful symbol of being a member of the American elite, it is owning your own private jet. Flying across the country in first-class on American Airlines was hardly the best way to touch the heart and soul of America, but at least he was in the same plane with his fellow citizens and had to go in and out of airports, where people approached him.

Arnold saw it otherwise. He had more money than most human beings but no more time, so he traded whatever money it took to buy a little more time. Schlepping up narrow roads to Mammoth was hardly his idea of pleasure. Arnold had a European attitude toward happiness. His life was not a restless pursuit of pleasure, running aimlessly from one diversion to the next. His work was finished for the day, and he was there with his friend, flying off to have fun. That did not wait until they got to the double-diamond runs to begin amusing themselves. They were already laughing and joking en route.

Thorsen helped himself to an ample breakfast served by the stewardess and had a glass or two of champagne. It was an exquisite morning to be flying high above southern California. Then one of the pilots came back to talk to

Arnold. "We can't land in Mammoth because there's bad weather," the pilot said. "But what about Heavenly Valley and Lake Tahoe?" The ski resort was another 200 miles north.

"Good," Arnold said, and returned to his breakfast. The plane landed at Lake Tahoe Airport in northern California, where a limousine and a ski instructor were waiting. Arnold and Sven made it to Heavenly Valley in time for the first run of the day. They skied with an instructor so they did not have to wait in line, and they made a good twenty-five straight runs before they had had enough. Arnold was back home in Los Angeles before dusk.

Arnold enjoyed skiing so much that he purchased a house in Sun Valley, Idaho, where he usually spent the Christmas holidays. Maria's brother Tim often went to the ski resort at the same time, as did a number of Hollywood celebrities whom Arnold numbered among his friends. When Arnold's political idol Ronald Reagan converted to the Republican Party in the early fifties, his close friends became wealthy Republican businessmen who advanced the movie star's political career. Arnold was every bit as Republican as Reagan, but he had almost no friends from the GOP. There were not that many conservatives in Hollywood, but he could have found some. If you looked around one of Arnold's parties in either Los Angeles or Sun Valley, there often was not a single other Republican in the room.

Before he bought the Sun Valley home, Arnold flew to Austria almost every December to go skiing at Schladming in the Styrian Alps. His mother spent part of the winter months in the ski village, and he saw much of Aurelia and skied with friends, among them the Austrian ski champion Charly Kahr. In the summer Arnold returned to his native land, where he tried as best he could to be part of the surroundings and enjoy a respite from celebrity. A local lawyer, Dr. Hans-Moritz Pott, happened to be high up in the Alps one afternoon, at a point where the shepherds took their flocks for summer pasture. The only structure was a stone building that served as a tavern for the herders. The attorney went into the building and was startled to see Arnold and Kahr off in the corner, having a drink, looking like a couple of grizzled shepherds.

In some ways, Arnold could be more himself in Styria than anywhere else. One year he flew there accompanied by Franco Columbu, Bobby Shriver, and Lou Pitt. Even though it was already evening, Arnold insisted on going shopping before everything closed. He was the king of shoppers, constantly replenishing his wardrobe. Although he intended to shop—and to shop meant to buy—he also wanted to say hello to an old friend who was the manager of a department store.

Arnold and his friends walked rapidly from the Grand Hotel Wiesler, where Arnold was given the finest suite, across a bridge over the River Mur, loping along toward the Hauptplatz, the plaza in the center of Graz. As they reached the Hauptplatz, they came across a group of schoolchildren returning from an outing. The teacher was startled to see Arnold and asked if the children might sing a song to him. "It was a coming home for him," Pitt said. "I could tell he was very touched by it. From where we were in the square to where the department store was, was maybe a thousand yards. Arnold is a talker, but he never opened his mouth and was just silent until we got to the building. And then we went in and bought Austrian jackets."

Arnold's most memorable moments in Styria were not always so sublime. Another year Sven was there next to Arnold's mother when he was giving a speech. "I'm so happy to be back here in Austria," he said, pausing a moment so the audience could imbibe his compliment, "because in this country, women have nice asses."

Arnold was a connoisseur of that part of the female anatomy, and it was like Martha Stewart commenting lyrically on a soufflé, but it was hardly appropriate. "His mom got so fucking upset with him, she was so embarrassed," said Sven. "We all looked at each other, as if to say, 'What is he doing now? What is he doing now?' But people loved it. He had this charming way, whereas if *you* said 'nice asses,' they would probably arrest you."

Arnold was right in his supposition that Maria would be a hands-on, all-consuming mother. Her brothers often made fun of their sister and all the help that she had, but they did so playfully, knowing that she used the help to enhance her life and her experience as a parent, not to push responsibility off on others. As she drove around, taking Katherine, Christina, and Patrick to school and various programs dressed in a running suit, she wondered at the woman she had become. She had always cringed when her mother had shown up at her school dressed like a bag lady, and here she was, looking about the same.

Maria planned her life so that during the week she was home with her children from about four to eight P.M. She did not make any calls. She did not answer e-mail or invite friends over. She was there for her children, watching over their homework, playing games with them, being totally involved with them.

She continued to work for NBC, trying to do serious work that her mother would watch with respect and admiration. She talked to her mother at least once a day, and always immediately after appearing on air. "My mother always calls and says, 'Congratulations, you did wonderful. You're so smart. I don't know how you do it,'" said Maria. "She does that for ten minutes and then if she thinks something wasn't well done, she says, 'Oh, I had maybe a little trouble following that piece.' But she always makes constructive criticism."

No matter what one did, it could always be a bit better. That was the way Eunice viewed her own life, and the way Maria came to view hers as well. She was a good woman, and "good" meant doing good work in the world, but she was sometimes tiresome in her goodness, unable truly to relax. Her mother was both her model and her goad. "Every time I call my mother, it's like, 'What's going on, what are people talking about?'" Maria said. "It's the issues. She's sending me speeches, articles. She's always running somewhere. She's just like on overdrive."

One day Maria was driving in the car with her daughter Katherine. "Mummy, look at me," the little girl said. "Who am I?" Maria turned to see her daughter with her face in a rigid grimace, her teeth bared, and her jaw clinched.

"I don't know," Maria said. "Who?"

"I'm Grandma."

Unlike many homes of the ultrawealthy, Arnold and Maria's estate did not have the pristine feel of a spread in *Architectural Digest*, but rather was a real home where children ran through the halls and plopped down on the sofas. Part of that was Maria's influence. Everyone thought of the Shriver home as a baronial estate where the family lived like American nobility. The reality, as Maria knew, was that when she and her brothers were growing up, the Shriver farm in Rockville was a "complete catastrophe." For the most part, it was a happy catastrophe, with children and adults running wild, meals served boardinghouse-style, with shouts across the table.

Maria wanted her children to feel free. Arnold had grown up poor, but his home life had been the one with rigid formality. He wanted none of that for his children. Both parents sought to make the children very much a part of their parents' lives. Arnold and Maria tried to have dinner with them each evening, when they would talk about the world. Part of this was a Kennedy tradition that went back to Joe and Rose Kennedy, but part was Arnold's Austrian background. "Each night they eat together and have conversations in the best old European way," said Albert Busek. "Many times they have wonderful guests who listen to the children. It's the best of America and Europe combined."

As an heiress of wealth and power, Maria had a much closer affinity to the realities of her children's lives than her husband. Her parents had tried to give her life experiences that would take her far beyond the narrow world of privilege, but she remained preeminently a child of advantage, mothering a new generation of wealth.

Arnold knew that his children would never feel quite the exhilarating hunger for life that their father had. He tried to give them discipline and not allow them to sink into the self-indulgent lassitude of inherited wealth. "I require that they do math every morning, spelling every morning, write their names, answer questions, and take care of their animals," he said. "If they want puppies, they have to feed them. I wake them up at 7 in the morning, even if they're still sleeping, and say, 'Look, the dogs are hungry; they're standing down there—let's go!'"

Arnold was proud of his kids' setting up a lemonade stand in front of their house, though there are few other neighborhoods where they could have earned a hundred dollars in no time flat. His children wanted a Rolls-Royce. Arnold denied them the pleasure of tooling around L.A. in the British luxury car. Instead, they suffered the deprivation of riding in a number of lesser vehicles, including a Mercedes, a Porsche, an antique El Dorado Biarritz convertible, a Jeep, a Hummer, or perhaps riding behind their dad on a Harley-Davidson motorcycle.

Arnold's family lived at a level of luxury that few Americans had ever even visited. As much as he tried to have his children feel the touchstones of life, it was difficult. As Arnold realized, "the kids know about the industry and they know what their fathers do and they're comparing notes in school of whose father's box-office grosses are bigger than the next father's." He brought his children to the set with their friends. "A movie set can become the best playground for children," Arnold mused. "Every day, I have a different child that comes with their friends. They do their homework in my trailer, when I study my lines and I can work with them." Although he meant that as a way to bond with his children, it also set them further apart from most of their peers, to whom their father was a Hollywood prince.

Arnold gave full rein to the childish part of him with his own children, getting down on the floor with them, playing their games, roughhousing like a big brother. He went out to his son Patrick's ballgames and stood on the field with other dads, cheering the team. As much as he tried to teach his children about life, Arnold understood that they never would or could experience life like other people. As he observed the hedonistic world of Hollywood, the best part of him stiffened and rejected the soft ease. He was the bad cop in the family. He was "the one that, you know, disciplines them a lot of times. My wife is also disciplining them. But I'm definitely the stricter one." His instincts to be tough were tempered always by the realities of his own child-hood. And yet he realized that as much as he suffered in his early years, in some ways his children risked suffering more from excess.

"You can't get away from it that they're going to be much more spoiled than I was," Arnold said. "You make sure they have great moral guidelines, and that they learn how to set goals, but they're never gonna be able to strug-gle through things the same way. I don't think so."

As strict as he tried to be, Arnold was always loving and sometimes indul-gent. His old Munich friend Albert Busek was there for Patrick's fifth birth-day in 1998, and it was an extravaganza worthy of Las Vegas. A special tent had been brought in, and there were all kinds of professional entertainment. "If they don't do it, they feel set back in terms of their friends," said Busek. "You're forced to do it. Or you have to live with the fact that you can't even do a birthday party for your child. Patrick was so high, he couldn't come down anymore. He calmed down, because Maria was strict with him, but he was at the edge. Everything was too much. I would never bring up my children that way, but I lead a different life."

Arnold always sought the joyful light of life. He still liked to drive over to Caffé Roma by himself for lunch with Franco or Sven. He still liked to get up on Sunday morning and head off on his motorcycle with a bunch of friends. As Christmas gifts, he went down to a do-it-yourself pottery store in Santa Monica and made gifts for his friends. He was an amateur artist of the Grandma Moses school and did paintings for his friends, too. He had prints made of them so he could give them to a number of people.

Maria was as energetic as her husband. They were a family that loved ath-letics, everything from skiing to Ping-Pong. On one occasion Maria and her mother were playing a game of doubles on their private tennis court against Arnold and Franco. It was not going well for the men. "You know what they are together?" Arnold asked Franco between points. "You take Eunice and Maria, they're over a hundred years old. Look how old she is. Why are we los-ing? What's wrong with you?"

Franco pointed out to his friend that the game was called "doubles," and if they were losing, Arnold shared the blame. The little pep talk did no good, and they lost the set. "I'm so embarrassed, I'm going to leave the house for three days," Arnold said. "How could we lose? You lost."

Franco responded, "I wasn't alone out there, Arnold. "You were playing, too."

The family had endless small intimate moments together but also great occasions. It was not just the children's birthdays that were special. Every July Maria planned a special birthday celebration for her husband, a gathering of their closest friends, who saluted Arnold in a manner both humorous and sentimental. "When in 2001 we had Arnold's birthday party in Sun Valley, I was the last one to talk," said Busek. "I was so overwhelmed by my emotion, I wasn't able to speak for half a minute. They clapped for me, and I said, 'Excuse me, but I love this country as much as my own.'"

That same July Arnold flew to South Africa to meet former President Nelson Mandela, to work with him to expand the Special Olympics in Africa. Before he went, he received a call from the Nobel laureate that at first he thought was a joke. "I'm your biggest fan," Mandela said. As massive as Arnold's ego is, it was astounding to him that the great African leader took such pleasure in his films.

Having his own jet allowed Arnold to take his kids with him without giving it a thought. The whole family flew to South Africa. Arnold had his children with him and let them join with the African leader as he returned by ferryboat to Robben Island so that they could see the tiny cell where he had lived most of his twenty-seven years of imprisonment.

The Schwarzeneggers lived in an exquisite 6,500-square-foot house with seven bedrooms and seven bathrooms on a cul-de-sac near Will Rogers Park in Pacific Palisades, shielded from the traffic below by a copse of trees. In 1993 Arnold purchased the 6,000-square-foot house next door from actor John Forsythe for about $3 million. Arnold turned the home into his office, including his own gym. Two years later he bought the four-bedroom, 5,000-square-foot home on the other side for about $2 million from another television star, Daniel J. Travanti. He tore that house down so he would have a lawn big enough for a massive tent when he wanted to give big parties. In 2001, as a Valentine's Day gift to his wife, he purchased a $3.2 million, five-bedroom house and made that part of the complex, too.

Arnold's private compound stood on 5.5 acres of land, but the homes were spread out. The following year he purchased a massive 11,000-square-foot home in Brentwood Country Estates, a gated community. The family's new five-bedroom, eleven-bathroom home sits on a six-acre knoll, so far above Los Angeles that the ocean is visible. He sold his newest property in Pacific Palisades to Maria's cousin Maxwell Kennedy for $3.4 million, while the two other houses in the compound were listed for sale for almost $18 million.

Despite his massive wealth, when Arnold's long-term secretary, Rhonda Columb, asked to borrow money from her boss so that she could buy a small house, Arnold turned her down. The rejection devastated a woman so devoted to him that she thought nothing of being there at dawn so that he could work before flying off to ski for the day. Yet when Columb became ill with cancer, he was magnificent to her, finding the finest medical care and watching over her.

Arnold was much the same when Art Zeller was dying. All through the years, Arnold had kept in touch with the bodybuilding photographer who had been there to meet him the day he arrived in Los Angeles. Zeller had taken many of the best shots of Arnold, and Arnold remembered. Seeing someone through his last days was draining, and Arnold could have avoided such duty but did not. In the aftermath, Joe Weider claimed that all the photos Zeller had taken were his property. Arnold said that they belonged to the estate and risked a lawsuit with Weider by paying Zeller's widow $100,000 for the collection. Although the money was a gracious gesture in memory of an old friend, there was an element of caution, too. Among the pictures were photos that might have embarrassed Arnold, including one of him in bed clutching a teddy bear.

CHAPTER THIRTY

True Lies

As hard as Arnold had worked out, he became the greatest bodybuilder in the world only because he started with such a strong, dynamic physique. He had inherited something else in his genetic mix, a family proclivity to heart problems. His grandmother had suffered from congenital heart disease, as did his mother. Aurelia's doctors had told her that she should have an operation, but she said that she was in God's hands, and if He wanted to take her, she was ready.

Early in 1997, as Arnold approached his fiftieth birthday, he learned that he had the same trouble as his mother and grandmother before him. Some individuals are born with two of the three flaps of tissue on the aortic heart valve grown together. At first, this creates no problems, but as a person grows older the valve has a hard time opening and closing and may become calcified or scarred. The better condition you are in, the longer it takes for symptoms such as shortness of breath or chest pain to manifest themselves, and by then serious damage had already been done.

Arnold had been born with a heart murmur. "It didn't stop my lifestyle," Arnold said. "My training camouflaged the problem. The murmur was getting stronger, and an ultrasound showed I had calcification on my aortic valve. I didn't want to think about it, but finally I decided to go in and get it fixed, so I could move on with my life. I was never really frightened. I did a lot of research, talked to four universities and picked the one I liked best."

The doctors told him that he could wait a few years for the operation. If he did not want to go under the knife, he could rely on medicine, but he would have to cut back on his physical activities. As Arnold was contemplating serious heart surgery for himself, forty-one-year-old Maria was at St. John's

Health Center in Santa Monica being fed intravenously for four weeks. Like her mother, high-strung Maria gave the world the impression that she was a woman of endless vitality, but she had a number of health problems. She was pregnant with their fourth child and was suffering from hyperemesis gravidarom, a serious, sometimes fatal condition in which pregnant woman vomit or are so nauseated that they suffer weight loss and malnutrition.

Arnold defined life as being able to live at the highest level of exertion of every kind. There was no question that he wanted the operation, which involved stopping the heart, removing the defective aorta, and replacing it. Although it might seem paradoxical that Arnold called it "the hardest decision I've ever made" while saying that "there was very little dwelling on it," that was precisely the psychological device Arnold used to deal with what was dark and threatening.

He had a beautiful life and a beautiful, seemingly healthy body, and he refused to dwell on all the dreaded possibilities. He could die, and he treated it as a walk in the park. On the day of the operation in April 1997, he swam laps at one in the morning, and at three Maria drove him to the hospital. His children arrived later, as did many of his Kennedy relatives.

When Arnold came out of the open-heart surgery, he told Sven that "it was like a train was parked on his chest, because they opened his rib cage." A pregnant Maria and their three children were at his bedside. Despite the pain, or perhaps because of it, he tried to will away his weakness. "I made the mistake to get up the next morning and go on the Lifecycle three hours after I woke up," he said. "The valve blew out again, and they had to put another one in. I learned quickly after that to wait a little longer." He had risen far too boldly and far too fast. He revived in dynamic fashion and was out of USC University Hospital after five days.

"When people see you almost as a machine, then they are shocked and amazed when something goes wrong with your body," Arnold said. "I was originally known as the guy with the perfect body, people found it hard to believe that my body was as vulnerable as the next guy's. I wasn't so much concerned how it would affect me. It was far more important to convince the world that it hadn't affected me. To convince the world I was OK and that I was back that was the big concern for me."

"For me and my career the image has been everything," Arnold reflected. "More important than the reality. The most powerful thing is what people perceive and believe about me." That was almost precisely what the Kennedy patriarch Joseph P. Kennedy had said about life. In Arnold's case, though, the truth of his life and the myth of his career had become so intertwined that it was almost impossible to see where reality ended and legend began. It was not a movie hero who had gotten out of bed immediately after his operation, but a mortal forty-nine-year-old man who damaged his heart again. There was no second take, only real consequences, resulting in a second operation.

Arnold had been home for less than a week when as he and Maria were driving three-year-old Patrick to preschool along Sunset Boulevard in their SUV, another vehicle came up beside them and the driver began videotaping Arnold. The first footage of the star since his operation would be worth thousands of dollars. The two paparazzi pursued Arnold's vehicle westward on the wide boulevard to the preschool on Montana Avenue in Santa Monica. Arnold and Maria claimed that the other vehicle nudged their car. "I felt the impact of the car and my wife started yelling, 'He hit us! He hit us! My God, he's crazy!'" Arnold said. He had been warned not to exert himself. "My heart was pounding," he said. "I could have died."

Arnold might once have shrugged off the incident, but he had become irritable during his recuperation. Much of that was probably the almost inevitable aftermath of his serious operation. He and Maria pressed charges, testifying against the men, who as a result were convicted of false imprisonment and reckless driving.

Arnold also fought back against those who he felt defamed him. There were rumors that his heart had been damaged by his use of steroids. It was a reasonable assumption, but Arnold insists that is not true. People around Arnold whispered about the possibility. He attacked those who dared profess the accusation publicly. The tabloid *Globe* ran a headline ARNIE'S GOT TICKING TIME BOMB IN HIS CHEST and said that he was "living in fear that after back-to-back operations on a defective valve, his heart will suddenly quit." Arnold sued, even though he might have to give a deposition detailing all sorts of personal matters. A little over a year later, the *Globe* settled by printing a retraction and making a donation to the Inner-City Games. He also sued a German doctor who said that because of the steroid danger, Arnold did not have much longer to live. This remark on a German radio show would have gone unnoticed if Arnold had not made such an issue of it. In the end, the physician lost the suit and had to pay Arnold $10,500.

Arnold had not been happy with his agent for almost half a decade, and still Lou Pitt had not gotten the message. Finally, in the spring of 1997, Arnold fired him, sending him off with a letter thanking him profusely for his decade and a half of service. In his place, he chose the husband of one of Maria's closest friends, Robert Stein of the William Morris Agency. As his career continued to decline, five years later in the summer of 2002, he fired Stein, who soon after left William Morris.

"I don't take any shit," Arnold told the British *Guardian* in 1999, talking about the retinue of PRs and minders who traveled with him. "I have to be a bit of a five-star general. I have no time for slacking off or failure. Everyone knows that I'm a tolerant guy, but everyone also knows I don't like laziness. If you want to be part of the team, then you have to go and kick butt. If you don't like that kind of pressure, then get the hell out. I need a team that is as enthusiastic and as quick and as organized as I am. I demand certain things. I don't blame anyone if they mess up. I just have to bring someone else in that can do the job."

Arnold still had that sense of humor with a one-sided edge that cut others but never himself. It was a part of Arnold that all his friends tolerated and some emulated. He did not care who you were if he wanted to stick it to you. At one party, with other people watching, he went up to one of the top television executives in America. "Look at the spot on your tie," he said. He reached out, seemingly to remove the offending stain, and chucked the man under the chin. It was funny to Arnold, but not to the executive, who never forgot his mini-humiliation.

For another man, the operation would have been an epiphany, a warning to slow down. Arnold's only change was not to work out quite as hard. He still rode his Harley in the Malibu Hills, still exercised an hour every day, and still slept only about four or five hours a night. He saved the evenings for his children. He was delighted when in September 1997 Maria gave birth to their fourth child and second son, Christopher Sargent Shriver.

There was a tender side of Arnold that only Maria and his children saw. Maria reflects: "No one has captured Arnold's softness, his saying 'What can I do for you?' Or 'I want to make you happy today. Can I take you to lunch? Can I take you shopping?' I think because everybody likes Arnold to be big and strong and knocking everybody down and not needing a woman—if it's the opposite, people go 'oops.'"

Arnold was in his fifties now, and though for years he had tinted his hair and had done everything he could to look young, he could hardly deny that he had lived half a century and his days as an action hero were limited. Since the perceived debacle of *Last Action Hero*, Arnold took the idea for an action/adventure film based on a French comedy to James Cameron.

Cameron had become a buddy. He was not only a member of Arnold's weekend motorcycle gang, but one of Arnold's crucial advisers. Cameron read his scripts and on one occasion rewrote part of one of them. As Arnold discussed the project, the director thought that the story of a James Bond–like secret agent who at home is just an ordinary father and husband resonated personally with the actor.

Cameron felt that Jamie Lee Curtis was perfect to play Arnold's wife. "I don't think she plays a mom," Arnold said. All sorts of other actresses were considered for the part, but Cameron kept coming back to Curtis.

"How much do you trust me?" Cameron asked Arnold.

"Of course I trust you," Arnold said.

"I mean how much do you *really* trust me?"

"All right, then I trust you completely," Arnold said.

"Well, then it's Jamie."

Cameron watched as Arnold's face clouded, irritated that the director was willing to play the face card of friendship to get his way, and knowing that he had no way out. Cameron feared that in winning he had lost. Arnold would make it so difficult on the set for Curtis that it might affect the entire movie. That did not happen, and the two clicked brilliantly together. He was so appreciative of Curtis's efforts that he agreed that her name join his above the title of *True Lies*. The stylish spoof became one of the big hits of the summer of 1994.

After *True Lies*, he collaborated for the third time with comedic director Ivan Reitman and costar Danny DeVito in *Junior*, in which he plays a genetic scientist whose experiments make him pregnant. Arnold had become so much a creature of marketing and deal making that as the London *Independent* suggested, "you feel he's not so much exploring his range as extending his franchise." The film is a series of lame, often embarrassing jokes. *Junior* did a disappointing $36.8 million in domestic gross when it opened during Christmas 1994 and was saved by Arnold's amazing worldwide popularity, earning $54 million overseas.

Arnold was still being paid as if he were the number one star in the world, thanks to his continued massive international box office. For the most part, he was like any brand name on its way down. Arnold had not made the complete devolution yet he risked endlessly repeating himself to oblivion.

In each film Arnold continued to convey what he always had, but increasingly the formulistic nature of his work became obvious. His 1996 action/adventure film, *Eraser*, was so recycled that Arnold deserved an award from the environmental movement. And yet the film delivered everything an Arnold film was supposed to, wild special effects, nonstop action, comic-book violence, and one-liners, and it proved one of the top hits of the summer of 1996.

His second film that year, *Jingle All the Way*, was even more calculated. The story of an absentee father who sets out to get the most sought-after gift of

246   Fantastic

the season for his son was overladen with devices to please the audience. "'Jingle' wants to warm our hearts and establish Schwarzenegger as a family man—but devotes so much time to goony violence and broad physical comedy that the last-reel schmaltz feels hollow and tacked-on," complained Edward Guthmann in the *San Francisco Chronicle*. The critics may have roundly panned the film, but Arnold was such a trademark that the film managed to jingle all the way to the bank, doing $125.7 million in business, split almost evenly between domestic and overseas markets.

Warner Brothers next signed Arnold to play Mr. Freeze in *Batman & Robin*, following in the illustrious footsteps of such previous Batman villains as Jack Nicholson, Jim Carrey, and Danny DeVito. Arnold was one of the greatest marquee names around the world, and the studio paid him $25 million for his six weeks' work, or about $800,000 a day, close to a record figure. The movie that opened in June 1997 was a lifeless pastiche. Arnold mugged his way through the film but was unable to breathe even momentary life into the critical bomb that nonetheless earned more than $237 million worldwide.

In the aftermath of his operation, Arnold kept a schedule that would have frazzled many men. In June he flew in his private jet to Graz for the opening of a bodybuilding museum in his honor in the gym beneath the newly named Schwarzenegger Stadium. He had to do no more than stand there and look at the homemade machines that he worked on three decades ago to see how life had changed. The equipment looked so primitive that it was as if it had been found in some ancient cave somewhere.

Celebrity greeted him everywhere. In October he jetted to Dublin to open the newest Planet Hollywood, where he was met by a crowd of two thousand Irish fans at St. Stephen's Green. He continued to promote the Inner-City Games, and he was an ardent fund-raiser for the Wiesenthal Center and the Museum of Tolerance. In Palm Beach he was the guest of honor of a dinner that raised millions for a Museum of Tolerance in Jerusalem.

Already by the early nineties Arnold was overseeing a fortune of probably well over a hundred million dollars. He still did not have any professional help managing his complicated investments, which were taking up a disproportionate amount of his time. He decided to bring in Paul Wachter to help manage his assets and investments. The Columbia University–trained lawyer not only had the Ivy League credentials that impressed Arnold, but he was a longtime friend with whom he felt comfortable. "People said, 'Be careful doing business with a friend,' said Wachter. "But it's been easier and more fun than I could have imagined."

Arnold was largely invested in real estate, but the attorney steered him into the stock market and some other sophisticated investments, including a 747 jet leased to Singapore Airlines. Wachter was highly successful and decided to take on several other wealthy clients. "I told Arnold that he should have a piece of the company," Wachter said. "He said, 'If I own a piece of the company, people will feel you're not independent and you'll have a hard time getting clients.' That's a good example of wisdom I wouldn't necessarily have seen."

Wachter also watched over Arnold's charitable donations. "In my business, I see what people give," the attorney said. "He's definitely in the most generous quadrant. For example, he was one of the first to give money after 9/11. He gave a million dollars the next day."

Most politicians use the word *friend* so often because they have so few real ones. The same is true of many celebrities, who bestow the term on subordinates and acolytes. Arnold was different. Although Maria did not like to have some of Arnold's friends around much, they remained his friends. Beyond his movie career, he had demanding business dealings, philanthropic pursuits, and political aspirations. But he always made time for his friends.

Jim Lorimer had retired and worked seven days a week putting on the annual Arnold Classic. In February 1998, when Lorimer received the Greater Columbus Hospitality Award, Arnold prepared a video to be played before the 650 guests at the annual meeting of the Greater Columbus Convention and Visitors Bureau.

Lorimer did not know about the video beforehand and stood at the podium, watching the screen. "What can you say about the man?" Arnold asked in remarks videotaped at his Santa Monica office. "He loves bodybuilding. He trains harder than anyone I know. All the bodybuilders love him, because he's been promoting the bodybuilding sport for so many years. Twenty-one years he's been promoting the bodybuilding championships in Columbus, Ohio. He loves his family, he's a great family man, he's a great . . . wait a minute . . . sorry, I'm talking about myself."

As the audience broke out laughing, the screen figure continued. "But let me tell you. He is really the greatest human being that I know. I want to congratulate you and I want to thank you for being my best friend and partner and I'll see you soon. As I always say, 'I'll be back.' "

Lorimer was touched that his friend had taken the time to do the video. After his inevitable jokes, Arnold had been very generous about their friendship. He was just starting to make his own comments when the back door of the ballroom opened, and in walked Arnold to the podium, where he embraced his friend.

"I said 'I'll be back,' and I always keep my promises," Arnold said. "It is great to be here, I tell you. Absolutely wonderful. You can imagine how thrilling it is to get up at four o'clock in the morning and to drive for one hour in a rainstorm in Los Angeles to the airport. And then to fly five hours through the wild, wild weather. To land here and drive for an hour here to the hotel for a little chicken lunch, I mean, it is really terrific."

Arnold stopped until the laughter subsided. "But I love to be here. Let's be honest. This man always presents that he is a low-key guy. It's a bunch of crap. He's an egomaniac, this guy. It's all vanity, believe me. All vanity. As a matter of fact, he's so bad that when he has an orgasm, he calls out his own name. Imagine."

Arnold turned toward his old friend. "You don't have to be embarrassed," he said. "They should know the truth, Jim, come on, now. But all I can tell you is that I don't want to get into your sex life at all. Otherwise, I should tell them that a Peeping Tom looked into his bedroom window and he fell asleep. That's to show you how active he is.

"But, anyway, we're really here to roast Jim Lorimer. What has happened is since 1976, we have been organizing in Columbus, Ohio, year after year. We love the town, this town has done everything for us, and people do everything for this town. So we are going to stay here in this town because of Jim Lorimer here. So this is the kind of influence this man has on me. Thank you very much, my friend."

Not even Lorimer credited how important such friendships were to Arnold, despite or because of the actor's world fame. For years whenever he visited Columbus, Arnold had stayed at the Lorimers' in their middle-class home in the suburbs. Arnold brought so many clothes that he overwhelmed their closets, and he decided that he had better start staying at a hotel. In October 2001, when Lorimer privately celebrated his seventy-fifth birthday, he did not even think of inviting Arnold, fearing it might embarrass his famous friend to have to decline. Lorimer was having a quiet time with twenty-five of his closest friends and associates at Bravo's, an Italian restaurant in Worthington, Ohio, when in the midst of the dinner Arnold walked into the room.

Arnold had not only great old friends but a healthy, vital mother. One of the continued joys of his life was the time he spent with his mother each year. It was a blessing, too, that when she was not with him, he knew that there were people watching over her. She had years before left Thal. When she was not up in the Alpine village of Schladming, she lived in the Styrian town of Weiz. When Arnold visited her there, he stayed at Gasthof Goldene Krone, a traditional Austrian inn where Maria and their children could experience something of what Austria once had been.

Almost every day, Arnold's mother made her way above the city to her husband's grave in the cemetery beneath the Gothic church. Seventy-six-year-old Aurelia went there on the first Sunday in August 1998 for what would have been Gustav's ninety-fifth birthday, and there by her husband's grave, she had a stroke. She was flown to Graz in a helicopter, but she was gone.

As soon as Arnold learned of his mother's death, he flew to Weiz. Arnold knew that his mother would have been no more comfortable with extravagance in death than in life. He gave her a simple funeral among friends, helping push the cart that carried her body from the church to the family burial plot.

He had never been touched before by a death in the way he was by his mother's. It was nothing that he would ever talk about to an outsider, nothing he wanted displayed to the world, but it was there. As tough as Aurelia had been on Arnold as a boy and as limited a view as she had of his ambitions, she had given him many things, including in some ways his ability to love. She was a touchstone in his life, and in her death she gave him something else he had not had before, an open emotionality, deep painful feelings that he did not attempt to hide.

Avenues of Relaxation

Arnold was like his classic Excalibur convertible, a complex piece of machinery that had to be perfectly tuned, or it did not run properly. He had his health back, but the operation had led to a disquieting period. He had lost his way creatively in recent years, and he was endlessly repeating himself in films that delivered neither at the American box office nor in critical acclaim. He was a fifty-two-year-old action hero who was not taking any chances. There were omens everywhere suggesting that his days as a great star might be ending.

Arnold's first film in two years opened in late November 1999. *End of Days* is a dark, apocalyptic thriller. In 1979 a newborn girl is wrapped in swaddling clothes and taken by a nurse to another room in the hospital, where she is washed with the blood of a freshly killed rattlesnake. Twenty years later she will give birth to the Antichrist if she mates with the devil between eleven P.M. and midnight on the eve of the millennium. All that stands in the way is an alcoholic, bearded former cop played by Arnold. After two hours of mayhem, the once-sodden hero turns pacifist and defeats the Prince of Darkness with his goodness.

"Idiotic beyond the point of redemption," wrote Peter Hyams in *Sight & Sound*, "this sinfully stupid farrago manages to insult audiences and critics, Christians and Satanists alike, reducing 2,000 years of fertile mythology to the level of an incoherent pop video." Arnold's acting merited an even worse response, if that were possible. "*End of Days* is dreadful enough to make most viewers consider gouging out their eyes in order to avoid seeing a second time the spectacle of the world's most wooden actor pretending to undergo a spiritual crisis."

It would have been natural for the studio to send out the megastar to shout the virtues of the film after his two-year absence from the big screen, but the film company so lacked faith in its aging star that, for the first time in his career, he was not the primary vehicle to promote the film. "I've seen the print ads for how long now, and I barely even realize that he's in the movie," a studio publicist told *Variety*.

That was clearly one of the reasons the $105 million film performed so disappointingly in the United States, taking in only $66.9 million. As so often in his career, the bottom line in Arnold's film was saved by its overseas business, $142.4 million in all. At least part of that success was due to the fact that the studio unleashed Arnold outside the United States.

He was scheduled to arrive at the premiere in London by hurtling up the Thames in a speedboat. That dramatic entrance was rained out, but thousands still stood outside in the sodden evening shouting, "*Hasta la vista*, baby," as Arnold walked past them into the premiere. Telling the hushed theater audience how great the film was, he was still the king—at least until the lights dimmed and *End of Days* appeared on the screen.

Not only did Arnold's film career seem to be going south, but Planet Hollywood had proved to be a financial defeat and a humiliating public beating. He had seen time and again that you could sell anything to anybody, and Planet Hollywood was as good an example of that as anything Joe Weider ever did. The idea was that if you had a few megastars arriving for the grand opening of a chain restaurant selling burgers and fries in a room full of movie memorabilia, fans would come and stand in line after the velvet ropes had been put away and the private jets departed. For a few years it worked, but when the magical dust of celebrity wore off, business dropped. Maybe it was in part that Arnold, Stallone, and Willis were getting long in the tooth and the kids no longer identified with them. And maybe it was just that the crowds had moved down the street to a new hype or that the chain had expanded too much, too fast. After the company went into Chapter 11, Arnold walked away with stock said to be worth about $200,000, not the estimated $10 million to $15 million it had been when he signed his five-year contract. Leaving was all the more bitter when he realized that the agreement allowed Planet Hollywood to continue using his name and image in promotions.

Arnold was not a man to obsess over momentary setbacks. He was already moving on to an elevated position in public life. He was considered a man of such influence that in May 2000, soon after he returned from a trip to China to promote the Special Olympics, he was asked by two Republican members of Congress, Mary Bono and Mark Foley, to call several undecided members to ask them to vote yes on a bill to normalize trade relations with China.

The Inner-City Games had expanded into a national program in twelve cities across America. Arnold went to corporate America for funding that he could combine with government and foundation money. He brought his marketing skills and something he had picked up from the Kennedy-Shrivers— knowing how to use people and their desire to get close to him and his name. Arnold, like the Kennedy-Shrivers, was much more generous with his time and his name than with his money, though he did come up with $450,000 a year to fund the ICG office in Santa Monica. He flew around the country in his private jet, visiting programs, traveling with his own hairstylist and makeup artist. It was Arnold the megastar people wanted to see, and they went away confirmed in the image they had seen on the screen, not whispering about what he once had been.

Whereas Arnold had perfect confidence that he had fathered all his accomplishments and deserved every accolade received, Maria was often uncertain that she merited the applause she was given. In August 1996 at the Democratic National Convention in Chicago, Maria scored the only interview with First Lady Hillary Clinton after she gave her address to the delegates. In a week bereft of drama, this passed as a major coup, but there were whispered asides that Maria had used her Democratic connections to arrange the interview. That was not said at the Republican National Convention when she snagged Elizabeth Dole, the wife of the Republican candidate, beneath the podium in an aggressive gesture that irritated some of her competitors. But always with Maria there were those who questioned whether she was merely play-acting a dilettante's game, and one of those questioning her was Maria herself.

In 2000 she was in New York City to host the *Today* show when the phone rang in her hotel room. She had just published a children's book, *What's Heaven?*, and the caller told her that not only had it made the *New York Times* bestseller list but she had just received a Peabody Award for a program on women getting off welfare. "And I hung up the phone and sat on the floor of my hotel room and wept for, like, half an hour," she told her friend Oprah Winfrey, "because I felt finally I had done something that had nothing to do with being a Kennedy, that had nothing to do with being married to Arnold, that I had accomplished something on my own. And that was at forty-three years of age—forty-three."

Although it would never appear on any list of her accomplishments, Maria and her family had a major role in inspiring Arnold to take a forceful, positive role in public life. During the Republican National Convention in Philadelphia, Arnold led a group to the Vaux Middle School to see the Inner-City Games program in action. Two weeks later during the Democratic National Convention in Los Angeles, Arnold took a number of big-city mayors to the Hollenbeck Center in East L.A. to observe the after-school program at work. He and Maria invited leading Democratic politicians and delegates to their home for a party. During that high-profile week, Arnold wrote an op-ed piece for the *Los Angeles Times* that could have been by a liberal Democrat. "We can help these children bridge the gaps created by hardship and hopelessness," he wrote. "We can help them get the drive, focus, attention, skills, and pride that lead to hope. We can get all our kids up to the same starting line."

Those were not the words of an op-ed piece as much as an early campaign speech of a man contemplating running for governor of California in 2002. Arnold watched the political scene with increasing fascination and, in some measure, with disappointment, even dismay. He took a visceral dislike to such Democrats as Governor Gray Davis, who to Arnold's way of thinking proclaimed his generous concern for the welfare of all Californians when he was beholden to special-interest groups that included the trade unions, teachers organizations, and the prison guards union.

Arnold did not like the bashing, belligerent talking-heads culture of America when he watched it on television or heard it coming from the mouths of would-be leaders. He was no fan of Bill Clinton, but he believed that his party could recapture the White House only by offering up a positive vision. He was tired of hearing "guys like [Pat] Buchanan" screeching, "We are anti-gay and we're anti-lesbian and anti-immigration. We are anti-taxation and anti-federal government."

Arnold, unlike most conservative Republicans, took no pleasure in the possibility of President Clinton's being hounded out of office because of his sexual peccadilloes. "That was another thing I will never forgive the Republican Party for," he told *George* in November 1999, after the impeachment trial failed in the Senate. "We spent one year wasting time because there was a human failure. I was ashamed to call myself a Republican during that period. Instead of devoting all this energy and all these hearings to how we're going to solve the problems of the inner cities . . . No, it's like, 'This man has to be removed from office because he's a national threat.' Yeah, that's a good one."

If the forty-second President deserved to be hauled out of the White House, tarred and feathered, and paraded down Pennsylvania Avenue for sexual misconduct, then a number of other politicians deserved to be carried along right behind him. Arnold had been born with a serious deficiency in hypocrisy. He was not about to join his conservative cohorts in raging against a President for his personal sexual conduct, in part because he had his own pattern of inappropriate sexual behavior.

When on the movie sets he spied a woman with a comely derriere walking up the stairs in front of him, he was apt to give it a pinch. He had on occasion grabbed at women's breasts, and he was full of sexual asides that would have caused a sailor to blush. Much of this was, as he later said, the rowdy, robust, macho atmosphere on his sets, but it was a mood that he established and it was far from a Hollywood universal. One woman journalist with impeccable credentials recalls being at an event with Arnold during which he reached up under the skirt of another woman for a pleasurable feel. When the evening ended, Arnold's publicist wanted to be assured that it was not part of her story, and, of course, it was not.

Arnold's unpuritanical sexual attitudes may have been largely European, but it would be unfair to blame his specific conduct on the Continent. Many men would have enjoyed such behavior if they thought they could get away with it without being slapped or rebuked. They could not, but Arnold could. He lived within a Hollywood world that sheltered and protected him. As bad as this conduct was, it was not a prelude to forcing himself on a woman. His pleasure was for the most part no more than a momentary touch or feel or the frisson of a shocking remark.

One of the most authentic witnesses to Arnold's conduct is Gigi Goyette, who says she first got involved with Arnold in 1975, when she was a sixteen-year-old television actress on *Little House on the Prairie* and he was a single bodybuilder. He saw her at World Gym one day and met her in Malibu, where she was riding her horse. Goyette told her friends later that she had sex with Arnold once and then he disappeared.

Arnold did not see Goyette again until fourteen years later, in 1989, at the first Arnold Classic in Columbus, where she was working for World Gym, helping with their franchising operation. Goyette says that the couple renewed their relationship, meeting every spring for the weekend of the Classic and generally at no other time. As Goyette tells her story, it was a relationship similar to that in the Neil Simon movie *Same Time, Next Year*, with one subtle difference. In apparent deference to Maria, Arnold did not want to have traditional sexual intercourse, but all kinds of rubs and massages. Goyette was a fearlessly erotic, voluptuous being with an insatiable sexual appetite, delighted to match her partner in whatever direction he chose to go.

Goyette looks at it all philosophically. "All this stuff that he did with all these women, these good-looking women, women he worked with," she said, "he grabbed their ass and said, 'Oh, you've got a nice ass, you got a nice body,' you know it's his way of making them feel comfortable, of complimenting them, because every woman thinks she's shoddy or she's looking bad or something's not right. When you've got a guy like that, saying something like that, it makes them feel so good."

Goyette's relationship with Arnold was unique, so she invented a new word to describe it. "I came up with the term 'outercourse' because it's like foreplay," she said. "It was whatever we wanted it to be. It wasn't the same all the time. Most of the time, it was just massages, really, and I think any stressed-out man in his position—maybe his wife wasn't there to relieve him—we'll get Gigi. Call Gigi. I was his avenue of relaxation."

Goyette says that the relationship continued generally no more than once a year until 1996.

Arnold may have had his dalliances and continued his rude, vulgar jokes and gamesmanship with his friends, but he was a serious man with serious ambitions. He knew that he was not going to be a movie star much longer. It was not simply that he was growing too old and his roles were getting tired. It was that he is a man who moves toward whatever is most joyful and gives him pleasure. That is why it was impossible to define him by the common categories of selfishness and selflessness. All his life he had ceaselessly promoted his own career and image. He still was doing so, but in recent years he had discovered that the highest joy was in helping others and doing what he thought was good.

That did not mean he had given up his personal ambitions; if anything, they were even greater, but he had meshed his aspirations with what he believed was good and right for his state and his country. Late in 2000 he signed up George Gorton, a political consultant close to former Governor Pete Wilson, to help him gear up for a possible run for governor in 2002 and to look into other possible races. Gorton is a feisty, unassuming man with a gift for candor. Arnold likes to be around people who are good at what they do and fun to be around, and Gorton scored an "A" in both categories. He bore his share of scars in the consulting game, including being pushed aside from running Wilson's lame campaign for the Republican presidential nomination in 1996.

At the end of that race, Gorton received a call that brought him and two of his colleagues to Moscow as consultants to Boris Yeltsin's campaign for the presidency of Russia. That episode became the subject of an HBO movie,

Spinning Boris, that was going into production as Gorton went to work for
Arnold. Arnold also signed on Wilson's former chief of staff, Bob White, a
shrewd, backroom operative and one of Gorton's closest friends.

The two consultants sat down with Arnold and gave him a primer course
on the costs of political life. "I urged him to make the race," said White, "but
I said to him and to Maria, 'Look, I have no doubt whatever about your ability as a campaigner. To the contrary, I think you may have the greatest natural
gifts as a campaigner that I've ever seen, but before you make the decision,
you need to understand that you're going to be under scrutiny of a kind that
you've never seen before.'" In the code words of politics, White was telling
Arnold that anything he had done previously in his life, including untoward
sexual conduct, would likely be fair game.

CHAPTER THIRTY-TWO

Patton's Retreat

A rnold was actively contemplating a political future when he flew to Great
Britain to promote his latest film, *The 6th Day*, in December 2000. As he
arrived at Heathrow, he already knew that the $80 million thriller about
cloning was his worst failure as a major star, in the end earning only $34.5 mil-
lion domestically. He was leaving behind a wife in Los Angeles who had had
what was probably the most difficult year of her life. That fall, Eunice had
become critically ill after an operation for a benign pancreatic tumor and for
weeks hovered between life and death. Maria flew back East to be at her
mother's bedside at Johns Hopkins in Baltimore, where Eunice lay comatose
in intensive care. Maria raged at the doctors, who she felt were not serving
Eunice well. She stayed there for weeks, but still her mother did not speak.
"That experience was really the first time that I came face-to-face with my
life without my mother," Maria told Oprah Winfrey afterward.

After about a month, Maria returned to Los Angeles to be with Arnold and
their family. Her children ranged from three to eleven, ages when being a
mom means endless chauffeuring. She was in the car one day when the cell
phone rang. "How are you doing, Maria?" her mother asked, as if all was right
with the world and always had been. Eunice's recovery was a miracle, but it
was a miracle that the Shrivers did not talk about. Eunice never talked about
the difficulties and problems of her own life but always looked at how she
could advance the lives of others. It was a lesson of immense moral force, but
the price was high. Maria, like her mother, pushed all her anxieties and
doubts into the closet of her mind and moved on.

Arnold may have felt his own need for a release from those weeks of endless tension. In London he indulged semi-publicly in the sort of conduct that

he had previously limited to his movie sets and other controlled environments. He acted wilder the farther from home he was, and he was an ocean and a continent away from Los Angeles. At fifty-three, he may also have felt the necessity to proclaim his virility in ways he had previously found unnecessary. Beyond that, this was just Arnold having fun.

Twenty-nine-year-old Anna Richardson claimed that during a television interview in his suite at the Dorchester Hotel, Arnold constantly talked about her breasts. "He kept saying how fantastic I looked and staring at my boobs," Richardson told the British tabloid the *Sun* afterward. "When I went to shake his hand he pulled me onto his knee, saying, 'I really want to know if your breasts are real.' I told him they are an F-cup. Before I knew what was happening, he circled my nipple with his finger and gave it a squeeze. He then said, 'Yeah, they are real.' I stood up and said, 'You're making me nervous.' He told me not to be nervous and pulled me back on his knee. I said, 'Can I go, please?' He said, 'Yeah,' and patted my bum as I went off."

It was a typical Schwarzenegger performance in that Arnold did his thing with an audience watching. He meant no harm, and to him it was a blissful romp. Arnold's spokesperson said later that both Arnold and Richardson were flirts, an allegation that so upset the journalist that in 2004 she prepared the legal groundwork for a libel suit.

Later that morning Arnold filmed a segment for a popular morning television show. Those who extrapolate the realities of British television from *Masterpiece Theatre* have likely not seen *The Big Breakfast*. The set includes a bed on which twenty-six-year-old Denise van Outen interviewed Arnold. "He stroked her THIGH and slapped her on the BUM before brushing his arm against her CHEST," described the *Sun*, heavily into capitalization. Van Outen had been startled when Arnold actually felt her bosom. "The stunned presenter said: 'You grabbed my breast then.' Then she quipped: 'I really liked it. Go on, have another go.' Arnie smirked and said: 'It was a handful. I never know if my wife's watching. I'll tell her it was a stuntman.'"

As in the previous incident, Arnold did not try to hide his conduct, and as one of the observers told the *Sun*, "The crew were quite shocked—but it made good telly." To Arnold it was nothing, a prank that he knew would be seen by a massive television audience.

That same day Arnold met with yet another pretty, young television journalist. During an interview for *Celebrity*, Arnold put his arms around the waist of thirty-year-old Melanie Sykes. In a still photo, Sykes poses with an extravagant smile while with her right hand she appears to be trying to remove

Arnold's hand. It was the kind of aggressiveness that most women have experienced at one time or another, and Sykes handled it smoothly.

The three incidents were sufficient for *Sun* gossip columnist Dominic Mohan to award Arnold his "Groper of the Year" award. "Groping" is not the most accurate description of his conduct, but it stuck with him from then on. The *National Enquirer* made the most of the story in its first issue of the new year, headlining ARNIE'S WIFE HITS ROOF OVER GRAB-HAPPY HUBBY over pictures of Arnold patting van Outen's bottom and Sykes apparently trying to pry Arnold's hand from around her waist.

Arnold had been the subject of numerous tabloid stories, and he did what he always did—ignored them. He paid increasing attention to the possibility of running for governor. He began to network actively, using his massive celebrity to draw to him people who would not have heeded the beck and call of most would-be candidates. One of those he called was Assemblyman Keith Richman of Northridge, outside Los Angeles.

Arnold felt an affinity for the moderate Republican, but the reality was that in Sacramento men such as the assemblyman and his counterparts among the Democrats were often dismissed as nothing more than weak-willed compromisers and panderers. That was largely because the California Republican Party was led by some of the most fervent right-wing politicians in America, their passions matched by the left-wing Democrats who dominated their party.

Arnold invited the politician to his home for dinner in January 2001. Richman had given up his medical practice to run for office, and both Arnold and Maria admired people who had done things and whose beliefs came from deep wellsprings of human experience. The assemblyman had taken a drop in salary to enter politics. "We talked about public policy," Richman recalled. "The recollection I have the most is really how much he knew about different public policy issues. This was someone who was interested in what was going on. He expressed his interest in being involved in giving back to the state of California. He had said that he had achieved beyond his wildest dreams, attributed that to California and America, and felt that he wanted to give back even more."

On February 1, 2001, Arnold read a column in the *Los Angeles Times* by George Skelton, one of the most respected political commentators in the state, about the 2002 gubernatorial election. Governor Gray Davis, whose best attribute was his political shrewdness, had ridden high in his first years in office as the California economy soared. But when the high-tech stock bubble had burst, billions of dollars stopped flowing into the state's coffers, and the private utilities were close to bankruptcy. Skelton portrayed Gray as an indecisive, almost fearful man in a time that called for boldness. Davis should have been in deep trouble, but as his chief strategist, Garry South, put it, you can't beat somebody with nobody, and "nobody" was the most likely Republican challenger, William Simon Jr., a wealthy rancher turned politician.

"South is right," concluded the columnist. "The governor's still a good bet for reelection. The Capitol longs for a Gen. Patton."

Arnold called Skelton from the trailer of the set for his newest film, *Collateral Damage*, at a water tunnel in Sylmar, California, to tell the reporter how much he appreciated the column. "Especially your last sentence when you said we need another Patton up there in Sacramento," Arnold said. "That's a really good line." The former tank driver announced boldly that if California needed its own General George Patton, Arnold was ready to play the role. "I saw in the last ten years that I'm getting much more pleasure out of that [helping people] than making money and making movies. It can lead—and will lead, probably—to some political office. I haven't really said this is the time. But, you know, the bottom line is if Davis goes on the way he is then you've got to say, OK, there's room for someone else. I have movie obligations through 2004. But I would sacrifice my, you know, $20 million a picture and all those things and forget about that to step in."

Arnold's announcement created such excitement among many of the party faithful that later in the month at the Republican state convention there were T-shirts for sale emblazoned "T2 in '02."

Just as it appeared that a well-orchestrated groundswell of support might lift Arnold to the 2002 nomination, an article appeared in the March 2001 issue of the glossy movie monthly *Premiere* called "Arnold the Barbarian" by John Connolly. The tabloid articles about Arnold's conduct in London had gotten the editors interested in doing a piece about Arnold's sexual conduct. Connolly, a brusque former New York City cop, says that he researched and wrote the article in less than a month.

During the research, Arnold's attorney, Martin Singer, called the magazine to complain. Arnold was one of the most litigious stars in Hollywood, a mark of that attitude not so much the lawsuits that were filed in his name but how often matters were taken care of long before the public knew about them. The attorney mentioned a number of sensitive matters about which he said

Arnold was prepared to sue. Singer says that "a lot of material that we referred to in our letter did not wind up in the story." That was true largely because the matters were not part of *Premiere*'s story anyway. Beyond that, the letter provided a blueprint for Connolly to investigate a number of new areas. In the end, however, the three British women were the only named sources about the actor's sexual conduct in a titillating piece filled with innuendo.

One of the earliest and most interested readers of the article was Governor Davis's strategist South. Davis feared that the megastar would come bolting into the race and overwhelm him. To stop Arnold in his tracks, South faxed copies of the *Premiere* article to political reporters across the state under the heading "A real 'touching' story—if you get what I mean."

Arnold was so upset with South's action that he had Singer threaten him with a lawsuit. South says that "not only did he threaten to sue me for libel— for e-mailing out an article that anyone could have bought on any newsstand—the last paragraph said, 'Oh, and by the way, this letter is itself copyrighted, and if you release any part of this letter to the press, I will further sue you for copyright infringement.'" Singer's letter was probably written more to placate his client and warn South to watch his conduct in the future than as a serious legal challenge.

Politics is not a sport in which you run off the field crying the first time your nose is bloodied, and Arnold's actions suggest that he was at this stage very much of a political amateur. For the most part, political journalists did not look favorably on a movie star running for governor. They read the article with great attention, and some viewed the scandal as the likely death knell to Arnold's political aspirations.

The tabloids had an unerring instinct for vulnerable flesh and competed with one another in a barbarian-style marketplace. The *National Enquirer* was not about to end its spate of Arnold stories. No sooner had the *Premiere* article appeared than the *National Enquirer* announced with glee the looming breakdown of Arnold's marriage, asserting that "in the wake of bombshell revelations of his sexual infidelities 'the buzz is that divorce is imminent.'"

The *National Enquirer* raised its attack to a new level by exposing Arnold's purported relationship with Gigi Goyette. Although she was paid for her cooperation, the article does not quote her. The story headlined ARNOLD's 7-YEAR AFFAIR was spread over two pages and included photos of Arnold with Goyette and called her Arnold's "mistress." "I was never Arnold's mistress," said Goyette. "The only thing he ever gave me was an old car. The article ruined my life, cost me my job, my reputation, everything."

In early March, Arnold's publicist announced that he had decided that "the timing's not right" for him to run for governor. The next day the publicist said

Arnold told her that although "there's a lot of contractual obligations and other obstacles, that does not necessarily count him out." In April Arnold opted out for good, citing contractual obligations. He told Gorton "that he had a deal to make *Terminator 3,* and he would be sued if he walked away from it because money had changed hands." That was a serious reason, but without the two salacious stories, Arnold may well have found some way to run.

After running its story about Goyette, the *National Enquirer* then published a follow-up, headlined ARNOLD'S DIRTY SECRETS—WHY HE CAN'T RUN FOR GOVERNOR. The tabloids are usually loathe to brag too loudly about any impact their scandalous stories may have on the American political process. In this instance, the *National Enquirer* trumpeted its supposed triumph in its April 26, 2001, issue: "For seven years, Arnold Schwarzenegger hid a mistress from his loving wife Maria Shriver—and hours after learning the EN-QUIRER discovered his sordid secrets, 'The Terminator' terminated his run for governor of California. Earlier this week, after we called his representative for comment, the star made a surprise announcement that he won't enter politics until his youngsters, ages 3 to 11, are older."

The *National Enquirer* not only took sole credit for Arnold's backing off his political ambitions (which was probably due more to *Premiere* and Arnold's other obligations) but in essence put him on notice that if he returned, they would be back with muck buckets at the ready. On May 15, 2001, in a follow-up story, the tabloid asserted: "Arnold Schwarzenegger terminated his plans to run for governor of California just hours after he found out the EN-QUIRER was publishing a story about his affair with sexy Gigi Goyette because he didn't want even more scandals uncovered if he made a bid for public office!"

For Arnold, the consequences of the stories were heavy. There were those within his own party who hoped that this would be the end of Arnold's political aspirations. That summer when a former chairman of the Republican National Committee was asked about Arnold running for office, the man said that his sexual conduct made it unthinkable.

PART FOUR

The Politician

Birth of a Candidate

O n the early morning of September 11, 2001, Arnold was lying in bed next to Maria with three of their kids when the phone rang. "Turn on the TV, there's been an accident," a producer from NBC told Maria. "A plane has crashed into one of the Twin Towers in New York." The couple turned on the television and, along with their children, watched a second plane crash into the World Trade Center and the scenes of horror and heroism in downtown Manhattan.

NBC called to tell Maria that she should go to LAX, itself a potential target. Arnold was the action hero, but that morning he was not headed off into a dangerous world, but his wife was. Maria's initial reaction was to dread covering a story that might end in more violence or another plane going down.

Arnold got up with his wife and went with her to drop the children off at school before Maria headed to her assignment. "Daddy, there are twenty or thirty buildings that planes have run into," one of the children said as they drove through the streets of Santa Monica. The child had watched the endless replays of the horrifying scene of terrorists flying the planes into the towers, seeing each one as a new building that had been destroyed. Arnold decided to turn off the television sets for a while.

"This means you can forget about your *Collateral Damage* movie," Maria said after they left the children at school. It had been Maria's idea for him to do the film, and now she was telling him that it was all over just as his newest film was about to open. As soon as he heard his wife's comment, he knew she was right. *Collateral Damage* tells the story of a firefighter whose wife and children are killed in a terrorist attack that destroys a Los Angeles high-rise. The hero sets out on his own to find and kill the notorious el Lobo, a Colombian terrorist, and he does so—killing both the mastermind and his cohorts by the dozens. Arnold did not make movies in which nineteen terrorists killed 2,792 innocent people while the ringleader Osama bin Laden sat safely, thousands of miles away. Arnold mowed the bad guys down by the score, picked up another weapon, and mowed down another score.

For once, Arnold had not been thinking about his career, only the images of the Twin Towers. "You're right," he told Maria. He called Warner Brothers, which had been trying to reach him to discuss postponing the release of the film.

In mid-October Maria flew to New York to host the *Today* show in place of Katie Couric, whose sister, Emily, had died from pancreatic cancer. Someone had mailed anthrax to Tom Brokaw at the NBC studios in Rockefeller Center. Maria walked into that building not sure about what she would face. Arnold and Maria's children were like most children in present-day America, too aware of the world and its ways even at tender ages. "What if something happens to you?" her eight-year-old son, Patrick, asked her, a question that was repeated thousands of ways in homes across America.

Arnold had no difficulty dealing with the anxieties of his children. One of his friends believed that fifty-four-year-old Arnold's greatest challenge would be dealing with his own anxieties about getting old, giving up part of what he always considered life. He still roared off on his motorcycle with his buddies, most of them in their fifties or early sixties. In December 2001 he had a motorcycle accident a couple of blocks from his home that left him with cracked ribs. He had ached terribly after his heart operations, but nothing like the excruciating pain he endured for weeks after the accident. "Every time you inhale, you're in a tremendous amount of pain," he recalled. "You can't get up by yourself, because you can't use your abdominal muscles. That contracts the ribs, and you're in tremendous pain again. When you cough, you think you're gonna die. It's a really wild thing."

By early February 2002 Arnold was well enough to promote *Collateral Damage* when it finally opened. The film did not do well, earning only $40 million in the United States and $55 million overseas. It may have done better if not for 9/11, but the larger problem was that the film itself is reminiscent of half a dozen other Schwarzenegger films. Arnold had the peculiar look of a movie star in late middle age: well preserved. He was a man in his mid-fifties who was running, jumping, shouting, and shooting in a film targeted at adolescent males a third his age. Arnold was winding down his career by making a marketer's decision, squeezing every dollar he could out of the brand name, milking it to the end.

Arnold knew that his days as an action hero were ending and that his plans to run for public office had become more difficult because of the stories about his sexual conduct. He was not a man to back away from what he considered an unfair onslaught by his enemies. As Arnold retreated from a possible campaign against the incumbent governor, he turned instead to an alternative that would establish him so firmly in the public mind that he would not have to retreat again.

Arnold's first public step toward the governorship was to find an initiative that he could back in the 2002 election. When the progressive Republican Governor Hiram Johnson instituted voter initiatives in 1911, the populist politician envisioned them as direct, participatory democracy. All citizens had to do was to go out and get signatures on petitions equal to 5 percent of those voting in the previous gubernatorial election. Then their proposed bill would be voted upon by the people of the state. To most Californians, it seemed a good idea. Hiram Johnson's populist initiatives were a glorious idea for wealthy Californians who had the means to put forth their own ideas, especially in the age of television and multimillion-dollar campaigns.

Over the years, Arnold had observed the initiative process at work. In 1978 Californians fed up with high property taxes voted yes on Proposition 13. The constitutional amendment, called the Jarvis Amendment, limits the tax on a residence to 1 percent of the assessed value at the time of purchase, with annual increases of no more than 2 percent. Arnold hated taxes, and he was a fervent supporter of the popular measure. He dismissed arguments that the Jarvis Amendment was inequitable and forced the state into all kinds of onerous user fees and hidden taxes.

In 1998, Arnold's friend Rob Reiner spearheaded an initiative that sought to increase the tobacco tax to fund early-childhood education. The measure squeaked through with 50.5 percent of the vote.

Reiner's initiative had given the director high visibility as a public-spirited citizen. Arnold sought an initiative to do the same for him. In many respects, Arnold was no longer the pro-NRA ultraconservative he had been in his early years in America. He still believed strongly in free enterprise as the great engine of economic and social advancement and in the unfettered entrepreneur as the crucial figure in the American economy, but he tempered that fiscal stance with a broad series of social concerns. He was a pro-choice, pro–gun control, pro–gay rights, pro–effective government hybrid Republican. If he had picked up some of these ideas from his wife and her family, he had embraced most from his own experience. Having worked with gays on the movie sets and worked out next to them in the gym, he believed that they should have the same rights as all Americans. He had worked with single professional women, too, and he knew why they were largely pro-choice. He understood that these issues were already decided by most Californians, and his party could not win there if it stood against such beliefs.

The consultant George Gorton listened long and well to Arnold. With his help Gorton came up with an initiative that showcased a candidate who was both a social progressive and a fiscal conservative, as well as an inspiring, idealistic juxtaposition to the endless homilies of the hollow men of Sacramento. Proposition 49 called for the state to take as much as $550 million from general revenues to vastly expand after-school programs. In a state with latchkey kids wandering the streets, this was socially progressive legislation at its best.

Arnold balanced his belief in the salutary benefits of government with an equally deep belief in fiscal responsibility. "Arnold kept saying to me, 'I don't want to raise taxes, and I don't want to take money from other programs,'" said Gorton. "We hit upon the idea that we would exercise what he called 'true leadership' by prioritizing money when it became available." The program would be funded only when the state revenues grew sufficiently to pay for it.

Gorton and Arnold had crafted legislation that could appeal to voters across the entire political spectrum. Arnold gave a million dollars of his money to the campaign, and he easily raised the rest of the $8 million. The after-school initiative was one of the few positives in a dreadfully dispiriting election, in which it was largely a question of which gubernatorial candidate was disliked less, the incumbent Davis or the Republican challenger William Simon Jr. The Republican candidate was so ineffectual that Arnold's polling included questions about his running for governor as a write-in. That was a fanciful idea, but it suggests how far beyond the usual politics Arnold was headed— not in his ideology, but in his strategy and willingness to go outside conventional wisdom.

Arnold's name and persuasiveness were enough to merit endorsements for his initiative from both the right and the left. Arnold had as much convincing to do among his Republican cohorts as among the Democrats. When he addressed the Republican caucus in Sacramento, he heard a litany of criticism from conservative legislators who feared that he was a closet liberal who had listened too long and too well to his Kennedy relatives.

The legislators soon learned that behind his omnipresent smile stood a man who could be not only forceful but intimidating. "I'm just excited to be out campaigning in the districts that endorse this," he said in the most innocent of voices. A few minutes later, one by one, the legislators came forward and endorsed Prop 49.

The campaign was a benign trial run. Arnold gave talks at colleges and was at the center of numerous rallies to which his celebrity drew great audiences. He visited the editorial boards of major newspapers. There he talked to reporters often startled to realize that this was no dumb movie star but an articulate advocate.

Arnold traveled where few Republicans had gone before. The very name of Willie Brown, the mayor of San Francisco and the Speaker of the State Assembly for fifteen years, was enough to send many Republicans into paroxysms of outrage at the Democratic warlord who had for so long bossed Sacramento. And yet there was Brown at San Francisco's Fairmont Hotel, attending a private reception in support of Arnold's Prop 49.

The African-American politician, like Arnold, was a dandy with an eye for the ladies and a gift of candor who said what he wanted to. "I called Gray," the mayor said, in words taken down by *L.A. Weekly* columnist Bill Bradley, "and told him to stop telling Simon to drop out. Because if he did, Arnold would be a write-in and he'd win." Arnold had the same weakness for truth as Brown. Instead of praising his party's candidate, he said that the race was "boring" and "pitiful."

Arnold headed off to lunch with Brown at the mayor's favorite haunt, the French restaurant Le Central, where they joined Phil Bronstein, the *San Francisco Chronicle* editor who was married to Sharon Stone, Arnold's costar in *Total Recall*. No one held court quite like Brown, but as always Arnold trumped everyone else. He was the center of a spirited luncheon. Arnold was still the raucous jokester, not thinking that it diminished his persona one bit. At one point a lobbyist friend of Brown's sidled up to the table, proud to show off his resplendent new sports coat to the clotheshorse of a mayor.

"Nice coat," Arnold said as he looked at the extravagant jacket. "Does it come in a men's?"

A vote for the after-school initiative was equally a vote for Arnold and his prospects as a political candidate. Prop 49 passed by a formidable 56.7 percent. It had been an exemplary campaign in every way, and now that it was over, the Republican Party saw Arnold as a legitimate contender for the gubernatorial nomination in 2006.

For the first time since 1982, Democrats won all statewide offices. Although Davis received only 47.4 percent of the vote, he had reason to believe that he could govern with only the most desultory and futile opposition from the Republican minority. There was even talk of Davis's running for President or Vice President. He was not a man to boast publicly, but on November 17, 2002, *The New York Times* reported that the governor of the most populous state in America "chortled" when talking about his management of California. "Unlike Washington, the Democratic Party stands for something in California," Davis said. "We've led America in a host of areas, including the first state to combat global warming, the first state to permit paid family leave. If you're in Congress, it's hard to go back to your constituents and say, 'Look what the Democrats have done.' You could do that in California."

Within weeks, Davis was at the center of an extraordinary confluence of circumstances that capsized his ship of state. He is surely right in his rueful lament that "when things were going so well we didn't deserve all that credit, and later we didn't necessarily deserve all the blame. That's just the nature of politics." His predecessor, Governor Pete Wilson, had pushed through the deregulation of electricity, but Davis had helped implement the measure. When rolling blackouts began in 2000, he received most of the blame. Governors of both parties elected in 1998 rode the wave of the booming Clinton economy, but in 2002 that economy was in trouble and so were the governors.

California is a state of economic extremes, roller-coaster revenues resulting in higher highs and lower lows. The state has a progressive income tax in which 10 percent of taxpayers pay about 75 percent of the personal income taxes. In 2000, when Silicon Valley was booming and money was easy, $17 billion poured into the state coffers from capital gains and stock options alone. Two years later, after the dot-com fizzle, that amount dropped to less than $5 billion.

When things were hopping, the legislature and Davis had gone on a shopping spree. Most of it was eminently worthwhile, investments in schools, health care for the young and the poor, added services for state and local government employees, whose numbers rose from 282,000 when Davis entered office to 326,000 in 2001. When times turned bad, no one wanted his special program gutted or his treasured group of state employees dismissed. And few wanted to endorse higher taxes. The state was faced with an accumulated deficit of an estimated $35 billion, and there were no easy answers—not in Sacramento, not anywhere.

Davis's personality and political style and the unique nature of California made the difficulties infinitely worse. The governor was an anomaly in the backslapping, good-buddy world of state politics, a politician who did not appear to like people and whom people did not like. He was roundly disliked by legislative leaders of his own party, and even by some members of his own staff.

Davis found money more reliable than love. He raised an unprecedented

$64 million for his reelection campaign. He spent an estimated $10 million of that in the Republican primary to help defeat former Los Angeles Mayor Richard Riordan, who would have run a far stronger campaign than the conservative Simon. Arnold did his best to help the moderate Republican, unsuccessfully lecturing his fellow party members that "they should not be told by Gray Davis who they should vote for [and] that to me the right choice is Dick Riordan, because he has a chance to beat Gray Davis."

If Davis did not sell out the state to raise money and win the election, he certainly mortgaged bits and pieces of it to such benefactors as the California prison guards union, the Indian gaming tribes, and the trade unions. Almost all politicians take special-interest money and do favors, but Davis did it in a blatant way that offended those who would perhaps not have noticed if he had been more subtle. To many, he did not seem a steward of all the people, but an advocate for a few chosen constituencies. Even in his reelection, 60 percent of the people in the state had an unfavorable opinion of him.

Beyond his low popularity, Davis had another problem: in the extraordinary political geography of California, the populous coastline is as Democratic as Sicily is Catholic and with as little regard for intruders of another faith. The more sparsely populated inland is inhabited by conservative Republicans who after years of defeat had come to believe that losing is the high price of principle.

Almost immediately after Davis's reelection, a group of right-wing activists set out to recall him from the office to which the voters had just elected him. In early May 2003 they were joined by Darrell Issa, a conservative congressman from San Diego County. He took $10 million of the fortune he had earned with the Viper auto alarm and used it to fund this recall movement to throw Davis out of office.

Recall is another of the early-twentieth-century reforms of the populist Hiram Johnson. The statute does not specify why an official should be recalled, but millions in the state were convinced that it was not to attack a governor who had just been reelected and who, whatever his faults, was not guilty of high acts of malfeasance. To force a new election, Issa and his cohorts did not need a majority of Californians, only 897,156 registered voters.

Issa paid solicitors to seek tens of thousands of names, but the voters signed the petitions because of inchoate anger boiling up across the state. For the most part, it was anger of the haves, not the have-nots. It was anger of millions of Californians worried that the dream of an endlessly bright horizon that they considered their birthright was ending. It was anger at electric blackouts and exorbitant fees for registering automobiles. It was anger at illegal immigrants streaming up from Mexico and outsourced jobs streaming out. It was anger at what they had lost in the stock market and what they feared they would lose in the future. It was finely honed anger that they turned on Sacramento and above all on the governor. By merely signing their names, they could send a message that he would never forget.

In the end, 1,356,408 certified signatures graced the petitions, and on July 24, Lieutenant Governor Cruz Bustamante set the new election for October 7, 2002. The October recall would be two elections in one, or one dependent on the other: a vote to see if Davis should be torn from his seat, and at the same time a second vote to choose his successor. Davis figured that he would beat back this challenge, but several Republicans announced that they would enter the race, including conservatives Issa, State Senator Tom McClintock, and Simon, while the moderate Riordan planned to run if Arnold did not.

Many others of both parties wrestled with their ambition, thinking that this might be their moment. And behind it and above it all stood Arnold, saying little and waiting.

Total Recall

A rnold knew that he had to treat his wife like a constituency of one who had to be wooed with all his acumen and savvy. The Jacuzzi was the perfect setting. It was there that Arnold went to relax and to talk leisurely of many things.

"We were sitting in the Jacuzzi one day and I said I wanted to run for Governor—and she started shaking and crying," Arnold said. That Arnold could even talk of that day many months later to members of the Hollywood Foreign Press Association said much about the difference between the two of them. Nothing emotional troubled him overwhelmingly, and he could blithely cough up the most intimate, sensitive moments of Maria's life. He hid some of his acts but none of his emotions, while she hid almost none of her acts and much of her emotions.

Maria was deeply troubled over the possibility of his running. She had married Arnold in part to avoid a life of politics. Now if her husband ran, he would expand his life and she would be doing most of the giving up. "It was very tough for her, but her mother—Eunice Kennedy Shriver—was in favor of me running, so she talked to Maria, and she finally agreed," Arnold said. "If she hadn't agreed, I wouldn't have done it, because my marriage and my family are the most important things." Maria's mother may have talked to her, but it was Maria's decision. She took weeks to give Arnold her answer. It was already midsummer, and Arnold had to make a decision. Much of what was going on at that point, the planning and preparation, he kept shielded from Maria. He tiptoed around her, waiting for her to say yes. "Everybody was mad about that," said Maria. "They felt what I was doing was unfair."

Before fifty-six-year-old Arnold could actively engage in politics, he had to finish off the worldwide promotion for *Terminator 3: Rise of the Machines.* The sequel directed by Jonathan Mostow was largely a remake of the first version, but this time Arnold plays the good Terminator, and a beautiful woman, Kristanna Loken, plays the bad. "*Terminator 3* is dumbed down for the multiplex hordes," wrote critic Roger Ebert of this highly derivative film, but Arnold was never concerned about reviews. What may prove his last starring movie did spectacularly around the world: $418.3 million in all, including $150.4 million in the United States and Canada.

"If Arnold hadn't run for governor, we would have been able to set up three or four movies in a row paying him huge money just off of *Terminator 3,*" Arnold's attorney Bloom ruefully regrets. "It did huge numbers and we really couldn't enjoy the success."

Arnold was faced with another matter that had the potential to damage or destroy his political future. Two years before, the *National Enquirer* had publicly warned that as soon as he entered the race, there would be a a Krakatoa of tabloid eruptions spewing the lava of supposed dalliances and untoward conduct.

The man sitting on the throne of the tabloids was the most unlikely of emperors. His name was David Pecker, a dapper studiously money-oriented former accountant who had risen to be the president of French-owned Hachette Filipacchi, a middling chain of magazines. In 1999 a venture capital group bought American Media, the owners of the leading tabloids, the *National Enquirer* and the *Star,* and installed Pecker as CEO. Six months later for $105 million, American Media added the *Globe,* the *National Examiner,* and the *Sun,* completing a monopoly of the supermarket tabloids. If American Media had purchased all the sports magazines or the newsmagazines, there would have been protests at the danger to a free press, but the tabloids were considered by most journalists as worthless rags. There were few complaints, though the publications had an enormous impact on American society that was largely unacknowledged by the upscale media that disdained them.

As Pecker celebrated his coup, the circulation of the tabloids was declining, in part a victim of their own success in the celebrity marketplace. They had increasing competition from mainstream media, with magazines and newspapers covering stories they never would have before, and in ways that had once been unthinkable. Entertainment shows on television scooped them, and the Internet raided their most provocative subjects. If that was not enough difficulty, Pecker had an unfortunate characteristic for a tabloid publisher—an overweening social ambition that led him to desire to know some of the very people his publications so profitably trashed.

Pecker's dream of walking away a billionaire by building a great empire rested not on the expansion of the tabloids but on acquiring other media. One of the few inviting properties was eighty-three-year-old Joe Weider's seven bodybuilding and fitness magazines. Weider was suffering from back pain, especially troubling to a man of such physical vitality, and he had decided it was time to sell. In a blind auction, held late in 2002, American Media successfully bid $350 million, $50 million more than the second-highest bidder and far more than some analysts thought the magazines were worth.

Pecker had bought magazines that for more than half a century had been stamped with the powerful personality of one man. Though part of the deal was that Weider's name stay on the masthead, he had to sit back in semi-retirement and watch his influence decline. In December 2002 Joe and Betty Weider met with Pecker and his wife at the Peninsula Hotel in Beverly Hills for a dinner commemorating the sale. Joe had overseen every aspect of his magazines, and he now sought to control what was no longer his.

Weider suggested that Arnold be given "maybe ten percent of the company" for publicizing the magazines "I know that you love Arnold, you trained Arnold, and he became a champion, and you're protective of him," Weider recalled Pecker saying. "We would never run anything [negative] about him."

In August, when George Rush and Joanna Molloy published Weider's account of the evening in their New York *Daily News* gossip column, Pecker vehemently denied it. "He got very upset because the board of directors will say, 'Well, he's not going to attack Arnold and lose sales,'" Weider said. "So he said, 'We're not going to use any of the old stuff about Arnold unless he does something new.' He [Pecker] wanted to please me because Arnold was important to me and he didn't want to hurt Arnold." Pecker has a slightly different recollection. He said that he told Weider: "There is one thing that I can tell you. We don't as a company rehash old stuff. Anything he does that's newsworthy, we're going to run if we can validate it."

The past would be a closed book. Although Pecker tried to suggest otherwise, it was a promise unlike that made to anyone else in public life. And Arnold was the sole beneficiary.

Pecker was not acting just to please Weider or merely to assure himself a seat at the table of the rich and famous. When Pecker walked into Arnold's Santa

Monica office on July 11, 2003, he had been the owner of the bodybuilding publications for six months, and he was lost in the wilderness. The office was enough to intimidate many visitors. It was enormous, stretching practically a whole floor of the building, with a pool table and so much memorabilia that it was like walking into an Arnold museum.

Pecker had never even heard of the Arnold Classic. That was ignorance akin to that of a baseball magazine publisher being ignorant of the World Series. He needed Arnold not only because he knew nothing about bodybuilding but because the magazines and the whole sport were in trouble. Its champions were often so built up on steroids and growth hormones that their enormous, overwrought physiques no longer bore any relationship to the human form as it has always been known. The magazines were largely dependent on supplement-and-vitamin advertising promising extraordinary physical gain, including the dietary supplement ephedra that the FDA banned early in 2004, claiming its use involved "an unreasonable risk of illness or injury." He needed Arnold because his face on the covers sold magazines, his monthly column "Ask Arnold" gave the publications credibility, and Arnold was not only the greatest figure in the sport but by far its most influential. At a level on which Pecker was largely incapable of appreciating, not only did he need Arnold, but so did bodybuilding.

Arnold was contemplating running for governor, and it was unthinkable that he would admit Pecker into his inner sanctuary for a meeting unless he had thoroughly checked him out and decided that they could do business together. Weider had already told Arnold that he had pointedly discussed with Pecker that if American Media wanted Arnold's help, they would have to leave him alone in the tabloids. Arnold says that he was not so foolish as to bring the subject up or in any way or seek some formal agreement. "There was no discussion about the *National Enquirer*," he said. "There were all sorts of people sitting there. It would have been inappropriate. Nor did I want to be on the record that I'm hassling him about another agenda."

Arnold did not have to say anything. "I think it's common sense," he observed. "Do you want to work with someone who you are attacking? You don't have to say anything. You don't have to be sleazy and make deals. It's human nature."

Arnold's preeminent concern at the meeting was bodybuilding. He knew that his beloved sport was in grievous trouble. "I was very impressed," Pecker told journalist Ann Louise Bardach of *Los Angeles* magazine. "It was the first time I met him. He was very articulate about bodybuilding, very articulate about the business side. He was very familiar with the magazines and with exactly how the bodybuilding industry worked."

Arnold had a detailed awareness of bodybuilding, from the precise form of exercises to the intricacies of financing and promoting major contests. When he was finished talking, Pecker wanted Arnold's involvement even more than when he had walked in the door. "I approached him about the concept of having a bigger role with all of the Weider titles," Pecker recalled, "but specifically with *Muscle & Fitness* and *Flex*."

Both men had something that the other desperately wanted and needed. In a time of turmoil and uncertainty within the bodybuilding world, Pecker needed Arnold as an anchoring force, to give America Media credibility and authenticity. As for Arnold, he wanted to see if Pecker truly cared about the future of bodybuilding. Arnold also needed to rid himself of the endless assault of the tabloids on his private life, an intrusion that was no longer just a mere nuisance and unpleasantness but a crucial challenge to his public life. In the volatile political arena, all it might take was one or two cover stories in the *National Enquirer* or the *Star* to set off the dogs of the media and possibly bring his campaign down. When Arnold showed Pecker out into the California sunshine, the publisher says that nothing had been agreed upon and the tabloid problem had not even been discussed, but by the evidence of what transpired, or did not transpire, everything had been understood.

Arnold turned to his beckoning political future. As Arnold met regularly with George Gorton and Bob White, the election itself boded to become a grotesque sideshow to the overwhelmingly serious problems facing a state whose economy was larger than all but five or six countries. Wall Street gave its dispassionate response to the recall by downgrading the state's bond rating three categories, to BBB, just levels above junk bonds, and the worst rating of any of the fifty states. Much of the rest of the country and indeed the world looked at the spectacle with derision, or a bemused sense of superiority.

"Those who see governance as a high-minded, intellectual pursuit, had best avert their eyes from California in the months to come," *The Cleveland Plain Dealer* editorialized, as Ohio's leading paper chronicled the low-minded goings-ons. *The Times* (London) placed the blame in part on their fellow countrymen, nineteenth-century emigrants with a "fondness for rabble-rousing" from the wilder reaches of the British Isles. "The result," the newspaper noted wryly, "was that Britain exported to California a culture associated with savage violence, lawlessness, an enthusiasm for magic and mysticism and high rates of illegitimacy, often the result of rape."

All it took was the $2,500 filing fee and sixty-five signatures to get your name on the ballot. The result was a motley hodgepodge of 135 candidates whose diversity proved that anyone could aspire to the highest office in California. Of course, there were the serious politicos. On the Republican side the candidates included State Senator Tom McClintock, a man revered by California conservatives for his principled adherence to their beliefs. He perused the state budget books for hours, liposuctioning fat and seeking justification for tax cuts. Peter Ueberroth brought a formidable record of having headed the 1984 Olympic Games in Los Angeles. Despite his defeat to Davis the previous year, Bill Simon decided to run again. Former L.A. Mayor Dick Riordan stood high in the polls among possible Republican candidates but not in the eyes of California's right wing, which considered him a virtual Democrat masquerading in the robes of a Republican. This time the centrist Republican would not have to run the gauntlet of a Republican primary and stood a good chance of winning the general election. He had not filed his papers, waiting to see what Arnold would do.

On the Democratic side, candidates were caught between supporting their elected governor, Gray Davis, and advancing their own careers if, in fact, Davis was voted down. Thus, while Lieutenant Governor Cruz Bustamante condemned the recall, in the end he also entered the fray, only too ready to save matters for the Democrats if Californians voted to remove Davis.

The fringe candidates included the pornographer Larry Flynt, making his first major public statement since trying to save Bill Clinton from impeachment by threatening to expose the sexual peccadilloes of Republican legislators. Voters had their choice of pornographers. If they did not like Flynt, they could vote for Mary Carey, a twenty-three-year-old porn star. If they preferred other kinds of entertainers, Gary Coleman, the pint-size TV star from the 1970s and '80s sitcom *Diff'rent Strokes*, threw his cap in the ring, as did the comedian Leo Gallagher.

In this extraordinary lineup, Arnold's possible candidacy seemed to straddle both camps, one boot planted among the serious politicos, the other in the celebrity world. As the *Times* described with partial accuracy, potential candidate Schwarzenegger was "a liberal Republican who posed nude for photographs, killed nearly 300 people on film, smoked pot, and missed the funeral of his Austrian father to attend a bodybuilding competition."

All during the summer leading up to the mid-August filing deadline and certification, there was speculation as to just what Arnold would do. "The essence of Arnold is that he wants to keep everybody guessing," said his friend Neal Nordlinger. "When he does decide to do it, he completely surprises people. He's an intensely private person in terms of what he wants to

Arnold's publicist Charlotte Parker was a key player in his rise to stardom. (Charlotte Parker)

For most of his career, Lou Pitt (center) was Arnold's agent. Also seated here is director James Cameron. (Lou Pitt)

Arnold's first starring role was as Conan the Barbarian. (Photofest)

The *Terminator* films turned Arnold into a worldwide icon. (Photofest)

Arnold, his nephew, and his closest friends on his wedding day. Left to right: Patrick Knapp, Franco Columbu, Albert Busek, James Lorimer, and Sven Thorsen. (Private photo)

On their wedding day, it was hard to tell who was happier, Maria or Arnold. (Private photo)

Arnold speaking at the Republican National Convention on August 31, 2004, in New York City. (AP/Wide World)

do. He doesn't reveal anything. That's the way he is in life, that's the way he is in business."

Arnold read the polls as a fledgling politician and as a movie star who had made films to please his audiences. The polls that summer said that there was only one candidate who could beat him and beat him soundly. That was Democrat Senator Dianne Feinstein, among the most highly regarded political figures in the state. Arnold was loathe to admit that anyone could best him at whatever he chose to excel in, and as he saw it over time, nobody could. The seventy-year-old senator was like Sergio Oliva in 1968, an opponent so formidable that the novice Arnold had avoided competing against him.

Earlier in her career, Feinstein had successfully fought back a recall when she was mayor of San Francisco, and she considered the gubernatorial recall a mugging of democracy. If she had been convinced that her candidacy was the only way to keep the governorship in Democratic hands, she probably would have run. But she read the same polls that Arnold did, and she knew that as long as he did not enter the race, the Democrats would likely win.

Gorton was talking to Arnold once or twice a day and dealing with scores of reporters, all asking the same question. Arnold never said definitively what he would do. At first the consultant was convinced that Arnold would run, but by early August Arnold was giving every indication that he would not. Arnold had reached the point where he was joking about the decision. "You know, if I were to run, what would you guys think if I announce on the Leno show?" he asked Gorton and his wife, Kiki. The couple laughed at Arnold's humor.

Gorton was also a consultant to Riordan, who intended to run if Arnold did not. Those last days of the month Arnold was meeting regularly with the former mayor of Los Angeles, discussing strategy for Riordan's campaign. "There wasn't any question but that everybody was settled and Arnold was not running," asserted Gorton. "So, what I had to do was to keep enough suspense that we could get the press there to hear Arnold's decision not to run. That's all we were trying to do."

Feinstein got the same message as everyone else, and she became convinced that Arnold was not running. That made her decision far easier. Freed from an unwanted obligation, on August 6 Feinstein announced that she would not be entering the race.

Later that day, Arnold was scheduled to go on *The Tonight Show* to announce his decision. At breakfast, Arnold and Maria discussed what he should do. In making up her mind, Maria had been as isolated as she had ever been in her entire life. No one understood fully what she was facing, not Arnold, not her mother, not her girlfriends. Maria realized the consequences of a political life for her husband. It was not the threat of assassination, the brutal attacks, or the endless obligations that threatened her. Her greatest concern was that Arnold would be consumed by a political life. "Someone like me looks to get out of it, versus with him it's 'Oh, this is brand-new. This is fun,'" said Maria. She saw how much Arnold loved politics. She sensed how it would take over his life. He would be reborn, but he would be reborn without her. "I knew when Arnold decided to run that my time was over," Maria said. Arnold hungered profoundly for political office. For Maria to say no was to lose her husband in another way.

Arnold showed Maria two announcements, one saying that he was not going to run and one saying that he was. "This is what I would say if it were me," she said, pointing to the press release backing out of the race. Then she pointed to the other positive announcement. "This is you. You are going for it and you should do what you want to do. And you shouldn't say my lines, because they're not your lines. Your lines are, 'I'm going for it.' You can't be me. You have to be you." She said, "Don't see me as an obstacle."

Arnold had lunch with Franco, celebrating his friend's sixty-second birthday at a Santa Monica club. For a man about to make the most important announcement of his life, Arnold was unshakably cool. He sat and chatted in German with Franco and other European friends for several hours, until it was time to change his clothes and be driven out to Burbank to tape the show. Arnold did not give Franco any indication of his decision. The muscular Sardinian had been around the Austrian Oak for too long to predict what his closest friend would do.

While Arnold was joking and talking to his friends, Riordan sat at his beach house with his advisers, including Congressman David Dreier, planning his race for governor.

Jay Leno is as much an aficionado of motorcycles as Arnold, and when his guest arrived at the NBC studios, the *Tonight Show* host insisted on showing Arnold his latest acquisition, a motorcycle with a motor that sounds like a helicopter. Arnold sat on the motorcycle. The two stars joked and made show-business small talk while a melancholy Gorton stood nearby, clutching press releases announcing Arnold's decision not to run.

When Leno left to get ready to tape the show, Arnold and Gorton were alone for a few minutes. "What is it?" asked Arnold, looking at his glum-faced consultant.

"I just hate to lose you as a candidate," Gorton said. "You'd be a great candidate, you'd be a great governor, and I just think you'd be terrific, and I'd just hate to lose you."

"Oh, well, let's do it," Arnold said, and Gorton walked away, sad that it was all over.

In three decades of promoting movies, Arnold had come to consider programs such as *The Tonight Show* as a kind of media home. He was perfectly comfortable making his decision public from the guest chair between Leno's monologue and the host's next guest. That way, Arnold controlled his announcement in an environment he had mastered. Even more important, he had a built-in audience of millions. He did not care if critics accused him of trivializing politics.

What Arnold presumably lacked as a politician was the gravitas of a serious candidate. Almost any political consultant would have told him it was madness to announce to a comedian on a late-night talk show. He should stand at the Hollenbeck Youth Center in East L.A. with a slew of Latino kids, and a podium full of prestigious politicians, but not take politics even further down the road of trivialization. "I do things my own way because my instincts are better than anyone else's researched thinking," said Arnold. "To me *The Tonight Show* was the most organic thing to do. I felt this was the best audience. The media were shocked. How dare he circumvent the *serious* press and talk to us afterwards when he does the fluff stuff, the entertainment stuff, first. Running for governor is a *serious, serious* thing, and how can he dare do that? I love that. I will decide how I am going to reach out to the people."

The trickster Arnold joked with the host, lulling the audience into thinking that this was just another celebrity interview with its scripted one-liners. "It's the most difficult decision I've ever made in my entire life, except for the one in 1978 when I decided to get a bikini wax," he told Leno.

Arnold kept it up, until it was clear to everyone out there that he was not going to run and was doing nothing more than creating false suspense. Then he struck. "The man that is failing the people more than anyone is Gray Davis," Arnold told Leno. "He's failing them terribly. And this is why he needs to be recalled. And this is why I'm going to run for governor of the state of California."

Sitting there in the front of the audience, Gorton could hardly believe what he had just heard. He was trying to make sense of it when his cell phone started going off, and he grabbed to shut it off. As Arnold reached for models to explain his candidacy, he turned to neither Lincoln nor Reagan, but the movies. And he culled his slogan not from Jimmy Stewart in the sentimental *Mr. Smith Goes to Washington*, but from the dark 1970s satire *Network*. "We're mad as hell, and we're not going to take it anymore," he told the television audience. That is the line that the maniacal, messianic Howard Beale tells his television audience. Beale improves his ratings by instructing viewers to open their windows and shout the slogan into the dark night.

"Do your job for the people, and do it well," Arnold warned California's politicians. "Otherwise, you are *hasta la vista*, baby," the action hero said, appropriating the line he used in *Terminator 2* to dispatch his nemesis.

Though Arnold had not been briefed beforehand by his campaign consultants, he designed a subtle, sophisticated piece of positioning. Obviously a man of innate political shrewdness, he attempted to inoculate himself from the kind of charges that he might well face. "They're going to throw everything at me," he confided to Leno. "That I have no experience, I'm a womanizer and a terrible guy."

Lights, Camera, Action

When Arnold called Dick Riordan after his *Tonight Show* appearance to explain his decision to run, the former mayor was all congratulations. He showed his true feelings the next day when he arrived at Arnold's office with Mike Murphy, a prominent campaign consultant who had been planning to work on the Riordan campaign and was meeting Arnold for the first time.

The plump consultant was disheveled. His clothes, it turned out, were designer-made, and if he looked like an unkempt bed, it was one with silk sheets and monogrammed pillows. His presence added another element of tension, in part because he had run former secretary of education Lamar Alexander's 1996 presidential campaign. On that occasion, Murphy had bested George Gorton and Bob White by helping drive Governor Wilson out of the race, a memory that still rankled the former Wilson hands. Beyond that, in a business of large egos, Murphy is thought by some to be a prima donna of the Pavarotti school, unwilling and unable to share his authority with anyone.

Riordan could not lash out at Arnold, but the former mayor insisted that Gorton leave the room before Murphy gave Arnold his private take on the campaign. Riordan felt that Arnold's campaign manager had betrayed him by not telling him of Arnold's plans; Gorton could hardly admit that he had known nothing at all.

As Murphy was laying out his thinking before he flew off to Puerto Vallarta to spend ten days with his girlfriend, the banished Gorton rushed back into the massive office. "Hey, we got to tell the *Today* show now," he said excitedly. "They want you tomorrow morning."

"Bullshit, George, they'll wait!" Arnold exclaimed. "It's me, for Christ's sake." As Gorton turned to leave, Murphy realized that he was dealing with someone who understood the game. The consultant was still planning to go off on his Mexican vacation, but the prospect of working the race had suddenly gotten much more inviting.

"California recently approved the nation's only paid-family-leave law," Matt Lauer, cohost of the *Today* show, said from its studios in Rockefeller Center. "Businesses say that's a job killer. Would you repeal it as governor?"

"I didn't hear your question," Arnold said as he fumbled with his earpiece in NBC's Burbank studios.

"I said California has the nation's only paid-family-leave law. Businesses are opposed to it. Would you repeal it as governor?"

"I-I will have to get into that, I mean, because, as you know, I'm very much for families, I'm very much for children and children's issues and all that stuff."

"Real quickly, are you going to make your tax returns for the past several years available to the press?"

"Say again?"

Regardless of all the times Arnold had been on television, he fumbled. At times he managed to overwhelm Lauer with his verbosity, but it had not been a good interview. He did not do much better in subsequent interviews with ABC and CBS. Later that morning his appearance in Bellflower at the opening of the Inner-City Games should have been a positive moment for the candidate, a perfect photo op, but after watching him mishandle the morning talk shows, the political journalists shouted out unpleasant, argumentative questions, trying to pin him down on myriad subjects.

That afternoon back at the Santa Monica office, Maria was furious. She did not blame her husband, she blamed Gorton for getting Arnold up too early. She blamed him for not prepping Arnold. She blamed him for letting Arnold get so tired. She blamed him for Arnold not being able to hear. Maria did not shout. She did not threaten. She spoke with chilly disdain and quiet anger. It was a sound that you never wanted to hear, and once you had been its victim, you never forgot.

In working on Proposition 49 and elsewhere, the campaign manager had contributed largely to Arnold's advance. It was hardly Gorton's fault that in the past weeks he had been concerned mainly about whether Arnold would run, not *how* he should run. Beyond that, Arnold had a movie star's attitude toward learning. He was not about to prep himself on scores of issues unless he was going to run, any more than he would memorize lines of a script that he might not film.

Gorton surely had enough capital with Arnold to survive the mistake, but

Maria was unforgiving. She was making her own enormous sacrifices, even giving up her job at NBC—at least during the campaign. When she walked into the office and said that the campaign staff had to be shaken up, there was no one to challenge her. In almost any other instance, Arnold would have protected Gorton, but not this time. "I felt that the campaign needed a massive operation run by someone who had presidential-level experience," said Maria. "From the minute that Arnold said he wanted to run, my focus was on putting the best team together to help him do that."

Arnold was not good at this sort of thing, but he called Gorton to his house and asked him if he would step aside and allow Bob White to take over as campaign manager. He said yes. White had been Gorton's closest friend, and their friendship became one of the casualties of the campaign. It took months for them to reestablish trust.

In the first two weeks of the campaign, Arnold did not head out to talk to voters and to the media. Although he was falling in the campaign's private polls, Arnold stayed largely at home or in his Santa Monica office, meeting with an endless stream of experts. They came and they sat and they droned on at a length and in a specificity to which few candidates would have subjected themselves.

Several of Arnold's advisers were appalled at this endless parade of academicians. They were used to briefing their candidate, and *brief* was the operative word, a ten-point memo, a fifteen-minute meeting, not these pedantic monologues when Arnold should have been out there greeting voters. But bodybuilding had taught Arnold that to win, you had to train more than anyone else. Although on one level it was far too late for that, he was trying to do the best he could, listening with intensity, taking what he needed and discarding the rest.

The truth was that Arnold was largely unprepared to run for governor. His appearance on the *Today* show was not an aberration but an accurate rendering of his lack of knowledge. "A lot of this for me was going on faith," said Congressman David Dreier, who after a phone call from Arnold became his most important political supporter in the state. "Faith in him, because of the fact that he had not done this, and I'll admit that there were a couple of times when I just had to swallow hard and think. One of the things was this notion of the [Bush] White House that a weakened Gray Davis going into the re-election campaign in 2004 might have been better than throwing Gray Davis out and having a Republican in there."

Despite Arnold's weaknesses, his popularity was enough to drive all the other credible Republican candidates except for Tom McClintock out of the race. Although there were many serious issues facing the state, by far the most crucial was the economic crisis. If he was to be a successful candidate, it was here that he would be tested first and hardest, and the advice he received would be the most crucial. One of the first economists to arrive at Arnold's Brentwood home was Arthur Laffer, best known for the Laffer curve, showing that raising taxes beyond a certain point decreases revenues since people have no incentive to work harder. Many mainstream economists view the Laffer curve the way physicists would a colleague who discovers that balls thrown into the air inevitably come down, but the American right wing has celebrated Laffer.

Former Governor Pete Wilson was also at the small meeting. Laffer relished his opportunity to talk about the politician he considers "the single worst governor in U.S. history—bar none." He raged against the Republican Wilson for raising taxes, when Laffer had the solution—eliminate all local and state sales taxes, property taxes, corporate taxes, gas taxes, and almost all other levies and impose a 5.85 percent to 6 percent flat tax.

Laffer also condemned several people who were not there, including Arnold's friend and adviser the billionaire investor Warren Buffett. "Rich don't make you smart or an honorable leader of men," Laffer said. Arnold was sending surrogates out to speak for him, and the immediate cause of Laffer's rage was an interview Buffett had just given to *The Wall Street Journal*. The Nebraska business sage had condemned Proposition 13. He pointed out that on his $500,000 Omaha home he paid $14,401 in property taxes while on his $4 million Laguna Beach property he paid only $2,264. He thought that neither fair nor good social or economic policy.

Laffer advised that if Buffett was his friend, Arnold should ask him to resign from the campaign. If Buffett was not a close friend, Arnold "should publicly dismiss him as an advisor." Laffer had similar suggestions for what Arnold should do with movie and television star Rob Lowe, another well-known backer. Lowe had entered politics at the 1988 Democratic National Convention in Atlanta, where he videotaped a sixteen-year-old having sex with another young woman. Laffer recommended that the candidate disavow any relationship with the *West Wing* star.

A few days later, another prominent economist made his way to Arnold's home; like Laffer, he sat outside on the patio with Arnold and a small group of advisers: Edward Leamer, a professor of economics, statistics, and management at UCLA.* A Republican, the professor had been on Governor Wilson's

---

*Professor Leamer is the author's brother.

Council of Economic Advisors. He had a very different take on the economic crisis.

Leamer described a government that overspent when times were good and did not cut back enough when times were bad. For four years Davis and the legislature had projected revenue growth that had not happened, and Leamer doubted that it would happen now, and he believed the next governor would have to wrestle with imponderable problems.

Arnold was dressed casually in shorts and a T-shirt, but there was nothing casual about the way he was listening. "I think you need a three-year plan," Leamer said. "You want to cut back spending to the supportable 1999–2000 level with roughly the same level of government employees. Include everything. Education. Everything. Since Davis entered office, about a hundred thousand jobs have been added to the public rolls in state and local government. You phase out those jobs over three years. And then you have a temporary tax increase of about $5 billion, a combination of sales and income. And the third year it's removed and you're back to normal. You're starting to have a state surplus to buy back the debt."

Arnold listened carefully and asked questions, and some of his advisers took notes. Leamer was not offering any magic bullet, no plan that could suddenly make things right. "But whatever you decide to do, Arnold, California voters need to understand what your plans are for the current deficit problem," Leamer said. "You really have to level."

"You don't understand the way the press operates," Arnold said. "You don't understand what would happen."

Leamer left that day full of contradictory feelings. He was impressed that Arnold had sat with him for close to three hours, asking probing questions. He had graduate students who could not follow him the way Arnold had, but he was troubled that Arnold dismissed his assertion that he had to be straight with the voters.

A few days later, on August 20, Arnold chaired a two-hour economic summit at the Hyatt Hotel near LAX. It was a shrewd strategy for the candidate with the least-impressive political credentials of any of the serious contenders to put together an "Economic Recovery Council" to advise him on the state's problems. Laffer had been invited to join the group of conservative businesspeople and a few academicians. He had turned the offer down because he was not sure just where the candidate stood. Laffer believed that Arnold had "all the portfolio assets to be a great leader but a great man with a bad plan is an emissary of the devil."

Although most of the council members did not realize it when they arrived, the gathering was wholly cosmetic. The only contribution most of the twenty-two-person panel would make to the campaign was to attend this two-hour gathering. The meeting began impressively enough as a pool of photographers and reporters were shown into the ballroom where Arnold sat between the cochairs, Warren Buffett and former Secretary of the Treasury and Secretary of State George Shultz. In his years since leaving government, Shultz's conservatism had become even more uncompromising. That was the sound he made into Arnold's ear.

As for Buffett, the Omaha billionaire was a moderately liberal Democrat. He had taken Arnold as his guest to the 2002 conference of European business leaders at Waddesdon Manor in Great Britain. The photographers ignored the rest of the panel and took numerous photos of the three men. Once the reporters were shown out, Arnold made a short introduction and the various panel members took turns speaking. There was no audience, except for campaign staff and security, and no press accounts of the discussion.

There was little diversity of opinion among the group. One after another the council members spoke mainly about lowering taxes and cutting business regulation, as if by such efforts alone the state's problems would disappear. Buffett was different. He sounded not like a sophisticated, world-traveled business leader but a simple man telling his 35 million California neighbors that if they did not do something, the bank was going to foreclose on their property. He explained how a month earlier the state had needed $11 billion in short-term loans so that it could meet its immediate financial needs. Wall Street felt that California was in such financial disorder that the state had to go out and get seven investment banks to guarantee that someone would be there to loan the state money. That cost the state $84 million in fees that could have been used for many useful purposes, and this would be only the beginning of what California faced if it did not get its house in order.

Leamer was the only other speaker who challenged the easy verities of the group. Arnold's associate Paul Minor, who had brought together many of the experts, told Leamer that he should speak frankly and openly. And so he did, saying some of the things he had said at Arnold's home about the necessity of a multiyear plan to cut expenditures and to raise taxes in the short term.

As soon as Leamer finished, Shultz cut the professor down for mentioning raising taxes, and no one spoke in his defense. Not during this meeting or anytime during the campaign did Arnold or anyone else mention the possibility of borrowing money by issuing new bonds—the primary method that Governor Schwarzenegger would use to deal with the short-term economic crisis.

When the meeting was over, Arnold walked out with Buffett and Shultz to give the first press conference of his campaign. Close to two hundred journalists waited for him, in its scope nearly unprecedented for a political press conference. Here was nearly the entire spectrum of the media, from major American newspapers to foreign press from five continents. There was everything from serious political magazines to the entertainment media to the tabloids.

The print reporters sat in row after row of chairs. Beyond them, traversing the entire room, stood twenty-nine television cameras and dozens of photographers darting back and forth, trying to get unique shots. In the back row with television cameras hovering over her sat Yvonne Abraham of *The Boston Globe*. "They're what's important," Abraham sighed, looking back at the cameras. "We don't matter any longer." That was only a momentary aside from a print journalist, but as Arnold looked out on the assemblage, it was not far from the vision he had of the gathering.

The cameras have always loved Arnold, and he looked to them as if seeking a friend in the crowd. "Well, first of all, thank you very much for this incredible turnout," he said as he scanned the room with a penetrating gaze. "I would have wished to have this kind of a turnout when I did *Last Action Hero*." He almost always began with a little self-deprecating humor, which immediately ingratiated himself with his audience. Then he turned serious.

"When I came to California thirty-five years ago, this was a place of great dreams," he said, touching each word with a hint of emotion. "This state said to the people everywhere, 'Come here. Work hard. Play by the rules and your dreams can come true.' What has happened to California? What has happened to that feeling? What has happened to the optimism that this state once represented to the world?

"Now, I believe that we all—in my heart—that we can bring that optimism back. The people of this state are working hard. They are raising their families, and they're paying their taxes. Our businesses are the most innovative on the face of this earth. We still have all the elements that made us great and prosperous. We have everything we need, except leadership."

There, in essence, was his campaign. Everything else was footnotes. He went on to talk about the overtaxed, overregulated Californians, many of whom had begun to leave the state. He would call a special session of the legislature to reform the horrendously expensive workers' compensation. He would institute a healthy business climate so businesses would not flee to Arizona or Nevada. He would bring down the high cost of energy in the state. He would call for a constitutional spending cap and "attack the spending deficit straight on." He would immediately call for an audit that within sixty days would "find out how bad the situation really is."

Arnold was startlingly lacking in details, and like a good defense attorney, he faced up to what would be the strongest criticism. "Before the carping begins about the need for the twenty-five-point plan on each one of those items, let me make one thing clear: that these problems were not created in two weeks," he concluded. "Nor will we be able to solve these problems in two weeks. Let me tell you something. One thing that the citizens of California can count on is that I would take action."

The action hero had spoken, and now he began answering the reporters' questions. Arnold believed that America needed a strong, authoritative leader who could bring order and discipline to the near anarchy of democracy. That began not in Sacramento but in his treatment of the media. He had an intimidating charisma that demanded respect and attention. He immediately made it clear that he would not tolerate the shouts and outbursts typical of so many press conferences. The reporters would ask their questions in an orderly fashion, or they would not ask them at all. "Excuse me! Excuse me!" he said before the journalists got the message and were shouting like traders on the floor of the Chicago Mercantile Exchange. "Even though I play a machine, I'm not a machine. So let me just answer one question at a time. Thank you!"

As he turned to face each questioner, it was much the way he had posed in bodybuilding competitions, always exposing the best part of himself. Arnold had not followed Laffer's advice to ask Buffett to resign. He preferred public humiliation. When he got the proper question, he was ready. "I told Warren if he mentions Prop 13 one more time, he has to do five hundred sit-ups," Arnold said, the trace of a smile crossing his lips. The revered billionaire was not often spanked in public, but he smiled, kept his mouth shut from then on, and maintained his friendship with Arnold. As for the whole question of Prop 13, Arnold employed the Reagan approach of answering with an anecdote. He told the story of an "old lady in Venice where I used to train in Gold's Gym [who] came out of her house [with] tears in her eyes," because the measure had passed and she would not have to sell her house. That did not answer the question, but it was far more emotionally satisfying, and Arnold moved on.

To a reporter from the Latin media, he had a richly empathic answer for his viewers ("I am very fond of the Latin community. I have done four of my movies down in Mexico"). To a reporter from *The New York Times* who asked about illegal immigration, he said that he would do something about that, too, and call on the President for help as well.

Arnold portrayed himself as the true people's candidate, unbeholden to the special interests, unlike the craven politicians in Sacramento. "I will be a governor of the people for change," he said. "The only thing that counts for me is the people." He dismissed the idea that people were interested in figures. They wanted action.

Gorton stood in the back of the room, watching the performance. He had been dropped as campaign manager after Arnold's spectacularly bad performance on the morning talk shows, but the consultant was still involved. He had begun that morning like a nervous coach sending a player into a game for the first time. As the press conference continued, he began listening with comfort and then with awe at what he considered "the best performance I've ever seen. It was better than Ronald Reagan."

None of the political reporters were as enthusiastic in their dispatches. For the most part, they were frustrated that they could not break through Arnold's persona. Whatever they asked, however tough their questions, he deflected them and posed a positive image of himself before moving on.

Arnold's last question of the day came from Jan Carl, a reporter from *Entertainment Tonight*. "I want to talk specifically about people who have gone on record as joining your campaign," Carl said. "What precise role is Rob Lowe going to have?"

The political journalists groaned audibly. They were serious reporters, and here they had to share their precious questions with a celebrity show.

"I have to tell you it's a very good question," Arnold said, and did an acrobatic transition into a lengthy monologue on how the Hollywood community wanted to help him because of all the work he had done with the Special Olympics, from Africa to China, plus all the work with education and children, before finally returning to Lowe. "Rob Lowe is not a senior adviser, nor is he an adviser," Arnold said. "But you know how it is in Hollywood, with the publicity agents and all of these things. The bottom line is that Rob Lowe is a very good friend and he was the very first one to say, 'My wife and I want to support you, any help that you need.'"

The media conference was over, but Arnold had one more thing he wanted to say. "I want to thank all of you for coming, because remember I am a strong believer in that if it was my bodybuilding career or my acting career, I could not have done it without the press," he said, pumping each syllable with sincerity. "You were always very helpful."

It was as if the journalists and Arnold were colleagues on a common quest. For some of the reporters, it was a compliment, but others found the remark strange, almost unsettling.

Arnold had as objective a sense of his public performances as anyone, and when he left that day, he knew he had scored magnificently. He had spent those two weeks listening to all those experts. Though he had rejected or found contradictory much of their advice, he had developed the confidence to deal with whatever the reporters threw at him. He drove back to his office in Santa Monica. When he was getting out of the car in the garage, he ran into Kiki Gorton, George's wife. He was effusive at how well it had gone.

"The reason why it went so great is because it's political press, it's news, it's entertainment press, you have them all there," Arnold said. Not only were they all there, but for twenty-five years Arnold and the entertainment media had been playing the same game. They wanted him to look good and he wanted to look good, and with all the coverage they were giving him, for the next forty-five days he might be able to stiff the political press.

A Fork in the Road

A rnold had another reason to be positive. A few minutes before the economic summit, he had met with Mike Murphy, who had just returned from his Mexican vacation. After a short discussion, Murphy drove out to LAX to meet the arriving private plane carrying Maria and her close friend Bonnie Reiss, a Democratic activist who was president of the Inner-City Games Foundation and a founding director of Arnold's All-Stars, his after-school program.

Maria was still supremely unhappy at the way her husband's campaign was being run. She had the Kennedy approach to problems—immediately seeking out the most prominent expert. That worked wonders if a dentist was needed, but it did not always work in politics, where Rolodexes dated quickly and were often full of the tried and the tired. In this instance, the people she talked to told her that Murphy was the best, and if he was the best, then Murphy was the man who should take over. "I called many people, and I said, 'I want the best operative in politics,'" said Maria. "People give you different names. And at the end of your research, you see which name comes up the most, and then you go after him. That was it."

After twenty years in politics, forty-two-year-old Murphy had grown tired of working ankle-deep in political blood and dreamed of a second life in show business. "If I had a choice between writing and directing my own little dark comedy or being the key political adviser for the president of the United States, I'd do the comedy," he told Gary Delsohn of the *Sacramento Bee*. In fact, his campaigns were their own little dark comedies. He was an ironist of high order, a funny man who fed the voters whatever lines brought the greatest applause. He had a reputation for running negative campaigns, but he used whatever worked, from saccharine to savagery. He was most famous for running Senator John McCain's campaign for the 2000 Republican presidential nomination, letting reporters ride on the candidate's bus and opening him up to the media in an unprecedented way. Reporters celebrated the campaign manager for that daring strategy. When Murphy talked about the campaign, he was like Field Marshal Erwin Rommel reminiscing about the brilliant success of the North African campaign, ignoring the minor detail that the Germans lost.

Murphy understood his own needs as well as his candidates', and his need was to run the show without interference. Once his terms were met, he agreed to take over the campaign. He had one problem. He had contracted to spend six days in the former Soviet republic of Georgia, consulting in the presidential campaign there, and Arnold or no Arnold, he could not back out of that commitment. And so he flew off to Eastern Europe, promising to return in a week.

Two days after his press conference, Arnold drove in a black GMC Yukon to Huntington Beach, a beachside town an hour south of Los Angeles, for his first campaign appearance. Arnold's campaign staff was not planning a major event there. He was to meet with a group of small businessmen at the Inka Grill and then visit several shops along Main Street, listening to the owners' complaints, make a few short remarks filmed by the camera crews, and drive back north.

The majority of the camera crews present were from the entertainment media, including *ET, Inside Edition*, and E!, and they had set up several hours before the event. As soon as people began hearing that Arnold would be there, they called their friends on their cell phones and changed their plans. By the time Arnold finally arrived at one P.M. a crowd of several thousand blocked the street surrounding the Spanish-style building where Arnold was to have his little meeting. They were not there because Arnold was running for office but because of his celebrity, and they were in a celebratory mood. Aides passed out blue JOIN ARNOLD signs. That was the campaign slogan—not join my crusade, not join my party, not join my cause, but join Arnold.

When Arnold left the restaurant and started walking down Main Street, a dozen beefy, buffed Huntington Beach police tried to keep the crowd back but were overwhelmed. He was wearing one of his regular-guy outfits, chino pants and a blue short-sleeved shirt with the top button undone. From a distance, it appeared he had been lifted up and was being carried along on the shoulders of the throng. He periodically looked up and nodded to the most distant members of the crowd, like an actor playing to the farthest seats in the gallery. When he finally worked his way back up the other side of the street, to a fountain where a microphone had been set up, the sound system did not work and the crowd could not hear what he was saying. They did not appear to care as they stood quietly, as if watching a silent movie.

At the end of the Huntington Beach event, Joe Mathews, a young *Los Angeles Times* reporter, happened to be standing near several of Arnold's staff, including Rob Stutzman, the chief spokesman, and another media aide, Karen Hanretty. He overheard them having a spirited discussion about the tumultuous event. An overly aggressive autograph seeker had nearly punctured an advance man with her pen, leaving the aide a ruined shirt as his souvenir of the event. There had been other frightening moments. The police blamed Arnold's people, and Arnold's people blamed the police, but it was clear that from then on, the candidate would have to campaign with more security.

This onslaught of humanity wanting to see and touch Arnold gave his advisers an excuse to wall him off physically behind barriers, just as they had closed him off from political journalists. It was an important story, but it did not appear in the *Los Angeles Times* the next morning, only at the end of the campaign, when Mathews wrote an excellent inside story of the campaign.

The young reporter's editors did not run the story, because they had a different agenda, which emanated from John Carroll, the editor. In his four decades in journalism, the unassuming, taciturn Carroll had become one of the most respected editors in America. He had been a correspondent in Vietnam and the Middle East for the *Baltimore Sun,* having received his education in American politics as the *Sun*'s White House correspondent covering the Nixon administration. After a stint at the *Lexington Herald-Leader,* he returned to the *Sun* in 1991 as its editor. Nine years later, he assumed the same position at the *Los Angeles Times,* the nation's fourth-largest newspaper. He was a reporter's editor who gave talented journalists the time and expense accounts to do serious investigative journalism. A measure of that commitment was the paper's five Pulitzer Prizes for journalism in 2003, though not for its coverage of the campaign.

Carroll is fundamentally a public moralist. The editor, like many journalists of his generation, has an overwhelming sense of decline in his profession and his country, to some degree. He celebrates the technological advances of his age, but with them has come what he calls "a tidal wave of pornography." The free press is sacred, and it, too, is being overrun by "journalistic pornography." It is all about money and ratings. When a story has the potential to create resentment, it is "seized like gold" and "cynically packaged as the inside story 'they' don't want you to know."

Sixty-one-year-old Carroll saw himself and his paper as being on a difficult search for the truth. Although its conservative critics considered the *Los Angeles Times* a liberal rag spewing its ideology in the guise of news, Carroll took the criticism of his paper as proof that he and his reporters were doing their jobs, and he was not about to stop simply because Arnold Schwarzenegger had come on the scene.

The editor kept coming back to the image of Nixon, whom he had observed firsthand. The editor saw distressing similarities between the autocratic disdain for the media on the part of Nixon's aides and a similar attitude from those on Arnold's staff. "When Richard Nixon was a candidate here in the late forties, early fifties, he did everything almost in the open that would foreshadow Watergate," said Carroll. "This paper was not covering that seriously in those days. If they had been, he never would have become President of the United States. That's not going to happen on my watch. We're going to cover his [Arnold's] character, and if the public likes his character as it is, knowing the facts, that's fine. But nobody's ever going to be able to say the *L.A. Times,* when John Carroll was editor, was asleep at the switch, and therefore a person with questionable character ascended to high office."

As Carroll saw it, the paper was the people's surrogate, asking the questions voters wanted asked and exploring the serious issues. What Carroll saw in Arnold's campaign was a "monumental collision" of civic values that he and his paper upheld and the more dubious aspects of show business. "It was new ground for the press, and our mission was to behave like the best of the old media," Carroll said, "to deal in facts, to force candidates to take positions on the issues to the extent that we can."

The editor believes that if a politician wants to become governor of California, the candidate is obligated to run the gauntlet of the free press, talking seriously to reporters, sitting with the editorial board, and holding him- or herself up to public scrutiny through the medium of the free press. When Arnold tried to avoid those meetings with the press, he was not simply walking away from an unpleasant few hours. He was trying to prevent the *Los Angeles Times* and other newspapers from doing a duty whose absence, Carroll believed, risked rendering democracy meaningless.

Arnold saw it differently. Early on in the campaign, he called Carroll and flattered him and his paper but then refused to sit down with an editorial board and reporters who were "experts on specific subjects" when he was "new to some of these subjects" and "didn't feel comfortable with that and though he would have things to say later on, he didn't want to do that now."

Arnold felt that the reporters and editors would try to trip him up on some esoteric fact that might matter to them but not to the voters.

The fact was that the California "free press" was largely Democrat-oriented, in which no major paper endorsed Arnold's candidacy. Arnold had already had a bad experience with the *Los Angeles Times* ten years previously when the paper had printed a false story about a preview of *Last Action Hero* and then refused to admit its error. He was so suspicious of the paper that during the campaign he told Fox News' Bill O'Reilly that "all of the [negative] stories are fed by the [Davis] campaign headquarters" and that the *Los Angeles Times* placed his opponents on page one and relegated him to "page 12 or page 20," an assertion that could be refuted simply by looking at a few copies of the daily.

Beyond his suspicion of individual newspapers and reporters, Arnold had an institutional problem with the print media. "It upset the press that until now they were the ones that delivered the candidates, they were the power brokers," said Arnold. "Now they're saying to themselves, 'What's going on with the position we used to have?' I think that's what upset the more serious press."

Even when reporters were sympathetic to Arnold, he and his staff disliked the reporters' intrusive craft. "In a traditional campaign, the press tail wags the dog, in many cases," Arnold's media adviser Don Sipple told the Institute of Governmental Studies postmortem conference on the recall election. "Well, Arnold Schwarzenegger was a well-known cultural icon; he did not need that. In order to be able to say what he wants to do and put forth his agenda, we had to go outside the mainstream media. So it was a conscious strategy of the campaign to do it that way."

Arnold and his advisers felt that the California and national newspapers were largely out to get them. "There's kind of an institutional 'gotcha' feeling about Arnold," asserted Mike Murphy. "The press had this attitude essentially saying, 'Well, we're in the complicated world of state politics, and he's a movie guy. He's an idiot, so we will harpoon him.' And so we built into our strategy not appeasing their view, which is that Arnold stands there and takes their questions every day for five hours until they can knock him out. That frustrated them a lot. They were highly critical for a long time because we didn't run the kind of campaign the press likes, which is a campaign about the press."

And thus was born an epic battle that was waged throughout the campaign. Day after day, the *Los Angeles Times* tried to force Arnold to take detailed stands on issues and respond to its insistent queries. Soon after Arnold entered the race, the paper gave all the major candidates a questionnaire asking how they would deal with the financial crisis. When everyone replied but Arnold, the paper pointedly left blank space where his comments would have gone. "After that, which I think got quite a backlash, he never ducked one of those things again," Carroll said proudly. "And he actually came out with positions on issues, not as many as some voters and certainly the newspaper would have liked, but he was much more responsive on issues than he had been. And I was pleased about that."

There was another issue about Arnold that troubled Carroll. The editor had no interest in movie gossip, but he knew that "for years, he'd [Arnold] had a reputation as a man who treated women crassly." Several of Carroll's editors had read the *Premiere* article, and the very day Arnold announced his candidacy, Carroll set his paper to the task of "see[ing] whether this reputation was warranted."

Carroll realized that millions of Californians had an emotional commitment to Arnold as the state's savior, and this project might end up creating a firestorm of criticism, especially since he and his paper were alone. "The *L.A. Times* itself was the only paper that pursued this groping thing," he reflected. "There was a fork in the road and the entire press corps went one way and we went the other way."

The editor is disdainful of the tabloid press, considering it not truly a part of journalism. He failed to grasp the essential fact that if the *National Enquirer* or the *Star* had pursued the story, a number of major American papers would probably have written about it. Nor did he understand that the most important story was not Arnold's individual sexual encounters, but why the tabloids had backed off covering them.

Carroll says that the paper did not investigate the sex lives of the other candidates because there was no spate of rumors about their conduct. That is true, but Arnold had been the most popular star in the world, and there were rumors about the sex lives of almost every Hollywood star. By every indication, Arnold's major opponents were men of admirable personal moral conduct, but even if they had not been, the *National Enquirer* would not have run stories on them. However Carroll tried to rationalize it, the *Los Angeles Times* set out to investigate what everyone—Arnold, his advisers, adversaries, and California's greatest paper—knew was the most vulnerable part of his candidacy.

Carroll assigned an entire task force to look into Arnold's sexual past, including Gary Cohn, a Pulitzer Prize–winning investigative reporter, who had just arrived at the paper from the *Baltimore Sun;* Robert Welkos, a seasoned Hollywood reporter; Carla Hall, a metro writer; and later in the investigation others, including Mark Arax, Tracy Weber, Megan Garvey, Sue Fox, and Anita Busch.

The reporters worked hectic, tense twelve-hour days, seeking out sources and trying to verify stories. Inevitably, Arnold's people heard rumors about the investigation, while several of the opposition camps waited eagerly for a story that might terminate the Terminator.

"We're Not Gonna Take It"

As Arnold walked toward the outdoor stage at California State University, Long Beach, on September 3, 2003, the heavy metal song "We're Not Gonna Take It" blared at rock-concert level. The candidate stepped purposefully along a pathway forged by two rows of bicycle racks. He ignored the shouts and screams of well-wishers pressed up against the temporary barricades, wanting an autograph, a word, or merely a look.

One of those standing there was Arthur Grace, a photographer who had worked on several of Arnold's films and had a sensitive awareness of Arnold's physiognomy. As Arnold walked past, the photographer thought he looked apprehensive and ill at ease. Unlike the times Grace had shot him on his movie sets, Arnold was not playing a role, repeating his lines for as many takes as it took. He was walking out into the unknown, giving his first major campaign speech.

About twenty feet farther ahead, Arnold was hit by an egg that splattered on the left shoulder of his yellow sports jacket. "Now, the man did not flinch," said Landon Parvin, a prominent speechwriter who had flown in from Washington to help with the campaign. "If he had flinched, looked at it, brushed it off, or ducked, the headlines would have been TERMINATOR HAS FEET OF CLAY. But he did not even miss a beat. To me, that was maybe the best thing that happened to him the first few weeks of the campaign. He just kept going, and people said, 'He is an action guy. He is a Terminator.'"

Mike Murphy, who had just returned from Eastern Europe to take control of the campaign, was equally impressed. He thought that Arnold moved forward like a tank, rolling ahead, paying no attention to the distraction.

Arnold took off his stained sports coat and walked up to the podium in his shirtsleeves. He gave a paint-by-numbers speech largely devoid of references to the two thousand students overfilling the amphitheater and spilling out onto the lawns beyond. Arnold was speaking to the bank of television cameras, providing a series of irresistible sound bites for the evening news. "I'm tired of hearing politicians say, 'We can't do this,' or, 'We can't do that!'" Arnold said. "I will be the governor who believes in what California can do."

Before departing in his black SUV, Arnold said a few words to the reporters. Murphy knew that the thrown egg would be the lead item in the papers and the footage on the local news shows. It had to resonate in the right way. He gave Arnold a line that could have come from one of his movies. "This guy owes me bacon now," Arnold said. "You can't just have eggs without bacon."

Murphy had never run the campaign of a movie star. He decided immediately that he would have to button down the campaign until he felt Arnold was ready. The campaign was flying in experts and scholars from all around the country to brief Arnold. "To Arnold's credit, he didn't just want a script," said Murphy. "He wanted to understand what he was doing, so he wanted to hear from the experts, because he knew the stuff he came out for he'd hold on forever."

That evening the five other top candidates would be confronting one another for the first time. Arnold told reporters that he had turned down all debates except for one on September 24 sponsored by the California Broadcasters Association. "When I was a bodybuilding champion, I didn't go to Mr. Venice Beach," Arnold said, smugly putting down the first debate. The real reason, however, he was not going to the debate was that such professional politicians as Tom McClintock and Cruz Bustamante might bury him under an avalanche of detail and specificity.

Arnold was no more ready to get waylaid by journalists. As Murphy and his colleagues saw it, the reporters were playing to one another, winning points by stumping the candidate. In the entire campaign, Arnold did not do a single long interview with a political journalist or another major press conference at which he would have to answer a full barrage of questions.

Arnold told the campaign consultant to treat him the way a director treats an actor. For the most part, all Arnold had to do was learn his lines and speak them well. "It's no different than when I start a movie and we hire a new director or a different producer and I say to people, 'I need you to tell me exactly what you need, and I don't want you to sugarcoat it,' " Arnold said. "He [Murphy] was like the Godfather on putting his thought in there. He mapped it out, and we followed the blueprint."

Maria felt more confidence now that the team she had selected of Murphy, Parvin, and White was in place, but she still had a sense that everything was not right. "Maria came only to a couple of the staff meetings," said Parvin. "At one of the early ones, she said that the real Arnold, the man she knew, wasn't getting out there. She was impassioned. The next day she came up to me and asked if she had been too much. I said no, that everything she said had been appropriate."

Maria may have avoided the formal staff meetings, but there was no one more crucial. She had absolute confidence in her judgment. Given her family background, she had more years of experience in campaigning than any of Arnold's advisers. "When I would say I don't want Arnold portrayed like this, everybody would be like, 'What a bitch,'" Maria said. "But you know what? I was right. There are a hundred people responsible for a successful campaign, and only one is responsible when it's a disaster. Going into it, I knew that if he didn't run, it was going to be my fault. If he lost, it was going to be my fault. And when he won, it's five guys who did it."

There had been a few protesters in Long Beach, and from then on Murphy made it difficult for the demonstrators to get near enough to bother Arnold. He set up a series of staged events at which Arnold could be at his best. His favorite devices were "Ask Arnold Town Meetings" with hand-picked audiences. To differentiate the similar events, Murphy attempted to give each one a theme.

One of the events was an all-immigrant evening at the East Los Angeles center where Danny Hernandez had started the Inner-City Games. The portable bleachers looked like a "We Are the World" Coke commercial, with every conceivable ethnic group present, all of them Republicans or otherwise suitably vetted.

Arnold had vowed not to accept any special-interest money, but in the end he took about $10 million in contributions, including substantial sums from real estate enterprises, entertainment companies, automobile dealers, and other business interests. He did not take money from trade unions and the Indian gaming tribes, as several of his opponents did. There was so much money that the campaign could even afford to rent an air-conditioning system that evening to cool the large building. The system made so much noise that soon after the meeting began, a young aide turned it off and the temperature rapidly began rising in the gym.

For the most part, these new Americans saw this meeting as an opportunity to ask Arnold what government could do for them. A Latin girl wanted books and more teachers at her elementary school. A European woman wanted help with her legal problem. A young Chinese woman wanted no more tuition hikes in colleges. Another immigrant asked for universal health insurance. A Burmese man wanted cheaper auto insurance and care for the homeless. "This is America, and these people need help," he said. "I'm okay, but these people need help."

Arnold thanked the man for his question and then went on to lecture him and the audience. He wanted their votes, but on this, the twentieth anniversary of his becoming a citizen, he wanted them to understand what he believed being an American should mean. "You are very adamant in the help that is needed, but I think it's one of the obligations we have as immigrants. We just can't think about what we can get from California. What can we get from this country. We have to think about what we can give back to our communities, to our states, to our nation. The question you have to ask is 'What do you do to help these people who are homeless?'"

These were not the words of speechwriters or the calculated campaign strategy, but something authentic and deep within Arnold himself. "It's very important that each one of us at night looks in the mirror and asks, 'What have I done today to help someone who needs help,'" he continued. "I remember one time when my father-in-law, Sargent Shriver, gave a speech at Yale University, where he said, 'Tear down that mirror in front of you that makes you look at yourself. And as soon as you've torn down that mirror, look beyond, and you will see the millions of people who need your help.'"

As a bodybuilder, Arnold had spent hours a day looking at himself in the mirror, and he had two mirrors to break, not one. He was still the proud, willful, self-involved man he had always been, but if he had not broken the mirror of endless self-regard, he had surely cracked it. He did what felt good, and he had come to realize that it felt good to help people. He was not like the Kennedys, believing that only with wealth and privilege comes the obligation to give back. This was a sentiment Arnold could have legitimately made one of the important themes of his campaign. But it did not fit with the strategy devised by Murphy and others, and he never again talked about breaking the mirror as passionately and persuasively.

The aide turned the air-conditioning back on after most of the meeting had been completed. That was way too late as far as Arnold was concerned. A star did not perspire; and by that definition, Arnold was not a star that evening but a sweat-soaked mortal. When Arnold left the event, he blew up for the only time during the campaign. "Jesus Christ, I'm spritzing like a mule out there!" he fumed. "Who turned off the fucking air-conditioning?" He ranted for about three minutes, showing a side of him most of his aides had never seen before. Then it was over. "All right, I'm done being mad," he said, and so he was.

Often during the campaign, Arnold turned to words offered by the speech-writer Parvin. He was another of Maria's finds. In mid-August, when the campaign was in its infancy, Parvin had gotten a call at his Virginia home to come out and bring clothes for a week, but the former Reagan speechwriter ended up staying for the entire campaign. He played a crucial role in crafting speeches that seemed as if they had hardly been crafted at all.

The first few days in California, Parvin sat in Arnold's office, listening to him on the phone and dogging his steps. At first, he found it excruciatingly difficult to grasp the man, but when Parvin began to understand Arnold, the speechwriter was startled at the way he found himself writing his speeches. "Basically, what I do for Arnold is, I talk to him and get the ideas from him, but what I do is then take that and write Reagan with a different cadence," he said.

Parvin realized immediately that when Arnold strode onstage, the stakes were higher than for most politicians. He was the action hero, and he had to deliver. Everything was short. The words. The speech. Everything but the man speaking. "Shortness is part of his comfort with being action-oriented," said Parvin. "He always wanted policy to do something. He just didn't want information. He wanted to know, 'What can we do?' And so, when he gives a speech, he needs that sense of movement. Short speeches. Short sentences. Repeating things several times, in different ways. And the more you move, the more action-oriented the speech, the more you're perceived as a leader."

Parvin enjoyed writing for Arnold more than for anyone since Reagan, but he saw that they were very different men. "Arnold built himself more than Reagan built himself," the speechwriter reflected. "Reagan felt the power of ideas. And Arnold feels the power of himself."

Unlike Reagan, who kept an emotional distance from almost everyone, including his own children, Arnold was passionate about the intimacies of family and personal life. One day, when Parvin was attending an important meeting outside on the patio at Arnold's house, the candidate's youngest son, five-year-old Christopher, ran barefoot up behind his father, put his hands over his eyes, and kissed Arnold. "I can't remember if Arnold gave him a kiss back or gave him a pat," said Parvin. "He didn't say, 'Don't. We're in the middle of something important.' And that impressed me." On another occasion Arnold was driving and talking on the cell phone to a staff member when the aide heard commotion. "When I say no, I mean no," Arnold said, and the aide realized he was talking to his kids jumping around in the backseat of the car.

Arnold's concerns went beyond his immediate family. During the campaign Kiki Gorton was bitten on the arm by a dog. Nearly fatal complications set in, and as busy as he was with the campaign, Arnold took charge, finding the proper medical care. "He saved my life," she said, not in a hyperbolic way but with sincerity.

In the sixty-two days of the campaign, Arnold traveled from one enclave of safety to another. Arnold talked to such friendly hosts as Oprah Winfrey and Larry King. When he did Sean Hannity's radio talk show, the conservative broadcaster asked Arnold's take on all the hot-button social issues, from abortion to gay rights, and Arnold got almost every one wrong—as least as Hannity saw the world. When Arnold was finished, instead of condemning Arnold, Hannity celebrated him.

Arnold gave scores of interviews to the state's right-wing radio stations. In their ideological fervor, they are more than a match for any liberal newspaper. The stations could have raged against Arnold as a false prophet befouling the temple of conservatism. Instead, they embraced him, arguing that with Arnold, Republicans could return to power in an overwhelmingly Democratic state.

Arnold's most dangerous antagonist was Governor Gray Davis. He was a relentlessly tough campaigner. "He's a machine," Bustamante said of him in 1997. "He is difficult to stop. He's like the Terminator. You blow him up and he just keeps on going. Strip him of all his flesh and he keeps coming. He's one tenacious son of a bitch." For most of his career, Davis had practiced the darkest of campaign techniques, one of the reasons even so many Democrats did not like him. At the beginning of the campaign, his own attorney general, Bill Lockyer, warned the governor about practicing more of his "puke politics." With such an admonition, Davis and his minions did not dare orchestrate negative research on Arnold but had to stand back and fume as Murphy and his staff whitewashed the entire state with a gloriously positive image of Arnold.

Robbed of his standard political maneuvers, Davis could only watch with awe, jealousy, and bewilderment, wondering how to compete with a man who is overlarge when he chooses to be and almost invisible when he chooses otherwise. "He is arguably the best-known Hollywood celebrity worldwide," said Davis. "In addition, because of his persona, and the figure he plays in the *Terminator* movies, he has a very commanding presence. That impacts all his relationships, be it the press, the legislature, or with an audience. During the campaign, his broadest appeal was to the entertainment press. From his perspective, he made good choices and essentially circumvented the political process and did so quite successfully."

For Arnold as well as all the other candidates, the debate on September 24 was hugely important. It was the one time that his opponents would have him in live sights in front of a massive audience watching on live television. If Arnold came across as a slogan-spouting celebrity out of his depth, wavering Democrats might return to the fold and vote to retain Davis or elect Lieutenant Governor Bustamante, while conservative Republicans would likely throw their lot with State Senator McClintock, who was one of their kind.

Arnold had listened long and well to the experts who had educated him in a series of mini-seminars. In the ninety-minute debate, Arnold showed himself fully versed on the state's major issues. From Arnold's perspective, the most dangerous person on the stage was McClintock, who could have savaged him as a liberal temptress who did not deserve the votes of principled Republicans. Instead, McClintock ignored Arnold and presented himself as a thoughtful, authentic conservative with a detailed knowledge of California's problems. "I wasn't there to criticize Arnold," said McClintock. "I believed I could contribute to the public policy debate, which was going on in California and which truly was unprecedented."

The debate also included Arianna Huffington, the one independent candidate and the only woman. Arnold had first been confronted by Huffington the Saturday after his announcement on *The Tonight Show*, when he and Maria had gone down to the County of Los Angeles Registrar-Recorder's office in Norwalk to file candidacy papers on the last day. The Brentwood liberal had rented a nearby hotel room so that she would be ready to muscle her way into Arnold's media coverage. An aide alerted her when Arnold was arriving, and she hurried to the office, pushed her way up the stairs, and stood next to Arnold so that her picture would also be on TV in the evening and in all the papers the next morning. Arnold had done a version of that approach when he was becoming a star, but it rankled him when people tried to trade on his celebrity.

Huffington had once been a conservative Republican married to a Republican congressman. She had jumped from the right bank of politics to the left, speaking with the same certitude as she had as a right-winger. Thanks to a divorce settlement, she was a multimillionaire, but the fifty-three-year-old foe of tax loopholes for the wealthy had in the past two years paid only $771 in federal taxes and no state taxes.

"The first thing I would do is close corporate tax loopholes," Huffington said, and then segued into an attack on Arnold with a transition obvious only to her. "And one more thing, Arnold . . ."

"Arnold? I like that," he said cutting her short, showing visible irritation at her patronizing tone. "I'll tell you one thing. Your personal income tax has the biggest loophole. I can drive my Hummer through it."

"Completely hypocritical of Arnold!" Huffington steamed a few minutes later. "Let me finish! Let me finish! You know, this is completely typical of the way you treat women."

Huffington's remark was greeted with a mixture of gasps, boos, and scattered applause. There was a look of disbelief on Arnold's face.

"That was a direct and personal attack on Mr. Schwarzenegger, so would you respond?" the moderator interjected.

"I would just like to say that I just realized that I have a perfect part for you in *Terminator 4*," Arnold said. It was a superb retort, so witty and quick that no one noticed he had not responded.

Several of his advisers expected Arnold to overwhelm his opponents, so they were mildly disappointed at his performance. Most people, reporters and voters alike, had underestimated how well he would do, which made him a winner. It certified him as a candidate with a legitimate right to run for governor. He was a lucky man, lucky that McClintock had not attacked him and lucky that Huffington had.

"The reason Schwarzenegger won the debate was because it wasn't about the issues, it was about Arnold Schwarzenegger," said John Feliz, McClintock's campaign manager. "The clip that showed every single day for a week after where they said Arnold Schwarzenegger handled himself well was not McClintock saying, 'You don't know the budget deficit from a hole in the ground.' It was not [Peter] Camejo [the Green Party candidate] saying, 'You don't understand the tax structure.' It was Arnold saying, 'I've got a role in *Terminator 4* for you.' "

Murphy was an impresario of the special moment, creating events where Arnold could stand as a man of action and independence. For the last days before the election, Murphy planned the splendid conclusion to it all, a spectacular four-day bus trip starting in San Diego and moving triumphantly toward a huge rally on the steps of the Capitol in Sacramento. Arnold would dominate the media coverage in the last week of the campaign, and on Election Day he would win a great and glorious victory.

Murphy had planned for every contingency except the *Los Angeles Times*. For weeks a team of reporters at the paper had been consumed by learning about Arnold's sexual life. They had picked up leads from many people, including a man often described as one of Arnold's close friends. They got help from a producer of one of his films and other Hollywood figures.

There were rumors about Arnold's having had an affair with an underage African-American extra on one of his films. They tracked down the young woman and determined that it was not true. They tried to locate Gigi Goyette, but she was nowhere to be found. The journalists had heard rumors that Arnold had had an affair with the flight attendant on his jet and that she had given birth to his child. They spent weeks finding the woman's name and traced her to a home outside Los Angeles, to find her married and living with her pilot husband and their young son. The reporter confronted her, and though the mother adamantly denied the allegation, the journalist felt that the boy looked like Arnold. The woman was so outraged at this intrusion into her life that she called Arnold's campaign and was eventually put through to campaign spokesman Sean Walsh. He called senior editor Joel Sappell, who was overseeing the investigation, and complained. Soon after, the *Los Angeles Times* dropped its investigation of the woman. Sappell insists that in no instance did the paper back off because of Walsh's complaints.

That story appeared three days before the election in London's *Daily Mail*, written and researched by the two reporters who had done the most to hurt Arnold's reputation, his biographer Wendy Leigh and John Connolly, who had written the 2001 *Premiere* article. That gave the *National Enquirer* entrée to run its one scandalous story on Arnold, but it appeared only after the election. "The only thing we were hunting was the 'love child' story," said Pecker. "We were working on it for six months. The woman always denied it. That's why we didn't run it the first time. We couldn't prove it."

Arnold's campaign was in the unsettling position of having no idea how far-ranging the *Los Angeles Times* was willing to go in its investigation of sexual conduct. The newspapers' reporters were at several disadvantages in pursuing this story. In the caste system of American journalism, the tabloid reporters are the untouchables, doing jobs that the higher castes would not and employing means that others won't. In this instance, the tabloids did not join their more highbrow colleagues in investigating Arnold's sexual past, but instead American Media promoted Arnold. With a full-page story and bold headline VOTE SCHWARZENEGGER! the *Star* looked like a campaign brochure. Another issue featured a paean to "Arnold and Maria's Family Life" and "Arnold: A New American Patriot," comparing the candidate with George Washington. If grocery-store shoppers wanted more of the heroic Arnold, they could buy *Weekly World News* with its revelation "Alien Backs Arnold for Governor," or plunk down $4.95 for a special 120-page magazine published by

American Media titled *Arnold, the American Dream*. "I made a lot of money on that," said Pecker. "A lot of money."

While their tabloid brethren celebrated Arnold's life, the reporters at the *Los Angeles Times* plowed through the garbage cans of his discarded past. The journalists did not pay for information, while their downscale colleagues on the tabloids would have shelled out thousands of dollars to get women to go on record with their groping allegations. Beyond that, the reporters had ethical concerns rare among the tabloids. "Some of these women I think I would have talked out of going on the record, because I knew what a cost it would have for them," said Gary Cohn. That was not a consideration the *National Enquirer* reporters shared when their story of Goyette's relationship with Arnold cost the woman her job and destroyed her future in Hollywood.

It was an uncomfortable business, asking women the kind of questions they had to ask. "I had some questions right about it at the beginning," said Cohn. "But what convinced me of the problem was sitting in the living rooms, listening to these women. No one pretended that their lives were ruined, but I concluded it was an important story."

As the days went by, there was considerable controversy within the newsroom itself about the issue. John Carroll seemed obsessed about doing the story of Arnold's sexual misconduct. Around him there coalesced an impassioned, dogged group of believers in the editor and this story. As Election Day drew near, more reporters were brought into the exploration of Arnold's sex life. But some other reporters and editors were increasingly queasy about the investigation, considering it an unseemly intrusion into the private life of a public citizen and beneath the dignity of one of America's great newspapers. Carroll not only did not care, he did not notice. His concern was to ensure that he had enough evidence to publish a solidly researched article that would stand up to the inevitable counterattack.

Thus, the editor pushed and urged his reporters forward—yet held the story back not because he wanted to launch an October surprise by publishing his revelations at the last minute but because the story was still too thin for a serious newspaper of record. The reporters must find more women willing to come forward.

CHAPTER THIRTY-EIGHT

The California
Comeback Express

On Thursday, October 2, six days before the election, the headline on the front page of the *Los Angeles Times* read: WOMEN SAY SCHWARZENEGGER GROPED, HUMILIATED THEM. The story that will forever be part of John Carroll's legacy as an American editor begins, "Six women who came into contact with Arnold Schwarzenegger on movie sets, in studio offices and in other settings over the last three decades say he touched them in a sexual manner without their consent."

There was nothing especially new in the article, only that this tabloid-like story was appearing in the pages of California's most prestigious newspaper. Of the six women, only two are named. One of them had already told her story in the tabloids, and the husband of the other had already spoken out against Arnold. One of the six accusations went back to the 1970s and two to the 1980s.

From the day the campaign began, Arnold's staff anticipated that someone would print a story of Arnold's purported sexual excesses, and they had actively scoped out how to deal with it. "When we did our focus groups going into this election, people had been spending twenty years going through the grocery lines in the supermarkets, seeing the *Globe*, the *Enquirer*, etc.," campaign spokesman Sean Walsh reflected after the election. "Most people shrugged, [thinking,] 'That's the way things go in Hollywood.' People have seen these types of stories about Hollywood people, not just Arnold but others, and there was some inoculation on these types of things. To the [*Los Angeles*] *Times* or other people in the media, it was a huge deal, some new breaking revelation, [but] those issues had been floating out in the consciousness for a long time."

When Mike Murphy saw the story online in the early-morning hours, he already had a good idea of its contents. Two days before, the *Los Angeles Times* had called Walsh to get Arnold's reaction to the specific charges. As Murphy read the story, he saw that the paper had printed the spokesman's denial. Walsh said that Arnold "has not engaged in improper conduct toward women" and called the charges "part of an escalating political attack on Schwarzenegger" in which "we believe Democrats and others are using this to try to hurt Arnold Schwarzenegger's campaign." Walsh was twice wrong. Arnold *had* engaged in improper conduct and the Democrats had nothing to do with the *Los Angeles Times'* reporting on Arnold's sexual conduct, but it was an effective way to challenge the credibility of the daily and make it appear a creature of the Democratic Party.

Murphy immediately set up a conference call with other top staffers. The campaign manager looked at the matter with the advantage of all the polling and focus-group data to help him know what would play best with the California voter. Arnold's staff would not have to block their candidate from intrusive interviews in the last days of the campaign, for he was already walled off. Murphy explained to the staff that they could stonewall for the next few days, but if they did, they would not be able to get anything else across. Instead, Murphy said that Arnold would be best to admit to some inappropriate behavior but cast it as nothing more than part of the whole rowdy movie business and say that he was sorry if he had ever done anything out of line. It was a version taken right out of the focus groups.

When Murphy met Arnold at the airport to fly to San Diego, he had a card typed up with what he thought Arnold should say. On the flight down, the two men talked and worked out the details. The kickoff rally at the San Diego Convention Center had been designed as the upbeat launch of the bus tour, but now Arnold was confronted with the toughest moment of his short-lived political life. As he waited to speak, wearing a white shirt and a black Arnold jacket, George "Duf" Sundheim, the chairman of the California Republican Party, saw Arnold standing with notecards in his hand. "He was pacing, looking up, and saying, 'I'm sorry,'" Sundheim said.

Arnold had used the words "I'm sorry" so infrequently that it was no wonder he had to practice them. Even so, as he began to speak, he could not bring himself truly to apologize but offered only a halfhearted act of contrition. "I know that the people of California can see through these trash politics," he began. He could have called what was done to him trash journalism. Gray Davis and the other candidates were blameless, and trash politics it was not.

"Let me tell you something, let me tell you something," Arnold said, trying to hold off apologizing for a moment more. "A lot of those, when you see those stories, it's not true." It was not likely that he could even remember whether or not he had groped a woman's breast at Gold's Gym in 1975 or grabbed and squeezed a woman's left breast as he walked down Nineteenth Street in Santa Monica in 1980. But surely he had done similar things over the years. Though he was more partial to butts than breasts, the stories were believable, for the most part. "But at the same time," Arnold went on, "I have to tell you that I always say that wherever there is smoke, there is fire."

Some of the audience let out gasps of disbelief, as if their preacher was standing in the pulpit confessing to multiple sins. "That is true," he insisted. "And so what I want to say to you is, yes, that I have behaved badly sometimes. Yes, it is true that I was on rowdy movie sets, and I have done things that were not right, which I thought then was playful. But now I recognize that I have offended people. And to those people that I have offended, I want to say to them, I am deeply sorry about that, and I apologize, because this is not what I'm trying to do."

Only three of the six alleged incidents took place on movie sets, but Hollywood had a lurid image in the public mind. It was as if the poor bodybuilder had been lured into sin on the "rowdy movie sets." When Arnold finished his short speech, the campaign theme song, "We're Not Gonna Take It," trumpeted that the moment of departure had arrived. Confetti started pouring down. A black curtain was dramatically pulled back, and there stood a gleaming blue bus with Arnold's picture and the words JOIN ARNOLD on the side, a moving billboard that the candidate was supposed to ride triumphantly five hundred miles north to Sacramento.

As the "California Comeback Express" set out behind a police escort, Arnold's bus, *Running Man*, was followed by the second bus, *Total Recall*, full of dignitaries and aides. After that came four buses, full of 220 journalists from twelve countries. Then followed television satellite trucks, more reporters in their rented cars, other candidates seeking scraps of publicity, political camp followers, and the merely curious.

As soon as the story hit the streets, the *Los Angeles Times* reporters started getting phone calls from other women claiming to be Arnold's victims. Gary Cohn, who had won his Pulitzer for a complicated, esoteric series about the dangers of dismantling old ships, was now noting whether it was the left or the right breast, and what the subtleties of the grope were.

Arnold's people were furious that the *Los Angeles Times* went ahead with further stories without giving them at least a day to check them out. Arnold kept saying that he did not remember, and the campaign could hardly get into the business of saying, no, that was not true; yes, that was true, demeaning themselves and their candidate by attempting to dabble in the details.

Groping was not the only dramatic new issue confronting the candidate. That first day on the road, Arnold faced another potential scandal that by itself could have been enough to derail his campaign. *The New York Times* published excerpts from George Butler's 1997 book proposal, in which the photographer called his friend a "flagrant, outspoken admirer of Hitler" and said that he had seen Arnold "playing Nazi marching songs from long-playing records in his collection at home" and that he "frequently clicked his heels and pretended to be an S.S. officer." This was buttressed by quotes about Arnold's fascination with Hitler from the outtakes of *Pumping Iron*, including the devastating line "I admire him for being such a good public speaker and for what he did with it." Although the timing of the story made it appear to Arnold an orchestrated example of "puke politics," *New York Times* reporter David D. Kirkpatrick asserts adamantly that the source had nothing to do with politics. Butler says that a book editor wanting to prevent Arnold from becoming governor leaked the proposal to the newspaper.

Butler told the *Times* in the next day's follow-up story that there was a typo in the proposal; Arnold had said he had *not* admired Hitler for what he did with his oratory ability. Butler says that he provided *The New York Times* with a thirty-three-page transcript of the *Pumping Iron* interview, which made it clear that though Arnold may have been somewhat obsessed with Hitler, he never for one moment expressed his admiration for the Nazi leader's actions.

Arnold rolled over the matter, blaming both the sexual charges and the Hitler story on Davis. "They have started the puke campaign, haven't they!" he told his audiences. "The puke campaign. They have started the puke campaign, because that is exactly what they know how to do." It was a powerful message, richly received. When he finished, he threw Arnold T-shirts into the crowd, shook hands and signed a few autographs, and ducked back into the bus.

With Arnold safely away from the restless pack of journalists, spokesman Rob Stutzman told reporters that the sexual allegations as well as the timing of the Hitler material were an orchestrated example of Davis's "puke politics." "Garry South promised us this campaign," Stutzman said as reporters huddled around him at a campaign stop. "Bob Mulholland promised us this campaign in its closing days and they're delivering on it." As the *Los Angeles Times* published seven more women's stories by the end of the weekend, Arnold's campaign spokesman replied with unmitigated anger. "Now the *L.A. Times* has put forth a casting call so that anyone can come forward, making any kind of claim in the final seventy-two hours of this campaign," Stutzman sputtered. "It's outrageous yellow journalism! It's unprecedented gotcha journalism, and we're not gonna sit back and take this from the *Los Angeles Times*!"

In the end, though, it was not the counterclaim of dirty politics that saved Arnold—it was his wife. During the six-week campaign, Maria had made occasional public appearances, but she was far more important behind the scenes. She had championed Murphy, brought in Parvin, and pushed several of the other aides into secondary spots. When she did not like what was going on, she could be harsh, almost shrewish, in her attacks, and several of the staff have fearsome memories of some of their encounters with her. Unlike many contemporary political wives, Maria saw no need to trumpet her own accomplishments but was totally comfortable in devoting herself to advancing her husband's campaign.

Early that morning, when Arnold was flying to San Diego, Maria was on the phone to David Dreier, discussing what Arnold was about to say and working out the best strategy. Later that day she addressed a Conservative Women's Leadership Association luncheon in Newport Beach. She said that the charges did not hurt "because I know the man I'm married to. I see women who work for him who admire him. He's been an extreme gentleman. I don't believe in gutter politics, and I don't believe in gutter journalism. He's taken the high road—he apologized, and that's courageous."

As soon as her other obligations were fulfilled, Maria joined her husband on the "California Comeback Express." When she stood next to Arnold on the stage during the bus trip, she gave credibility to him that no other endorsement could have made. Although she photographed well and smiled bravely, there was at times an almost haggard, haunted look to her, as if she had taken on all the burdens of the campaign and Arnold had taken all the joys. Two years earlier she had reportedly been outraged by her husband's purported conduct in London. These accusations were so much worse, but she stood with him now, as if she had made her own decision about what mattered in her marriage and in her life. Despite all that she knew, if she could stand here, accepting and loving her husband for what he was, then certainly California voters could accept him, too, and make him their next governor.

"I have known this man for twenty-six years," Maria said as she introduced him at a rally at the P-R Farms in Clovis. "I've been married to him for seventeen. He's an extraordinary father and a remarkable husband and a terrific human being. He has the character to govern. He has the temperament to govern and he is a leader for all of you."

Maria, however, was a Democrat, while the Republicans considered themselves on a higher moral plane. Their candidates spoke from pulpits of high virtue, or they dared not wear the robes of a Republican. "The line we used to use is that Bill Clinton could do it as a Democrat, but a Republican can't do it," said Dreier. "It's tolerated from a Democrat, but not tolerated from a Republican."

Arnold may have been a Republican, but he was not going to retreat from the battleground merely because the *Los Angeles Times* was pointing a scolding finger at him. If Arnold could overcome these charges and win acceptance not only from the voters but from right-wing radio programs and conservative publications, then he would change American politics before even serving a day in office. Citizens in this vanguard of American states were being asked to either ignore or excuse conduct that only a few years ago would have destroyed a public career. In a sense, they were being asked to jettison the last relics of their Puritan morality and act more like Europeans.

Over the weeks of the campaign, many reporters had grown increasingly restive, their moods darkening even more during the last days, when they felt like little more than campaign props. Most of them had been unable to ask Arnold even a single question. One by one, a few prominent national and California journalists were ushered onto *Running Man* for a few minutes with Arnold. One of the anointed was Charlie LeDuff, who looked more like a motorcycle runner for the networks than a *New York Times* reporter. He had grown disdainful of the whole calculated process. "Arnold's a really bright guy, a smart guy," LeDuff said. "But it's this whole game we're playing. I do 'gotcha' and you do 'can't get me.' So, we get no answers."

Arnold still had a gift for candor that was at times a dubious blessing for a politician. In his interview with the NBC anchor Tom Brokaw, he made one of the few errors of his campaign. "Well, first of all, a lot of it is made-up stories," Arnold told Brokaw, a longtime family friend. "I have never grabbed anyone and pulled up their shirt and grabbed their breasts and stuff like that. This is not me." What he could not say and joked about to his close friends was that he was not in truth even interested in breasts. Had he been accused of pinching a butt, he would not have denied it so readily. In talking to Brokaw, moreover, Arnold had certain advantages that other candidates would not. He was not a hypocrite whose pious musings now stood exposed. Nor had he made a bold defense of his conduct ("I did not have sex with that woman") that might have come to haunt him later.

Instead, Arnold accused the governor of orchestrating the sexual allegations. "Well, it—the *Times* and also, you know, the . . . the campaign, because Gray Davis is running a dirty campaign," he said. "This is all part of it."

When Brokaw tried to probe the sexual allegations further, Arnold deflected his questions by pushing the problem into the future. He told the TV journalist, "As soon as the campaign is over, I will—I can get into all of those kind of specifics and find out what is really going on, but right now I'm just really occupied with the campaign." It was a pledge that he could not conceivably fulfill, or his first months in office would be nothing but endless tabloid-like stories as he dug through the sordid allegations, sorting out the true from the half-true, and the half-true from the false.

Up and down the length of the state, the conservative radio stations rallied to Arnold's defense. They almost universally supported Arnold while condemning the *Los Angeles Times* for its sordid exposé. In one of the abiding ironies of the campaign, the largest political victim of the allegations turned out to be not Arnold but McClintock. Although some of his supporters turned toward Arnold as the likely winner, others were so outraged by the liberal newspaper's smutty stories that they protested by deciding to vote for Arnold. "Tom lost about ten or fifteen points because of the *Los Angeles Times* groping story," said McClintock's campaign manager, John Feliz. "That's what collapsed us. And it was the most frustrating experience of the entire race."

As for the growing crowds on Arnold's journey northward, they cared nothing about the allegations. For the most part, they saw Arnold as the last blessed hope for the Golden State. They often waited several hours for Arnold to arrive, and yet even before his ten-minute stump speech was over, some of them appeared restless. They did not want to listen to lengthy speeches but only to a spirited avowal that Arnold would change things, cast the moneychangers out of the temple of California democracy, and set things right again.

Arnold had begun the campaign as a good speaker, but he was ending it as a great one, shaving the lines that drew the weakest responses and highlighting those that bought the audiences to paroxysms of emotion and passion. His stump speech was a curious one, for it combined two emotions that are rarely so closely linked—optimism and anger. Arnold was a buoyant spirit in his element in front of these growing crowds. "What has happened to that optimism that the state represented to the rest of the world?" he asked rhetorically. "The optimism that was the envy of the rest of the world. They've put a spending cap on those skies."

And then came the anger. "We are mad as hell and we're not gonna take it," he said, plumbing the electorate's anger. "This is like a war and we're in the trenches. We have to fight it. To my twin Terminators, *hasta la vista*, baby." To accentuate Arnold's message, "We're Not Gonna Take It" was played as he walked onstage, further revving up the crowd's anger. When protesters dared shout out a slogan or raise a sign for another candidate, they were lucky if they were not pummeled or pushed and were mercly escorted out.

On the first day of the bus trip, Arnold stopped at Riley Elementary School in San Bernardino, west of Los Angeles. Here homes are still affordable and massive population growth spawns diverse jobs and economic possibilities. It is an area full of young, ambitious, restless, politically undefined Californians who have climbed partway up the mountain of success, and fear that they may be pushed back down. They were the bedrock of Arnold's support, such areas giving him 60 percent of their votes. "We're Not Gonna Take It" was their anthem. They weren't gonna take the tripling of their car tax, but they were gonna take the unprecedented rise in property values. They weren't gonna take the illegal immigrants pouring across the border, but they were gonna take the fruits and vegetables on their tables picked by them. They weren't gonna take anyone touching sacred Prop 13 and upping their property taxes, but they wanted better schools and more cops and a leader who could figure how to give them what they wanted.

The journalists were irritated with the walk-on role they were playing in this drama, and many in the crowd were angry at the reporters as the corrupt purveyors of a scurrilous attack on their beloved Arnold. At a rally on the third day in Pleasanton, the journalists marched sullenly into the outdoor setting and stood behind a wall of bike racks. As Arnold took to the stage, LeDuff and a TV cameraman pushed for position. The two men got in such a jostling match that they starting flailing at each other, trading punches rather than trading places.

While this battle of the media raged, farther down the line, a group of five women activists who had infiltrated the scores of journalists threw off their jackets and exposed their pink sweaters identifying them as members of Code Pink, a radical feminist organization dedicated to world peace. "No groper for governor!" they chanted. "No groper for governor!" As the protesters tried to shout down Arnold's words, the audience turned back angrily to the reporters. Members of the audience were so convinced of the media's connivance with the anti-Arnold forces that they believed the protesters were from the national media. "Fucking NBC!" someone screamed. "Asshole *Los Angles Times!*" another Arnold supporter yelled.

On Sunday afternoon on the great lawn leading to the steps of the Capitol in the shadow of Davis's office, up to 10,000 supporters stood waiting for Arnold to speak. Since the *Los Angeles Times* story, the campaign had tried to counter the image of Arnold as misogynist with a twinkle in his eye. Rows of cheering women stood on the podium as a background to Arnold's speech. Dee Snyder, the leader of Twisted Sister, sang "We're Not Gonna Take It." This time the song sounded purged of its anger, almost elegiac.

The event signaled the end of the bus tour, and Arnold addressed the massive crowd in positive fashion, leaving out the negative jibes that he had made in the past few days. "I, when I go in there, when I become the next governor, I will make sure the California economy will become again the powerful job-creating machine that it once was," Arnold said. "This state will once again run on all eight cylinders, rather than on one cylinder, the way it is right now."

Protesters shouted oaths but were drowned out by supporters, and the mood was almost euphoric. Two days later, before cheering supporters, Arnold mounted the podium at the Century Plaza Hotel in Los Angeles with Maria at his side to accept a victor's ovation. In one of the most dramatic political stories of the new century, the voters had overwhelmingly cast Gray Davis out of office (55.4 percent yes to 44.6 percent no). And they had elected Arnold in a landslide, giving him 48.6 percent of the vote, followed by 31.5 percent for Bustamante and 13.5 percent for McClintock.

Standing behind Arnold were not Republican politicians and campaign staff members, but a long line of Shrivers. "It was probably the first time in history that a candidate won from one party and everybody standing directly behind him is from the other one," said Maria's brother Anthony Shriver.

In this celebratory moment, Arnold tried to reach out to all Californians and enlist them in his attempt to change the state that had given him so much. "I will not fail you," he said to the wildly enthusiastic crowd and to the millions watching on television. "I will not disappoint you, and I will not let you down. The first choice that we must make is the one that will determine our success. Shall we rebuild our state together or shall we fight among ourselves, create an even deeper division, and fail the people of California? Well, let me tell you something. The answer is clear. For the people to win, politics as usual must lose."

The Golden Dream by the Sea

The California flag was draped vertically from the upper reaches of the Capitol so that the state bear looked as if it were climbing perpendicularly upward, defying the laws of gravity. On the broad expanses of lawn beneath the white neoclassical building, a large audience of well-wishers had assembled on November 17, 2003, to witness the inauguration of Arnold Schwarzenegger as the thirty-eighth governor of California.

There is no more exalted moment in American democracy than an inauguration. No matter the rancor and the passions of the campaign, a peaceful, civil transfer of power takes place, and for one brief moment between the heat of the campaign and the cold reality of governing, all is promise and possibility. Even by that standard, this was a special day. For all the sideshow diversions of the recall campaign, the people had made their clear, definitive choice. As if to defy that judgment, Governor Gray Davis displayed graciousness in defeat that he had rarely exhibited in his public life, standing in front of the largely Republican throng before disappearing and returning to his 1,000-square-foot condo in West Hollywood.

There was an interest in the swearing-in ceremony rarely seen in American politics other than for the inauguration of a President. The 7,500 invited guests were for the most part members of the Republican gentry, ladies in fine cloth coats that were hardly necessary on the warm, sun-dappled day, alongside their prosperous husbands in conservative suits. Crowded onto the grounds were more than 700 accredited journalists from fourteen countries. On a platform behind the audience stood 130 cameras, including those broadcasting the inauguration live around the world to countries such as Russia and Japan.

Walking into the event with Maria and their four children, Arnold held his six-year-old son, Christopher, by his hand and told the boy to smile for the cameras. He and Maria had sheltered the children from the publicity, but not on this momentous day. Arnold was fifty-six years old, but he was a young father with four children under the age of fourteen. The scene evoked the same emotions that JFK and his family once did, that politics is not a denatured alternative to life but part of a good, full life.

"I am humbled, I am moved, and I am honored beyond words to be your governor," Governor Schwarzenegger declared as he began his inaugural address, each word pressed with sincerity. He was the least humble of men, but there was no reason to doubt him. He grasped the overwhelming trajectory of his life, and it was a wondrous thing that he, Arnold Schwarzenegger of Thal, Austria, could be standing there that morning.

"President Reagan spoke of America as a shining city on a hill," Arnold said. "I see California as the golden dream by the sea. Perhaps some think this is fanciful, but to someone like me, who came here with absolutely nothing and gained absolutely everything, it is not fanciful to see California as the golden dream. I have taken the oath to uphold the constitution of California, and now with your help and with God's, I will uphold this dream that is California."

Inauguration weekend was full of parties and celebrations. One of the smallest of the gatherings was a cocktail party for the board of Special Olympics International. The group was holding its biannual meeting in Sacramento so that board member Maria could take part easily. When Arnold got up to say a few words, he turned to his mother-in-law. "Eunice got me involved with Special Olympics," Arnold said. "And I realized it felt good to do good, and whatever makes me feel good, I like to do." In recent months Arnold's friends had noticed a startling transformation in the man. He was still the egocentric, self-centered, fun-loving Arnold they had always known, but there was a deeper, philosophical quality to him. He had a full measure of what the Greeks considered the most unique and highest form of love, *agape*, a love of humanity. Which did not mean that he would necessarily be a good governor, merely that his most exalted emotions came from doing what he thought was good.

As soon as Arnold was sworn in, he walked into his office in the Capitol, signed a bill terminating the hated tripling of the car tax, and called the legislature back into special session. He had kept his promise to the voters, but with a mere signature on a piece of paper, he entered fully into the maelstrom of politics. The so-called car tax is a fee that Californians pay to register their vehicles. The money goes directly back to the counties and cities to make up in part for the revenues lost because of the Prop 13 limitation on property taxes. Now the municipalities and local governments were deeply threatened.

Arnold had vowed not to raise taxes, in part because he said it was wrong for the people to pay for the sins of the politicians. But the people almost always pay for their leaders' foibles—if not now, then later. Instead of socking it to Californians in 2004, he proposed a $15 billion bond issue, including $4 billion to cover the lost car-tax revenue, plus $10.7 billion to replace a questionably legal bond from the previous administration. He promised to make deep cuts in wasteful government programs and to stop the expansion of many social services.

On Arnold's first day in office, the Capitol was already inundated with protesters. On one side of the massive building, several hundred citizens listened to speakers condemning possible cuts in services for the disabled. There were people in wheelchairs, amputees, and other sufferers of dramatic magnitude.

Arnold had called the legislature into special session to deal with the crisis, but the Senate opened like a Rotary Club meeting. One senator celebrated his wife of twenty years on their wedding anniversary, while his colleague introduced a constituent who happened to be in town. How difficult it would be for Governor Schwarzenegger to translate his rhetoric into reality could be judged by the confidence with which President Pro Tem John Burton, Arnold's greatest Democratic adversary, wandered the floor of the Senate, joking amiably with members from both parties. In Burton's office, the phone was ringing off the hook from frightened Californians who were worried that Arnold would pillage their schools, take away their welfare payments, or lower their disability checks. Call after call came in, if anything only stiffening Burton's resolve to prevent the governor and the Republican minority in both houses from making draconian cuts.

Burton had served in Congress in the seventies when his brother, Phil, was one of the most powerful men in the House of Representatives. Phil was a man of the left with the hard-nosed strategy and detailed knowledge of a nineteenth-century ward boss. Indeed, to Phil, America was one great ward, and he knew the nuances of every district. John learned at his brother's feet, and brought those same skills to Sacramento.

John Burton said that he had not changed his politics in three decades, though the world had changed. The mildly disheveled, shambling politician no longer had a great vision of social democracy in the future. He gauged his success by how much he was able to turn government into a machine to benefit those without voices or money: the underprivileged, minorities, and the deprived. He was as perceptive of the hypocrisies of the right as he was blind to those on the left.

Burton did not care much what the press said and turned a deaf ear to the pundits who were bemoaning the excesses of the legislature that had led the state to its unprecedented deficit. He did not see it that way, and felt that he bore no responsibility. "Somebody tell me what we wasted money on?" he asked angrily. "Did we waste money on getting more kids into Healthy Families? Waste money on providing Cal Grants dollars for needy students? How about all the bullshit tax cuts that were put in? I mean, the state's in trouble because they indexed the income tax. They did away with the inheritance tax. They went on a tax-cutting frenzy, and no matter what you do, if you don't have money coming in, you're going to end up in the toilet."

Burton knew that he was no match for the megacelebrity who had set up shop in the governor's office. "I got a press conference in a back room," he said. "He's got a convention." Burton did have certain advantages in his struggle. He came from a San Francisco district that celebrated his ideological purity and listened to his often vitriolic attacks on the Republicans with relish. Since this was Burton's last hurrah, due to term limits, he was especially motivated to stick it to Arnold and his party.

When Arnold suggested that the legislature find a way to give some of the lost money back to the local communities, Burton gave Arnold a sweet taste of what might be in store. "I'm not the guy who took the money away," Burton yelled to reporters. "Who likes someone to throw a turd in the punch bowl at their daughter's wedding? Not I."

If Burton and his liberal colleagues were not problem enough for Arnold, on the right side he faced such men as Senator Tom McClintock, Burton's ideological opposite. Although the right-wing Republican from Thousand Oaks would never use the intemperate language of Burton, he was just as opposed to a number of Arnold's proposals.

McClintock was considered by his colleagues to be a man so obsessed with principle that his uncompromising stature had become a fetish. His best political friends were not his colleagues in the California Senate, but the Founding Fathers whose words he studied with diligence. He was all for cutting billions of dollars from the budget, stripping the government of most of what men like Burton had imposed, returning it to a size and function that Thomas Jefferson would have recognized. If Arnold had called him on the day after the election to ask him to help decide what must be cut, he says that he would have arrived with his pruning shears at the ready, but that call did not come.

McClintock is a man of few words, and especially since the recall, he was listened to carefully. The senator was adamantly opposed to Arnold's attempt to use bonds to wiggle his way out of the financial crisis. To many Californians, the word *bond* has an esoteric ring to it. McClintock pointed out rightly that it is no different from borrowing on your credit card. Sooner or later, you have to pay the money back with interest. Bonds are generally not used to fund the ongoing expenses of the state, but for schools, roads, and bridges that would benefit citizens who have not even been born yet. "It is not appropriate to use bonded indebtedness for ongoing expenses," McClintock argued. "Just on the simple principle that our children will have their own roads to build and buildings to paint without having to pay for services that were obsolete thirty years ago. So, I mean, that's just very bad public policy and very bad family policy."

Faced with two such intransigent legislators, the new governor would clearly have as much difficulty with the Republican right as with the Democratic left. Both McClintock and Burton are intelligent, perceptive men, but like so many of their colleagues, neither considered compromise a worthy attribute. And they did not march alone. After the 2000 census, Republicans and Democrats had gerrymandered the state so that most legislators had solid, almost untouchable majorities. "Currently in California, legislators, in effect, choose their voters, instead of the voters choosing their legislators," wrote political columnist Daniel Weintraub in the *Sacramento Bee.* "The result is that most of the state's 120 legislative districts heavily favor either the Democrats or the Republicans, and the likely outcome in almost all of them is known well in advance."

"It ends up driving the political debate to the extremes of both parties," said Assemblyman Keith Richman, one of the beleaguered moderates. "The special-interest groups are setting the political agendas and the political orthodoxy for both parties. On the left you've got public employee unions and the trial attorneys, and on the right you've got anti-tax groups, the club for growth, the social conservative groups, and there's no subtlety in their messages. If you don't toe the party line, they literally threaten you to say they're going to take you out."

This situation has led to, among other things, endless posturing and divisive, extreme rhetoric of the sort rarely heard on the floor of the U.S. Congress. "Everybody wants to make the evening news and the next day's paper," said Assemblywoman Sarah Reyes, a liberal Democrat from Fresno

County. "They know the higher a fireball they throw, the more likely they are to be able to get in the paper."

Arnold read his polls as carefully as he did the overnights when one of his films opened. In his way, he tried to figure what was best for what he considered an optimistic, freedom-loving people. That was true of his concern for fiscal responsibility, his lack of concern for economic inequality, and his progressive stance on social issues. "Any candidate worth electing must begin by recognizing how California—the sixth largest economy in the world—makes its money," wrote James Flanigan in the *Los Angeles Times*. "It relies mostly, of course, on more than 1 million individual enterprises, 95 percent of which employ fewer than fifty people. In other words, this is a small-business state. And yet, perversely, its laws and regulations seem more suited to the old industrial world of big companies and struggling labor unions."

Whatever they earn, most Californians live close to the economic ground and feel the rumblings of the economy in the way those working for great corporations often do not. They were sympathetic toward Arnold's attempt to limit onerous government regulations to make the state more hospitable to business pursuits.

His limitations were the limitations of optimism. He flew to Las Vegas for the day and hooted it up to Nevadans to come on back and bring their businesses with them. He set up billboards in Nevada and Massachusetts brazenly wooing business to the Golden State. That tactic was crowd-pleasing, if not to the governors of Nevada and Massachusetts. He beckoned millions to come West to the golden shores, but nobody asked too much about where all these new people were going to live when there was already near-gridlock on the freeways and the builders were pressing farther and farther into the hinterlands. He did not focus much on the crumbling infrastructure of the state, the roads that needed be widened, the bridges that were weak, the schools that had to be built, all of the massive projects for which there was insufficient money. He did not look much at the dark side of things, and neither did most of his fellow citizens. His optimism was the crucial quality Arnold brought to Sacramento, not a thought-out ideology. Arnold was exhorting Californians to return to the future, taking the optimism and entrepreneurial energy that was so much part of the American past, propelling it forward into a new century.

When the proper time arrived, the Democrats were ready to unleash a firestorm of rhetoric on the new governor. Some thought that might not even be necessary. They predicted that as soon as this movie star arrived in Sacramento, he would deflate, just as the giant Arnold balloon had at the 1993 Cannes Film Festival. But when he walked in to talk to the Assembly's Democratic Caucus his first week, many of them proved as starstruck as moviegoers outside a premiere at Grauman's Chinese Theatre.

In politics, the best speeches often occur not before the public but in front of one's peers, and Arnold put on a stellar performance before the Democrats. "He came in and he told us about how he was inspired to public service by the Kennedys, by Eunice Shriver and Sargent Shriver, and on and on and on, and how Teddy Kennedy is the smartest man he knows," said Reyes. "He played the Kennedy card for all it was worth."

Arnold laid out to the Democratic legislators his California Recovery Plan. It included the $15 billion bond issue and a second bill to put a cap on state spending, to be voted upon in the special March election. He also called for a radical reform of the state's workers' compensation program.

They were all measures about which most Democrats had legitimate doubts. What made the Terminator a threatening character was that even his most benign gestures had an ominous ring to them. Arnold gently, oh so gently, suggested to the Democratic legislature that he would be back in the fall to campaign for those who supported his economic recovery plan. He did not say he would campaign against anyone who opposed his plan, but the idea of this mammoth character strutting across one's district sent shivers of fear into those Democrats in marginal districts, and in their natural insecurity most politicians believe that their district could be marginal.

"I've met Bill Clinton, but, man, this guy is just as good as him at speaking and dodging the issue," said Reyes. "Arnold engages you, he says he wants to work with you, but he never answers your questions. Arnold doesn't unveil all his cards. Best poker player I've ever seen. I told the caucus afterward, 'That man's good. I've seen a lot of politicians, and he's good.'"

One of the crucial matters for which he needed the support of the Democratic majority was the repeal of a bill granting illegal immigrants the right to drivers' licenses, which had been signed by Davis during the campaign. The majority of Californians shared Arnold's doubts about the legislation, but not the labor unions, liberal organizations, and many Democratic politicians. Burton said that racism was involved in the attempt to kill the law. "What the fuck do you think?" he asked. "Because they were talking about Mexicans, all right, they were talking about people of brown color and people with accents. That's what the fuck it was about.'"

Burton's charge rankled many Californians. "His absurd 1960s-era claim of 'racism' can hardly account for the massive resistance to the illegal alien drivers' licenses in a state as liberal as California," said syndicated columnist Jill

Stewart. "Many were furious because it's a first step to getting all sorts of other documents in an era of terrorism, plus many others were outraged because it seemed to reward people who broke the law to be here. The subtext is the strategy to build up the unions with the warm bodies of illegal aliens."

The Democratic politicians did not want Arnold to take the popular issue to the public, and they went along with rescinding the bill with his promise to help develop new legislation that would have the kind of safeguards that he could approve. Arnold wanted a special color or code on the license that would show that it was clearly different, and he gave a clear indication that if such a bill came to his desk, he would pass it.

The staff Arnold assembled suggested a man comfortable with diversity in ideology. One of those Arnold first thought of naming his chief of staff was his brother-in-law Tim Shriver, the CEO of Special Olympics International. Shriver would have been someone Arnold knew "would cover my back," but he had other obligations and that discussion did not get very far. Instead, Arnold picked Pat Clarey, who had been Wilson's deputy chief of staff. She was a political moderate who oversaw a staff that on the right included the most important initial appointment, finance director Donna Arduin, who had filled similar positions in Michigan, New York, and Florida. Communications director Rob Stutzman was also a conservative with a fierce antagonism against what he considered a biased liberal media. The right-wingers were matched on the left by several important appointments. Senior adviser Bonnie Reiss was supposed to oversee the attempt to keep filmmakers working in California and also handle the after-school programs. She was such a close friend of both Arnold and Maria that she had as much access as anyone in the administration. She was a shadowy presence, giving few interviews in part because her ideology was anathema to most of Arnold's supporters. The other strong liberal force in the administration was the new head of the California Environmental Protection Agency, Terry Tamminen, who had been introduced to Arnold during the campaign by Maria's cousin environmental leader Robert F. Kennedy Jr.

Arnold selected Congressman David Dreier to head the transition, and he assembled an eclectic team. Dreier had to deal with critics who charged that the campaign had been overloaded with Wilson people and that Arnold would be largely their pawn as governor. On election night, there had been two VIP suites of celebrants, one full of a rowdy, beer-drinking crew headed by Murphy and his associates, and the other suite laden with preppy Wilson people. These latter aides were moving into the new administration in large numbers. During a transition meeting, members of the team worried aloud that the governor-elect might appear to have been captured by the Wilson people and was not his own man. "Wait a minute," Arnold said. "The last successful governor of California was a Republican, and why in the world would we not take advantage of expertise that is there?"

It was a mark of self-confidence. "There were people who were worried that somehow the Wilson forces were going to overshadow and control Arnold," said Dreier. "But nobody controls Arnold."

Arnold was both an inspiring and a difficult boss. He infused the administration with infectious optimism, but he was not a systematic administrator, and his subordinates at times found endlessly waiting on him difficult. He and Maria were both demanding perfectionists, and if they were dismissive of those who fell short, they were richly laudatory to those who came through. Unlike many politicians, they were largely understanding of their demands. At the staff Christmas party, Arnold and Maria thanked the spouses whose husbands and wives worked interminable hours. "While the first months were hard, he makes you feel great," said Donna Lucas, deputy chief of staff. "Both Maria and the governor have high standards. Good is not good enough. Maria will stay up all night preparing for a press conference or a speech."

Arnold did not quite have the philosophy of Conan the Barbarian, who, when asked what the best thing in life was, replied, "To crush your enemies, to see them driven before you, and to hear the lamentations of the women." Arnold settled for first defeating and then belittling his foes. In his first public act since losing ignominiously to Arnold, Lieutenant Governor Bustamante introduced the new governor for his first State of the State address to the legislature in January 2004. When the diminutive politician stepped back from the podium, the senators and assemblymen gave Arnold a wild, hooting reception unlike anything that had been heard in these chambers for years. "Thank you. Thank you very much. Thank you. Wow, this looks good. I like that," Arnold said. Then he looked down at his former opponent: "This was all for you." If former Governor Davis had made such a remark, he would have been roundly rebuked for his public nastiness, but it was just more of Arnold's playfulness.

Unlike Conan, Arnold was civil and cordial to his defeated opponents as long as they deferred to him and publicly acknowledged their defeat. Davis did everything but wear a sackcloth. The former governor showed up at various events in which Arnold starred and he was merely a featured player shuffling along at the edge of the spotlight. Davis tried to develop a relationship with Arnold. "I don't know why he calls," Arnold said in February 2004. "But he tells me how well I'm doing. Isn't that fantastic? He's coming over for dinner tonight."

From his bodybuilding days, Arnold took his penchant for exaggeration and institutionalized it as one of the primary techniques of his governorship. When Superior Court judge Loren McMaster ruled that Arnold would have to repay $4.5 million that he had loaned his campaign, any other politician would have struggled to defend the way he had wiggled around campaign laws and now had to open his own wallet up to pay an amount that even he found painful. But no, the judge's decision was "fantastic," and most of the press coverage was of Arnold's bizarre cheerfulness rather than the ruling.

When Arnold entered the recall election, he had vowed, "I don't need to take any money from anybody" because "I have plenty of money myself." That was true, but he did not like to spend his own money, though he had put up $12,850,000, all of it before he won election. Since he was constantly flying around California, giving speeches, promoting various initiatives and plans, and extolling the state everywhere from Las Vegas to Tokyo, New York to Jerusalem, he needed millions of dollars that most elected officials would not have found necessary.

He had savaged Gray Davis as a creature of moneyed interests, yet in his first year in politics Arnold took in an awesome $26.6 million, including his own contributions, an average of $72,000 a day, twice that of his predecessor. "He's taken more money from special interests than anyone in this state ever has," said David Fink, a policy advocate at the Foundation for Taxpayer and Consumer Rights. "He hasn't changed the political culture in Sacramento. It's the status quo. He made everyone believe in him, that he wasn't the typical politician, and he's just like everyone else."

Arnold took 95.8 percent of the money from businesses, including real estate developers, investment companies, and high-tech corporations. As he saw it, these were not special interests but the fundamental concern from which the good affluent lives of Californians have grown and will continue to grow. Special interests were those narrowly targeted groups such as the prison guards unions, the Indian casino owners, and the teachers unions that had so successfully pursued their interests in a Sacramento ruled by Democrats.

Money is not the mother's milk of politics, as Speaker of the California House Jesse Unrah once famously remarked, but the heavy cream. Too much is as dangerous as not enough. Arnold was a man of personal integrity, but his administration was swamped with money that came almost exclusively from business interests, with only .5 percent from unions.

During his term in office, Davis had squirreled his money away for a future race, but Arnold spent most of his out campaigning. Arnold was the action governor, and the action governor did not spend his days in his office in the Capitol. He derived his energy and optimism from his forays out among the people, and he had barely arrived in Sacramento before he was out campaigning again, pushing for the passage of his California Recovery Plan. On one early December day alone, he did four radio interviews in the morning before a noon rally at the West Valley Mall in Tracy, seventy miles from Sacramento.

Tracy, a town of 70,000 in the Central San Joaquin Valley, is a raw, working person's community. The new mall, the place to go in Tracy, is anchored by a Target and a Dollar Store. The several thousand people who congregated in the food court to hear Arnold were from all over America and much of the world—white Protestants, Mexican Americans, Asians, African Americans—all seeking opportunity in a place where homes were cheap and jobs plentiful. The fast food was like Tracy itself, both generic and diverse—Charley's Steakery, Burger King, Dairy Queen, Orange Julius, Chinese Gourmet Express, and Taquería Los Gallos.

Most of those who stood waiting for Arnold had no deep knowledge of his recovery plan; they simply believed in him. They did not care that he had backed off his promise to investigate the sexual charges against him or that he was not discovering the massive institutional corruption that he had asserted was so much a part of Sacramento. He was hope. "It's important that you bring a new dimension into politics," reflected John Jackson, a landscape contractor who had moved to Tracy from Iowa. "In all civilizations there's a sharing in the same interests even if people don't know it. All of a sudden we can be excited about the future." One of those excited was thirty-five-year-old Leticia King, an immigrant from Mexico, holding her nine-year-old son, Nicholas, by the hand. "Arnold impresses me that he came to Tracy," she said. "I took my son out of school to learn about politics."

Gone was most of the inchoate anger of the campaign, transformed into an equally inchoate hope, tied not to a clear ideology but to a sense that the future would be better. The theme song of this new campaign was Bachman-Turner Overdrive's "Takin' Care of Business," the sounds reverberating through the food court. When Arnold arrived, he was greeted like a great star who had miraculously descended on Tracy. Teenage girls swooned. Two giddy teenagers jumped up on chairs and screamed, "I love you." Others held up videos and DVDs, hoping he would sign them.

Arnold's Sacramento opponents criticized him for grandstanding in shopping malls from San Diego to Tracy instead of being at the capital with them, trying to work out a compromise before the December 5 legislative deadline to put the two measures on the March ballot. But he was sending them a message, delivered by the television cameras that captured his sound bites. He did not speak so much in sentences as in slogans and applause lines. He bid "*hasta la vista*, baby" to the car tax and licenses to illegal immigrants, the line from *T2* bringing the biggest applause of the day.

"I want all of you to flex your muscles once again and call your legislators," he said as he had time and again in past days. "Do I have your promise?"

"Yes!" they screamed. He asked them again, and they screamed louder. And he asked them a third time, and they screamed loudest of all.

Arnold was the pied piper leading his followers to an unknown destination, but follow him they did, inundating the legislators with urgent phone calls imploring them to back Arnold's plan, whatever it was.

Late in the afternoon on December 5 a cherubic school choir stood in the rotunda of the Capitol, singing Christmas carols to no one. On this, the legislative deadline for the March ballot, the Republicans and Democrats were supposedly trying to work out a compromise before midnight, but there was little sense of urgency. The legislators nibbled away at the buffet set out for them before they entered the chambers. The Republicans insisted upon a spending cap that would prevent the continued expansion of state government, while the Democrats sought a cap that could allow government to serve the increased needs of Californians once good times came again. Neither side budged, and the midnight deadline approached with little more than shrugs and halfhearted rationalizations.

Near midnight, Arnold walked up from his first-floor office to visit with Republican legislators in a conference room behind the Assembly chambers. He had been in office less than three weeks, and he was being handed what almost anyone would have considered a devastating defeat. He could boast about backing a spending cap initiative for the November ballot, but that was almost a year away. Long before that, if the Davis-backed bond issue was found to be illegal, the state would find itself in a fiscal crisis unprecedented in its history. Nonetheless, the governor was smiling—not a masked grimace, but an authentic expression of his emotions. He loved it when life was on the edge, and the difference between hope and despair no thicker than a dime. He flashed his anger at Democrats, who had not been willing to compromise as much as he felt the Republicans had, but he was resolute and fiercely confident about taking the matter to the people and letting them decide.

Those on the right and the left could walk out into the Sacramento night proud that they had defended their honor, but those in the middle could leave only with a sense of futility. One of those moderates was Assemblyman

Keith Richman, who kept thinking about the dysfunctional legislature as he flew down to Los Angeles for the weekend. By the time he reached his Northridge home, he decided that he would make a last attempt to seek a workable compromise.

Richman had learned that in California politics the center is a no-man's-land between enemy encampments, booby-trapped and endlessly dangerous. And yet it was to the center he went in search of solutions. He called his colleague and friend Joe Canciamilla, a moderate Democrat and coleader with Richman of a bipartisan group that for months had been quietly seeking a solution. They collected the signatures of nineteen members who were part of that beleaguered center calling for new negotiations. The two men convinced Secretary of State Kevin Shelley to extend the deadline for the March 2 ballot.

Despite his bravado among Republican legislators, Arnold flew back to his Brentwood home cognizant of the difficulties that might be in store for his new administration. Maria listened to her husband and discussed the situation with several of the governor's informal advisers, including Leon Panetta, Clinton's former chief of staff. Maria was a participant in a conference call with several of Arnold's aides discussing the budget parley. Arnold agreed to talk to the bipartisan group and reopen negotiations.

Arnold was a natural mediator. When he brought departing Assembly Speaker Herb Wesson or Burton into his office with other politicians and aides, he had a disarmingly casual manner about him. It was hard sometimes to realize that they were not a group of friends sitting around, playing penny-ante poker, but adversaries at a table with the highest of stakes. Arnold showed his hand to no one, and though he made compromises that his more conservative aides considered excessive, he did so because in legislative politics there is rarely final victory, only battles won. Arnold agreed to what was not really a solid spending cap, but a measure that would hold back massive increases in spending. With that in place, the Democrats voted to put Prop 57, the $15 billion bond issue, and Prop 58, the measure to hold down future state spending, on the ballot and then went home for Christmas.

With the legislators gone, the governor played the card the Democrats had not anticipated. He called a press conference and, flanked by a formidable alignment of police chiefs, fire officials, and local politicians, announced that he would invoke his emergency powers and make cuts in the budget on his own and pay $150 million out of the state coffers to local government. The legislature had not meant to give the governor the right to make such munificent grants, but he had seized it. This was a massive usurpation of the presumed power of the legislature, but there was very little the elected officials could do about it, especially when local communities throughout the state applauded the governor.

The move did nothing to solve the financial crisis exacerbated by the new governor's rescinding the car-tax increase, but it was a dynamic, popular gesture. "It's the only way you get anything done around here," said former Governor and Oakland Mayor Jerry Brown. Judged by Arnold's high popularity rating, it was a sentiment shared by most Californians.

CHAPTER FORTY

Cigar Nights

When in Sacramento, Arnold lives in a penthouse suite at the Hyatt Regency Hotel across from the Capitol. He and Maria talked about buying a house, but the governor is so comfortable with hotel living that it seems likely he would serve out his term staying at the hotel. He loves the sensation of travel, weightlessly moving through time and space. Even the transient feeling of a hotel room appeals to him. He generally spends no more than three or four days a week in Sacramento, flying home to Los Angeles, where he works out of his Santa Monica office. He often gets in his jet and zooms off to Sun Valley, Idaho, for the weekend, with few knowing where he is going.

If he is in Los Angeles on the weekends, he often goes off for a motorcycle ride with his buddies. Franco Columbu does not like to go roaring up to the house on Sunday mornings, so Arnold's closest friend waits for him on the side of the highway in Pacific Palisades. Sure enough, at seven o'clock, just when he said he would, Arnold comes revving up, ready to ride up into the hills, wearing black leather pants and a black leather jacket, looking like the Terminator.

Of course, it is not the same. Even with his friends there are security people following behind just out of sight. In Sacramento he sometimes travels the one hundred yards or so from the hotel to his office in a three-car motorcade. That might seem excessive for a man whose natural tendency would be to walk briskly across the exquisitely tended Capitol grounds while greeting the tourists, but he has come to accept a cocoon of security.

When he traveled to Washington in February 2004 for the National Governors Association's meeting, neither his entourage nor the welcome he received fit a mere governor, even from the greatest of states. Instead, they befitted a revered world leader. The excitement among the legislators when he walked into the U.S. Capitol was reminiscent of the crowds outside the Academy Awards squealing at a glimpse of their favorite star. His mini–press conference in the catacombs was a riotous gathering of scores of reporters. In the evening there was a major fund-raiser at which both Arnold and President Bush were present. "And here the President was standing in one room and Arnold was in the other," recalled speechwriter Landon Parvin. "And they were just as excited to see Arnold as they were the President."

Arnold read the enthusiasm his presence evoked the way a television executive read the overnight ratings. By that criterion, there was no more successful politician in America. He was overwhelmingly happy. He told Jim Lorimer that he liked nothing better than the feeling of living life on the outer edge of his energy and ability. Even by that standard, when something is gained, something is always lost, even if it is not always recognized. Arnold's true friends had stopped calling as much, a mark of their concern for him, not the lack of it. They saw how busy he was, and they simply did not want to impose, but that limited one of the most precious parts of his life.

His professional life increasingly interfered with his moments of personal pleasure. He invited journalist Charlie LeDuff to join his friends one Sunday on the motorcycle rally. Though it made for vivid copy on the front page of The New York Times, it also made for a day of everyone playing himself rather than being himself. For a decade, Cigar Night at Schatzi on Main had been like a monthly birthday party, a gala celebration with Arnold and his friends. Once he became governor, he invited big contributors to his table or raised tens of thousands of dollars by using part of the restaurant as a site for a campaign event.

In an attempt not to lose touch with his friends, Arnold piggybacked his time with them onto his most serious political endeavors, inviting his buddies to be there when he was having important meetings. Having them there served a second purpose, lightening up often-ponderous discussions. When Albert Busek visited from Munich, he attended meetings as if a cabinet secretary, but one always ready to pull out a camera. "It was such a hilarious scene," Busek recalled of one meeting. "I photographed it from a high angle, Assembly Speaker Fabian Nuñez looking serious and Arnold and Senator Burton telling stories, but sharp in the content, in a way humorous." To the amazement of many and the consternation of some, Arnold had managed to hit it off with John Burton.

Burton asked Arnold if he knew about the royal hunting lodge at Mayerling at which Crown Prince Rudolf murdered the beautiful young Baroness Marie

Vetsera and then committed suicide in 1889. It was a famous Austrian tale, but Arnold had never heard about it, or had forgotten. He did his best to maintain his credibility by having Albert respond to Burton's exam. "Arnold was glad I knew," said Busek. "Burton wanted to be a winner that he knew something that Arnold didn't know." Burton stuck the needle in again by giving the governor on his birthday not only roasted coffee beans from his San Francisco home, but the movie *Mayerling*.

For the governor, humoring the leader of the opposition was worth every smile as they traded jokes. Arnold's favorite place to take legislators that he wooed was not his private office but his smoking tent in a patio outside the Capitol offices. He was not about to violate the no-smoking ordinance, but he had figured out a way to circumvent the law and display his disdain for political correctness. He liked nothing better than a fine illegal Cuban cigar. He did not inhale but used it as a manly prop, a neat bit of stick-it-in-your-face, anti-PC, agitprop by the legendary action man of Hollywood. Women now and then shared a cigar with the governor, but for the most part it was a stag enclave.

Arnold's day began earlier than almost anyone else's and ended late, and through most of it he was rarely alone. The worst job in his administration was that of the scheduler. Arnold did not like to be pinned down, and he often made his plans at the last minute and then as likely as not would change them. If he was having an interesting discussion on the phone, he did not care if that backed up his appointments for the rest of the day, he kept right on talking.

This pattern was particularly maddening to the old Wilson hands, accustomed to a governor who scheduled everything to the minute. Beyond that, the staff had as difficult a time figuring out where their boss stood on different issues as the journalists who covered him did. He was as much his own man to them as he was to the public, and he would not be hemmed in by the more ideological of his aides.

As much as Arnold loved Maria, he would never have done for her what she had done for him. She had essentially given up a career that she loved so that he could follow his destiny. For several months Maria had negotiated with NBC, hoping to somehow maintain her two-decade-long position at the network. "There was an article in the paper saying I was politically involved, and it was downhill from there," she told Marie Brenner of *Vanity Fair*. "I had been in TV a long time. I knew what a conflict of interest was. I

knew what my integrity was. I said, 'We can work this out.' They said no."
There were simply too many conflicts of interest, and in the end Maria left
NBC with an agreement that she might return to the network to do special
programs.

Maria had an office in the Capitol, where she tried to spend a day each
week. She was a figure of suspicion to conservatives, who feared her Svengali-
like influence on her husband, pushing him to take liberal stances on a variety
of issues. Arnold trusted Maria's voice, but he no more acceded automatically
to her suggestions than he did to anyone else's. Nonetheless, there was no
one as crucial to his decision making, her agenda not to push her husband to
the left as much as to ensure that his decisions get hammered out with intelligence and tempered with foresight.

Maria was so painfully thin that some of those close to her worried about
her health. Whereas the governorship had carried Arnold up to a level of passionate intensity that even he had not known before, Maria seemed even
more high-strung and nervous. She had always sought authenticity in whatever she did, but she risked becoming an endless photo op, shuttled from one
event to another. At Thanksgiving she went to the Sacramento Food Bank to
hand out donated turkeys. It was a wild media moment, but she was gone
within an hour, the photos all taken, the video in the TV cameras, the appropriate quotes given to the newspapers.

Arnold obsessed over nothing but endlessly moved on, discarding whatever was unpleasant and negative and carrying forward only what inspired
and moved him. Maria obsessed over almost everything, from a quote about
her in the newspaper to what she would say at her next event. Arnold's
friends were a joyful diversion from the world. Maria's circle of women often
played into Maria's insecurities and obsessions. Some of them subtly put
other friends down, trying to ingratiate themselves to Maria.

Maria's natural inclination would have been to spend her time on a cutting-
edge social issue. She was, however, such a lightning rod for conservative Republicans that she could not afford to become a public symbol of the more
politically progressive aspects of the administration. "The first lady has a traditional office, the office of special projects," communications director Rob
Stutzman told the *Los Angeles Times*.

Maria bridled under the limitations of her position, everything from the title "first lady" itself and the omnipresent security to the shackling of her own
political concerns. She decided to focus on women—not women and welfare,
not women and abortion rights, not women and equality, but celebrating what
she called "remarkable women."

Maria's first major initiative was an exhibit of California's "Remarkable Women" at the California State History Museum, including a line of "remarkable women" jewelry. The exhibit was so successful that Maria sought to expand it into a full-fledged California Women's History Museum.

Maria was rushing in to take the only museum in the state devoted to California's history, albeit an obscure, neglected facility, and turn it over to one constituency. "What's wrong with that?" the *Fresno Bee* editorialized. "The same thing that would be wrong with the Smithsonian Institution closing down the National Museum of Natural History and replacing it with a dinosaur museum because of the popularity of a blockbuster dinosaur exhibit."

Maria was a woman of almost overwhelming enthusiasm, energy, and persistence. Though Tom Stallard, the president of the board, said that he had "the highest praise for her work ethic," he also felt that "she may not be aware that she really has the ability to run over others." There had been a relentlessly celebratory tone to the "Remarkable Women's Exhibit," and Stallard feared that the new museum would be full of "*People* magazine kind of stuff." The criticism was exacerbated when documents made public from the museum's consultant stated that Edwin Schlossberg, married to Maria's cousin Caroline Kennedy, would be designing the women's museum. The apparent choice of Schlossberg without competitive bidding or vetting suggested Kennedy family nepotism. "He was never hired," said Maria, bristling at the idea that she would do such a thing. "He was never paid a penny, nothing. I asked him if he would come up and give me ideas about how that museum could be saved. That's all."

Maria had gone about changing the museum with what some of the board members thought was an imperious manner. Although almost no one wanted to risk offending Maria, Stallard and two other board members resigned. Maria placated the critics and brought the political leadership of both parties to her cause by expanding her idea into a new California History Center that would have space for the state archives, California history exhibits, and a full-fledged women's museum.

Maria remained the first and last of her husband's crucial advisers. She sat in on meetings first ladies had not attended before, and she gave her forthright opinion on most of the important issues facing California. She was not the liberal goad her right-wing critics imagined her to be. Her transcendent goal was to give her husband advice that would help make him an effective, popular leader. Some of Arnold's staff rustled with nervousness whenever she appeared. She had eyes that went from adoring looks at her husband to chilly disdain for those who fell short in advancing her husband's future.

As during their entire relationship, some of Arnold's associates profoundly admired Maria and appreciated her contributions, while others dreaded to hear that the first lady would be at a meeting. "There's a lot of 'Who the hell are you?' " said Maria. "I say to Arnold, 'Why don't I just wait outside or people are going to go nuts.' And he says, 'No, no, no, I want you in there. I want you.' And believe me, I know anytime I give my opinion about a speech or I do anything, people are like, 'What is she doing?' "

In September 2004 Maria hosted a powerful, inspirational TV special chronicling Roy Horn's partial recovery after being mauled by a tiger during the Las Vegas show of Siegfried and Roy. Maria's greatest public accomplishment during Arnold's first months in office was a conference on women held in December. Previous first ladies had chaired similar events, but nothing like the forum that took place at the mammoth Long Beach Convention Center. Ten thousand women heard speeches by women notables including Oprah Winfrey, Sheryl Crow, and Queen Noor of Jordan. The event was ripe for masculine disdain. *The Washington Post*'s William Booth described the day as "a little pop. A little schlock. Mixed in with you-go-girl messages of surviving breast cancer and making a mint—bringing home the bacon and frying it up in the pan."

The larger political point was that these participants were here mainly because of forty-nine-year-old Maria, not her husband. Probably the only other person in America who could have brought together such an eclectic, enthusiastic, and enormous group of women was Maria's close friend Oprah Winfrey.

"Oprah said to me the other day, 'You're doing exactly what you were always raised to do,' " said Maria. "If I had overshadowed Arnold, I would have been tarred and feathered. So you know I'm very savvy about how these things work. The first lady's office in Sacramento is busier than the one in the White House, period. There's more mail coming in there than to the governor's office. I must be doing something right. But there's not enough room for two people at the same level. It's just impossible, and I'm aware of that."

Unlike Senator Hillary Rodham Clinton and Teresa Heinz Kerry, who when introducing their husbands at the 2004 Democratic Convention spent most of the time touting themselves, their achievements and goals, Maria considered it her transcendent public role to advance her husband's career. Whenever she introduced Arnold, she used every ounce of energy and rhetorical force to project a bold image of the man she loved.

Maria knew that even in the most loving of marriages, one partner made it work, and it was usually the woman. If she had wanted to run for governor, Arnold would likely not have given up his movie career, and she was making sacrifices he would not have made. Maria had in some ways become a traditional wife, viewing her children and her husband as her preeminent concern.

"My fight for Arnold's time today is strictly for my kids," she insisted, "not even for myself. And never do I have any kind of time. He's the one who will fight for time for me. He'll be like, 'I don't have enough time with you.' I understand the job, and I understand the public need for him, because I grew up in the middle of that. But I'll be damned if I don't get time for my kids."

The criticism that Maria had not found herself as first lady or was squandering her days with an endless series of trivial, insubstantial matters rankled her to her core. "Listen, that's all I've heard my whole life," she said. "If your uncle was President, should you really leave town to become a reporter? Is that really good enough for you? You're moving to Baltimore, and you're a Kennedy. Is that really good enough for you? You're living in a studio. Is that really right? When Arnold wins, 'I hope you're going to be like Hillary Clinton' or 'I hope you're not going to be too much like Hillary Clinton.' 'Aren't you co-governing?' 'Aren't you going to cure poverty?' 'Aren't you going to be as big a deal as President Kennedy?' Well, guess what? I'm not.

"I think Arnold's the happiest he's ever been," Maria said wistfully. "This is definitely not where I thought I would be. But I think for any woman sharing her husband with the world 24/7 would be a mixture of tremendous joy and pride and also a 'there he goes' kind of thing. It's very hard for anybody in that situation. He has a job. I don't have a job. My job is raising my kids. That's what I'm doing. And I'm concentrating on two aging parents. And the rest of it is helping Arnold and doing whatever I can do for women."

Arnold was constantly looking for action. He sought out issues and ideas that he could forcefully sell to California voters. When Arnold set out to campaign for Props 57 and 58, the two initiatives were far down in the polls, with only a third of Californians favoring the measures. It seemed unlikely to many that even Arnold would be able to get jaded, tired voters to sign on to the two measures: a $15 billion bond issue and a second bill limiting future spending, which pleased neither conservatives nor liberals.

Arnold loved to be out on the campaign trail, especially if the stakes were high, the challenge great, and the audiences large. His governorship was almost a constant campaign. Several days a week he flew to controlled events all across the state. He did not generally give interviews, and his people made sure that reporters did not get close enough even to shout out their questions.

He had an agenda to push, and he would no more indulge the journalists in their far-ranging questions than talk about anything but his film when he had had a new movie coming out.

Nothing was missed in creating the desired image. At some of the stops, the staff set up special stands from which photographers and cameramen could take photos and video of Arnold's best profile before he moved back onto the campaign bus. For the first few months some of the reporters had asked only the gentlest of questions, in part hoping to get an exclusive interview. That had not happened, and the governor's communications office spent most of its time keeping the media at bay.

At the end of the initiative campaign, Arnold went off on a one-day bus trip from Los Angeles to Fresno, in the heart of Silicon Valley. The final event at the Martin Luther King Library offered a startling picture of the power and the authority Arnold had amassed. Northern California was bathed in the bluest of Democratic blues, but on the stage behind Arnold stood much of the Democratic leadership, a group that six months before would have considered it unthinkable to be anywhere near him.

There was Senator Dianne Feinstein, who had almost run against him and now was a proud supporter of Props 57 and 58. She told the audience that Arnold had "brought a very strong breath of fresh air to this state." And there stood one of the icons of the American left, Dolores Huerta, who along with César Chávez had founded the United Farm Workers of America. "We're tired of his lies," Huerta had said during the recall campaign. "And, hey, we're tired of his groping!" But now she added her stature to this cause. The whole stage was largely Democrats, from the Secretary of State to the Fresno mayor, from state senators to assemblymen, from La Raza to the NAACP, all gently jostling to stand nearer to Arnold so that the moment would be memorialized in a politically useful photograph of them with their dear friend and governor.

"You flexed your muscles once before," Arnold said, his words pumped with energy and enthusiasm, speaking as always primarily to the cameras. "You flexed your muscles and you voted me in. You sent me to Sacramento to clean house and to take care of this mess. And this is what I'm doing. I'm creating action. One after another, all the promises I have made I will keep. I need your help. The massive weight we must lift off our state alone I cannot lift it. But together we can. I want you to be my power lifters. Help me lift off this weight."

Arnold sold the propositions with a compelling, irresistible grandiosity, the same way he sold his movies. The initiatives were compromises that left the state's problems sitting largely where they were, but he made them sound like the first day of a grand, compelling journey that would bring back the golden days of California. On Election Day, March 2, 2004, Proposition 57, the "economic recovery" bond issue, passed by 63.4 percent, and Prop 58, the "balanced budget" initiative, passed by a walloping 71.1 percent. By any definition, it was a formidable victory, giving Arnold a position of authority greater than any governor in at least a generation.

Three days later, Arnold flew off to Columbus for the sixteenth annual Arnold Classic. When he and Jim Lorimer had started the competition in 1989, they had envisioned it as a major bodybuilding event. Not even Arnold could have prophesized what it had become, an all-around sports event with more participants than the Olympics and 100,000 people walking the exhibit halls and cheering the competitors. Of the twelve thousand athletes taking part, only thirty were bodybuilders, half of them women. The Greater Columbus Convention Center was a beehive of competition. Even the endlessly energetic Arnold could not visit all the events, from gymnastics to cheerleading, martial arts to table tennis, fencing to weight lifting. In the center in the main hall was a six hundred–booth exhibition promoting primarily food supplements and nutritional products.

When Arnold called Columbus his second hometown, he was not merely flattering the Ohio city. He had partial ownership of Easton Town Center and although there were hundreds of volunteers, the Arnold Classic was a profit-making enterprise owned by Arnold and Lorimer. The governor's major new philanthropic pursuit, the two-year-old After School All-Stars program, had chapters in fifteen cities, including a program in Columbus. On the evening of his arrival, he attended a fund-raiser for the All-Stars, gave out awards at the Ms. International Fitness and Figure International contest, and then returned to the annual World Gym dinner that was honoring Joe Weider.

Arnold knew that his eighty-four-year-old friend and mentor was in bad shape. Weider should have gone to the dinner in a wheelchair, but he was a man of such overweening pride in his own physical well-being that he insisted on walking into the banquet room at the Hyatt on Capitol Square. It had been thirty-six years since Weider had brought Arnold to L.A. And nothing was the same. Most of the World Gym franchisees had nothing of the devotion to bodybuilding that had possessed Joe Gold when founding first Gold's Gym and then World Gym. Although most cared about physical fitness, a few could just as easily have purchased a Jiffy Lube or a McDonald's franchise. Seated with them were many of the past greats of the sport—Lou Ferrigno, Frank Zane, Reg Park, Mike Katz—men who had won their last trophies long ago. Several of them were unsettled by the transformation of their sport and bewildered by Arnold's ascent to the governorship of California. They could not erase from their consciousnesses the image of the rowdy trickster they had known and competed against.

Life waited for Arnold. When he finally arrived in the middle of the dinner, he received a standing ovation. Another man might still have been savoring his victory in the initiatives just three days before, but Arnold was a man of monumental focus—and now it was the bodybuilders' turn. It was not the governor of California standing there before them, but the most revered figure in the sport. He was supposed to be celebrating Joe Weider that evening and giving him an award for his lifetime service to the sport, but Arnold almost always managed to talk about himself.

"If Joe Weider's magazine hadn't existed, I never would have known about Reg Park," Arnold said, looking out at the South African champion, "and would never have been inspired to get into bodybuilding and to come over here. When Joe invited me, that was the great beginning of making my dream a reality. Ever since I came to America, Joe opened up his arms to me.

"On top of that, he has been an unbelievable human being. After I was through with bodybuilding, he took complete interest in my movie career. He came many times to the set. He was even at rehearsals and always there at my side. Every step of the way. After-school programs. And my campaign. Contributing. Writing letters. Leaving messages. So, ladies and gentlemen, the great Joe Weider."

Arnold had spent little of his time saluting Weider for his many contributions to bodybuilding, but Joe heard what he wanted and needed to hear— namely, that Arnold cared deeply for him and appreciated what he had done. The two men had had their difficulties over the past three and a half decades, but when Arnold made his own spiritual accounting of those who had helped him in his life, Joe was up there near the top of the list.

Painfully, Joe made his way up to the podium and stood there a moment as the applause rose and the guests gave him a standing ovation. "Arnold, we all know, is a great man," Weider said in his heavy accent. "We all know that he is a fabulous human being. And most important, I wish everybody knew him the way I do."

All his life Weider had celebrated his own name and accomplishments wherever he could stamp them. But on this occasion, when he had the right to talk of himself, he spoke only of Arnold. "His friendship, being in his company, it's one of the greatest joys a human being could have," Weider asserted. "When he talks to you and is with you, you feel like a king. And when he leaves, you feel pretty bad. He's got a heart of gold. He's loyal. He's dependable. I don't know how to describe him."

Joe started to cry as he reached for words that were not there. "One of my greatest joys and successes in this world is to have found Arnold," Weider went on. "And I figured every sport needs a hero. And I thought at that time that Arnold would be that man. And he would exalt the sport. Which he did. And his success I feel is my success. When he gets ahead and grows, I grow. It confirms to me that I made the best decision of my life."

When Joe left the podium, he stumbled and began to fall. Arnold was so busy with well-wishers that he did not notice, but Ferrigno jumped up from his seat and helped Weider back to his table.

Saturday morning. Arnold had his picture taken with the 1,800 fans who had paid $350 for the VIP tickets for the weekend, many of them primarily for this moment. The crowd stood in a long line, waiting for their ten seconds with Arnold. He grasped the person's arm and smiled, and the Polaroid photo looked as if the governor was standing with one of his closest friends.

That afternoon, in the Grand Exhibit Hall, publishing magnate David Pecker was to make an important announcement with Arnold standing beside him. Arnold had agreed to serve as executive editor of *Muscle & Fitness* and *Flex*, American Media's two major bodybuilding magazines. He was to be paid $250,000 a year for his efforts for a minimum of five years. The money was to be given to charity, and it was largely a public relations gesture, but it was not often that the owner of America's tabloids announced a formal business relationship with a leading public official. It was yet another reason why it was unlikely that the *National Enquirer* and the *Star* would be delving into Arnold's past.

Weider, waiting in his wheelchair, was ready to rise and join Arnold and Pecker on the temporary stage. These had been Joe's magazines, and this was a moment he relished. As Pecker chatted quietly with his entourage, he had a different view.

"I felt this agreement was a milestone," Pecker said. "The Weiders never did it." Joe had not been willing to share the top of the masthead with Arnold, and it rankled Pecker that now Weider sought to elbow his way into yet another moment of public glory. Beyond that the day before, *USA Today* wrote, "When Weider sold the magazines, he told the New York *Daily News* that he had gotten assurances from AMI chief David Pecker that the company's celeb tabloids would stay away from Schwarzenegger. Now that deal seems cemented." Just before going onstage, Pecker said to Arnold that there was little time, and he did not want to share it with Weider. "You make the decision," Arnold said. And so as Arnold and Pecker walked forward to thunderous applause, Weider sat by himself in his wheelchair. It was a cruel farewell to his creations, but he had been royally paid and he could not let go of what was no longer his.

That evening Arnold attended the finals of the bodybuilding championship named after him. When Arnold and his contemporaries had walked out onstage to pose, the outline of their bodies was enough to tell them apart, from Oliva's massive thighs and dancer's waist to Zane's elegantly wrought frame, from Columbu's solid figure to Arnold's rough-hewn form. As the top contenders walked out onstage that evening, they were so devoid of unique physical form that they appeared almost interchangeable. Nor was there any of the dramatic competitions like those between Arnold and Oliva that had so enriched the sport. "There are no personalities being developed in the sport right now," Arnold admitted. "They walk out slow and act like they can't move, and they all have the same kind of music. I fall asleep."

Arnold had an exquisitely perfected body, but these men have bodies that bear almost no relationship to the human form. They are the creatures as much of science as sport, shimmering, stained-brown behemoths lumbering around backstage. They were kept apart in a separate hotel, where they were fed up to a dozen times a day. They often weigh fifty or seventy-five pounds more than the bodybuilders of Arnold's generation of comparable height. Yet there is not a pinch of fat on their bodies. They are nothing but sheaths of muscle.

Scores of pages of ads in the muscle magazines feature pictures of the mammoth champions promoting supplements that are sometimes of questionable value and untested safety. The crowds buy the magazines and the supplements that promise the muscles of Hercules, and pay a premium price for tickets to see these suprahuman figures. The hard-core fans were in attendance that evening, 4,000 of them in the theater and 15,000 watching on pay-per-view.

The bodies had grown so much in the years since Arnold competed that Zane said that if he were young again he would have to enter the women's competition. The road to a championship leads so directly to steroids, human growth hormones, and the illusion of health and strength that when the teenage grandson of Arnold's mentor Reg Park wanted to become a bodybuilder, his father talked him out of it.

This year, DEA agents had arrived at the Arnold Classic to serve a few subpoenas to supplement dealers and others. Insiders fear that one day the feds will come down on bodybuilding in full force, the sport's image will be decimated, and the new executive editor of *Flex* and *Muscle & Fitness* will suffer from his continued involvement.

Saturday evening after the event, Arnold went back to the Hyatt on Capitol Square to join a group of about ten friends, who sat in the back room of the bar, talking and smoking cigars. As late as he stayed up, the next morning he was up early to head over to the same theater where the night before the champions of the sport had walked. About a thousand people gathered there for Arnold's personal seminar.

The man speaking at the podium was wise in the ways of bodybuilding, wise in the ways of the world beyond, and generous in imparting that wisdom. He was not talking about hard-core bodybuilding but about getting in shape physically, mentally, and spiritually. To Arnold, working out was not an occasional diversion, but one of the crucial, indispensable elements of a full life. That was Arnold's central message. Working out enhances your physical health, but it also supports psychological well-being and spiritual richness.

"Your number one priority should be exercise," he said. "It's like sleeping and eating. There are certain things that you need to do in order to survive. Therefore, you have to make adjustments. Maybe you have to get up earlier or go to bed later. Right now you can imagine the kind of responsibilities I have. It's from early morning till late at night. But I still get in my workout, a half hour of cardiovascular training in the morning, and in the evening I work out with weights for a half hour or sometimes an hour. My workout continued throughout the entire campaign. Every single day I work out, seven days a week. The day is twenty-four hours. So if you work hard for fifteen hours, well, there's still nine hours left. So what's your problem?"

Girlie Men

When Arnold returned to Sacramento, he faced a daunting list of promised reforms. High on his agenda was workers' compensation. Insurance companies, the medical establishment, lawyers, and other special-interest lobbyists had helped create a program that was the most expensive in the nation for employers, yet often delivered inadequate benefits to affected workers. For years legislators had been working to reform the program, and Davis had signed a bill that went part of the way.

Arnold, however, took to his bully pulpit and made Californians aware that, individually and collectively, they were being hurt. He took what most would have considered an esoteric concern and made it a hot-button issue for millions of Californians. For a month and a half, he held the sword of a November ballot initiative over the heads of the legislators as they pushed forward in a hurried process that allowed almost no time for scrutiny by most of the legislators or the media. Arnold did not care. He wanted action, and when he threatened, it was not bluster.

While the legislators tried to work out a compromise, he went out on the hustings again, getting signatures for a ballot initiative. "This is what the people want to see," he told a crowd at a Costco in Burbank. "They want to see an action governor—not someone who sits around the office in Sacramento, not doing anything." Arnold immensely enjoyed standing in the public arena, but the purpose this time was to force the legislators to reform the system.

Arnold got his bill by mid-April, and in the end even the often-critical *Los Angeles Times* admitted that the legislation was "expected to wring billions of savings from an insurance system often blamed for causing business to flee the state."

In January 2004, Ken Auletta wrote a piece in *The New Yorker* about President Bush's attitude toward the press that was widely read within the Schwarzenegger administration. Auletta argued that "perhaps for the first time the White House has come to see reporters as special pleaders—pleaders for more access and better headlines—as if the press were simply another interest group, and moreover, an interest group that's not nearly as powerful as it once was." Arnold was doing precisely that in a far more thorough way even than the Bush administration. He was changing the fundamental way that the press covered the governor in California.

Arnold's attitude toward the media had grown originally from his experience with bodybuilding and the Weider publications. These magazines projected a mythic image that had only a casual relationship to what the innocent would call truth. As a movie star, Arnold had an immensely disciplined approach to projecting precisely what he wanted to project, and that was a gigantic, legendary being. Over the years, he had developed a justifiable suspicion of the press, but his attitude now was not simply about containing the damage that he might suffer from what he considered biased liberal journalists. As he saw it, all journalists could be a problem, and they had to be contained and harnessed to his will.

Arnold usually fed reporters like squirrels in the park, throwing a few peanuts at them. The next time he showed up they scurried around him again, ready to scramble for a few more peanuts. He had no favorite reporters. Arnold might pontificate to the Hollywood Foreign Press or give mini-interviews, shuffling the scribes in and out as he had promoting his films, but he almost never gave extensive, on the record, one-on-one interviews to political reporters. He was no longer the recipient of frequent segments on *ET* and *Extra* as he had been during the campaign, but their absence was compensated for by the California television stations, several of which had added Sacramento bureaus to cover the governor, and by the national media's fascination.

His was an immensely disciplined administration. Arnold's close associates hardly ever talked to the press, and there were almost no leaks. "Staff members still prefer to remain tight lipped," communications director Rob Stutzman said. "Can't imagine any of us believe it serves the governor to talk about the administration until it comes to an end." Although most of those within the administration found it an immensely satisfying spectacle watching the reporters standing outside the gates, a few close to the governor thought it was a mistake. They felt that Arnold should go in and meet with the editorial boards of the *Sacramento Bee* and the *Los Angeles Times*. He should let reporters quiz him at length and spend extensive time with him. They felt that he was so good at what he did that he could only win.

Arnold was all about control, though, and if he could not have control, he was not about to run the risk. When his positive poll numbers sat comfortably at 65 percent, who was to say that he was wrong?

Arnold's largest problem was passing the 2005 budget by the July 1 deadline. All during the campaign he had belittled squabbling among petty legislators unable to resolve their differences, annually leaving the state in weeks of uncertainty and crisis. He vowed that with him at the helm, the ship of state would sail on a steady course, without the frantic last-minute bickering and compromises.

Arnold was committed to what seemed a logical impossibility. He did not want to make draconian cuts in government services, yet sought a balanced budget that did not involve tax increases. Economic growth was the genie that could solve that dilemma by increasing the state's revenues without raising tax rates. It would almost take a second California Silicon Valley technology rush to create that level of growth to refill the state's coffers. Although neither his own Department of Finance nor the Legislative Analyst's Office nor many private economists thought it likely, Arnold proceeded rhetorically as if a surge in growth was almost inevitable.

Arnold was a font of endless optimism, biding his time with patch-and-paste temporary fixes on the broken machine of government until the great engine of the California economy took hold creating vast new tax revenues. In other words, he did what his predecessor had done—pushed the problem into the future and hoped for future revenue growth. That magnitude of hope never seemed to hang well on Gray Davis's slim body, but it fit perfectly with Arnold's oversize persona.

Arnold went to the California Teachers Association and got it to give up $2 billion in legally mandated funding in exchange for an agreement that he would not be back to ask for cuts again. He did essentially the same thing to the cities and counties to get them to cough up $2.6 billion in property tax revenue over the next two years, and to the public universities to cut back enrollment temporarily. He was not mortgaging the future but was promising that the future would be good enough to render his promises inviolate.

The roughly $5 billion in temporary spending cuts did little more than offset the revenue loss from the vehicle-license-fee reduction Arnold had promised. He needed to find about $10 billion more. But he was caught between

Democrats, who felt it their sacred duty to protect social programs, and Republicans, who thought it their equally sacred duty to cut enough funds to balance the budget. Arnold had countless discussions and meetings with legislative leaders of both parties. When he played up to them, he was the most genial and conciliatory of men, with a good word for everyone, nicknames for everybody at the table, and cigars all round, enveloping them in a backslapping camaraderie worthy of Lyndon Johnson. When it was time to get tough, he did not merely wave a stick in front of the troublesome politicians, he brandished a bludgeon.

When Arnold had been running for office, he had raged against the waste and excess in Sacramento, but now that he sat in the governor's seat, trying to cut the budget, he saw that after a point he was not cutting programs, he was cutting people and hurting individual lives. He had said he wanted to temporarily suspend new enrollment in the expensive Lanterman Act that provided in-home services for the disabled, but after his mother-in-law lectured him on that subject, he changed his mind. He contented himself with trying to hold down the dramatic increase in such programs, in the end agreeing to undo about a billion dollars in cuts from his original budget proposal, primarily for social services. He needed the Democratic votes to pass his budget, and he was not going to be seen as the scourge of poor children and the developmentally disabled, whatever the price to his promise of a balanced budget.

For all his avowals that he was different, Arnold did not get his budget passed by the July 1 deadline. As the days passed, he displayed his frustration in bolder and bolder rhetoric. In mid-July at a speech at an Ontario mall, he fumed at the Democrats: "They cannot have the guts to come out there in front of you and say, 'I don't want to represent you. I want to represent those special interests: the unions, the trial lawyers.' I call them girlie men. They should get back to the table, and they should finish the budget."

The phrase "girlie man" resembled the friendly insults that Arnold and his bodybuilding friends had hurled at one another on the floor of Gold's Gym. The precise phrase came from a parody on *Saturday Night Live* in which Dana Carvey and Kevin Nealon played muscle-bound, brain-limited versions of Arnold. The phrase set off a firestorm of criticism, especially from gay activists and feminists. "It's really painful to hear the governor resort to such blatant homophobia," said State Senator Shelia Kuehl, a liberal Democrat from Santa Monica. Burton was more philosophical. "I don't know what the definition of 'girlie man' is," Burton said. "As opposed to his being a he-man? I can't think of a way to have the he-man and the girlie men join hands around the Capitol and sing 'Kum Ba Ya.'"

Arnold had found the phrase funny, and he was damned if he was going to apologize. He was a one-man wrecking crew, flailing away at political correctness with his verbal sledgehammer. He was going to stick it to the legislators in language that would leave welts that would not soon go away—and by the end of the month, girlie men or no, he had his budget.

Arnold was probably mistaken when he concluded that his provocative attack at the Ontario mall had anything to do with the legislature's agreeing to a $105 billion budget with a projected deficit of $5–$7 billion. The Democrats almost unanimously voted for the budget. Since twelve of the fourteen Republican senators voted against the bill, many of the girlie men out there were in his own party. The bill itself bore all the nicks and scratches of endless infighting and was hardly exemplary of the new politics that Arnold had promised to bring to the people of California.

The governor stood with an expansive smile on his face, asserting that he was filling the glass of California politics with wine of a new vintage. The question was whether it was leaking out through a hole in the bottom faster than he was pouring. Daniel Weintraub, a political columnist for the *Sacramento Bee*, thought that it was no apparition—the glass was slowly filling. Weintraub, a fierce critic of politics as usual in Sacramento, appreciated what Arnold had been up against. The governor had cut the projected deficit of $15 billion at least in half and the budget by about $10 billion. He had done a masterful job of negotiating with teachers, the public university system, Indian tribes, and others, working out concessions that had seemed almost unthinkable.

"It would have been nice to see the governor reach higher for the kind of long-term budget reforms the state dearly needs," Weintraub concluded. "But Schwarzenegger has just taken a chunk out of California's persistent budget shortfall while cutting taxes and building important new political alliances with school leaders, local government officials, university administrators, and the freeway builders and labor unions that constitute the transportation lobby. Not a bad start for a novice."

Others looked at that same glass and said that any fool could tell that the glass was cracked and it was emptying out. One of Arnold's most compelling critics has been Senator Tom McClintock, who looked with dismay at a Republican governor who proudly perpetuated massive deficits and trumpeted his appalling failure as a triumph. Economists shook their heads, too, at a budget that merely pushed the fiscal day of reckoning into the future. The state Legislative Analyst's Office estimated that there was fully $17 billion of borrowing in the budget and projected that the deficit would grow from about

$5 billion to almost double that in two years. Beyond that, the promises that Arnold had made to the teachers and counties and others would only exacerbate the problem by the time of the 2007 budget.

Arnold did his usual brilliant job of selling his budget as a successful resolution of a dangerous stalemate, and at least 65 percent of Californians continued to approve of their new governor. That in itself was an extraordinary achievement—especially when measured against the calamitous situation at the time of Governor Davis's recall. It was all a matter of perspective. Those like Weintraub, who understood how difficult it is to achieve great things in the inbred, provincial, self-protective world of Sacramento politics, applauded Arnold and appreciated his accomplishment. Many of those who stood furthest back from the daily world of politics and were most serious about the magnitude of the crisis argued that the governor had merely postponed tough decisions.

Not the Last Chapter

In his speech at the 2004 Republican National Convention, Americans across the nation saw in Arnold what Californians had been experiencing for the past year: a feverishly exciting spectacle of provocative sound bites, fervent exhortations, and optimism. The speech turned Arnold into an important national political figure, the most talked about new Republican politician in America.

There was increasing talk and speculation about a constitutional amendment to allow a foreign-born citizen to run for the presidency. The prohibition against a foreign-born President is the one surviving inequality institutionalized in the fundamental document of American governance. The argument against changing the Constitution is that it is dangerous to tinker with what works. The argument to amend arises from the conviction that in a nation of immigrants, if a man or a woman can mow your lawn, wash your dishes, fight for you in Iraq, educate your children, and build your technology, then after being a citizen for twenty or thirty years he or she certainly should have all the rights of native-born Americans. Well before Arnold became governor, politicians on both sides of the aisle, from Senator Orrin Hatch to Ted Kennedy, favored such an amendment.

In September a small independent group began placing radio ads calling for a constitutional amendment. Such a change requires a two-thirds majority in both houses of Congress, followed by ratification by three-fourths of the states. The never-utilized alternative involves a constitutional convention and ratification by three-fourths of the states.

Those ads and favorable editorials led to a nativist backlash. For Arnold's prospects, the issue had been defined in the worst possible way. When the front page of *USA Today* on December 3, 2004, headlined SHOULD THE CONSTITUTION BE AMENDED FOR ARNOLD? the answer was a resounding "no!" A Gallup poll showed that two-thirds of Americans were opposed to amending the Constitution. As long as it appeared to be a revision to benefit one man, that was unlikely to change.

Although Arnold favored the constitutional amendment and privately aspired to becoming President, he knew that he should distance himself from the issue. He had to get on with the mighty tasks facing him in California. Arnold did not have to risk himself in the elections of November 2004, for his governorship ran two more years, but he, nonetheless, became almost as central a figure as if he had been standing for election himself.

There was little Arnold could do to deliver California for the incumbent, George W. Bush. California was one of the few states the Republicans conceded to the Democrats. Just as important to most Californians were the special ballot propositions. Arnold had a slate of initiatives he was backing, and some he opposed. He traversed the state, appearing on talk radio and advancing his case in television advertising.

Among the propositions Arnold was keen to defeat were two separate initiatives seeking to expand the Indian gaming tribes' casinos. He looked hard, long, and critically at a proposition that would have dramatically weakened the "three strikes and you're out" law that imposed long terms on multiple offenders. His opposition pleased conservatives, but not his championing of another dramatic, unprecedented initiative that called for the state to invest $3 billion in stem cell research. In backing it, Arnold set himself against the Bush administration, fiscal conservatives, and even a number of economists who found the measure quixotic and irrational.

Arnold felt little of the rapport with the younger President Bush that he had with his father, George H. W. Bush. Although Arnold found plenty of time to campaign in California, he insisted he was too busy to go out of state to campaign for the President. Although the Bush administration had not given California the aid that Arnold hoped it would, the two men needed each other's support. Ohio promised to be one of the crucial states in a close election, and Arnold's popularity there had the potential to make a difference. After negotiations, Arnold agreed to introduce President Bush in Columbus on the Friday before the election. Arnold flew first to Cleveland, where Joe Weider was recovering from back surgery. Joe had suffered a temporary relapse, and as Arnold sat by his bed at the Cleveland Clinic, he was not even sure that Weider recognized him. From there, he traveled to Columbus— where huge crowds were assembling to hear the President.

Arnold walked along a runway to the podium at Nationwide Arena to engulfing applause. Unwilling to be upstaged, the President and First Lady stepped out right behind him, entering to an even more thunderous welcome. For ten minutes, Arnold had the unfamiliar experience of having to stand there while 20,000 people applauded not him but the First Couple. As Arnold was introducing the President, Bush stood behind him, occasionally whispering to his wife and making gestures to some of those in the audience. In his ten-minute introduction, Arnold implored the audience to "roll up [their] sleeves—to post yard signs, climb into the trenches" to assure victory for the President; but Arnold's sleeves were firmly buttoned and there were no signs in his yard.

On election night, Arnold could take some credit for Bush's victory in Ohio. In California, Arnold scored an overwhelming personal success on the initiatives. By coming in hard and strong against tampering with the "three strikes" legislation, he turned almost certain passage into a ringing defeat. The casino proposals were defeated, too, and the stem cell proposition won by a landslide. When it came to issues that he cared deeply about and articulated in the media, the governor had shown he was almost unbeatable.

Despite Arnold's success, his party did not pick up a single seat in the state legislature or the congressional delegation. California remained a land of impregnable one-party mini-states. A proposition had been added to the ballot that would have begun to change that political map by creating open primaries after which the top two candidates would run in the general election. Since the measure would have pushed candidates to the center in search of votes, it was adamantly opposed by professional politicians in both parties. Though Arnold supported the measure, he did not actively campaign for it, and it went down to defeat.

For his first anniversary in office, every major paper in the state wanted to interview Arnold. It was a matchless opportunity for the governor to make his case to journalists when he did not need them instead of waiting until he did. His communications director turned everyone down. "You want to communicate, and summing up one year in office, do you sit down with eight or nine newspapers or do you sit down for an hour with Larry King?" asked Stutzman. "You sit down with Larry King in a medium that's better suited to this governor, and if he makes news, the California press crops is going to cover it anyway."

As 2004 came to an end, Arnold had a list of accomplishments to celebrate, not least of which was changing the way Californians looked at themselves and their future. At the end of the Davis administration, 76 percent of Californians had felt that the state was headed in the wrong direction. After a year of Arnold's governorship, the number had shrunk to 38 percent. Such a turnaround was unprecedented in recent Californian history. Arnold's success, derided by critics as a triumph of style over substance, had taken all of his media acumen and political skill to change attitudes. The cheerful excitement Arnold brought to governing was the essence of the man, and it spilled over onto almost everyone who came in contact with him.

Nor had Arnold hidden behind his popularity to avoid contentious issues. He vetoed a bill raising the minimum wage, arguing that it would only hurt business growth at a time when he was trying to accelerate the economic engines. Although he was consistently pro-business, he confounded those who sought to pigeonhole him ideologically. During the campaign he had been wrongly accused of intending to abolish the state Environmental Protection Agency. As governor, he proved to be in the forefront of that issue. He not only appointed a certified liberal as his environmental chief, Terry Tamminen, but backed him to the hilt. The governor approved bills to dramatically cut automotive greenhouse gas emissions and groundbreaking legislation permitting hybrid autos to drive in carpool lanes. He created an enormous 25-million-acre nature conservancy in the Sierra Nevada. Tamminen's work so impressed Arnold that he named him cabinet secretary in November 2004.

When Mayor Gavin Newsom of San Francisco started issuing marriage licenses to gay couples, Arnold displayed political acumen in dealing with the controversy. If he took a firm position, he risked offending either the gay and lesbian community and their liberal supporters or the conservative religious community and those who sided with them. Californians had spoken out strongly on this issue by passing Proposition 22, banning gay marriage. Arnold did not address the issue itself but the legality of Newsom's action. He implored Democrat Attorney General Bill Lockyer, his possible opponent in the next election, to use his authority to end the illegal unions. "I don't have to concern myself about anything else," he declared, refusing to be drawn into the issue any deeper.

Arnold had been elected to office to resolve the budget crisis and return California's financial solvency. In his first year in office, he had nibbled around the edges of the great economic problems that faced the Golden State, leaving the intransigent issues. During his first months, he had negotiated with resolve and shrewdness to wring concessions from teachers, local governments, and other groups, but he could not go back and ask more of them. The initiatives passed by Californians in the last quarter-century severely limited what Arnold could do as governor. Because of Proposition 13, towns and cities deprived of property tax revenues looked to Sacramento for help. Proposition 98 mandated the state spend at least 38 percent of general revenues on education while Proposition 42 required the state to spend gasoline taxes only on the roads. Arnold had been instrumental in getting the voters to approve Proposition 58, which meant that he could not go out and float a bond to pay for ongoing expenses. Elizabeth Hill, the state's nonpartisan legislative analyst, predicted a budget deficit of $6.7 billion to $10 billion. "I think what this forecast tells me is we still have a lot of hard work to do, that we really haven't addressed the large structural imbalance facing the state," Hill told a November 2004 press conference.

Arnold's critics argued that he had a historic opportunity to change the nature of California politics. If he did not face the state's problems straight on, the failure would lie not within the political system or the exigencies of time or fate, but largely with Arnold himself. Some media observers claimed that Arnold was a tepid leader, who spoke loudly and carried no stick. *Sacramento Bee* columnist Daniel Weintraub, for example, wrote: "The most frustrating thing about Arnold Schwarzenegger as governor is how often he promises to be revolutionary and instead turns out to be, if not ordinary, certainly not the mold-breaking force he has the potential to become."

Los Angeles Times columnist George Skelton quoted the governor: "The reason why I'm against taxes is because the people consistently are against taxes." "Those are not the words of a strong leader," Skelton thundered. "They sound like a scared politician who's a follower. A strong leader chooses the right course and persuades the people to follow."

Arnold bristled at such a suggestion. "I promised when I ran for office not to raise taxes," said Arnold. "When you look at any poll, the reason my numbers are so high is simply because people trust me. People don't trust government, and people definitely don't trust the media. Therefore, I won't listen to him [Skelton] or to the government people about raising taxes. I only listen to my own instincts.

"I am not here in Sacramento to please any writers or to please anyone out there in a popularity contest. When I walk away, I want the people for the next ten years to have the benefit of it. That is the idea. That is what I'm here for, to trim government, to streamline it, to make government a better servant, and to take care of some of the problems that the legislators never can do. It's what the people and I together will be able to do. It's as simple as that. There will be courageous and strong moves with no backing down and no changes."

On January 5, 2005, the governor gave his second State of the State address to the legislature. A year before, he had been greeted with the thunderous applause of a great star and a novelty act, but now the greeting was more subdued. The man standing at the podium was no longer perceived by the legislators primarily as a creature of Hollywood. His hair was a more natural brown, and he had little of the exaggerated persona of a man stepping out of cartoonlike movies. These physical manifestations of the change were the least of it. He had transformed himself into a consummate politician, and there was no one in the chamber who did not appreciate the magnitude of that change.

Arnold was the leader of a minority party in one of the most heavily Democratic states in the nation, yet he presented himself as a leader holding a great mandate to transform the Golden State. In the twenty-eight-minute address, he set forth an agenda that might radically transform California politics. The politicians in the chamber listened intently, for Arnold was attempting to wrest power from some of the most powerful constituencies in the state, including the politicians themselves. He was doing what few elected leaders would have even imagined doing, declaring war on the California political system itself.

Arnold had all but told Californians to read his lips that there would be no tax increases, but he probably could have successfully sold the merits of a temporary tax increase. He had wrestled with that option for months. In the end, because of either deeply felt principle, ideological delusion, or a little of both, he decided to submit a budget that would be balanced not by a tax increase but by cuts in programs and services and by applying mandated money for education and road building to general expenses, "We don't have a revenue problem," he claimed, ignoring that his own pledges to local government after rescinding the raised car tax had cut $5 billion out of state funds. "We have a spending problem."

The governor knew what was in store for him. "The special interests will run TV ads calling me cruel and heartless," he foretold, addressing both legislators and the attendant press. "They will organize protests out in front of the Capitol. They will try to say I don't understand the consequences of these decisions. Let me tell you something. I am well aware there are lives behind the numbers.

"Tomorrow, I will convene a special session to address the financial, educational, and governmental reforms that civic responsibility demands," he announced. He was seeking a radical reform of the budget system, proposing legislation that would cut expenditures across the board when they rose above revenues.

It was akin to a declaration of war. There was silence as the legislators weighed the consequences of the governor's words. When campaigning for Prop 58 a few months before, the governor had said in television ads that the initiative "tears up the credit card for good. It requires a balanced budget every year without borrowing so we never get in this mess again." And now he was telling Californians that the mess was still there and that he needed a new hose to sweep away the detritus of the past.

On and on the governor went, targeting ways in which the state budget could be overhauled. He inveighed against the generous pension plans that were one of the primary reasons Californians took on government jobs. In five years the state's annual pension obligation had grown fifteen fold, to $2.6 billion. "For new employees, we must move from a defined benefit to a defined contribution system," he said.

Arnold also wanted to infuse the discipline of the marketplace into the public schools. "We must financially reward good teachers and expel those who are not," he said. "The more we reward excellent teachers, the more our teachers will be excellent. I propose that teacher employment be tied to performance, not to showing up."

Arnold sought to introduce the same discipline of a competitive marketplace into a California politics that was a series of monopolies. He intended to change it into a genuine two-party state, not impregnable fiefdoms of one party or the other. "I will propose that an independent panel of retired judges—not politicians—determine California's legislative and congressional districts," he said. "They can draw fair, honest district lines that make politicians of both parties accountable to the people. The current system is rigged to benefit the interests of those in office, not the interests of those who put them there. And we must reform it." His proposal threatened entrenched Republican politicians as much as Democrats and set the governor against much of the political establishment.

Arnold had other reforms, too, large in scope and ambition. In his first year, he had authorized a massive California Performance Review, involving contributions by 275 state employees, consultants, and academicians who produced hundreds of reform recommendations. The idea was to rationalize government and purge Sacramento of what he considered the parasites that fed off it. The first agency he set out to reform was probably the most troubled and the most difficult to change of all governmental institutions—a state prison system in which the prison guards union had wrested inordinate control. Among his other proposals, he intended to abolish almost one hundred boards and commissions that he said provided lucrative political patronage for over a thousand appointees. "No one paid by the state should make a hundred thousand dollars a year for only meeting twice a month," Arnold said.

The governor told the legislators that it was time to go forward with these reforms. In doing so, he would confront the toughest of the special interests, the politicians themselves. "What I propose will demand sacrifice from all of us," he concluded, "but it is nothing compared to the sacrifice of thousands of Californians in uniform. Many have left their blood and their buddies in the sands of a foreign land. When we ask them to risk their lives for democracy over there, how dare we not take the risk to reform our democracy here!"

There had been legitimate doubts about whether Arnold was more than a preening movie star who read his polls like a script and imagined that popularity was the same thing as accomplishment. His State of the State speech made it clear that this was a man willing to take risks that few contemporary politicians would have taken. Millions were adamantly opposed to parts of his agenda. Much of what he sought would almost inevitably find its way onto the ballot of a special initiative election, and Arnold would have to spend his second year in office as he had his first, campaigning to seek from the people what he could not wrest from the legislature.

Arnold's love of ringing ripostes and stinging phrases led him to oversimplify several of the crucial matters that he sought to reform. Although some of the commissions and boards he sought to abolish were hapless boondoggles, others were crucial watchdogs. Within a few weeks of his State of the State speech, he backed off and called for further review. His plan to bring down a terrible swift sword on expenses whenever they reached beyond revenues sounded bold when spoken from the high pulpit of office, but it was politically unrealistic and probably economically unsound. Conservative and moderate Republican groups were soon planning more nuanced approaches to control government spending and seeking Arnold's support for their initiatives.

Other than economic reform, no issue is more important to the future of California than a public education system that within a generation has deteriorated from one of the best in the nation to one of mediocrity. Yet all Arnold said about education in his speech was that he wanted merit pay for teachers. Beyond that, when he condemned what he considered union excesses and did not praise the good work of individual teachers, prison guards, or nurses, he made foes where he might have made friends.

His opponents had already begun to pick many of these proposals apart so that there was nothing left but contradictions and troubles. Those who believed him far too much a creature of big business were fiercely opposed to what they considered largely ersatz reforms. Most of these opponents did not even begrudgingly appreciate the audacity of his act. He had fancied that he could dance nimbly around the press, and now in the most dangerous moment of his political journey, his journalistic detractors gave him little quarter.

"The governor is sitting on the knee of the state Chamber of Commerce boss like a wooden dummy, and he's got the gall to deplore the influence of special interests," wrote one of his most acerbic critics, *Los Angeles Times* columnist Steve Lopez. "Listen to me, Arnold. This has got to stop. Are you listening? What does the average Californian have to do to get your attention? OK, I'm getting out my checkbook."

"Just a few days ago, Schwarzenegger said that the state's budget mess was the result of politicians promising people more than the state could afford to deliver," wrote the *Sacramento Bee*'s Weintraub. "Now he knows firsthand just how easy it is to fall into that trap."

"The question political insiders are starting to ask about Gov. Arnold Schwarzenegger is potentially one of the most damaging that can be asked about a politician," wrote the *Los Angeles Times*' Skelton. "Can you believe him? Can you trust him? Will he keep his word? Actor Schwarzenegger prospered in a world of make-believe. Gov. Schwarzenegger is expected to deal in truth, even if most politicians do bend it. Trust. Integrity. They're a politician's stock in trade—more important even than 'reform.'"

Political journalists often spend their time chronicling the natural hypocrisies of politics, but the very boldness of Arnold's assertions had come back to haunt him. He had promised that he would have an audit that would uncover massive waste in Sacramento, but he found that it was not institutional corruption that was bleeding the state dry but the very structure of government. He had promised Californians that he would "tear up the credit card and throw it away," but he had kept one in his back pocket that he planned to use to borrow $6 billion over the next two years. He had promised California's teachers that if they would give up $2 billion in legally mandated money for one year, that would be the end of their sacrifices, and now he sought to dun them again. He dulled their pain by increasing school funding $2.9 billion, but that still left them at least $1.4 billion short of what they were owed.

He stood waist deep in millions of dollars of campaign contributions almost exclusively from business, and he was willing to stick it to almost everyone except for California's corporations. No one could have expected him to back the punitive measures that some Democrats wanted, but there were tax loopholes and excessive write-offs that he could have sought to end.

Out of his impregnable optimism, Arnold had believed that the economic tide would rise to cover over the budget deficit. Although the tide had risen significantly, it was not even close to the high-water mark of 2000, and Arnold was faced with nothing but unpleasant choices. In a lesser politician, these matters would have torn away at his credibility, and the drumbeat of criticism would finally have affected his popularity. Arnold spoke so loudly and boldly that much of this denigration was hardly heard, and if it was heard was not believed, but he was clearly worried that the attacks from the press and Democrats might take their toll.

For the first time in fourteen months in office, Arnold went to the offices of the *Sacramento Bee* in January 2005 and sat down with their editorial board to try to explain himself. "I have a very, very positive outlook on this year," he said. "I tell you that this is going to be the year that things change very drastically because I have the feeling for it. I always see things ahead of time. I see things way ahead of time. When people say, 'You won't be Mr. Universe, Austrian farm boy,' I say, 'I see.' And they could not figure that out, and I did. I was totally convinced that it would work. I saw myself as a great action star. I never saw myself as a musical star or something like that. I saw myself as an action star and that's exactly what I did. And I saw myself as the governor. And I see that we can turn our state around. I get the feeling that the people of California see this as their opportunity to participate and change things.

"The ex-governors said to me on Inaugural Day, 'This is going to be a wonderful day for you, probably the happiest day.' Which is not true. I've had many, many happy days. I'm a very happy guy. I'm a very happy guy, and I'm a very happy guy in my job even in the most difficult circumstances."

For the first time, Arnold's poll numbers began to decline from the formidable 65 percent approval rating to around 55 percent, but he remained disdainful of those who attacked him. At the Republican Party state convention in February 2005, he revved the rhetoric up a few more notches, defining this as a battle between good and evil, light and darkness. "We're going right there where all the evil is, and we're going to fix this problem once and for all," he told the Republican faithful. He warned his fellow party members that his opponents were planning to raise $200 million to defeat his reform initiatives. "I say, bring it on!" he said, daring them to challenge him.

Arnold had single-handedly created a political drama worthy of a Hollywood scriptwriter. "In most states, nothing is going on this year," Arnold told columnist George Will. "So attention will be given to what is going on here," wrote Will. "If Schwarzenegger successfully employs the plebiscitary mechanism this year, he will approach reelection next year ranked among the state's most transformative governors. And ripples raised by the boulders he is throwing into this nation-state's political pool will roll eastward across the country."

Even while Arnold boasted how his reform agenda would change California, he was handing his opponents the weapons with which they could bludgeon him. In December 2004, when a small group of protesters interrupted his speech before a massive audience of women in Long Beach, Arnold shouted out that he would "kick their butts." As always, he took pleasure in provoking a reaction, confronting his opponents and belittling his enemies. As a young bodybuilder he had called his American opponents "cowards" and, similarly, as a politician he had called the Democratic legislators "girlie men." It seemed then Arnold could get away with remarks that would have embroiled almost any other politician in controversy. When the governor unlashed his rhetorical thrust on this occasion, it is not even clear if he knew who the demonstrators were.

These women were nurses signaling their anger at his opposition to a law signed by his predecessor, Gray Davis, mandating that there should be no more than five patients per nurse in hospitals in California. In a state with a massive financial crisis and a shortage of nurses, the new governor had opposed the measure, only for the courts to overrule him. To the nurses and their union he appeared little more than a bully, picking on one of the few truly benighted occupation groups in the state. He had hoped to overcome the protesters with his rhetoric, but the nurses, their union, the other public employee unions, and the Democratic strategists grabbed hold of his words and turned them against the immensely popular governor. For over a year they had fought largely weaponless against a formidable opponent, but they were weaponless no longer.

Arnold's intention had been to make 2005 his "year of reform." He could have easily done that by backing a populist agenda that included several measures of clear benefit to most Californians and would have won wide adherence across the Golden State. Instead, he put forth an uncompromising agenda, whose benefits would fall primarily to the next generation of Californians. He sought to end the gerrymandered state legislature by having judges redraw the lines. In his first year in office he had backed an initiative that he promised would balance the state budget in future years and allow the state to "throw away the credit cards." He saw now that this measure was inadequate and he sought a stiffer, more draconian measure that would cut spending whenever the state was in deficit. He sought to end the immensely generous, defined-benefit pension plan for state employees, which would have imposed an onerous obligation on Californians for decades to come and instead, proposed to give new employees 401K pension plans in which they would manage their own retirement monies.

Arnold laid out the basis of his reforms in his State of the State address in January. The speech faced many of the crucial issues and was a daring attack on the political establishment. But, following Schwarzenegger's pattern, the address had been cobbled together in secrecy and was not vetted by a broad range of political insiders who would have probed the weaknesses. Much of it was set forth in a haplessly inept way, proffering proposals – many of which had to be withdrawn or reshaped.

The worst mistake was his backing of the initiative to reform the state pension system. As written, the resulting initiative probably would have taken pensions away from the widows of fallen police officers and firefighters. That could have been remedied in separate legislation, but it was appalling slovenliness not to have realized this and the public employee unions saw this error as their opportunity to cripple the popular governor. At some of his public events, Arnold began to find more protesting police officers, firefighters, and nurses outside than he did supporters inside.

If he had had a better relationship with the Californian press, the governor may have been able to overcome this attack, but that too was affected by the patterns of his past. Arnold has always considered himself a self-created product, and if journalists are going to exploit that product they are going to do it on his terms and in a way that benefits him. Consequently, reporters who had not been allowed close enough to be able to write intimately of the triumphs of Arnold's first year in office were more than happy to stand in the street and chronicle the troubles of his second year. In their articles they chose not to explore the extent to which these spontaneous protests had been orchestrated by the public employee unions and the Democrats. Ordinarily, it is is unlikely that citizens would march in the streets to protest about these kind of abstract issues, which largely did not even affect them. Schwarzenegger was proposing his pension reform for new employees only, so none of these chanting protesters would have diminished retirements. As for the nurses, they had won. The hospital staffing was law, despite the governor trying unsuccessfully to throw out the law in the courts. The purpose of the attacks was to show him up. This man, who had lived by the sound bite and evocative image was now dying by them.

The noise grew so loud that Arnold held a press conference in April to announce that he was backing-off his support of the flawed pension initiative. The governor could have done what JFK did after the Bay of Pigs and apologize. President Kennedy took the full blame and his polls shot up. It seems Schwarzenegger is incapable of truly apologizing for anything; instead, he danced nimbly around the issue before saying that what had happened was "terrific." Arnold's polls continued to fall.

A more introspective, self-critical leader might have backed off, but Arnold insisted on going ahead with a special election in November 2005. He did so in part because his first year in office had been an endless drama, and he wanted to make the second act like the first. He had a profound psychological need to be out there among the masses, weaving a spell of words and images that transcended the often humdrum day-to-day business of governing.

Thanks to inept planning, he was left with a motley collection of initiatives, which he wrapped in gaudy packaging to sell as the basis of "The Year of Reform." He had initially proposed merit pay for California's teachers in his State of the State address, but that metamorphosed into a proposal to postpone granting tenure from two years to five years. He had made a passionate case to end the gerrymandered legislature by having a panel of retired judges redraw the lines. Although there was debate whether even this could be done before the 2008 election, he forged ahead on that idea. He was righteously concerned with the legislators' proclivity to overspend, and he sought to control it. He also agreed to support a measure that would end the public-employees union using members' dues for political purposes without first seeking the approval of the individual members.

Arnold's opponents brilliantly portrayed the governor as a dangerous reactionary. For the public-employees unions the so-called check-off initiative over their members' dues was virtually a life and death struggle, and they fought with tens of millions of dollars and fierce acumen. They sensed that Arnold was damaged, and in the next few months they followed the trail of blood until they had cornered a grievously wounded politician who pretended that he had nary a scratch.

In a summer of discontent Arnold's popularity continued to tumble until it stood at around 35 percent. Wherever Arnold went he was dogged by taunting protesters and he appeared only before controlled audiences. He denied the poll numbers that showed the initiatives failing, and pretended that all was right.

No great scandal haunted Arnold. There was not a declining economy for which he might be blamed, and no immense new crisis faced him. Yet Californians seemed to have grown tired of Arnold's cartoon-like character, his pithy sound bites, his ceaseless cheerleading.

In November, all four of the initiatives failed, and even Arnold could not find a positive spin to put on the results. He had long dreamed of becoming president but he had awakened in a cold dawn where he might not even be reelected governor. His whole engine of ambition had been driven by an immensely optimistic life force but that had been throttled down.

Arnold's life had been one long first act, endlessly repeating the same techniques and playing the same roles as bodybuilder, movie star, and politician. Now he would have to reconnect to the Californian electorate in a new way. He was fifty-eight-years old, and his days as a Hollywood action star were over. He was getting old. He would have to find worthy new challenges, and face them in different ways.

If the last chapters of Arnold's life were to be a thick and worthy tome, they would have to be written in different colors and different tones. This was probably the most difficult challenge of Arnold's life, doubly difficult because he seemed not even to realize that he faced it.

Notes

CHAPTER ONE: The American Dream

3 Arnold's favorite word was *fantastic: Los Angeles Times*, Feb. 1, 2004. When reporter Joe Mathews noted Governor Schwarzenegger's constant use of his favorite word, the governor tried valiantly to kick the habit, replacing *fantastic* with other, less satisfactory superlatives.

3 "fantastic job": *Sacramento Bee*, Jan. 6, 2004.

4 Everyone was looking at him: This chapter is based largely on interviews with Governor Arnold Schwarzenegger. The author's interviews with Congressman David Dreier, Mike Murphy, and Landon Parvin were also invaluable. The author was on the floor of the convention the evening of the speech.

5 "People asked me if I still lift weights": Interview, Landon Parvin.

5 Maria would not allow: *San Jose Mercury News*, Dec. 26, 2004.

6 "Thank you, thank you": Author was present.

7 "The hell with that": Interview, Governor Arnold Schwarzenegger.

7 "moved to tears by": E-mail from Julie Nixon Eisenhower, Feb. 16, 2005.

7 "trying to find the middle": Ibid.

7 "blatant homophobia": *Los Angeles Times*, July 18, 2004.

8 Arnold held tough: *New York Times*, Sept. 12, 2004.

8 "was not apologetic": Interview, Governor Arnold Schwarzenegger.

CHAPTER TWO: A Man from Thal

11 near the boathouse: Interviews, Governor Arnold Schwarzenegger and Dr. Karl Gerstl; Arnold Schwarzenegger and Douglas Kent Hall, *Arnold: The Education of a Bodybuilder* (1977), p. 13.

12 "Now, that may make you think": Arnold Schwarzenegger, "The Education of an American," speech to the Perspectives 2001 Conference, Sacramento, Calif., Sept. 21, 2001.

12 "Arnold learned how to get along": Interview, Peter Urdl.

12 "most of the people": Markus Joroschka and Gerhard Dienes, eds., *Europea Erlesen Graz* (2003), p. 61.

12 "the wild people beyond the Semmering": Interview, Barbara Gasser.

13 one table in the establishment, the *Stammtisch:* On the author's weeklong visit to Thal, he was accorded the honor of sitting at the special table at the Café-Restaurant Thalersee by owners Karl and Elif Kling, lifelong friends of Arnold Schwarzenegger.

13 Arnold's mother worked in the kitchen sometimes: Interview, Karl Kling.

14 "I was a little kid": Nigel Andrews, *True Myths: The Life and Times of Arnold Schwarzenegger* (1995), p. 15.

14 Arnold snuck in to see: Transcript of interview with Arnold Schwarzenegger by Joan Goodman conducted in 1987 for *Playboy* (Jan. 1988).

14 "He would correct it": Transcript of *Playboy* interview.

14 the Parents' Day: Interview, Governor Arnold Schwarzenegger.

15 "My hair was pulled": Betsy Morris, "Arnold Power," *Fortune* (Aug. 9, 2004).

15 "I have seen one kid": Interview, Governor Arnold Schwarzenegger.

15 "I rebelled against my father": Ibid.

15 "I think being a disciplinarian": Ibid.

16 the "Chained Dogs": *Los Angeles Times*, Aug. 14, 2003.

17 "He was a rascal": Interview, Franz Hörmann.

17 "Arnold was a mama's boy": Interview, Sepp Heinzle.

18 she was "Frau Schwarzenegger": Interview, Karl Kling.

18 family of outsiders moved to the village: Discussion with Herta Kling-Schmidbauer.

18 "With my father's death": Interview, Governor Arnold Schwarzenegger.

CHAPTER THREE: The Hedgehog

20 "I scraped up the *pfennigs*": "The Education of an American," op. cit. Schwarzenegger has told several stories about how he first saw the magazine. He told Rick Wayne for an article in the August/September 1976 *Muscle Builder/Power* that he saw the magazine in 1962 while he was working out, purchased the publication, and started following Reg Park's routines.

21 "Reg became my idol": Rick Wayne, "Reg Park . . . a Hero's Hero," *Muscle Builder/Power* (Aug./Sept. 1976).

21 "the Sandow Trocadero Vaudevilles": David L. Chapman, "Sandow: The Man Who Made the World Mad for Muscles," www.sandowmuseum.com.

21 Bernarr Macfadden: Charles Gaines and George Butler, *Pumping Iron: The Art and Sport of Bodybuilding* (1974), pp. 128, 130.

21 "performance art": Interview, Frank Zane.

21 Thanks to "Dynamic-Tension": Gaines and Butler, pp. 129–30.

22 "Maybe I was competitive with my brother": *Time* (Dec. 20, 1990).

22 "I wouldn't overthink it": Interview, Governor Arnold Schwarzenegger.

22 "Some people are by nature depressed": Ibid.

22 "the exploration of the universe": Kay Redfield Jamison, *Exuberance: The Passion for Life* (2004), p. 32.

23 Marnul invited his young acolyte: Interview, Kurt Marnul.

23 When Arnold looked back: Transcript of *Playboy* interview.

24 "When I discovered what he was doing": Jack Neary, "Arnold: Lover of Life," *Muscle Builder/Power* (June 1979).

24 "We used to joke around": Interview, Franz Baumgartner vulgo Großhofbauer.

25 "Arnold has always been a personality": Interview, Dr. Karl Gerstl.

25 "From your second son": Interview, Alfred Gerstl.

25 As Arnold admits: Interview, Governor Arnold Schwarzenegger.

25 Dr. Ignaz Gerstl: Helene Maimann, "I Am a Maccabean" (translated by Matt Gaffney), Kausfiles.com.

25 "To the Catholics I was a Jew": Interview, Alfred Gerstl.

26 "Arnold was not shy": Interview, Dr. Karl Gerstl.

26 "We paid very little attention": Interview, Governor Arnold Schwarzen-
    egger.

27 "Arnold was influenced by the fact": Interview, Alfred Gerstl.

27 One day Knaur handed him *Pfaffenspiegel:* Schwarzenegger and Hall, p. 32.

27 "Knaur had a big impact": Interview, Governor Arnold Schwarzenegger.

27 "the Jews had too often shown serious": Wolfgang Sotill, *Es gibt nur einen
    Gott und eine Menschheit* (2001), p. 125.

28 "outraged—so filled with rage": Associated Press, Nov. 4, 2003.

28 "there exists a great chasm": Sir Isaiah Berlin, *The Hedgehog and the Fox*
    (1953).

28 "I saw the other bodybuilders": Schwarzenegger and Hall, p. 27.

29 "Jesus Christ, you should see some of the women": Ibid., p. 32.

29 One evening he and his classmate: Interview, Peter Urdl.

29 "No, that one doesn't fit me": Interview, Johann Strebel.

CHAPTER FOUR: Helping Hands

30 had the misfortune: Interview, Johann Strebel.

31 "I was interested in Arnold": Interview, Albert Busek.

31 "Who are you?": Interview, Dr. Franco Columbu.

32 "It clicked like the chemistry": Ibid.

32 "Freddy would say" : Interview, Governor Arnold Schwarzenegger.

33 "I had become a hero": Schwarzenegger and Hall, p. 38.

33 He was so strong: Interview, Johann Strebel.

33 From my earliest recollection, I've always had": Julian Schmidt, "Arnold,"
    Muscle & Fitness (Aug. 1991).

34 "Putziger had agreed immediately": Interview, Albert Busek.

34 "Arnold was mad as hell": Ibid.

34 "Why you got such a little bed": Interview, Dr. Franco Columbu.

35 "We called him the 'muscle locomotion'": Interview, Albert Busek.

35 "I was working": Interview, Governor Arnold Schwarzenegger.

35 "did not have to kiss ass": Interview, Anthony Shriver.

36 Invited inside, Arnold was a compelling witness: Andrews, p. 27.

CHAPTER FIVE: Paying the Price

37 "at least fifty huge guys": Schwarzenegger and Hall, p. 47.

37 No one knew him": Interview, Dianne Bennett.

38 "It is a visible process and a riveting one": Gaines and Butler, p. 25.

38 "special creations of science": Schwarzenegger and Hall, p. 49.

38 Arnold's hair reminded: Rick Wayne, *Muscle Wars: The Behind-the-Scenes Story of Competitive Bodybuilding* (1985), p. 89.

38 "Considerable time was spent": John C. Grimek, "Arnold Schwarzenegger, the Austrian Powerhouse," *Muscular Development* (Nov. 1973).

39 Arnold wanted to know: Wayne, p. 61.

39 "Do you think a man can get": Interview, Rick Wayne.

40 Dianne Bennett had put together: Interview, Dianne Bennett.

40 "it made the entire four years": Schwarzenegger and Hall, p. 51.

40 "Why do you write so big?": Transcript of *Playboy* interview.

42 "When Arnold did squats": Interview, Albert Busek.

42 "He learns from other people": Ibid.

CHAPTER SIX: The Trickster

43 "During the training": Interview, Dr. Franco Columbu.

44 "These people are nothing": Wayne, p. 91; interview, Rick Wayne.

45 "His corduroy trousers": *Mail on Sunday* (London), March 1, 1998.

45 "He came from a stern background": Interview, Dianne Bennett.

46 "Before that, when I was just a young bodybuilder": Schwarzenegger and Hall, p. 61.

46 lined up a series of shows: Interview, Reg Park.

46 "I consider myself a sponge": Interview, Governor Arnold Schwarzenegger.

46 "Steve Reeves was the typical hero": Ibid.

47 "this foolish self-conscious smile": Schwarzenegger and Hall, p. 61.

47 a man of reserve: Interview, Jon Jon Park.

47 The best that Reg managed: *Muscle Builder/Power* (Sept. 1976).

47 "I understand you bring out the current Mr. Universe": Interview, Reg Park.

CHAPTER SEVEN: Mr. Universe

49 "He was helping me, giving me instructions": Schwarzenegger and Hall, p. 73.

49 "I sent him out as a spy": Ibid.

49 Arnold was asleep: Interview, Governor Arnold Schwarzenegger.

49 "Fantastic!": Schwarzenegger and Hall, p. 73.

49 "I was going through my routine": Interview, Dennis Tinerino, *Arnold Schwarzenegger: Made in Britain*, Channel Four Television.

50 "I was already the greatest": Schwarzenegger and Hall, p. 78.

50 "I would think Arnold was in awe": Interview, Bill Pearl.

50 "Come on, you guys": Interview, Dennis Tinerino, *Schwarzenegger: Made in Britain*.

51 "We would sit down to dinner": Interview, Reg Park.

51 at the age of nineteen: Interview, Jon Jon Park.

51 "Marion was an incredible woman": Interview, Governor Arnold Schwarzenegger.

51 "Arnold fell in love with my wife": Interview, Reg Park.

51 "feels inferior if she has to prepare": Rick Wayne, "Reg Park: A Hero's Hero," *Muscle Builder/Power* (Aug./Sept. 1976).

51 "Arnold could hardly speak a word of English": Interview, Jon Jon Park.

51 "I want to win the Mr. Universe": Interview, Reg Park.

52 "I almost made myself thrown out": George Butler, *Arnold Schwarzenegger: A Portrait* (1990), p. 25.

52 "I was talking to three camps": Interview, Governor Arnold Schwarzenegger.

53 "He told Joe, 'Hoffman'": Interview, Dr. Franco Columbu.

53 the July 1968 *Muscle Builder/Power:* Weider constantly tweaked the titles of his publication so that in a given year there might be several manifestations of a single magazine.

53 "He's wearing dark glasses": Ben Weider, "The Battle of the Giants: 1968 Mr. Olympia," *Muscle Builder/Power* (Aug. 1968).

53 "Arnold was definitely excited": Interview, Kurt Shusterich.

CHAPTER EIGHT: Joe Weider's Greatest Creation

54 "seemed damned sure of himself": Wayne, p. 104.

54 "Don't worry about Arnold": Interview, Frank Zane.

55 cried himself to sleep: Schwarzenegger and Hill, p. 93.

55 "The idea was to just wipe everyone out": Wayne, p. 107.

55 he thought his defeat had been terribly unfair: Interview, Governor Arnold Schwarzenegger.

55 "Even if he had won": Interview, Joe Weider.

55 circulation of his magazines: Joe Weider, "It's Now or Never," *Muscle Builder/Power* (July 1970).

56 "I sensed that this man would be a great idol": Interview, Joe Weider.

56 "I hope it will be a year": Dick Tyler, "The Austrian Oak," *Mr. America* (May 1969).

56 go back to Germany: Joe Weider, "Arnold Schwarzenegger—New Phenomenon," *Muscle Builder/Power* (May 1969).

56 Paul Graham: *Boston Globe*, April 26, 1986; interview, Bill Grant.

56 "transported two stolen Mustangs": *United States* v. *Paul Maxwell Graham*, Complaint for Violation of U.S.C. Title 18, Jan. 29, 1969.

57 "He said that he had some legal problems": Interview, Governor Arnold Schwarzenegger.

57 best man at Graham's [wedding]: *Daily Telegraph* (Sydney), Dec. 14, 1999.

57 "I spoke to Arnold": Interview, Joe Weider.

57 "I knew Arnold was a penny-pincher": Ibid.

57 "Arnold, anything you want": *Los Angeles Times*, Aug. 23, 2004.

57 Gold had already given him a nickname: *Los Angeles Times*, July 13, 2004.

58 "If you got up on the second-floor balcony": Interview, Dick Tyler.

58 "Oh, it was just wonderful": Interview, Charles Gaines.

59 "Arnold told me,": Interview, Joe Weider.

59 "Here, Joe, give us the money": Interview, Dr. Franco Columbu.

60 "Yeah, because we need to know": Ibid.

60 "Arnold was different": Interview, Frank Zane.

60 "It seemed like all the other guys": "In the Picture," interview by Peter McGough, *Flex* (Sept. 2003).

60 "My kids told me": Interview, Bill Grant.

60 "Mentally most people have no connection": Robert Hayes, "Arnold Schwarzenegger," *Interview* (Dec. 1976).

61 He saw in his mind's eye: Transcript of *Playboy* interview.

61 "If he ever went to the gym by himself": Interview, Frank Zane.

61 He attended classes at other schools: Transcript of *Playboy* interview.

61 Zane tutored him: Ibid.

62 "Some of the bodybuilders were a little intimidated": Interview, Betty Weider.

63 "Joe's a promoter": Interview, Governor Arnold Schwarzenegger.

63 "But the very fact that he brought me to America": Ibid.

63 "Weider was very instrumental": Ibid.

64 "I read how Joe trained this champion": Peter McGough, "Anatomy of an American Icon," *Muscle & Fitness* (July 1997).

64 one memorable day in the early 1970s: Interview, Gene Mozee.

64 "He lit a candle": Interview, Governor Arnold Schwarzenegger.

65 "'Why are you making a statue of yourself?'": Interview, Joe Weider.

CHAPTER NINE: The "Wow" with the "Pow"

66 "what current fashions": Joe Weider, "Growing Up with Our Readers," *Mr. America* (March 1969).

67 "Sock it to me, baby": Dick Tyler, "Savage 'Terror Bombing' of the Sexiest Legs in Hollywood!" *Mr. America* (Sept. 1969).

67 "When he came to California": Chick Sipes, "They Call Him 'Sexy' Schwarzenegger Now," *Mr. America* (Aug. 1949).

67 "the laboring class still produce the most babies": "Sexual Excitation in the Human Male," *Mr. America* (Feb. 1970).

67 "masturbation is nature's way": Saul Lucks, M.D., "Masturbation," *Mr. America* (July 1970).

68 "You are so lovely": Dick Tyler, "More Adventures with Arnold," *Muscle Builder/Power* (March 1971).

68 "Arnold wanted to stop": Dick Tyler, "Probing Questions at Arnold Schwarzenegger—Mr. Universe Winner," *Mr. America* (June 1969).

69 "I just fucked her": Interview, Gene Mozee; *Los Angeles Times*, September 29, 2003.

69 "Not many people had the guts": Interview, Gene Mozee.

69 "He looked so sad": Interview, Joe Weider.

69 Sometimes people would bring these girls": Interview, Dick Tyler.

70 "There were some bodybuilders": Interview, Betty Weider.

70 "leis upon leis": "They Call Him 'Sexy' Schwarzenegger Now," op. cit.

70 "The restaurant had plenty of beautiful women": Arnold Schwarzenegger, "Tropical Training in Hawaii," *Muscle Builder/Power* (Jan. 1970).

70 "And don't worry": Dick Tyler and Ed Giuliani, "Gossip Round-up," *Muscle Builder/Power* (June 1969).

70 "The economic connection between bodybuilders and gays": Alan M. Klein, *Little Big Men* (1993), p. 93.

70 "I remember in Gold's Gym": Interview, Bill Dobbins.

71 Bud Parker, the editor of *Muscle Builder*: Wayne, p. 110.

71 "How the champs met their rent": Ibid., p. 116.

71 "30 to 80 percent of the men": Klein, p. 196.

71 Arnold was a "good tease": Wendy Leigh, *Arnold: An Unauthorized Biography* (1990), p. 65.

72 posed for the celebrity photographer Francesco Scavullo: Cliff Jahr, "A Sex Symbol for the Seventies?" *New Times*, Oct. 15, 1976.

72 "I was sort of skittering around": Interview, Bill Dobbins.

CHAPTER TEN: Mr. Olympia

73 "In Europe I had limited information": Interview, Governor Arnold Schwarzenegger.

73 "Some of the guys would come in, complaining": Interview, Dick Tyler.

74 "I knew the fans would remember": Arnold Schwarzenegger, "I Challenge You, Sergio," *Muscle Builder/Power* (Dec. 1971).

74 "Things are great here in London": "Letters to the Editor," *Muscle Builder/Power* (Feb. 1970).

75 "I don't know if it was rebellion": Interview, Barbara Outland Baker.

75 "He had poor table manners": *Ottawa Citizen*, Oct. 3, 2003.

75 "So there was a rough diamond": Interview, Barbara Outland Baker.

76 "It was funny to hear him speak": Ibid.

77 "Every time Arnold said something in German": Interview, Dr. Franco Columbu.

77 "He'd sometimes drive down": Interview, Jon Jon Park.

78 "Please let me remind you": "Letter from Arnold," *Flex* (July 1994).

79 Photographer George Butler: Interview, George Butler.

79 "We separated it out": Interview, Governor Arnold Schwarzenegger.

CHAPTER ELEVEN: *Hercules in New York*

81 "We European bodybuilders have little respect": Arnold Schwarzenegger, "American Bodybuilders Are Paper Tigers!" *Muscle Builder/Power* (Oct. 1970).

82 "I did this interview": "The Restless Icon," interview by Jim Schmaltz, *Flex* (Jan. 2000).

83 "Damn it, Arnold!": Wayne, p. 119.

83 "I was shit": Interview, Reg Park.

83 Oliva showed up: Interview, James Lorimer.

83 "To make sure I would have an even easier time": "I Challenge You, Sergio," op cit.

84 "Whenever he says to me": Interview, James Lorimer.

84 "His eyes were as clear": Ibid.

85 "Don't pump, Arnold.": Interview, Joe Weider.

86 Arnold learned afterward: Interview, Governor Arnold Schwarzenegger.

86 Franco, who understands Arnold's bodybuilding psychology: Interview, Dr. Franco Columbu.

87 "there's a little meat on this chicken": Interview, Governor Arnold Schwarzenegger.

87 "He's already lost": Interview, Dr. Franco Columbu.

87 "It's very clear": Interview, Governor Arnold Schwarzenegger.

88 shoot her husband in 1986: *Chicago Tribune*, July 25, 1986.

88 *Sergio, I'm so sorry.* "I Challenge You, Sergio," op. cit.

CHAPTER TWELVE: The Greatest

90 "I called this guy": Interview, Dr. Franco Columbu.

90 "Franco climbed up on the roof": The National Journal Group, The Hotline, Sept. 12, 2003.

90 "After a while, he said to me": Interview, Joe Weider.

91 Arnold had amassed $28,000: *Los Angeles Times*, Sept. 3, 1989.

91 borrowed $10,000 more: Interview, Governor Arnold Schwarzenegger.

91 "The first money he got from shows": Susan Peters, "Schwarzenegger, Inc.," *California Business* (June 1986).

92 "You know, I think you really need": Interview, Barbara Outland Baker.

92 "From then on, each time I made a move forward": Interview, Governor Arnold Schwarzenegger.

93 "When I made a phone call home": Ibid.

93 "He used any kind of trick": "In Conversation with Sergio Oliva" by Brian D. Johnston, at www.exercisecertification.com/articles/olivainterview .html.

94 "Certainly Sergio was great enough": Rick Wayne, "Has Success Spoiled Arnold?" *Muscle Builder/Power* (Aug. 1973).

94 "They call him [Weider] the 'Master'": "In Conversation with Sergio Oliva," op. cit.

94 "Arnold was going to go onstage": Interview, Joe Weider.

95 "I have never claimed to be a weight lifting champion": Wayne, p. 136.

CHAPTER THIRTEEN: Games Arnold Played

96 In September 1972: Interview, George Butler.

96 "from old, well-off Southern stock": Charles Gaines, *Stay Hungry* (1972), in "About the Author."

97 "Well when you ski or shoot": Ibid., p. 51.

97 "The thing that inspired Michelangelo": Ibid., p. 95.

97 "There was a lot of pulling and tugging": Interview, Charles Gaines.

98 "The body builder is the sculptor": *Newsweek*, March 17, 1975.

98 "very possibly the most perfectly developed man": Gaines and Butler, p. 22.

99 "Everybody has weak points": Interview, Frank Zane.

99 "When was the last time": Interview, George Butler.

99 "Arnold was definitely our Pygmalion": Ibid.

100 "Here's my lover boy": Interview, Burton Hersh.

100 Morris considers the most agonizing, secret moments: The author attended one of Eric Morris's classes.

100 "Probably he told me more": Interview, Eric Morris.

101 "Arnold would say, 'You know, we have such a perfect life'": Interview, Barbara Outland Baker.

102 "Are you serious?": Interview, Burton Hersh.

CHAPTER FOURTEEN: *Pumping Iron*

103 There was a painting of flowers from Holland: Armand Tanny, "Arnold— His Life and Good Times," *Muscle Builder/Power* (June 1975).

103 He hired several bodybuilders: Ibid.

104 he sought decent dressing rooms: Ibid.

104 "Why don't you call it *Pumping Arnold*": Interview, Frank Zane.

104 "There is no doubt in my mind": Arnold Schwarzenegger, "He's Big . . . He's Scary . . . and I'm Training like Crazy," *Muscle Builder/Power* (Jan. 1975).

105 "I wanted to prove myself perfect": Interview, Lou Ferrigno.

106 "I knew the more outrageous I was": "I'll Look Back," interview by Peter McGough, *Flex*, April 2003.

106 "My relationship to power": Butler, p. 34.

107 "I admired Hitler": *New York Times*, Oct. 4, 2003.

107 "You can easily understand": Deirdre Henderson, ed., *Prelude to Leadership: The European Diary of John F. Kennedy* (1995), p. 74.

107 Douglas Kent Hall, his collaborator: *New York Times*, Oct. 4, 2003.

107 "Nazi marching songs": Ibid.

108 "Is a pump better than coming?": Twenty-fifth anniversary DVD of *Pumping Iron*.

108 "if Arnold wins": Interview, Dr. Franco Columbu.

CHAPTER FIFTEEN: The Promoter

109 "I'm done competing": Interview, James Lorimer.

109 Afterward, Arnold went to the insurance company executive's house: Ibid.

110 "Too many bodybuilders": Arnold Schwarzenegger, "Bodybuilders Are Too Greedy," *Muscle Builder/Power* (Oct. 1977).

110 "The fact is that Arnold could have won": Interview, Frank Zane.

111 While Arnold was rotated: "A Sex Symbol for the Seventies?" op. cit.

111 "Arnold Schwarzenegger type": *New York Times*, Feb. 23, 1977.

111 "Arnold may look like he's all rock": *New York Times*, Sept. 7, 1976.

111 BORING THINGS THAT ARE SORT OF FUN: *Washington Post*, June 2, 1977.

112 "It is one thing to make a movie": John Simon, "Bungle Gym," *New York*, May 3, 1976.

112 "Arnold got a lot of his knowledge": Interview, Bobby Zarem.

113 At the various tables sat Andy Warhol: *New York Times*, Jan. 13, 1977.

113 "What do you think of that?": Janet Charlton, "They Loved Him with Clothes On," *Muscle Builder/Power* (April 1977).

114 "At least fifteen women propositioned me tonight": Ibid.

114 "take a walk for a while": *Los Angeles Times*, Oct. 3, 2003.

115 "How's this for a lift?": Anonymous interview.

115 "Arnold used to love to shock people": Interview, Bill Dobbins.

116 "Schwarzenegger is the first personality since Bruce Lee": *Washington Post*, Feb. 19, 1977.

116 "bodybuilder of sorts": Janet Charlton, "The Smallest Trophy He Ever Won," *Muscle Builder/Power* (May 1977).

116 "Rocky" came up to Arnold's: Ibid.

CHAPTER SIXTEEN: The Maria Factor

118 In August 1977: Interview, Bobby Zarem.

118 "He asked, had I ever heard of the tournament": Interview, Lawrence Kubik.

118 "the highlight of the day": *New York Times*, Aug. 28, 1977.

119 "that's brighter than I am": "A Sex Symbol for the Seventies?" op. cit.

119 "When Arnold first met Maria": Interview, Lawrence Kubik.

120 "part of this pack": Maria Shriver, *Ten Things I Wish I'd Known—Before I Went Out into the Real World* (2000), p. 7.

120 "Growing up, people would come up and say": Interview, Maria Shriver.

121 "I can remember staying overnight": Interview, Theo Hayes.

122 she wore the same gown: Rose Kennedy, *Times to Remember* (1974), pp. 22–23.

122 "Maria didn't necessarily have the physique": Interview, Anthony Shriver.

123 Theo Hayes was so upset: Interview, Theo Hayes.

123 "I wish I'd known how creative": Shriver, p. 120.

123 Maria's own mother: Interview, Dr. Herbert Kramer.

124 "I was in shock": Interview, Betty Weider.

124 "I found him there, crying": Leigh, p. 166.

124 She never found time: Shriver, p. 15.

125 "Smell it": Interviews, Dr. Franco Columbu and Maria Shriver.

125 "She always says that the first time she met me": Andrews, p. 69.

126 "I said, 'No, I want to go'": Interview, Governor Arnold Schwarzenegger.

126 "He wanted everything to be perfect": Interview, Bill Dobbins.

126 "She picked me up": Nancy Collins, "Pumping Iron," *Rolling Stone* (Jan. 17, 1985).

CHAPTER SEVENTEEN: "Part of the Entertaining Show"

127 "If there's one thing I should do, it's the unexpected": Peter Manso, "Conversation with Arnold Schwarzenegger," *Oui* (Aug. 1977).

127 "Get up there, Arnold": Interview, Eric Morris.

128 "I don't care if I ever become an actor": Interview, Betty Weider.

128 "The first movies that were offered to me": Interview, Governor Arnold Schwarzenegger.

129 "It's not like you can go to Nat and Al's deli": Interview, Craig Rumar.

129 "more of a weight": *New York Times*, July 20, 1979.

130 "Well, you handled that well": Interview, Craig Rumar.

130 "His accent was much thicker": Interview, Lawrence Kubik.

130 "If I have to choose": Interview, Dino De Laurentiis.

130 "I saw the terrific discipline and confidence that he had": Interview, Lawrence Kubik.

132 "It was a picture of him on his back.": Interview, John Milius.

133 "In the early days, when I photographed Arnold": Butler, p. 52.

133 "I always find": Robert Strauss, "Arnold Schwarzenegger," *Enterprise Incidents* (Sept. 1984).

133 about fifteen guns: Dale Dye, "Cyborg Terminator: The Ultimate Merc," *Soldier of Fortune* (Dec. 1984).

134 "Great, Arnold": Jack Neary, "Olympia Report: Arnold's Victory Creates Controversy & Bitterness," *Muscle & Fitness* (Feb. 1981); interview, Frank Zane.

134 "Yeah, Arnold": Interview, Frank Zane.

135 "world-class physique": "Olympia Report: Arnold's Victory Creates Controversy & Bitterness," op. cit.

135 "Are you going to compete?": Interview, Frank Zane.

135 "Actually, I just start my training now": Butler, p. 138.

135 "So this afternoon": Ibid., p. 141.

136 "let them fight a little": Interview, Dr. Franco Columbu.

136 Arnold injected cortisone: "Olympia Report: Arnold's Victory Creates Controversy & Bitterness," op. cit.

137 raised his friend's arm: Interview, Dr. Franco Columbu; Butler, p. 146.

137 "You know the applause": Interview, Governor Arnold Schwarzenegger.

138 "as long as he was in respectable shape": Butler, p. 145.

138 "If Jimmy Carter goes to Ronald Reagan": Interview, Frank Zane.

CHAPTER EIGHTEEN: Arnold the Barbarian

141 "We're going to use the dog-training technique": Interview, John Milius.

141 riding horses in the countryside: Interview, Gerry Lopez.

142 "naughty puppies." Interview, John Milius.

142 "When you're dressed like a barbarian": Interview, Sven-Ole Thorsen.

143 "The wolf almost got my ass": Interview, John Milius.

143 "Sandahl, take off your shirt": Interview, Sandahl Bergman.

143 "Pain is momentary": Interview, John Milius.

143 "What are you doing?": Ibid.

144 "At the end he was in as good a mood": Interview, Gerry Lopez.

144 "You know, I love making movies": Interview, Sven-Ole Thorsen.

144 "You can talk about opposites attract": Interview, Sandahl Bergman.

144 largely naked woman: Interview, Gerry Lopez.

145 Milius and Lopez went up into the hills: Interview, John Milius.

146 "Everyone in Hollywood is an assassin": Interview, Craig Rumar.

146 "Our contract had come to an end": Interview, Lawrence Kubik.

146 "He's always been the master of his own destiny": Interview, Lou Pitt.

146 "My father always disliked that film": Interview, Raffaella De Laurentiis.

147 The studio had booked one of the three theaters: New York Times, March 16, 1982.

147 "There's not one actor in the U.S.": Interview, Dino De Laurentiis.

CHAPTER NINETEEN: Paying the Price

148 "the flatness of Schwarzenegger's performance": *Time* (May 24, 1982).

148 a dull clod with a sharp sword": *Newsweek* (May 17, 1982).

148 displaced from its top spot: John Flynn, *The Films of Arnold Schwarzenegger* (1993), p. 48.

149 "a forceful voice": United Press International (Nov. 1, 1983).

149 his hair was already turning gray: *People* (June 7, 1982).

149 "After years of pounding": Rick Wayne, "Arnold Goes to Jail," *Muscle & Fitness* (Oct. 1983).

150 "Just tell me what you want": Interview, Charlotte Parker.

150 In the next two decades: *Terminator 2: Judgment Day* is one example of Schwarzenegger's muscle in the international market. That film earned $205 million domestically and $312 million overseas. Action/adventure films usually do well internationally, but even his comedies did well outside the United States. *Twins* earned almost as much overseas ($104.7 million) as domestically ($111.9 million), while *Kindergarten Cop* did slightly better ($110.5 million) abroad than in the United States and Canada ($91.5 million). These figures, as well as all other film grosses, are from a highly useful Web site, Film Studies Web Resources, sponsored by Penn State University Libraries.

150 "Being from Austria": Interview, Governor Arnold Schwarzenegger.

151 "I sat, and I had dinner with the reporters": Interview, Charlotte Parker.

152 It's neither a man nor a bird, but it could be a moose": *New York Times*, June 29, 1984.

153 "Schwarzenegger has acquired a reputation": "Schwarzenegger, Inc.," op. cit.

153 "90 percent of my investments": Ibid.

154 "Of course, he's having a a great time": Interview, John Milius.

155 "Now I want to embody the whole American ideal": PR newswire (Sept. 14, 1983).

CHAPTER TWENTY: *The Terminator*

156 "I was already tired": "Pumping Iron," op. cit.

157 As the two men sat together: Interview, James Cameron; *Terminator* anniversary DVD.

157 "Mike Medavoy, the studio head, told me": Interview, Governor Arnold
    Schwarzenegger.

158 "I chose to play the villain": *Richmond Times-Dispatch*, Nov. 18, 1984.

158 Pitt made a point of counting: Interview, Lou Pitt.

158 seventy-four words: *The Independent*, March 18, 2001.

158 "The thing that I learned from my acting teacher": Interview, Governor
    Arnold Schwarzenegger.

159 The Terminator does not run: Transcript of *Playboy* interview.

159 "I was lying on the hood": Robert Strauss, "Arnold Schwarzenegger Is
    Terminator," *Enterprise Incidents* (Dec. 1984).

159 "I have to just smile": Peter McGough, "Conversation," *Flex* (Nov. 1995).

160 Parker was so upset: Interview, Charlotte Parker.

CHAPTER TWENTY-ONE: Chasing Sly

162 "I would have walked away": Interview, Charlotte Parker.

162 Arnold started giving fifty thousand dollars: Interview, Rabbi Marvin Hier.

163 "How many Austrians": Ibid.

163 Arnold made his involvement: *Los Angeles Times*, Nov. 21, 1989.

165 "I said to myself": Interview, Governor Arnold Schwarzenegger.

165 "All that flag waving": *News of the World*, Nov. 17, 1985.

165 "I see him working out in the gym": Jean Vallely, "The Promoter," *GQ*
    (July 1986).

165 "Stallone's ingenious comic-strip artistry": *Newsweek* (Dec. 23, 1985).

CHAPTER TWENTY-TWO: *Red Sonja*

167 Arnold and Nielsen were spotted traveling together: Leigh, pp. 216–18.

167 "I said, 'I have a girlfriend'": Transcript of *Playboy* interview.

168 Nielsen's alleged lesbian affair: *London Telegraph*, July 20, 1987.

168 "I felt I should do a favor": Flynn, p. 85.

168   "We were at a screening": Interview, Sandahl Bergman.

169   "We talked about how you expand a career": Interview, Lou Pitt.

169   "I'm not knocking myself out for you": Interview, Charlotte Parker.

170   dubious honor: Andrews, p. 123.

170   "Yeah, it's a good movie": Interview, Sven-Ole Thorsen.

170   *Parade* reported: *Toronto Star*, Jan. 16, 1986.

171   "I'd be angry at hearing my name": *News of the World*, Nov. 17, 1985.

171   "Watch out, Rambo!": Kirk Honeycutt, "'Commando' Is a Clone," *Daily News*, Oct. 4, 1985.

CHAPTER TWENTY-THREE: The Good Life

172   Warhol, Wyeth, Dalí, and Chagall: Lynn Darling, "How Much Bigger Can Arnold Schwarzenegger Get?" *Esquire* (March 1985).

172   Arnold sitting at the dining-room table: Interview, Theo Hayes.

172   "Most of the people there": Interview, Neal Nordlinger.

173   He spent more money on his apartment buildings: Transcript of *Playboy* interview.

174   "idols": Ibid.

174   he wanted to keep that to himself: Ibid.

174   He believed, too, that he loved America: Ibid.

174   "I set a goal": "Arnold's Vision," *Flex* (Dec. 1984).

175   "A lot of people are very sensitive": Interview, James Lorimer.

175   "What I am most happy about": "The Promoter," op. cit.

175   "What does it mean?": Transcript of *Playboy* interview.

177   "Arnold used to say when he went to the gym": Interview, Sven-Ole Thorsen.

177   "I can't believe Arnold lets you do that": Interview, Maria Shriver.

177   He saw the emotional energy: Transcript of *Playboy* interview.

178   Maria says that: Interview, Maria Shriver.

178   "Arnold, you've been going with this girl": Interview, James Lorimer.

178   "I had to make a wrenching decision": *New York Times*, Oct. 21, 1985.

179   "Girls were always chasing him": Interview, Theo Hayes.

179 She sucks in her cheeks": *Washington Post*, October 7, 1985.

179 When she was criticized for posing: *Los Angeles Times*, Jan. 20, 1986.

179 "I'll be taking": Marvin Kitman, "Blues at 'The CBS Morning News,'" *New Leader* (July 14, 1986).

181 "She felt originally": Transcript of *Playboy* interview.

181 elegant violet dress: *Boston Globe*, April 27, 1986.

181 "It's amazing how nice she is": Interview, Governor Arnold Schwarzenegger.

181 "I don't know if you're talking about three": Interview, Maria Shriver.

181 "reprisal actions against the partisans": *The Economist*, April 26, 1986.

182 "Maria looked like Gloria Swanson": *Chicago Tribune*, May 1, 1986.

182 "That was a caddish thing to do": Interview, George Butler.

CHAPTER TWENTY-FOUR: Raw Deals

185 "We fly back and forth": UPI, May 16, 1986.

185 "Maria worked the same hours": Interview, Sandy Gleysteen.

186 "Maria took a kid": Interview, Betty Weider.

186 "Hey, sweetheart": Anonymous interview.

187 she usually spent three months: Transcript of *Playboy* interview.

187 Maria points out: Interview, Maria Shriver.

187 One of Arnold's: Transcript of *Playboy* interview.

187 when they went out with him: Ibid.

188 "She is extremely smart": *Los Angeles Times*, Aug. 4, 1991.

188 "Before we shoot the first frame": Ibid.

188 he kills forty-two people: *The Advertiser*, July 3, 1986.

189 SCHWARZENEGGER BEATS SLIMY SLY: *Toronto Star*, June 6, 1986.

189 "Arnold is absolutely brilliant": Interview, Charlotte Parker.

190 "People were jealous": Interview, Governor Arnold Schwarzenegger.

190 "I hate to do interviews": Brian Donion, "The Star of Conan Depends on His Mind as Well as His Muscle," Charlotte Parker press clipping, July 1984.

191 "I don't want them to sell the Kennedy shit": Transcript of *Playboy* interview.

191 "I was just so angry": Interview, Charlotte Parker.

191 "There's one condition": Interview, Joan Goodman.

191 "She had ambition and ego equally": Ibid.

192 "He just hits me the wrong way": Transcript of *Playboy* interview.

192 "His beef was that he'd criticized Sly": E-mail from Barry Golson, Aug. 8, 2004.

192 "Was what I said about Sly presumptuous?": Interview, Governor Arnold Schwarzenegger.

193 Arnold went on *Good Morning America*: *Los Angeles Times*, Jan. 3, 1988.

193 "what it created was him [Stallone] hating me": Interview, Governor Arnold Schwarzenegger.

193 "We were sitting on these high chairs": Interview, Wendy Leigh.

193 "I never did anything to the f—er": *South China Morning Post* (Hong Kong), Aug. 9, 1997.

193 Stallone said that Arnold's father: The author several times requested an interview with Sylvester Stallone through his publicist Michelle Bega. She said, "We have decided to let Mr. Schwarzenegger's remarks stand for Mr. Stallone as well."

193 The publicist says she told Leigh: Interview, Charlotte Parker.

194 "I'll get you an agent": *South China Morning Post* (Hong Kong), Aug. 9, 1997.

194 "I think of Schwarzenegger every night": Ibid.

194 "this is better than getting four blow jobs": Interview, Wendy Leigh.

195 In December 1989: The Press Association Limited, Dec. 21, 1989.

195 Her publisher was not about to publish: Interview, Wendy Leigh.

195 "Both were people I know": *Chicago Tribune*, May 31, 1990.

195 "urgent, demanding pleas": Neal Koch, "The Terminator at Work?" *Columbia Journalism Review* (Jan.–Feb. 1991).

196 "was not a word of truth": *Editor & Publisher Magazine* (July 31, 1993).

196 "I feel somewhat responsible": Interview, Governor Arnold Schwarzenegger.

CHAPTER TWENTY-FIVE: "You Are What You Do"

197 Hollywood joked that he would have to fight an alien: Flynn, p. 111.

198 "Arnold, give me a fucking break": Interview, Sven-Ole Thorsen.

199 Bennie Dobbins: Flynn, p. 139.

199 "What the fuck is wrong?": Interview, Sven-Ole Thorsen.

199 "even though the Austrian-born star": *Washington Post*, June 17, 1988.

199 In December 1988, Arnold: Interview, Lou Pitt.

199 "Hey, Barry": Ibid.

200 "The risk to the studio was tremendous": Ibid.

200 "Look at it, fifteen thousand dollars": Interview, Sven-Ole Thorsen.

200 Arnold received 17½ percent: *Business Week*, July 24, 1989.

200 "like a kid that's funny, humorous, and lighthearted": "Schwarzenegger on Life in the Governor's Mansion" with Renée Montagne, *Morning Edition*, National Public Radio, Aug. 4, 2004.

201 "If I'm going to do it": Interview, Ronald Shusett.

202 "[Bleep] him": Jack Mathews, "Arnold to the Rescue," *Los Angeles Times Magazine*, Sept. 10, 1989.

202 "an audacious script": Interview, Paul Verhoeven.

202 "Arnold just told them": *Los Angeles Times*, Sept. 10, 1989.

202 Early on, when Caralco: Ibid.

202 "So, it was a tough time": Interview, Paul Verhoeven.

203 considered impatience his worst weakness: Transcript of *Playboy* interview.

203 "What impressed me was his ability": Interview, Paul Verhoeven.

203 On the set Arnold: *Los Angeles Times*, Sept. 3, 1989.

204 "the thing I love about Mexican women": anonymous interview; Connie Bruck, "Supermoderate!" *The New Yorker*, June 28, 2004.

204 "There's certainly a mean-spirited part": Interview, Lou Pitt.

204 "I have to tell you something": Interview, Ronald Shusett.

205 Shusett handed Arnold a tape: Ibid.

CHAPTER TWENTY-SIX: The Sins of the Father

207 "It's really great to be part of the delivery": Andrews, p. 164.

207 "When I'm at home with my kid": Ibid., p. 164.

207 "We took Katherine with us on a couple stories": Interview, Sandy Gleysteen.

207 "How lucky am I?": Shriver, pp. 76–77.

208 "You can can send your tax-free contribution": *New York Times*, Oct. 8, 1992.

209 flew across the Midwest: Interview, James Lorimer.

209 "I've had people write to Bush": Interview, Wendy Leigh, and *South China Morning Post* (Hong Kong), Aug. 9, 1997.

209 drug bust: *Sports Illustrated*, March 20, 1989.

210 "Arnold, man, I've got to talk to you": Interview, Danny Hernandez.

210 served as executive commissioner: *Los Angeles Times*, July 25, 1991.

210 "Everywhere we went, there was support": Interview, Danny Hernandez.

211 "Look, I'm in a sort of a difficult situation": Interview, Rabbi Marvin Hier.

211 The *Los Angeles Times* had done its own investigative reporting: *Los Angeles Times*, Aug. 14, 2003.

211 "We cannot say with absolute certainty": *Los Angeles Times*, Sept. 9, 2003.

212 Almost every major studio head: Associated Press, June 14, 1991.

213 Rich managed the apartment building: Andrews, p. 120.

213 "We are talking today about a bodybuilder turned 'actor'": Quoted in Andrews, pp. 222–23.

213 "He hated everybody": Interview, Joe Weider.

213 Charles Fleming: Interview, Charles Fleming.

214 "had a lot of courage": Quoted in unpublished manuscript by Lacy H. Rich Jr.

214 "All right, so what if the rumors—confirmed for *Spy*": Charles Fleming, "He's a Kennedy. He's Best Friends with George Bush . . .," *Spy* (March 1992).

214 "whisper things like 'Senator Schwarzenegger'": Interview, Charles Fleming.

215 "Coming in October will be the most complete outing": Fax to author from Lacy H. Rich Jr.

CHAPTER TWENTY-SEVEN: Number One

216 In June 1990, while shooting parts: *Los Angeles Times*, June 29, 1990, interview, James Lorimer.

216 "ballsy": Ibid.

216 Hummer general manager Mike DiGiovanni: Interview, Mike DiGiovanni.

217 "They see me as both American and European": *Time* (Dec. 24, 1990).

217 "When he got into the Hummer and cigars": Interview, Lou Pitt.

218 "I think that probably my imagery": Interview, James Lorimer.

218 wanted to purchase the army tank: *Washington Post*, July 15, 1994.

218 drive the tank: Interview, James Lorimer.

219 $94 million: Flynn, p. 183.

219 $12 million Gulfstream: Ibid., p. 190.

220 "a lot of smoking Derringers, but no smoking guns": Interview, George Butler.

221 "destroy any of such photographs": Film Purchase Agreement between Pumping Iron America, Inc., and Arnold Schwarzenegger, July 12, 1992, at www.thesmokinggun.com.

221 "This is a weekend read": Interview, Lou Pitt.

222 "I just feel we are at a time": *Boston Globe*, June 17, 1993.

222 "Having a kid come into a movie": *New York Times*, May 30, 1993.

222 "The best thing would have been": Ibid.

223 "I never got back": Interview, Jake Bloom.

223 "It's very easy to blame": Interview, Maria Shriver.

CHAPTER TWENTY-EIGHT: *Last Action Hero*

225 The driver drove into Cannes: Interviews, Anita Busch, Sid Ganis, and Duncan Clark.

225 Columbia had only twelve and a half minutes of footage: *Hollywood Reporter*, Cannes Satellite Edition, May 15, 1993.

225 "huge, large. It's monstrous. It's gigantic": *Hollywood Reporter*, Cannes Satellite Edition, May 17, 1993.

225 Columbia's plan to pay $500,000: *Washington Post*, May 30, 1993.

226 *Last Action Hero* cups at Burger King: *Business Week*, April 12, 1993.

226 "I hate the fucking line.": Interview, Danny Simon.

226 "Everyone in this town is jealous": *Sunday Mail* (London), June 20, 1993.

226 What happens in Hollywood": Interview, Governor Arnold Schwarzen-
     egger.

226 "Hollywood is a cannibal": Interview, Neal Nordlinger.

226 "actors, directors and film industry executives to social": *Los Angeles Times*,
     June 6, 1993.

227 "We suffered, because the *L.A. Times* didn't care that day": Interview, Sid
     Ganis.

227 "his article sought only to convey the rumors about a screening": *New York
     Times*, June 17, 1993.

227 "a film was previewed in Pasadena": *Variety*, June 14, 1993.

227 Fleiss later claimed: Lynn Hirshberg, "Heidi Does Hollywood," *Vanity Fair*
     (Feb. 1994).

227 "Sources close to alleged Hollywood madam": *Hollywood Reporter*, Aug. 30,
     1993.

228 "a joyless, soulless machine": *Variety*, June 14, 1993.

228 "the last, big, loud, ugly thing": Quoted in *Orange County Register*, June 18,
     1993.

228 "an awkward mixture of overproduced action." *Los Angeles Times*, June 18,
     1993.

228 "First of all": *Seattle Post-Intelligencer*, June 17, 1993.

228 the attack went from the film to Arnold personally: *Daily Variety*, June 21,
     1993.

229 "Part of the problem is of your own making": Ibid.

229 cost about $120 million: *Variety*, Oct. 3–9, 1994.

230 Neither does this film: Interview, Neal Nordlinger.

230 "You upset Arnold": Interview, Charlotte Parker.

230 "Maria is unbelievably protective": Interview, Governor Arnold Schwar-
     zenegger.

230 "I have a support system": Ibid.

230 "Maria means well": Anonymous interview.

231 "Arnold's friends could not": Ibid.

231 "Charlotte Parker was a hardworking": Interview, Governor Arnold
     Schwarzenegger.

231 "I said, 'Well, what'": Interview, Maria Shriver.

232 "I don't think Arnold believed in it": Interview, Lou Pitt.

CHAPTER TWENTY-NINE: Private Lives

233 John Milius, another of Arnold's: Interview, John Milius.

233 Thorsen helped himself to an ample breakfast: Interview, Sven-Ole Thorsen.

234 The attorney went into the building: Interview, Dr. Hans-Moritz Pott.

235 "It was a coming home for him": Interview, Lou Pitt.

235 "His mom got so fucking upset": Interview, Sven-Ole Thorsen.

235 from about four to eight P.M.: Shriver, p. 79.

235 "My mother always calls": Interview, Maria Shriver.

236 "complete catastrophe": Ibid.

236 "Each night they eat together": Interview, Albert Busek.

237 "I require that they do math every morning": *Houston Chronicle*, June 24, 1996.

237 a number of lesser vehicles: Andrews, p. 209.

237 "the kids know about the industry": Transcript of *The Oprah Winfrey Show*, June 11, 2003.

237 He brought his children to the set: Ibid.

237 "the one that, you know, disciplines them": Ibid.

238 "You make sure they have great moral guidelines": *Houston Chronicle*, June 24, 1996.

238 "If they don't do it, they feel set back": Interview, Albert Busek.

238 "You know what they are together": Interview, Dr. Franco Columbu.

239 "When in 2001 we had Arnold's birthday party": Interview, Albert Busek.

239 "I'm your biggest fan": Interview, James Lorimer.

239 returned by ferry boat: Associated Press Online, July 13, 2001.

239 purchased the 6,000-square-foot house next door: Property Transfer Record for Los Angeles County, 14215 Sunset Boulevard, Pacific Palisades, CA 90272.

239 he bought the four-bedroom, 5,000-square-foot home: Property Transfer Record for Los Angeles County, 14205 Sunset Boulevard, Pacific Palisades, CA 90272.

240 clutching a teddy bear: Interview, Melvin Sokolsky.

CHAPTER THIRTY: *True Lies*

241 His grandmother had suffered from congenital heart disease: *The Mirror* (London), June 10, 1997.

241 Aurelia's doctors had told her: Interview, Albert Busek.

241 Some individuals are born: *Pittsburgh Post-Gazette*, April 18, 1997.

241 "It didn't stop my lifestyle": *Scottish Daily Record & Sunday Mail*, Dec. 10, 1999.

242 suffering from hyperemesis: *USA Today*, March 10, 1997.

242 "the hardest decision": *USA Today*, April 23, 1997.

242 "there was very little dwelling on it": *Scottish Daily Record & Sunday Mail*, Dec. 10, 1999.

242 "it was like a train was parked on his chest": Interview, Sven-Ole Thorsen.

242 "I made the mistake": *The Mirror* (London), Dec. 10, 1999.

242 "When people see you almost as a machine": *The Guardian* (London), Dec. 10, 1999.

242 "For me and my career": Ibid.

243 "I felt the impact of the car": *Los Angeles Times*, Jan. 31, 1998.

243 ARNIE'S GOT TICKING TIME BOMB: *San Jose Mercury News*, Sept. 4, 1998.

243 had to pay Arnold $10,500: *Daily News*, Dec. 2, 1999.

243 the husband of one of Maria's closest friends: *Los Angeles Times*, July 29, 2003.

243 five years later . . . he fired Stein: Express Newspapers, *Daily Star*, July 19, 2002.

244 "I don't take any shit": *The Guardian* (London), Dec. 10, 1999.

244 chucked the man under the chin: Anonymous interview, OTR.

244 "No one has ever captured": Interview, Maria Shriver.

245 "you feel he's not so much exploring": *The Independent* (London), Dec. 8, 1994.

245 *Junior* did a disappointing $36.8 million: www.worldwideboxoffice.com.

246 "'Jingle' wants to warm our hearts": *San Francisco Chronicle*, Nov. 22, 1996.

246 In June he flew his private jet: *The Guardian* (London), July 25, 1997.

246 In October he jetted to Dublin: *The Mirror* (London), Oct. 17, 1997.

247 "In my business, I see": Interview, Paul Wachter.

247 "What can you say about the man?": Tape of event, courtesy of James Lorimer.

249 gave her a simple funeral: *Scottish Daily Record & Sunday Mail*, Aug. 6, 1998.

CHAPTER THIRTY-ONE: Avenues of Relaxation

250 "Idiotic beyond the point of redemption": *Sight & Sound* (Feb. 2000).

251 "I've seen the print ads": *Variety*, Nov. 29, 1999–Dec. 5, 1999.

251 He was scheduled to arrive at the premiere: *The Guardian* (London), Dec. 10, 1999.

251 worth about $200,000: *Newsday*, March 7, 2000.

251 signed his five-year contract: *USA Today*, Jan. 26, 2000.

251 he was asked by two Republican members of Congress: *Ottawa Citizen*, May 25, 2000.

252 traveling with his own hairstylist and makeup artist: Tom Dunkel, "Millennium Man," *George* (Nov. 1999).

252 "And I hung up the phone": Transcript of *The Oprah Winfrey Show*, April 14, 2000.

253 Arnold led a group: *Philadelphia Inquirer*, Aug. 31, 2000.

253 We can help these children bridge the gaps": *Los Angeles Times*, Aug. 16, 2000.

253 "guys like [Pat] Buchanan": "Millennium Man," op. cit.

254 "All this stuff that he did with all these women": *Schwarzenegger: Made in Britain*.

256 "I urged him to make the race": Ann Louise Bardach, "Taming the Hydra-Headed Carnivorous Beast," *Los Angeles Magazine* (Sept. 2004).

CHAPTER THIRTY-TWO: Patton's Retreat

257 Eunice had become critically ill: *Boston Globe*, Oct. 28, 2000.

258 "When I went to shake his hand.": *Los Angeles Times*, Oct. 2, 2003.

258 she prepared the legal groundwork: *Sunday Mail* (London), Oct. 31, 2004.

258 "He stroked her THIGH": *The Sun*, Dec. 12, 2000.

259 Dominic Mohan to award Arnold his "Groper of the Year": Ibid.

259 ARNIE'S WIFE HITS ROOF OVER GRAB-HAPPY HUBBY: *National Enquirer*, Jan. 2, 2001.

259 "We talked about public policy": Interview, Assemblyman Keith Richman.

260 "South is right": *Los Angeles Times*, Feb. 1, 2001.

260 "Especially your last sentence": *Los Angeles Times*, Feb. 5, 2001.

260 "I saw in the last ten years": Ibid.

260 T-shirts for sale: *Washington Post*, March 29, 2001.

261 "a lot of material": "Taming the Hydra-Headed Carnivorous Beast," op. cit.

261 the letter provided a blueprint: Interviews, John Connolly and anonymous interview.

261 "A real 'touching' story": *Washington Post*, March 29, 2001.

261 "not only did he threaten to sue . . .": "Taming the Hydra-Headed Carnivorous Beast," op. cit.

261 "in the wake of bombshell": *National Enquirer*, Feb. 27, 2002.

261 The story headlined ARNOLD'S 7-YEAR AFFAIR: *National Enquirer*, April 26, 2001.

261 "I was never Arnold's": Interview, Gigi Goyette.

261 "the timing's not right": *Los Angeles Times*, March. 7, 2001.

262 "that he had a deal": Interview, George Gorton.

262 "For seven years": *National Enquirer*, April 26, 2001, promotional material at www.nationalenquirer.com.

262 "Arnold Schwarzenegger terminated his plans": "Taming the Hydra-Headed Carnivorous Beast," op. cit.

262 That summer when a former chairman of the Republican National Committee: Anonymous interview.

CHAPTER THIRTY-THREE: Birth of a Candidate

265 "Turn on the TV": Andrew O'Hehi, "Entertaining Arnold," *Salon*, Feb. 8, 2002.

265 "Daddy, there are twenty or thirty buildings": Ibid.

265 "This means you can forget about your": Ibid.

266 She walked into that building: Transcript of *The Oprah Winfrey Show*, Oct. 26, 2001.

268 "Arnold kept saying to me": Interview, George Gorton.

268 Arnold's polling included questions about his running: *LA Weekly*, Sept. 20, 2002.

269 "I'm just excited to be out campaigning": Interview, George Gorton.

269 "Does it come in a men's?": *LA Weekly*, Nov. 22, 2002.

270 "when things were going so well": Interview, Governor Gray Davis.

270 10 percent of taxpayers pay about 75 percent: *New York Times*, Dec. 9, 2002.

270 numbers rose from 282,000 when Davis entered office to 326,000 in 2001: Ibid.

270 an estimated $35 billion: *Los Angeles Times*, May 4, 2003.

271 an estimated $10 million: *Los Angeles Times*, Nov. 3, 2002.

CHAPTER THIRTY-FOUR: Total Recall

273 "We were sitting in the Jacuzzi": *Los Angeles Times*, October 12, 2004.

273 "It was very tough for her": Ibid.

273 Much of what was going on: Anonymous interview with senior campaign staff member.

273 "Everybody was mad": Interview, Maria Shriver.

274 "'Terminator 3' is dumbed down": *Chicago Sun Times*, July 7, 2003.

274 "If Arnold hadn't run": Interview, Jake Bloom.

274 Six months later for $105 million: *Fortune* (Nov. 1, 2004).

275 "maybe ten percent of the company": "Taming the Hydra-Headed Carnivorous Beast," op. cit.

275 "He got very upset": Interview, Joe Weider.

275 "There is one thing that I can tell you": "Taming the Hydra-Headed Carnivorous Beast," op. cit.

276 "an unreasonable risk": Consumer Alert, FDA, Dec. 30, 2003.

276 Weider had already told: Interview, Governor Arnold Schwarzenegger.

276 "There was no discussion": Ibid.

276 "I think it's common": Ibid.

276 "I was very impressed": "Taming the Hydra-Headed Carnivorous Beast," op. cit.

277 "Those who see governance": *San Francisco Chronicle*, July 30, 2003.

277 "fondness for rabble-rousing": Ibid.

278 "a liberal Republican who posed nude": Ibid.

278 "The essence of Arnold": Interview, Neal Nordlinger.

279 "You know, if I were to run": Interview, George Gorton.

279 "There wasn't any question but that": Ibid.

280 "Someone like me looks": Interview, Maria Shriver.

280 "This is what I would." Ibid.

280 "Don't see me as": Interview, Governor Arnold Schwarzenegger.

280 Arnold had lunch with Franco: Interview, Dr. Franco Columbu.

280 Riordan sat at his beach house: Interview, Congressman David Dreier.

281 "Oh, well, let's do it": Interview, George Gorton.

281 "I do things my own way": Interview, Governor Arnold Schwarzenegger.

282 "They're going to throw everything at me": *Contra Costa Times*, Aug. 7, 2003.

CHAPTER THIRTY-FIVE: Lights, Camera, Action

283 His clothes, it turned out: This metaphor is from an interview with Bill Bradley.

283 "Bullshit, George, they'll wait!": Interview, OTR.

284 The consultant was still planning: Interview, Mike Murphy.

284 "California recently approved": NBC News Transcripts, *Today*, Aug. 8, 2003.

285 I felt that the": Interview, Maria Shriver.

285 "A lot of this for me": Interview, Congressman David Dreier.

286 "the single worst governor": Arthur B. Laffer, "An Afternoon with Arnold," Laffer Associates, undated.

286 "Rich don't make you smart": Ibid.

286 He pointed out that on his $500,000 Omaha home: *Wall Street Journal*, Aug. 15, 2003.

286 "should publicly dismiss him": "An Afternoon with Arnold," op. cit.

286 he videotaped a sixteen-year-old: *Los Angeles Times*, Aug. 1, 1989.

287 "all the portfolio assets": "An Afternoon with Arnold," op. cit.

288 2002 conference of European business leaders: *The Times* (London), Sept. 28, 2002.

288 Leamer was the only other speaker: Interview, Professor Edward Leamer.

289 "They're what's important": Discussion with Yvonne Abraham.

290 As he turned to face each questioner: The author was present.

291 "the best performance I've ever seen": Interview, George Gorton.

292 "The reason why it went so great": Interview, Kiki Gorton.

CHAPTER THIRTY-SIX: A Fork in the Road

293 "I called many people": *Sacramento Bee*, July 11, 2004.

293 "If I had a choice between writing": Ibid.

294 When Arnold left the restaurant: Author was present.

295 Joe Mathews, a young *Los Angeles Times* reporter: Interview, Joe Mathews.

295 "a tidal wave of pornography": *Los Angeles Times*, Oct. 12, 2003.

296 "When Richard Nixon was a candidate here": Interview, John Carroll.

296 "experts on specific subjects": Ibid.

297 "all of the [negative] stories": *The O'Reilly Factor*, Sept. 10, 2003.

297 It upset the press": Interview, Governor Arnold Schwarzenegger.

297 "In a traditional campaign, the press tail wags the dog": Transcript of University of California at Berkeley Institute of Governmental Studies 2003 California Recall Postmortem Governor's Race, October 18, 2003. Note: This is an invaluable, unique discussion among most of the principal consultants in the campaign speaking with candor and insight.

297 "There's kind of an institutional 'gotcha' feeling": Interview, Mike Murphy.

298 "After that, which I think got quite a backlash": Interview, John Carroll.

298 "The *LA Times* itself": Ibid.

CHAPTER THIRTY-SEVEN: "We're Not Gonna Take It"

300 As Arnold walked toward the outdoor stage: Author was present.

300 As Arnold walked past: Interview, Arthur Grace.

300 "Now, the man did not flinch": Interview, Landon Parvin.

301 He gave Arnold a line: *Sacramento Bee*, July 11, 2004.

301 "To Arnold's credit, he didn't just want a script": Interview, Mike Murphy.

301 "It's no different than when I start a movie": *Sacramento Bee*, July 11, 2004.

302 "Maria came only to": Interview, Landon Parvin.

302 "When I would say": Interview, Maria Shriver.

303 Arnold thanked the man: Author was present.

303 "Jesus Christ, I'm spritzing like a mule out there!": Anonymous interview.

304 He was another of Maria's finds: Marie Brenner, "Arnold and Maria," *Vanity Fair* (Jan. 2005).

304 "Basically, what I do for Arnold": Interview, Landon Parvin.

304 "I can't remember if Arnold gave him a kiss back": Ibid.

305 "He saved my life": Interview, Kiki Gorton.

305 Sean Hannity's radio talk show: CNN.com/Inside Politics, Aug. 28, 2003.

305 "He's a machine": *Los Angeles Times*, April 11, 1997.

305 "puke politics": *Sacramento Bee*, Aug. 1, 2003.

305 "He is arguably the best-known Hollywood celebrity worldwide": Interview, Governor Gray Davis.

305 "I wasn't there to criticize Arnold": Interview, Senator Tom McClintock.

306 The Brentwood liberal had rented: Interview, Bill Bradley, and anonymous interview.

306 paid only $771 in federal taxes: *Los Angeles Times*, Aug. 14, 2003.

307 "The reason Schwarzenegger won the debate": Institute of Governmental Studies transcript, op. cit.

308 He called senior editor Joel Sappell: Anonymous interview.

308 Sappell insists that in no instance: Interview, Joel Sappell.

309 "I made a lot": Interview, David Pecker.

309 "Some of these women I think": Interview, Gary Cohn.

CHAPTER THIRTY-EIGHT: The California Comeback Express

311 "He was pacing, looking up, and saying, 'I'm sorry'": "Supermoderate!" op. cit.

313 "flagrant, outspoken admirer of Hitler": *New York Times*, Oct. 3, 2004.

313 David D. Kirkpatrick asserts adamantly: Interview, David D. Kirkpatrick.

313 Butler told the *Times* in the next day's follow-up story: *New York Times*, Oct. 4, 2004.

313 "They have started the puke campaign, haven't they!": The author was on the bus tour.

314 Maria was on the phone to David Dreier: Interview, Congressman David Dreier.

314 "because I know the man I'm married to": *Los Angeles Times*, Oct. 4, 2003.

315 "The line we used to use": Interview, Congressman David Dreier.

315 "Arnold's a really bright guy, a smart guy": Interview, Charlie LeDuff.

315 "I have never grabbed anyone": NBC News Transcripts, *Dateline NBC*, Oct. 5, 2003.

316 "Tom lost about ten or fifteen points": Institute of Governmental Studies transcript, op. cit.

317 They were the bedrock: Joel Kotkin, "Baseless," *New Republic Online*, Oct. 8, 2003.

318 55.4 percent yes to 44.6 percent no: Official election returns, Office of California Secretary of State Kevin Shelley.

318 "It was probably": Interview, Anthony Shriver.

318 "I will not fail you": *Los Angeles Times*, Oct. 8, 2003.

CHAPTER THIRTY-NINE: The Golden Dream by the Sea

319 The California flag was draped vertically: Author was present.

319 disappearing and returning to his 1,000-square-foot condo: *Los Angeles Times*, Nov. 18, 2003.

320 Arnold held his six-year-old son, Christopher: *New York Times*, Nov. 18, 2003.

321 One senator celebrated his wife: Author was present.

321 Phil was a man of the left with the hard-nosed strategy: Laurence Leamer, *Playing for Keeps: In Washington* (1977).

322 "Somebody tell me what we wasted money on?": Interview, Senator John Burton.

322 "Who likes someone to throw a turd": *Sacramento Bee*, Nov. 21, 2003.

322 If Arnold had called him: Interview, Senator Tom McClintock.

323 "It is not appropriate to use bonded indebtedness": Ibid.

323 "Currently in California": *Sacramento Bee*, Oct. 31, 2004.

323 "It ends up driving the political debate": Interview, Assemblyman Keith Richman.

323 Interview, Assemblywoman Sarah Reyes.

324 "Any candidate worth": *Los Angeles Times*, Aug. 13, 2003.

325 "What the fuck do you think?": Interview, Senator John Burton.

325 "His absurd 1960s-era claim": E-mail from Jill Stewart.

326 "would cover my back": Interview, Governor Arnold Schwarzenegger.

327 "Wait a minute": Interview, Congressman David Dreier.

327 "While the first months were hard": Interview, Donna Lucas.

327 "To crush your enemies": Flynn, p. 40.

327 "Thank you. Thank you very much.": Official transcript of Governor Arnold Schwarzenegger's State of the State Address, Jan. 6, 2004.

328 "I don't know why he calls": *New York Times*, Feb. 13, 2004.

328 "fantastic": Associated Press Online, Feb. 28, 2004.

328 "He's taken more money": *San Francisco Chronicle*, Nov. 17, 2004.

328 Arnold took 95.8 percent of the money from businesses: The Institute on Money in State Politics, www.followthemoney.org.

329 The several thousand people who congregated in the food court: Author was present.

329 "It's important that you bring a new dimension": Interview, John Jackson.

329 "Arnold impresses me": Interview, Leticia King.

330 Late in the afternoon on December 5: Author was present.

330 Near midnight, Arnold walked up: *Sacramento Bee*, Dec. 15, 2003.

331 The two men convinced Kevin Shelley: Interview, Assemblyman Keith Richman; *Los Angeles Times*, Dec. 13, 2003.

331 pay $150 million: *Sacramento Bee*, Dec. 19, 2003.

332 "It's the only way": Ibid.

CHAPTER FORTY: Cigar Nights

333 Columbu did not like to go roaring up to the house: Interview, Dr. Franco Columbu.

333 In Sacramento he sometimes traveled: *Los Angeles Times*, Oct. 24, 2004.

334 The excitement among the legislators: Author was present.

334 "And here the President was standing": Interview, Landon Parvin.

334 He told Jim Lorimer that he liked nothing: Interview, James Lorimer.

334 He invited journalist Charlie LeDuff: *New York Times*, Feb. 13, 2004.

334 "It was such a hilarious scene": Interview, Albert Busek.

335 giving the governor on his birthday: *Los Angeles Times*, April 14, 2004.

335 "There was an article in the paper": "Arnold and Maria," op cit.

336 At Thanksgiving she went to the Sacramento Food Bank: *Marin Independent Journal*, Nov. 27, 2003.

336 "The first lady has a traditional office": *Los Angeles Times*, Dec. 17, 2004.

337 Maria's first major initiative: *San Jose Mercury News*, May 2, 2004.

337 "What's wrong with that?": *Fresno Bee*, Nov. 6, 2004.

337 "the highest praise for": *San Jose Mercury News*, Dec. 26, 2004.

337 Edwin Schlossberg: *Los Angeles Times*, Oct. 13, 2004.

337 "He was never hired": Interview, Maria Shriver.

338 "There's a lot of": Ibid.

338 "a little pop. A little schlock": *Washington Post*, Dec. 8, 2004.

339 "I think Arnold's the happiest": Interview, Maria Shriver.

340 At the end of the initiative campaign: Author was present.

340 "brought a very strong breath of fresh air": Author was present; *Contra Costa Times*, March 1, 2004.

340 "We're tired of his lies": *Los Angeles Times*, Oct. 5, 2003.

340 "You flexed your muscles once before": Author was present.

341 passed by 63.4 percent: Official voter returns, Office of California Secretary of State Kevin Shelley.

341 On the evening of his arrival: Author was present.

342 "If Joe Weider's magazine hadn't existed": Author was present.

343 Weider, waiting in his wheelchair, was ready to rise: Author was present.

343 "I felt this agreement": Interview, David Pecker.

343 "When Weider sold": *USA Today*, March 5, 2004.

344 "You make the decision": Interview, David Pecker.

344 "There are no personalities being developed": "The Flex Interview: The Restless Man," *Flex* (Jan. 2000).

344 Zane said that if he were young again: Interview, Frank Zane.

344 the teenage grandson of Arnold's mentor Reg Park: Interview, Jon Jon Park.

CHAPTER FORTY-ONE: Girlie Men

346 "They want to see an action governor": *Governing Magazine* (July 2004).

346 "expected to wring billions": *Los Angeles Times*, April 18, 2004.

347 "perhaps for the first": Ken Auletta, "Fortress Bush" *The New Yorker* (Jan. 19, 2004).

347 "Staff members still prefer": E-mail from Rob Stutzman, Dec. 27, 2004.

349 agreeing to undo about a billion dollars in cuts: *Sacramento Bee*, May 14, 2004.

349 "They cannot have the guts": *Los Angeles Times*, July 18, 2004.

349 "It's really painful to hear the governor": Ibid.

349 "As opposed to his being a he-man?": Ibid.

350 twelve of the fourteen: *Los Angeles Times*, July 30, 2004.

350 "It would have been nice": *Sacramento Bee*, Aug. 3, 2004.

350 The state Legislative Analyst's Office: *Orange County Business Journal* (Aug. 9, 2004).

CHAPTER FORTY-TWO: Not the Last Chapter

353 A Gallup poll showed: The Gallup Organization, Gallup Poll Tuesday Briefing, Dec. 7, 2004.

354 Arnold had the unfamiliar experience: Author was present.

354 "You may want to communicate": Gary Delshon and Margaret Talev, "Travels with Arnold," *American Journalism Review* (Dec./Jan. 2005).

 76 percent of Californians: *Time* (Dec. 20, 2004).

355 "I don't have to concern myself": *California Journal* (April 1, 2004).

356 "The most frustrating thing about Arnold Schwarzenegger": *Sacramento Bee*, Dec. 26, 2004.

356 "The reason why I'm against": *Los Angeles Times*, Nov. 4, 2004.

356 "I am not here in Sacramento": Interview, Governor Arnold Schwarzenegger.

359 "The governor is sitting": *Los Angeles Times*, Jan. 19, 2005.

360 "Just a few days ago, Schwarzenegger": *Sacramento Bee*, Jan. 20, 2005.

360 at least $1.4 billion short: *San Francisco Chronicle*, Jan. 21, 2005.

361 "I have a very, very positive outlook": *Sacramento Bee*, Jan. 19, 2005. While the author has abridged these comments, he has not changed any of Governor Schwarzenegger's words.

361 "We're going right": *Sacramento Bee*, Feb. 12, 2005.

361 "In most states": *New York Post*, Feb. 13, 2005.

361 "If Schwarzenegger successfully employs": *Kansas City Star*, Feb. 12, 2005.

Bibliography

Andrews, Nigel. *True Myths: The Life and Times of Arnold Schwarzenegger*. New York: Carol Pub. Group, 1996.

Arnold, Katie. *Chemical Pink: A Novel of Obsession*. New York: Forge, 2001.

Baldassare, Mark. *California in the New Millennium: The Changing Social and Political Landscape*. Berkeley: University of California Press, 2000.

————. *A California State of Mind: The Conflicted Voter in a Changing World*. Berkeley: University of California Press, 2002.

Blitz, Michael, and Louise Krasniewicz. *Why Arnold Matters*. New York: Basic Books, 2004.

Braudy, Leo. *From Chivalry to Terrorism: War and the Changing Nature of Masculinity*. New York: Knopf, 2003.

————. *The Frenzy of Renown: Fame & Its History*. New York: Oxford University Press, 1986.

Brunner, Walter. *Thal*. Graz: Verlag Josep Riegler, 1994.

Butler, George. *Arnold Schwarzenegger: A Portrait*. New York: Simon & Schuster, 1990.

Columbu, Franco, with George Fels. *Winning Bodybuilding*. Chicago: H. Regnery, 1977.

Columbu, Dr. Franco, with Lydia Fragomeni. *The Bodybuilder's Nutrition Book*. Chicago: Contemporary Books, 1985.

Davis, Mike. *Ecology of Fear: Los Angeles and the Imagination of Disaster*. New York: Metropolitan Books, 1998.

Draper, Dave. *Brother Iron, Sister Steel: A Bodybuilder's Book*. Santa Cruz, Calif.: On Target Publications, 2001.

Flynn, John. *The Films of Arnold Schwarzenegger*. Secaucus, N.J.: Carol Pub. Group, 1993.

Fussell, Samuel Wilson. *Muscle: Confessions of an Unlikely Bodybuilder*. New York: Poseidon Press, 1991.

Gabler, Neal. *Life the Movie: How Entertainment Conquered Reality*. New York: Knopf, 1998.

Gaines, Charles. *Stay Hungry*. Garden City, N.Y.: Doubleday, 1972.

Gaines, Charles, and George Butler, photographs. *Pumping Iron: The Art and Sport of Bodybuilding*. New York: Simon & Schuster, 1974.

Gamson, Joshua. *Claims to Fame: Celebrity in Contemporary America*. Berkeley: University of California Press, 1994.

Henderson, Deirdre, ed.. *Prelude to Leadership: The European Diary of John F. Kennedy*. Washington, D.C.: Regnery, 1995.

Jamison, Kay Redfield. *Exuberance: The Passion for Life*. New York: Knopf, 2004.

Kegan, Robert. *In Over Our Heads: The Mental Demands of Modern Life*. Cambridge, Mass.: Harvard University Press, 1994.

Klein, Alan M. *Little Big Men: Bodybuilding Subculture and Gender Construction*. Albany: State University of New York Press, 1993.

Leamer, Laurence. *Playing for Keeps: In Washington*. New York: Dial, 1977.

Leigh, Wendy. *Arnold: An Unauthorized Biography*. Chicago: Congdon & Weed, distributed by Contemporary Books, 1990.

Linder, Bert. *Condemned Without Judgment: The Three Lives of a Holocaust Survivor*. New York: S.p.i. Books, 1995.

Marshall, P. David. *Celebrity and Power: Fame in Contemporary Culture*. University of Minnesota Press, 1997.

Morris, Eric. *Acting Imaging and the Unconscious*. Los Angeles: Ermor Enterprises, 1998.

Paris, Bob. *Gorilla Suit: My Adventures in Bodybuilding*. New York: St. Martin's Press, 1997.

Pearl, Bill, with Kim Shott. *Beyond the Universe: The Bill Pearl Story*. Jamaica, N.Y.: Agni Press, 2003.

Pope Jr., Harrison G, Katharine A. Phillips, and Roberto Olivardia. *The Adonis Complex: The Secret Crisis of Male Body Obsession*. New York: Free Press, 2000.

Reisnger, Marc. *A Dangerous Place: California's Unsettling Fate*. New York: Pantheon Books, 2003.

Schickel, Richard. *Intimate Strangers: The Culture of Celebrity*. Garden City, N.Y.: Doubleday, 1985.

Schrag, Peter. *Paradise Lost: California's Experience, America's Future*. Berkeley: University of California Press, 1999.

Schwarzenegger, Arnold, and Douglas Kent Hall. *Arnold: The Education of a Bodybuilder*. New York: Simon & Schuster, 1977.

Shriver, Maria. *Ten Things I Wish I'd Known—Before I Went Out into the Real World*. New York: Warner Books, 2000.

Sotill, Wolfgang. *Es gibt nur einen Gott und eine Menschheit.* Graz, Austria: Verlag Styria, 2001.

Starr, Kevin. *Americans and the California Dream, 1850–1915.* New York: Oxford University Press, 1986.

———. *Coast of Dreams: California on the Edge, 1990–2002.* New York: Knopf, 2004.

Tyler, Dick. *West Coast Bodybuilding Scene: The Golden Era.* Santa Cruz, Calif.: On Target, 2004.

Wayne, Rick. *Muscle Wars: The Behind-the-Scenes Story of Competitive Bodybuilding.* New York: St. Martin's Press, 1985.

Zane, Frank Zane. *Mind, Body, Spirit.* New York: Thunder's Mouth Press, 1997.

Bodybuilding Titles

Junior Mr. Europe (Germany)	1965
Best Build Man of Europe (Germany)	1966
Mr. Europe (Germany)	1966
International Powerlifting Championship (Germany)	1966
NABBA Mr. Universe, Amateur (London)	1967
NABBA Mr. Universe, Professional (London)	1968
German Powerlifting Championship	1968
IFBB Mr. International (Mexico)	1968
IFBB Mr. Universe, Amateur (New York)	1969
NABBA Mr. Universe, Professional (London)	1969
NABBA Mr. Universe, Professional (London)	1970
Mr. World (Columbus, Ohio)	1970
IFBB Mr. Olympia (New York)	1970
IFBB Mr. Olympia (Paris)	1971
IFBB Mr. Olympia (Essen, Germany)	1972
IFBB Mr. Olympia (New York)	1973
IFBB Mr. Olympia (New York)	1974
IFBB Mr. Olympia (Pretoria, South Africa)	1975
IFBB Mr. Olympia (Sydney, Australia)	1980

Films

Hercules in New York (1970)

The Long Goodbye (1973)

Stay Hungry (1976)

Pumping Iron (1977)

The Jayne Mansfield Story (1980)

Conan the Barbarian (1982)

The Terminator (1984)

Conan the Destroyer (1984)

Red Sonja (1985)

Commando (1985)

Raw Deal (1986)

Predator (1987)

The Running Man (1987)

Red Heat (1988)

Twins (1988)

Total Recall (1990)

Kindergarten Cop (1990)

Terminator 2: Judgment Day (1991)

Last Action Hero (1993)

True Lies (1994)

Junior (1994)

Eraser (1996)

Jingle All the Way (1996)

Batman & Robin (1997)

End of Days (1999)

The 6th Day (2000)

Collateral Damage (2001)

Terminator 3: Rise of the Machines (2003)

Around the World in 80 Days (2004)

Index